THE NATIONAL ARMY MUSEUM BOOK OF

WELLINGTON'S ARMIES

Also in this series

The National Army Museum Book of the

BOER WAR

Field Marshal Lord Carver

The National Army Museum Book of the

ZULU WAR

Ian Knight

The National Army Museum Book of the

TURKISH FRONT 1914–1918

Field Marshal Lord Carver

Wellington at Waterloo

THE NATIONAL ARMY MUSEUM BOOK OF

WELLINGTON'S ARMIES

BRITAIN'S CAMPAIGNS IN THE PENINSULA

AND AT WATERLOO 1808–1815

Andrew Uffindell

SIDGWICK & JACKSON

in association with

The National Army Museum

First published 2003 by Sidgwick & Jackson
an imprint of Pan Macmillan Ltd
Pan Macmillan, 20 New Wharf Road, London N1 9RR
Basingstoke and Oxford
Associated companies throughout the world
www.panmacmillan.com

ISBN 0 283 07348 9

1 3 5 7 9 8 6 4 2

A CIP catalogue record for this book is available from
the British Library.

Typeset by SetSystems Ltd, Saffron Walden, Essex
Printed and bound in Great Britain by
Mackays of Chatham plc, Chatham, Kent

Foreword

Two hundred years ago this year, on 18 May 1803, war was resumed between France and Great Britain after the collapse of the short-lived Treaty of Amiens, which had provided a respite in a conflict beginning with the declaration of war by Revolutionary France in 1793 and continuing until its final resolution by the defeat of the Emperor Napoleon by the Duke of Wellington on the battlefield at Waterloo on 18 June 1815. The contents of this volume accurately reflect its title, being concerned especially with that decisive phase of the war from 1808 when the then Sir Arthur Wellesley was sent to Portugal.

The war of 1793–1815 against Revolutionary and Napoleonic France is central to the displays at the National Army Museum (NAM), and a permanent gallery entitled 'The Road to Waterloo' was opened by the Duke of Wellington in 1990 to mark the 175th Anniversary of the Battle of Waterloo. This was accompanied by a book of essays of the same title. This war is the earliest for which the NAM has good archive coverage, with the collection being boosted especially by the donation in July 1967 of the Military Manuscripts Collection of the Royal United Service Institution, which included the papers of Brigadier-General Robert Long and General Armand Philippon, as well as the Visitors' Book from Napoleon's grave on St Helena.

Other outstanding or unusual acquisitions include the 7th Hussars papers of the Marquess of Anglesey; the letters and diary of Lieutenant James Gairdner, an American officer in the 95th; and the papers of Lieutenant-General Sir Stapleton Cotton, later Viscount Combermere, Major-General George Murray, Wellington's Quartermaster-General in the Peninsula, Lieutenant-Colonel Richard Hussey Vivian, Captain William Tyrwhitt-Drake, and, from the former Middlesex Regimental Museum Collection, the correspondence of Lieutenant-General Sir Hew Dalrymple.

Andrew Uffindell is well qualified to collate these varied and disparate collections to produce a coherent and balanced account of Wellington's armies, being the author, co-author, or editor of five books on this period and, as the Editor of the *Newsletter* of the Society of Friends of the National Army Museum, fully conversant with the rich holdings of original manuscript material in the NAM.

In addition to Andrew Uffindell's efforts, it is appropriate to acknowledge the contribution of Dr Peter Boyden, Assistant Director (Collections), Dr Alastair Massie, Head of the Department of Archives, Photographs, Film and Sound, and Ian Jones, Head of the Photographic Department in the NAM, who have been assiduous in their support for Andrew Uffindell during the period that this volume has been written. Finally, as always with this series, the support of Sidgwick and Jackson is gratefully acknowledged, especially in the person of Ingrid Connell, without whose wholehearted support this well-edited mainly unpublished original archival material would not have appeared in print.

Ian G. Robertson

Director, National Army Museum

17 February 2003

Acknowledgements

I wish to record my gratitude to Ingrid Connell, of the publishers, for her tremendous support and guidance during the production of this book; and to Nicholas Blake, my copy-editor. Similarly, I am greatly indebted to the staff of the National Army Museum, particularly the Director, Mr Ian G. Robertson; Dr Peter Boyden, Assistant Director (Collections); and Dr Alastair Massie, Head of the Department of Archives, Photographs, Film and Sound, who generously advised me throughout this project, as well as commenting on the manuscript. I am also very grateful to their assistants for their unfailing helpfulness while I was researching this book in the Reading Room. I would also like to thank Ian Jones, Head of the Photographic Department, and his assistants for producing the illustrations. Additionally, my thanks go to John Richards, who drew the sixteen superb maps; as well as Julian Humphrys, Rogan Faith, the staff of the British and Bodleian Libraries and my friends, colleagues and family for their help and encouragement over the past two years.

Contents

List of Illustrations

All the illustrations are from the National Army Museum's collection. The numbers after the description are the Accession and the Photograph, or Negative, numbers.

Section One

of Foot, formed in line two ranks deep, counter-attacks a French infantry column in the afternoon of 28 July 1809. In fact, hand-to-hand fighting was rare: the French, already shaken by a volley, usually broke and fled as the British charged. The 40th Regiment, as part of the 4th Division, was attacked twice in the afternoon by General Jean-François Leval's infantry division. Although this watercolour by Richard Simkin depicts French soldiers, Leval's division was actually composed of German and Dutch units in French service. Leval was completely repulsed and lost nearly a quarter of his men. (1959-09-70 / 2519)

9. The 3rd Division counter-attacks the French at the Battle of Busaco, 27 September 1810. In the left foreground is the 88th (or the Connaught Rangers) Regiment of Foot, while the Portuguese 8th Regiment is immediately above, led by an officer waving his hat. Note, on the right, the French reserves far below in the valley. (1971-02-33-507-10 / 97703)

10. Marshal André Massena. He commanded the French invasion of Portugal in 1810, but was outgeneralled by Wellington. (Bk 17874 / 29487)

11. Wellington in Portuguese Marshal-General's uniform, with the ribbon and star of the Order of the Bath, 1809. The maps refer to his four recent victories at Roliça, Vimeiro, Oporto and Talavera. (1960-07-186-1 / 3840)

12. Lieutenant-General Sir Stapleton Cotton, later Viscount Combermere, served as Wellington's cavalry commander for much of the Peninsular War. He is seen here as a full general in c. 1827. (1968-06-119 / 3581)

13. Lieutenant-General Sir Rowland Hill, c. 1819. One of Wellington's most reliable and popular generals, he was known to the men as 'Daddy Hill'. (1962-10-108 / 1577)

14. Lieutenant-General the Hon. Sir Galbraith Lowry Cole, the commander of the 4th Division in the Peninsula. (1973-10-18 / 20110)

15. Lieutenant-General Sir Thomas Picton. He took command of the 3rd Division in February 1810 and led it for most of the rest of the Peninsular War. He was killed at Waterloo at the head of the 5th Division. (1969-12-1-1 / 11010)

16. The Battle of Fuentes de Oñoro, 5 May 1811. In a celebrated incident, Captain Norman Ramsay of the Royal Horse Artillery galloped his two guns through a swarm of French cavalry to safety. (1972-08-2 / 8364)

17. Fuentes de Oñoro. Two British soldiers are carrying a stretcher, probably made from a blanket and two poles, while regimental surgeons tend the wounded. Note the battalion sitting down to rest on the right. Welling-

Section Two

He lost about 500 men a year in this way in the Peninsula, with a disproportionate number being from his foreign troops, such as the Chasseurs Britanniques and the Brunswick Corps. 'Desertion towards the enemy' was liable to result in a death sentence; other cases were usually punished by flogging or transportation. (1964-01-4 / 764)

Section Three

List of Maps

Key to Maps

☐	Allied Infantry
◸	Allied Cavalry
■	French Infantry
◣	French Cavalry

Introduction

Britain has never had a greater military commander than the Duke of Wellington.

This book follows his campaigns against the French between 1808 and 1815. Wellington had previously commanded armies in India, where between 1797 and 1805 he had helped the Governor-General, his brother Richard Wellesley, second Earl of Mornington, to lay the foundations of British imperial power in the subcontinent. But his fame lies primarily in his six-year struggle against the French occupation forces in the Iberian Peninsula and his subsequent defeat of Napoleon himself at Waterloo. These years transformed him from a junior lieutenant-general into Field Marshal the Duke of Wellington, a legendary figure to his men and a commander renowned throughout Europe.

His relentless string of victories was primarily responsible for restoring the British army's prestige and self-confidence following its defeat in the American War of Independence (1775–83) and its mixed fortunes in the wars against Revolutionary and Napoleonic France from 1793. Napoleon's defeat remains one of the British army's finest achievements. Its regiments under Wellington acquired some of their most famous battle honours, proudest trophies and traditions that have stood them well in adversity. Wellington's victory at Waterloo also marked the dawn of Britain's imperial splendour and gave her a sense of national destiny that lasted until its destruction amid the appalling losses of the Battle of the Somme in 1916.

This book is not intended to cover every aspect of such a vast topic as Wellington's armies. Instead, its purpose is to add to existing knowledge by describing his operations through the eyes of the participants whose letters, diaries or other papers are held in the archives of the National Army Museum. The richness of these remarkable collections has made it necessary to be selective. But the quoted extracts are as representative as possible of the range and diversity of the source material. Priority has been given to documents that contribute new information, and to accounts by soldiers who actually witnessed the events that they described. It was common for letters received by families at home and for soldiers' memoirs to be copied for private or other purposes either at the time or soon afterwards. Wherever possible, the extracts quoted in this volume are from original documents, although some contemporary and near-contemporary manuscript transcripts have also been used. Of the material that has not been incorporated, a considerable amount consists of photocopied, or recently transcribed, primary material, along with some original papers that were not considered relevant for inclusion in this book. This additional material may be identified in the Museum's Reading Room.

I have used the background text to put the extracts in context, particularly where the Museum's collections offer limited coverage of specific events. For example, there are few first-hand accounts of Wellington's crossing of the River Douro at Oporto in 1809, or of the Battles of Barossa and Albuera in 1811. In contrast, the coverage of Talavera and of Waterloo is particularly full. In addition, the Museum's sources sometimes present a detailed picture of minor actions that are merely mentioned in the standard histories of Sir Charles Oman and Sir John Fortescue. A good example is the action on the River Bayas on 19 June 1813, two days before the Battle of Vitoria.

The National Army Museum's papers are particularly valuable in showing what the soldiers thought at the time. They include, for example, some fascinating letters written immediately after the Battle of Waterloo. The result is a freshness and an immediacy that are usually lacking in even the best written of secondary accounts.

The documents quoted in this book were written mostly by subaltern officers, but include several from both the high command and the rank and file. Wellington himself is strongly represented, particularly through a collection of letters to his cavalry commander in the Peninsula, Lieutenant-General Sir Stapleton Cotton. These are particularly valuable in showing his intentions and understanding of developments as they occurred. Two of Wellington's senior subordinates, Marshal William Carr Beresford and Lieutenant-General Sir Thomas Graham, are also included, while Lieutenant-General Sir Thomas Picton's character is shown in a remarkable letter about the Battle of Busaco. The papers of Major-General Robert Long describe several battles from the perspective of an outspoken cavalry brigadier and offer an insight into the machinations that led to his replacement in 1813. Similarly, a collection of letters from the commander of an infantry brigade, Major-General Andrew Hay, provides valuable new evidence about the Battle of Vitoria and the storming of the fortress of San Sebastian in 1813. But there is nothing from some of Wellington's other, equally colourful, subordinates, such as Major-General Robert Craufurd, and none of the letters in the archives from Lieutenant-General Sir Rowland Hill was sufficiently pertinent to quote.

The National Army Museum tells the story of the British soldier and naturally its archives for the Napoleonic period are overwhelmingly from British participants. It does possess the Order Book of the French General Armand Philippon, who gallantly defended the fortress of Badajoz, but other French original sources must be sought elsewhere.

Coverage of the Portuguese contingent of Wellington's Peninsular army is more satisfactory. The Museum has accounts from British officers seconded to the Portuguese army to help regenerate it as an effective fighting force. They include Brigadier-General Charles Ashworth, who commanded a Portuguese infantry brigade in 2nd Division, and one of his subordinates, Captain Richard Brunton of the 6th Caçadores.

The Spanish contribution to Wellington's success is represented only by intelligence reports supplied to Wellington's army in 1810 by the Spanish General the Marquess de La Romana. It must be remembered that the bulk of the French troops in the Peninsula were tied down by the activities of the guerrillas and by the Spanish regular armies which despite frequent defeats and severe handicaps continually re-formed and maintained the struggle for six years. It was because of this that Wellington with his relatively small army was able to have such an impact.

The Waterloo Campaign presents similar gaps. Only 40 per cent of Wellington's troops were British or from the King's German Legion, a formation of largely Hanoverian exiles that formed part of the British army. The rest of Wellington's army was supplied by the United Netherlands and various German states. None of these foreign contingents is represented, although the Museum does hold a detailed letter from Lieutenant James Hamilton of the 2nd Line Battalion of the King's German Legion. Similarly, the only account in the National Army

Museum of the Prussian army's operations during the campaign comes from Captain William Cameron of the British Quartermaster-General's Department, who happened to be sent to the Prussian Headquarters as hostilities began.

The British sources in the Museum are themselves disproportionate in origin. In the Waterloo Campaign, 68 per cent of Wellington's British troops were infantrymen, while 17 per cent were in the cavalry and 15 per cent in the artillery. Yet in the Museum's sources for the campaign, the infantry and cavalry are equally well represented and the artillery not at all. One result is that the cavalry action at Genappe on 17 June is more prominent than the role of Lieutenant-General Sir Thomas Picton's 5th Division in the Battle of Waterloo the following day. Furthermore, the Foot Guards and light infantry regiments are better represented than other infantry units.

Yet the idiosyncracies of the collections also highlight more obscure aspects of the campaigns or add fresh information. For example, the papers of Lieutenant-General Sir Hew Dalrymple give a clearer picture of the controversy surrounding the Convention of Cintra, which marred Wellington's first command in the Peninsula in 1808. Similarly, the Museum's four detailed accounts of the Battle of Vimeiro are all from the same brigade and offer a fascinating combination of perspectives. Occasionally, the authors of the Museum's sources even refer to each other, most notably when Major Lord Fitzroy Somerset and Lieutenant-Colonel William Warre describe the capture of the French Governor of Badajoz in 1812.

The National Army Museum's sources cover not only the fighting but also the internal organization and everyday life of Wellington's army in the Peninsula, a fascinating topic in its own right. Rather than attempt to explore every aspect of Wellington's army, which could not be done adequately in a book this size, I have exploited the strengths of the Museum's collections to highlight areas which have often received little attention, such as the army's postal service and the experiences of prisoners of war. The select bibliography at the end of the book serves as a guide to further reading.

As far as can be ascertained, about three-quarters of the sources quoted in this book have never before been published. Of those that have, most are now out of print. Previously published extracts were often edited and quoted out of context or without explanation. The extracts in this book have been transcribed directly from the documents, without the addition of punctuation or the correction of spelling, except where indicated in square brackets. The intention has been, wherever possible, to let the eyewitnesses speak for themselves.

To avoid confusion, I have referred throughout this book to the River Douro, although the section that flows through Spain to the Portuguese border is called the Duero.

The dust jacket shows the ribbon of the Waterloo Medal. This was the British army's first campaign medal to be awarded without distinction of rank to every officer, NCO and soldier. It was introduced on Wellington's own urging and became the model for future campaign medals.

Lieutenant Standish O'Grady fought at Waterloo with the 7th (or The Queen's Own) Regiment of (Light) Dragoons (Hussars) and wrote to his father on 16 September 1815:

> ... I hear from Paris that the Army are to wear Medals for Waterloo officers privates & all[.] I think they ought to give us another for the Spanish Campaigne it is hard on those Regiments who have been thro' Portugal Spain & France to lose this [Waterloo] medal because they were [instead] fighting hard for us in America – ...

But Peninsular veterans had to wait until 1848 for similar official recognition through the issue of the Military General Service Medal 1793–1814. Senior officers had received awards such as the Army Gold Medal and Army Gold Cross at the time of the Peninsular War, while some junior officers had been decorated by Britain's allies, notably Portugal. But there was no comprehensive British award for Peninsular service until 1848. The omission was made good by individual regiments, which produced their own awards to recognize campaign service or specific acts of gallantry. In 1815, for example, the 53rd (or the Shropshire) Regiment of Foot gave medals to fifteen of its sergeants who had distinguished themselves in the Peninsula. Such decorations lacked the comprehensive nature of an official campaign medal, but were rich in variety and indicated the strong sense of unit pride that sustained Wellington's regiments. Their campaigns are described in the pages that follow.

1

Napoleon Intervenes in the Peninsula

1807–8

By July 1807, Napoleon was master of Europe. Less than three years after his coronation as Emperor of the French on 2 December 1804, he had crushed Austria and Prussia and made Russia seek peace by smashing her army at Friedland. On 25 June 1807, he met Tsar Alexander I at Tilsit, 320 km north of Warsaw, and agreed to divide the Continent into French and Russian spheres of influence.

The Peace of Tilsit secured Napoleon's dominance of Europe as far east as the River Vistula and virtually isolated Britain, his most inveterate enemy. Only Sweden and Sicily, the refuge of the King of Naples, continued openly to oppose him on the Continent and they both required British support and protection. Napoleon was determined to undermine Britain economically through a Continental Blockade and to challenge her maritime supremacy by combining his resources with Russia's and creating a fleet powerful enough to overwhelm the Royal Navy. He launched a massive ship-building programme and planned to seize the fleets of two neutral countries, Denmark and Portugal, as well as that of Sweden, which would be invaded by Russia in 1808.

But Napoleon's economic warfare proved less effective than he had hoped and led him to overstretch his military resources as he tried to consolidate his hold on Europe and close its remaining ports. He was also foiled in his attempt to seize the Danish and Portuguese fleets. Britain audaciously sent an expedition to Copenhagen at the end of July 1807 and forced the Danes to surrender their ships on 7 September, before Napoleon could invade by land. Meanwhile, Napoleon had issued Portugal with an ultimatum on 12 August, demanding that she declare war on Britain. Portugal tried to avoid such a drastic step, for she had traditional ties of friendship with Britain and depended on food imported from overseas. Napoleon declared war on 22 October and five days later signed the secret Treaty of Fontainebleau with Spain, Portugal's traditional enemy. Spain had been allied to France since 1796 and at war with Britain from then until 1801 and again from 1804. Napoleon arranged for a French corps under General Andoche Junot to march across the Peninsula and occupy and partition Portugal with Spanish help. Junot's advance guard reached Lisbon on 30 November, a day after the Prince Regent had sailed, with the court, fleet and treasury, for the safety of the Portuguese colony of Brazil.

Napoleon had now closed Portugal to British trade, but was also determined to establish greater control of Spain in order to secure Junot's rear, exploit Spanish resources more effectively in the war against Britain and further his increasingly grandiose ambitions. He remembered that Spain's loyalty had been uncertain during his 1806 campaign against Prussia and was keen to avoid a war on two fronts in the event of any future conflict in central Europe.

Spain had declined dramatically since the height of her power in the sixteenth century. She still had the largest overseas empire of any European country, including nearly all of Latin America, the Philippines, several Caribbean islands and large tracts in the south and west of North America, but had been cut off from the resources of these colonies by the Royal Navy and had lost much of her fleet at the Battle of Trafalgar in 1805. She was one of the most backward states in Europe, but attempts at reform encountered bitter resistance from conservative elements of Spanish society, particularly the nobility and the Catholic Church, and the situation was worsened by an economic crisis and a succession of natural disasters. Napoleon had nothing but contempt for the weak Spanish Bourbon King, Charles IV, and his chief minister and favourite, Manuel de Godoy.

Napoleon gradually pushed troops into the north and north-east of Spain, ostensibly to secure Junot's communications. Then, in February and March 1808, he had frontier fortresses at either end of the Pyrenees seized by stealth to gain control of the two main routes into Spain. Finally, he placed his brother-in-law, Marshal Joachim Murat, in command of all the French troops in the country and ordered him to occupy Madrid. The Spanish royal family intended to flee to South America. But the deep divisions within Spanish society came to a head on 17 March with a revolt at the royal palace of Aranjuez, 45 km south of Madrid, which forced Charles IV to abdicate two days later in favour of his equally unprepossessing son, Prince Ferdinand, Prince of Asturias. Both Charles and Ferdinand appealed to Napoleon, who opportunistically summoned the Spanish royal family to France under the pretence of mediating in the quarrel. He then persuaded both father and son to abandon their claims to the throne, to make way for his elder brother, Joseph Bonaparte, who would rule Spain as a dependent kingdom.

Napoleon now had 90,000 troops in Spain and did not expect serious resistance. Popular resentment had initially been centred on the widely detested Godoy, who had been arrested during the revolt at Aranjuez. But the Spaniards were soon antagonized by the indiscipline and looting of the French troops and also by the removal of Ferdinand, who was widely portrayed by Godoy's enemies as Spain's potential saviour. An insurrection in Madrid on 2 May was quickly crushed, but was followed by revolts that exploded across the country. Provincial councils, or *juntas*, organized resistance and appealed to Britain for money and weapons. Napoleon unwisely dispersed his troops in an attempt to crush the main centres of the insurrection, exposing them to defeat piecemeal. Junot was cut off in Portugal by the revolts and had to concentrate the majority of his troops around Lisbon, leaving most of the country, like Spain, in a state of revolt.

These events boosted Britain's fortunes at a critical time. Her exports rose dramatically with the opening of new markets in Latin America. Her navy no longer had to maintain a blockade of the Peninsula and Napoleon at a stroke had lost twenty-four Spanish ships-of-the-line and seven French, seized in the Spanish ports of Vigo and Cadiz. Furthermore, the way was open for Britain to land an army on the Continent to mount an effective and sustained challenge to Napoleon's power on land. For the British, the Iberian Peninsula was an ideal theatre of war. It lay 700 km from Paris and had poor internal communications, making it difficult for the French to manoeuvre: apart from Switzerland, Spain was the most mountainous country in Europe. The Pyrenees could be readily crossed by an army only at either end, next to the sea, while the mountainous terrain of much of the countryside had hindered the development of a road net and provided many strong defensive positions. The few good roads that did exist were mainly centred on Madrid and were usually guarded by fortresses at key locations. Of Spain's rivers, only the Ebro and Guadalquivir could be used as avenues of communication, the others being accessible to boats only for limited stretches near the sea and often enclosed in steep valleys with no room for the construction of roads. Both Spain and Portugal were sparsely populated and had limited resources, making it difficult for large French armies to live off the country. Even the more fertile plains would become exhausted by the prolonged presence of large numbers of troops. In contrast, Britain through her maritime supremacy could readily supply her forces by sea, and, if necessary, evacuate them to safety.

Nine thousand British troops had already been assembled at Cork in southern Ireland. They had originally been earmarked for an expedition against the Spanish colonies in South America, but now that Spain was no longer an enemy they were redirected to the Peninsula. Their command had been entrusted to Lieutenant-General Sir Arthur Welles-ley, the future Duke of Wellington.

*

Wellesley was one of the most capable officers in the British army, but had yet to establish his reputation on the European stage. He was thirty-nine years old, slim, physically fit and of medium height, being five feet nine inches tall. He had short, dark brown hair, penetrating blue eyes and a distinctive aquiline nose. He spoke quickly and decisively and had an unusual, whooping laugh, but tended to be reserved on first acquaintance. He was nicknamed 'the beau' for his smart appearance. During the Peninsular War and at Waterloo he mostly wore civilian clothes rather than a uniform, usually a blue or grey frock coat, white waistcoat, white or grey pantaloons with black boots, a low cocked hat and sometimes also a blue or white cloak, or grey greatcoat. He had married Catherine Pakenham in April 1806, but found that they were ill-matched in temperament. Yet despite their unhappiness, they produced two sons, in February 1807 and January 1808, and remained married until Kitty's death in 1831.

Wellesley was a well-rounded and experienced commander. He had spent nine of the fifteen years since the outbreak of war with Revolutionary France in 1793 on active service, first in Flanders (June 1794 to March 1795), then in India (February 1797 to March 1805) and Denmark (August to September 1807). He had also commanded a brigade in an abortive expedition to Hanover in northern Germany during the winter of 1805–6. Few British generals had as much recent experience. His achievements were particularly impressive in India, where he had

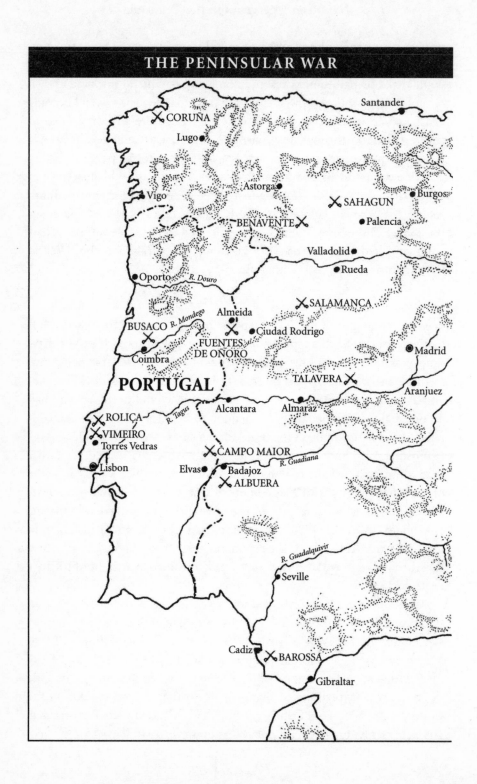

THE PENINSULAR WAR

Santander

✗ CORUÑA

Lugo●

Astorga●

Vigo● ✗ SAHAGUN ● Burgos

BENAVENTE ✗ ● Palencia

Valladolid●

● Rueda

Oporto● *R. Douro*

✗ SALAMANCA

Almeida●

BUSACO *R. Mondego* ✗ ● Ciudad Rodrigo

Coimbra● FUENTES ● Madrid

DE OÑORO

PORTUGAL TALAVERA ✗

● Aranjuez

R. Tagus Alcantara Almaraz●

✗ ROLIÇA

✗ VIMEIRO

● Torres Vedras

✗ CAMPO MAIOR

● Lisbon Elvas● *R. Guadiana*

Badajoz●

✗ ALBUERA

R. Guadalquivir

Seville●

Cadiz● ✗ BAROSSA

● Gibraltar

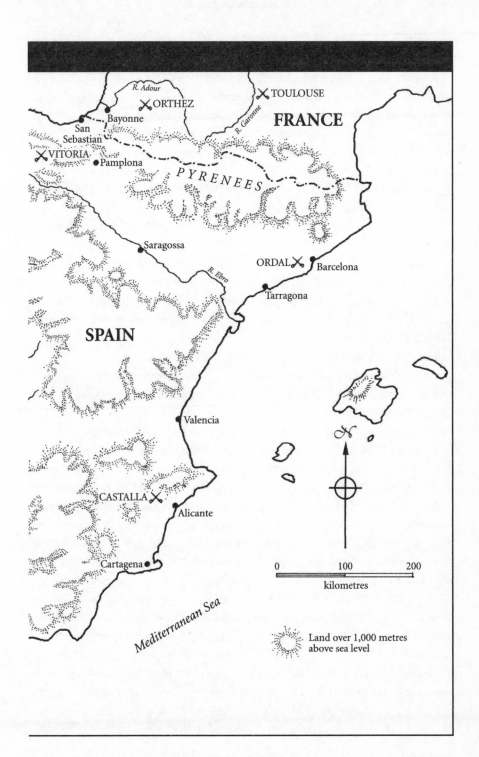

R. Adour

✕ ORTHEZ

✕ TOULOUSE

Bayonne

FRANCE

San
Sebastian

R. Garonne

✕ VITORIA

● Pamplona

P Y R E N E E S

● Saragossa

ORDAL ✕

Barcelona

R. Ebro

Tarragona

SPAIN

● Valencia

N

CASTALLA ✕

● Alicante

● Cartagena

0   100   200
kilometres

Mediterranean Sea

Land over 1,000 metres
above sea level

successfully pacified the state of Mysore and had then won major battlefield victories as an independent commander at Assaye and Argaum during the Second Maratha War (1803–5).

Wellesley had supplemented his practical experience by setting aside a couple of hours each day for private study. He read widely about his opponents and the areas in which he was operating. He had also acquired political, administrative and diplomatic experience, particularly in India, where he had governed the city of Seringapatam, negotiated peace treaties and advised his brother Richard, the Governor-General from 1797 to 1805. He had helped Richard extend British control and influence and had thereby played a key role in laying the foundations of British imperial power in India. After his return to England, he had won election to the House of Commons in April 1806 and a year later had joined the Duke of Portland's Tory Ministry as Chief Secretary for Ireland. He was an outstanding administrator, with a flair for mathematics and finance and a thorough and well-organized mind. He had demonstrated, particularly in India, his mastery of logistics and ability to collect, process and use a mass of intelligence.

Wellesley's self-confidence stemmed largely from his background. He was born in Ireland in the spring of 1769 as the third surviving son of Garret Wesley, the first Earl of Mornington. His family belonged to the Anglo-Irish Protestant Ascendancy, which dominated Catholic Ireland from Dublin. Such a background bred a natural authority and self-belief. Yet Wellesley was a late developer and after three undistinguished years at Eton had been sent in 1786 to the Royal Academy of Equitation at Angers in France to prepare him for a career in the British army, his mother having decided that he was unfit for anything else. It was only in his mid-twenties that he fully dedicated himself to his profession. He was indebted for his start in life to Richard, his brilliant elder brother, who had taken over as head of the family following his father's death in 1781. It was Richard who purchased for Wellesley an ensign's commission in the 73rd (Highland) Regiment of Foot in 1787 and used his money and influence to advance his subsequent career, particularly in India.

Wellesley believed in seeing and doing as much as possible himself and often assumed personal command of a battalion at a critical point. He led by example and enjoyed the trust of his troops, who knew his concern for their well-being and determination to avoid unnecessary casualties. He was courageous but not rash. In India, he had become accustomed to attacking boldly, for he knew that a disciplined and well-led army with a reputation for invincibility could overthrow a much larger native force. He retained this aggressiveness, but it was tempered in the Peninsula by the knowledge that Britain lacked the manpower to replace his army if it was destroyed. He could not take unnecessary risks or purchase success with heavy casualties and instead was flexible and pragmatic. He was able to think ahead and appreciate the connections between his operations and the wider war against Napoleon, yet at the same time he was forceful and self-centred in arguing for resources.

Wellesley's decisiveness enabled him to transact business quickly and efficiently and also contributed to his notorious abruptness with fools and pedants. He enforced an iron discipline to stamp out neglect and preserve order. He did not hesitate to shoot or hang looters as the only way to preserve the efficiency of his army and avoid antagonizing the local inhabitants. He insisted on undivided responsibility and refused to have a second-in-command in any meaningful sense. His self-reliance and autocratic character, and a concern to avoid leaks, also tended to make him reluctant to share his plans with his subordinates as much as he might have done.

He was devoted to duty and public service and had shown in India that he was incorruptible. He discouraged cheering and despised the veneration that Napoleon evoked, but it is easy to exaggerate his reputation as a cold and aloof commander. He was sometimes sparing of praise in his written despatches, but made a point of encouraging his troops and subordinates verbally during a battle. He insisted on units being efficient and well disciplined, but was less concerned with their parade-ground appearance. His explosions of temper were sudden and ferocious, but rarely lasted long and rebukes often ended with an invitation to dinner.

*

Wellesley had been promoted to lieutenant-general on 25 April 1808 and on 14 June he was formally given command of the 9,000 troops at Cork. Before leaving London, Wellesley dined with a friend, John Wilson Croker, who would be taking care of his Irish duties in Parliament during his absence. Wellesley at one point was deep in thought and explained that he was thinking of the French whom he was going to fight. He had last seen them thirteen years before in the Low Countries, but had studied their subsequent campaigns. He thought that they could be defeated with steady troops, especially as he, unlike most of Napoleon's Continental opponents, was not afraid of them.

Napoleon had won his stunning victories of 1805–7 only at a heavy cost in casualties and had filled the gaps in the Grand Army, his main offensive weapon, by enrolling the men due to be conscripted in 1808 and 1809 a year or two early. Furthermore, since he had not expected significant opposition in the Peninsula, he had not gone there himself and had sent mainly second-rate and often temporary units of conscripts or reserve troops under mediocre commanders, instead of formations from the Grand Army, which remained in Central Europe. Many of the battalions that Wellesley initially encountered under Junot in Portugal had previously been guarding the French coasts rather than gaining combat experience. During the Peninsular War, Wellesley encountered units of varying quality and never had to face the Grand Army in its heyday; nor did he have to fight Napoleon himself until Waterloo. His initial victories in Portugal were crucial in establishing the moral superiority of the British troops over their opponents and this was reinforced as the war progressed. The steady rise in the experience, efficiency and self-confidence of Wellesley's army accompanied an erosion in French morale under the impact of a string of defeats and the strain of occupying a hostile country.

The British army had a poor reputation in 1808, partly as a result of its demoralizing defeat in the American War of Independence (1775–83), followed by more recent failures during the Wars of the French Revolution (1793–1802), and partly because of the small numbers it had available for operations within Europe after providing garrisons for bases and colonies around the world. But Wellesley demonstrated in the Peninsula that much had been done to regenerate the army and that its low standing was no longer valid.

Many of the army's initial problems stemmed from its massive expansion following the outbreak of war with Revolutionary France in 1793, with a tripling in the size of the regular army within two years. It was also difficult to adapt the army's administration to a wartime footing, especially given the deliberate diffusion of control to allay traditional fears of a military dictatorship. Such problems overshadowed the progress that had already been made in the aftermath of the American War of Independence, including the adoption in 1792 of Major-General David Dundas' *Principles of Military Movements* to provide a uniform system of infantry drill and hence enable battalions to operate efficiently together. The situation steadily improved, particularly after the King's second son, Frederick Augustus, Duke of York and Albany, superseded Lord Amherst in chief command of the army in 1795. The Duke undertook a series of reforms which strengthened the discipline and internal administration of the army, enforced the observance of Dundas' drill regulations and improved the professionalism of the officer corps and the welfare of the private soldiers. He also presided over the introduction of permanent regiments of riflemen and light infantry, which enabled the British to contend on more equal terms with the powerful French skirmishing screens, particularly as Napoleon did not have rifle units. Improvements were also made in the cavalry and, under the Master-General of the Ordnance, in the artillery and the design and provision of weapons.

From 1793 to 1808, units of the British army fought in the Low Countries, Ireland, Denmark, Egypt, the Mediterranean, Cape Colony, India, the Far East, the West Indies and South America. Although many expeditions ended in evacuation, this was largely due to poor planning and leadership, inadequate logistical and medical support or simply inferior numbers and unreliable allies. The actual regiments were essentially sound, as was demonstrated by their steadiness in battle, and they helped win some notable victories against the French, for example Famars, Lincelles and Villers-en-Cauchie during the ultimately unsuccessful campaigns in the Low Countries in 1793–95.

The British army's growing potential was emphasized by the expulsion of the French from Egypt in 1801. A British expedition under Lieutenant-General Sir Ralph Abercromby executed a superbly planned amphibious landing in Aboukir Bay and then decisively defeated a veteran French army at the Battle of Alexandria. The quality of the British infantry was confirmed during Lieutenant-General Sir John Stuart's expedition to Calabria in southern Italy in 1806, when they routed a French force at the Battle of Maida. The British during these years never suffered sufficiently high casualties to undermine the efficiency of their units, in contrast to the qualitative decline in Napoleon's army and, indeed, in those of his Continental opponents. Furthermore, Lord Castlereagh as Secretary of State for War and the Colonies from

July 1805 to January 1806 and again from March 1807 increased the army's strength by encouraging Militiamen to transfer to regular service. He thereby established a disposable force of 40,000 men, with a fleet of transport ships, ready to intervene on the Continent as soon as it was required.

Wellesley on disembarkation in the Peninsula would have to weld his various units, and the departments of his headquarters which were theoretically responsible directly to superiors in London, into a cohesive, efficient and self-confident army. He would initially be weak in numbers, particularly in cavalry and artillery, and would have to improvise a system of logistics using mostly local transport. But he had superbly trained and disciplined battalions even at the start of his Peninsular campaigns and could depend on their steadiness and tactical efficiency. These infantry battalions would be the essential building blocks of his success.

2

The Road to Coruña

1808–9

Wellesley sailed from Cork on 12 July 1808 and while at sea acquired a basic understanding of Spanish by using a dictionary and a Spanish translation of the Book of Common Prayer. He preceded his army in a fast frigate and on 20 July reached Coruña at the north-western tip of Spain to confer with the local Junta and assess the situation in the Peninsula. The Spaniards were keen to accept money and weapons, but had been at war with Britain until as recently as 5 July; they suspected her motives and did not want her troops.

Wellesley then sailed southwards to Oporto in Portugal, where he arrived on 24 July and gained further intelligence. He knew that Junot had concentrated most of his troops around Lisbon and hence resolved to disembark at Mondego Bay, 160 km north of the city.

Second Captain William Eliot was with Captain Henry Geary's Brigade of 9pdr guns. He explained in a letter dated 27 July:

> we sailed from Cove [of Cork] on the morning of the 12th inst with a fine breeze which however, unfortunately got round to the opposite quarter, and continued to blow against us for near a week excepting two or three days which were perfectly calm[.] on the 22nd we made cape Ortegal and lay to for 2 days whilst the Frigates went into Ferrol & Corruna where Sir A Welesley was recieved in the most cordial manner by the natives & on his joining the fleet again brought with him ribbons with death or liberty & [the Spanish King] Ferdinand the 7th which the natives had given him, and on his arrival had illuminated the town[.] whilst off Cape Finisterre we fell in with the Amazon Capn W. Parker. I went on board & collected all the news & he supplied us with a few articles we were in want of. On the 26th we lay to close off Oporto and this morning anchor'd here [Mondego Bay]. the bay appears strongly fortified and is in possession of the

Portuguese who have lately risen on the French and driven them out.
6000 are encamped about 20 miles nearer Lisbon. Sir A.W. is gone
on in the Frigate and it is generally believed we shall debark here,
in order to attack the French in the rear. Gen[l] Junot has not more
than 16.000 men in the country and those much distributed 10.000
of them in or near Lisbon[.] the Portuguese are arming and training
in every village and only want good officers to lead them arms &
ammunition we can supply them with. . . .

In fact, Junot had 26,000 troops. Wellesley began landing on 1 August
and was joined by nearly 5,000 reinforcements from Gibraltar. He learnt
that more troops would arrive shortly and that he would be superceded
in command, for he was one of the most junior lieutenant-generals in
the army and could not reasonably be left in command of a force that
would eventually total almost 40,000 men. Lieutenant-General Sir Hew
Dalrymple would take over as Commander-in-Chief, with Lieutenant-
General Sir Harry Burrard as his second-in-command. It was a bitter
blow, but Wellesley hoped to defeat the French while he was still in
charge.

He marched southwards and found 4,300 French troops under
General Henri Delaborde at Obidos, 70 km north of Lisbon. Delaborde's
aim was to cover the concentration of the rest of Junot's army and after
a preliminary skirmish on 15 August, he withdrew to a position near the
village of Roliça. Wellesley attacked on the 17th, seeking to turn both his
flanks. Delaborde fell back once more, this time 1.5 km to a steep ridge
cut by gullies. Wellesley again sought to outflank him and after hard
fighting drove him from the battlefield.

Lieutenant Thomas Blackwell of the 36th (or the Herefordshire)
Regiment of Foot vividly described the Battle of Roliça in his journal.
He accompanied a force of 4,500 men sent under Major-General Ronald
Ferguson to turn Delaborde's eastern flank. Ferguson lost his way and
arrived late, but posed sufficient threat to encourage Delaborde to retreat:

Marchd from Calanes [?] reached Ovidas [Obidos] at 8 AM[.] here
the army was formed in order of Battle & soon after moved on left
in front – The inhabitants of this village afraid for the French did not
receive us with that enthusiasm with which we had been accustomed
since our landing[:] looking over the walls of their fortifications they
beheld us pass in silence. – Soon after passing this place a Rifle man

came back & told us the French were near – We could now perceive them in a valley at the foot of pass a [illegible] – Gen Ferguson seeing them advancing formed his Brigade [illegible] and smashed their attack – seeing this they retreated to the pass – the 5th 9th & 29th having arrived in front of the hills forming this pass immediately ascended the almost perpendicular heights by ravines – but suffered much from the enemies fire – not daunted in the smallest at this they soon gained the summit & forming on the plain charged – and assisted by several guns playing on the enemy soon routed them. – The French perceiving that little more than ½ their numbers had completely beat them [the French were in fact outnumbered] & afraid of being surrounded by that part of our army they saw advancing began their retreat which their General La Bord executed in good stile.

Lieutenant William Coles of the 40th (or the 2nd Somersetshire) Regiment of Foot was also with Ferguson's turning force. He wrote to his father on 19 August:

... We commenc'd our march about 150 miles from Lisbon and are arriv'd now within 30, have met with no opposition except at the pass of Obidas where the French had taken up a very strong position. It is impossible to explain the advantages possess'd by the Enemy at the time of attack. in fact it is one of the strongest positions in Portugal, which is saying a great deal as the Country is mountainous; and capable of much defence. I will not speak of the attack; as it was here & there our Rifle Corps fell in promiscuously with the advanced posts of the Enemy, who commenc'd the action, the Right Brigade supported follow'd & By the undaunted Bravery of the Soldiery, the French were oblig'd to Retire to the Neighbouring Hill, where they Rallyd their Troops and remained prepard for the second attack. this was not delayd long, our whole Body was pushed forward, and with Considerable loss at length obtaind the summit of the Hill, where the French met us with determind courage, Several Vollies were fir'd on Both Sides, But when our Artillery was enabled to act the French were affraid that the loss occasiond By a heavy fire would be too great to be sustaind, as their Force was Inferior to ours and thought it prudent to make a Retreat, which was a very admirable one; myself Being in the Light Infantry had the opportunity of seeing much, tho

not foremost, as the action commenc'd before our Brigade could
Reach the Ground – . . .

After Roliça Wellesley advanced 21 km south-westwards to cover the
disembarkation of two brigades of reinforcements at the mouth of the
River Maceira. But Sir Harry Burrard arrived offshore on the evening of
20 August, judged correctly that Wellesley was underestimating Junot's
numbers and ordered him to remain on the defensive. Fortunately,
Burrard did not land immediately and so Wellesley was still in command
when Junot attacked on the morning of the 21st with 13,000 men.
Wellesley shifted his army eastwards in response to Junot's obvious
attempt to outflank him and beat off the initial assaults on the village of
Vimeiro and its adjacent hill. Further east, another two French attacks
were defeated by two British brigades, one of which was commanded by
Major-General Ferguson.

The Battle of Vimeiro saw the first demonstration of Wellesley's
highly successful defensive tactics. He placed his battalions behind a
ridge to conceal and protect them from artillery fire, but deployed strong
screens of light infantry on the forward slopes to counter the skirmishers
that led the French attacks. His guns were distributed along his front to
fire on the French as they approached. The French infantry used a
variety of formations for particular circumstances, but tended to advance
in columns for ease of manoeuvre, intending to deploy into line for
greater firepower if they encountered serious resistance. But Wellesley
unexpectedly counter-attacked before they could deploy, and his battalions, each formed in a two-deep line with every man able to fire his
musket, overthrew the French columns with a volley at short range
quickly followed by a cheer and a bayonet charge. The French had
difficulty in coordinating their attacks over the rough terrain and
Wellesley was able to defeat a succession of assaults by concentrating
superior numbers at each threatened point.

Four eyewitnesses from Major-General Ferguson's brigade describe
the success of these tactics at Vimeiro. An anonymous soldier of the 71st
(Glasgow Highland) Regiment of Foot recorded:

 . . . the bustle around was great. there was no trace of a day of rest
 [it was a Sunday]. Many were washing their linen in the river, others
 cleaning their fire locks; every man was engaged in some employment. In the midst of our preparations for divine service, the French

columns began to make their appearance on the opposite hills. 'To arms, to arms!' was beat, At half-past 8 O Clock, Every thing was packed up as soon as possible, and left on the camp ground.

We marched out two miles, to meet the enemy, formed line, and lay under cover of a hill, for about an hour, untill they came to us. We gave them one volley, and three cheers three distinct cheers. then all was as still as death. they came upon us crying and shouting to the very point of our bayonets. Our awful silence and determined advance, they could not stand. they put about, and fled without much resistance. At this charge we took thirteen guns and one General.

We advanced into a hollow, and formed again then returned in file, from the right in companies, to the rear. the French came down upon us again[.] We gave them another specimen of a charge, as effectual as the first, and pursued them three miles.

In our first charge, I felt my mind waver; a breathless sensation came over me. the silence was appalling. I looked alongst the line: it was enough to assure me. the steady determined Scowl of my companions assured my heart, and gave me determination. How unlike the noisy advance of the French! . . .

Captain William Warre served as ADC to Major-General Ferguson and wrote to his friends on 17 September:

. . . We had received information on the Even^g of the 20th that the enemy intended to attack us next morning, but this was generally discredited. We were, as usual every morning, under arms an hour before day-break & remained after day break longer than usual, when not perceiving any thing of the Enemy, the troops were dismissed & Genl Ferguson & his staff again retired to our straw at a house about ½ a mile from Camp at the town of Vimeiro, about 8 I was woke by a Serjeant, who told me our piquets of the 40th on the left were driven in & the enemy advancing – I ran to tell Genl Ferguson & we were soon on horseback & on the Hill on the left, from whence we had a full view of the french army on its march to attack us in two strong columns, the strongest & principal attack was on our centre & the other against the hill and the left of our position, which was seperated from the centre by a deep Valley covered with vineyards occupied by our light troops, & to the top of which Genl F. ordered his brigade to advance to wait their attack.

Sir A Wel_ly arrived soon after as I had been sent to tell him of the attack, & perceiving the intention of the Enemy, ordered Genl Bowes & Genl Acklands brigades to support Genl Ferg.'s & made his dispositions in the most cool & masterly stile as from our commanding situation we could see all the movements of the French & our own army.

. . .

the Column that was to attack us, had a round to make & did not arrive till long after the centre was engaged, they advanced in column, Cavalry, infantry, & artillery with great confidence & were well received by our light troops, as soon as they were within reach, Genl Ferg. ordered his brig^de viz the 40th 36th & 71st [illegible] to charge them, which was done with all the intrepidity & courage of British soldiers & the Enemy retired before us keeping up a sharp fire, a part of them rallied, but Genl F. hurraed the 36th a very weak tho' fine Reg^t to charge which was done in great stile three successive times, till being very much thinned in some disorder from the rapid advance (I was sent back to hasten the support which was far behind[)], the gallant little regiment forming to rally again under cover of a Hedge of American aloes tho' much pressed, I just returned in time to join the 71st who were charging 6 pieces of the enemy's cannon that were retiring, & the fire at this time from the enemy being really tremendous, I had my poor horse shot under me the first day I rode him, having just received him from Porto. The first Ball broke his fore leg & immediately another just grazed the calf of my leg & killed him, I mounted the horse of an orderly that was shot at the same moment, but he was so dead tired I could not get him on, & having the cloak shot thro' before me, I thought it best to dismount, & join the 36th which reg^t I remained with the rest of the action, the Enemy attempted to rally & advanced with drums beating but the 71st charged them so manfully that they retired in confusion & the retreat became general, thus ended this glorious day in which the valor & intrepidity of gallant fellows was most conspicuous, their appearance w^d have made a stone feel in such a cause, as to Genl Ferg. all I could say would not be half what he deserves in praise his gallantry & judgement decided the day on the left, my only astonishment & that of every body else is how he escaped, he was always in advance & in the hottest Fire, animating every body by his noble example. . . .

Lieutenant Coles of the 40th Regiment wrote:

... Altho we expected that an Action would take place, I believe the Genl [Wellesley] had not the most distant Idea that it would take place so soon or that we should be fortunate enough to become the attack'd party – our position being rather confin'd and the cause of the French having arriv'd at a desperate pitch, Junot I suppose, conjectur'd that his only chance of success was, in surprising us, and directing his force against one weak quarter. He accordingly made a feint attack on our Right, then withdrew his force and by a circuitous rout[e] brought the whole of his Army to bear on our Left, our Genl being Inform'd of this maneeuvre took care not to [illegible] a Sufficient number to the Right, as to weaken the left wing, and by a concentration of his force at that quarter where the real attack was to be made by the Enemy He in great measure frustrated their Plan, and render'd Their Intention useless – The attack by the Enemy, tho not making the Impression that was expected, was well Regulated and Skilful, their Rifle Men [the French skirmishers in fact carried ordinary muskets] coverd the operations of the Main Body so well that many Individuals who were in the advance had not a conception that the French intended to make the Engagement general, however as their Light troops extended, the more we had occasion to be prepar'd, and the whole army excepting one Brigade was assembled on the rising of an Hill, and their appearance coverd by a constant fire from the advanc'd Light Infantry and our Rifles[.] However it became soon necessary to withdraw them, in order to give scope for action, and likewise Ground for our army – the Light Infantry Retird by Degrees under a most desperate fire and no sooner had they attaind the Flanks of their respective brigades than the action became general . . .

Lieutenant Blackwell was with the 36th Regiment:

Gen Ackland had no sooner landed with the 2ᵈ & 20ᵗʰ Regᵗˢ [one of the two brigades of reinforcements] than the French Columns appeared – in front of the lines of the 50ᵗʰ [?] a little above the village of Vimeiro – our drums beat to arms our Battˢ were formed and marchd & took possession of a hill on the left of the village – from our position we could see the enemies columns sweeping along in all directions – our Camp was soon attacked on all sides – When the right was warmly engaged we saw with confidence of the result several columns advancing to the attack of our position, our artillery now began a well directed fire – our Rifles and skirmishers [illegible] – but were soon driven in by the rapid advance of the French – the left of their line extending beyond our right the Gren[s] 1st & 2[d] Companies are detachd to [illegible] the thing – awaiting their approach with the greatest steadiness notwithstanding a galling fire which was kept up during their advance – When the enemy came within 60 yards our detachment began to throw in vollies amongst them – 8 rounds were expended by the time they had gained 40 yards – the men [illegible] now gave three cheers and charged – they [the French] retreated precipitately. Col [Robert] Burne now dashed in amongst them with the 7 Companies and after keeping up a hot fire for a quarter of an hour charged scattered them w[it]h dreadful slaughter – the firing which had continued for 3 hours ½ now ceassed – the silence only disturbed by the bussings [kissing] of congratulation and shouts of joy – . . .

Wellesley wanted to take immediate advantage of his victory by cutting Junot's line of retreat to Lisbon. But the lacklustre Burrard had now disembarked and refused to allow him to pursue. That night, Sir Hew Dalrymple also arrived and confirmed Burrard's decision. He had served competently as Governor of Gibraltar since 1806, but was fifty-eight years old and had seen active service for only one of the forty-five years that he had been in the army. On 8 August, he had written to his wife, who had hoped to join him at Gibraltar:

Our plans of meeting are over for the present, & I am to take the Field. You probably heard [in England] of the high honour that had been confer'd upon me, (and that in the most flattering manner,) before my letters reach[d] you to encourage your coming out.

The Command I have got is very important & very extensive as to numbers, and I am officially told that it has been bestow'd upon me 'His Majesty highly approving of the Zeal & Judgement which has mark'd my Conduct under the late important Events which have taken place in Spain.'

I carry the 42[d] Reg[t] with me & have many Volunteers from this Garrison, of which I am instructed *during my absence* to leave General Drummond in the Command; do I wish to return here? I dont know, but *If I come* [back] I shall have a house ready to receive you.

The Phœbe Frigate is orderd to take me on board, and C[aptai]ⁿ Oswald who commands her is an intimate, & very happy with his commission; alas!! I fear I shall have to sail a good deal; But I feel about that, less than I did about Bells voyage.

I fancy my present Command, though it may lead to the House of peers, is not in the direct road to the Stock Exchange; but on this I am but slightly informed.

Despite the bitter controversy that followed his short period in command, Dalrymple did in fact receive a baronetcy in 1814, after protesting about his treatment. His lack of self-confidence is revealed by his letters. While negotiating with the Spanish Government as Governor of Gibraltar in June 1808, he had informed his wife in a decidedly uncertain tone:

... How my measures may be approved I know not, I have had no authority or Instructions & little time for Consideration, before decisions were made; But when I feel disposed to *hesitate* I shall retire *from service* ...

After arriving in Portugal, he wrote in similar vein on 12 September from his headquarters at Dáfundo, 7 km west of Lisbon:

When [Captain] Adolphus [Dalrymple, a son] left me I inhabited an Elegant Villa of the Marquis of Marialoz at Cintra: that he probably described – From thence I went to an ancient Seat of the Marquis de Pombal at D'Oeyras [Oeiras], that was very ancient very [illegible], & very pompous Immense Gardens & Walks in the Dutch stile but rather fine[.] am in good [illegible], my bed was under a Crimson Damask Canopy, and I slept under a Quilt of Crimson & Gold; for the purpose [of] a more ready communication with Lisbon I am now at the [illegible] but luxurious Villa of a Merchant, [illegible] & close to the Tagus, The Rooms are fitted up in the Elegant stile of an Expensive Mistress, & my Family & Staff are amply accomodated, Here I live whilst the Duties I am call'd upon to perform are of a magnitude and Importance, that I often think as much too large for my Talents, as the Houses I inhabit are for my Fortune or Establishment. ...

The French sought an armistice on the day after Vimeiro, with a view to negotiating an evacuation of their army back to France. The British for their part would thereby evict the French from Portugal without the need for further fighting and without having to besiege several French-held fortresses. The French wanted to be transported in British ships, since they had been cut off by the Spanish uprisings. The French occupation forces in Spain had abandoned Madrid at the beginning of August and fallen back to the River Ebro in the north-east after a humiliating defeat in which a corps of 17,600 men under General Pierre Dupont had been forced to surrender at Bailen to General Francisco Castaños, the commander of the Spanish Army of Andalusia.

The armistice in Portugal was signed on 22 August by the French representative, General François Kellermann. Wellesley, who was instructed to sign by Dalrymple, realized that in any case the chance had been lost to secure a quick result by military means. A definitive convention was signed eight days later by Kellermann and Dalrymple's Quartermaster-General. But the Convention of Cintra provoked immediate controversy, not least as it left the French free to fight again; they also tried to take much of their loot. The British Government was unable effectively to counter the popular outcry, since Dalrymple failed to send a copy of the convention until nearly a week after it had been signed. Dalrymple also neglected to include Portuguese representatives in the negotiations. They particularly resented the inclusion of clauses allowing French residents to remain in Lisbon for a year and providing for the protection of Portuguese subjects who had collaborated during the French occupation.

Portugal lacked a formally recognized government. The Prince Regent had nominated a Council of Regency on his departure for Brazil in 1807, but it needed to be reconstituted following the French occupation, for several of its members had collaborated while a Supreme Junta had emerged under the Bishop of Oporto to resist the French. Dalrymple re-established the Council of Regency on 18 September and its new composition included the Bishop of Oporto. The Supreme Junta was then dissolved, leaving Portugal with a single, recognized government. Despite inefficiency and some opposition within the Council, Portugal was effectively a dependent state of Britain for the rest of the war.

A further 11,000 British reinforcements had now landed in Portugal under Lieutenant-General Sir John Moore. Wellesley and Moore each commanded a division under Dalrymple, and Second Captain Eliot of the Royal Artillery complained to his wife on 23 September:

... we are yet under the hedges all the troops which came with Sir J
Moore &c being accomodated before those who sustained the whole
of the hard work & because they are *better clothed* & wear more *Pipe
Clay* so much for military appearances. were we sure of remaining
the winter here I should wish above all things to have you come out
but a winters passage with the uncertainty of remaining in the
country I think are much against it. consult your friends & if they
think it adviseable, come if you can . . .

Such resentments were not shared by an unidentified captain in
Wellesley's division. He noted on 28 August that at Torres Vedras:

... It was a pleasing & interesting sight to see the officers & men of
Sir. J. Moore's army & our's, who had met each other for a length of
time congratulating each other on their meeting in a Foreign
Country, the former wishing us every joy on our late victories. –
none but those who are daily exposed to scenes of danger, can feel
that sweet sensation that is imparted by mutual & desinterested
friendship.

He also recorded on 1 September how the soldiers felt about the
Convention:

... Though we had not met with any party of the Enemy since the
Battle of Vimiero, an unpleasant circumstance had nearly occurred
this morning, which might have led to most serious consequences; a
French Party of Cavalry approached too near our Piquets, and as
[although] the Convention was not officially communicated to the
army, we well knew that cessation of hostilities had taken place,
notwithstanding which our Sentries fired on this party & with great
difficulty could they be persuaded that they were not come to attack
us; such was their hatred to the French, indeed they seemed anxious
to have an opportunity of breaking the truce & recommencing
hostilities. . . .

The captain took the opportunity offered by his being sent on a
detached duty to visit Lisbon on 10 September. Two French gendarmes
escorted him past numerous sentries and through a crowd of inhabitants
who were cheering the English. They left him at an inn, where he was
ushered by the French landlord into the coffee room:

... which I was not a little astonished to find full of French officers.
I felt rather awkward at first, but was soon relieved from my
unpleasant situation, by the whole rising from their seats, & present-
ing me a place near the head of the Table, showed me every polite
attention imaginable, & by a manner peculiar to the French soon
made me forget I was a stranger. an aide de camp of Genl Laborde
[Delaborde] was present, he was particularly attentive, by ordering
the Landlord to provide a handsome supper, which was soon served
up: The conversation became general, & the wine going round our
spirits soon became exhilirated, & we did not retire untill late, with
mutual civilities; and I must confess, that I did not hear during the
whole evening any insinuation relating to our national enmity, but
much the reverse; Their *friends* the Portuguese, they honored with
Epithets of the grossest nature. . . .

Five days later, he saw the 18th Regiment of (Light) Dragoons
(Hussars) march into Lisbon:

... nothing could exceed the beauty & magnificent appearance of
this Corps. The noble appearance of the men, their size, magnificence
of their uniform & horse appointments & the beauty of the horses
themselves astonished the great numbers of spectators who were
assembled to see them: a visible deference was apparent between this
Reg^t and a body of French Cavalry who were not yet embarked,
indeed they themselves acknowledged the superior quality of our
horses.
    Though these exterior appearances are of little consideration to
our own countrymen, it is astonishing the effect they have on
Foreigners, who judge of the respectability & power of a nation, by
those whom that nation deputes to defend or plead for their rights.
with pleasure I heard many spectators remark, how powerful a nation
the British must be, who could send out such a formidable &
respectable body of men.

The French, as agreed under the Convention, sailed between 15 and
30 September. The unidentified captain described how the British
actually had to defend the last of the French from the inhabitants:

... as their [French] numbers decreased the mob became more
sanguinary; at last an almost general attack was made on all those
whose imprudence had detained them from the Body of the Troops.

numbers were murdered in this manner, & had not the timely arrival of some parties of our Troops put a stop to these assassinations, probably the streets of Lisbon would have become a scene disgraceful to the most uncivilised savages. Some of our officers had it in their power to save many from the grave, & were under the necessity of acting offensively on the mob to save these devoted wretches, & often the protection of a British officer was barely sufficient to protect them from the stiletto.

The conduct of our Soldiers was admirable, parties were seen protecting the French at the risk of their own lives (many British being dangerously wounded in the affray) & with their Bayonets charged conveying their protegés to the quay.

Wellesley by now was keen to return home, being frustrated by his impossible situation. On 17 September, he wrote a private letter to Moore. Despite his outstanding reputation as a soldier, Moore was outspoken and had recently clashed with Government ministers, whom he had suspected of deliberately trying to deprive him of the command in the Peninsula. Wellesley addressed this issue directly:

I write to you upon the subject to which this letter relates with the same freedom with which I hope you would write to me on any point on which you might think the publick Interests concerned.

It appears to me to be quite impossible that we can go on as we are now constituted; the Commander in Chief must be changed; & the Country & the Army naturally turn their eyes to you as their Commander. I understand however that you have lately had some unpleasant discussions with the King's Ministers, the effect of which might be to prevent the adoption of an arrangement for the Command of this Army, which in my opinion would be the best, & would enable you to render those Services at this moment for which you are peculiarly qualified.

I wish that you would allow me to talk to you respecting the discussions to which I have adverted, in order that I may endeavour to remove any trace which they may have left on the minds of the King's Ministers, which might have the effect which I have supposed. Although I hold a high Office under the Gov[t] I am no party Man; but have long been connected in friendship with many of the persons who are now at the Head of affairs in England; & I think I have sufficient Influence over them to induce them to listen to me upon a point of this description, more particularly as I am convinced that they must be as desirous as I can be to adopt the arrangement for the Command of this Army which all are agreed is the best.

In these times My dear General a Man like you should not preclude himself from rendering the Service of which he is capable by any idle point of form. Circumstances may have occasioned & might justify the discussions to which I have referred; but none can justify the continuance of the temper in which they were carried on; & yet till there is evidence that it is changed it appears to be impossible for the King's Ministers to employ you in the high situation for which you are the most fit, because during the existence of this temper of Mind, there can be no cordial or confidential Intercourse.

In writing this much I have perhaps gone too far, & have taken the permission, for which it was the Intention of this letter to ask; but I shall still send it, as it may be convenient to you to be apprized of the view which I have already taken of these discussions, as far as I have any knowledge of them, in deciding whether you will allow me to talk to you any further about them. If you should do so, it would probably be most convenient for both to meet at Lisbon; or I can go over to you, if that should suit you better.

They met the following day. Moore shared Wellesley's views of Dalrymple's incompetence but refused to enter into any intrigue. Wellesley sailed for home on the 20th, while Burrard and Dalrymple were soon recalled. The Convention had caused public outrage in Britain, where it was seen as having thrown away the fruits of the victories of Roliça and Vimeiro as well as being dishonourable. The controversy was fanned by the press and overshadowed the benefits of the Convention. Wellesley found himself along with Dalrymple and Burrard as one of the three scapegoats, for opponents of his family saw an opportunity to make political capital out of the controversy. The Government was obliged to summon a military Court of Enquiry to investigate the circumstances and all three generals were required to give evidence. Dalrymple in a letter to his wife on 26 September offered a robust defence of his actions:

... You will have heard a great deal about the Convention made with the French & I understand [words missing] Ministers took a very early opportunity to exclaim against it, whether they are right or wrong I shall not say just now, but I have enough to offer if necessary.

Burrard came just in Time for the Battle of Vimeiro, and I came just in Time for the suspension of arms; he declined all honour from the first, and I disdain any great portion of honour for the second. I approved it of course, because I knew nothing about the state of affairs in Portugal; because Sir Arthur Wellesley did know that state, *and because* he was perfectly acquainted with the *views of H.M. Government*; but certainly those articles signed by Sir Arthur were not disapproved by him, indeed I do not think it likely he would wish to shrink from the degree of responsibility which must naturally attach to him. I must also say, that [words missing] now, knowing as I do, I entirely approve [of] the Convention although one or two more articles, (the last perhaps within Lisbon which would probably have been destroy'd) the loss of a thousand or 1500 men, & the winter Blockade or siege of Elvas & Almeida, would have cut the French to pieces or caused them to lay down their arms; but then the Portuguese instead of seeing the [enemy] Destroy[ed] or arrested in his progress tranquillity, and a great deal of property restored, would have suffered all the [illegible] above described, without either [illegible] or redress. This is my private Opinion *now*[.] The day I came I had no Opinion about the matter, but was astonished to find all the histories I had before heard, meer fables. . . .

In fact, Wellesley had favoured taking a tough line with the French and had protested to Dalrymple about some of the details of the armistice before signing it as he was directed.

Dalrymple's feelings on returning to England were not wholly adverse. He wrote to his wife on 29 September:

Last night Adolphus [came] with orders for my return to England, I therefore look forwards with joy to meeting my family after more than two tedious years of absence.

. . .

Let this be a lesson to us my sweet woman to look for happiness elsewhere than in popular applause, particularly in a Country Governed by Newspapers; the Exaggerated commendations which perhaps helped to obtain me this high distinction were certainly not justified by any thing I had it in my power to do, I mean any of those things that could point me out as capable of Commanding an army larger than that of the Duke of Marlborough, believe me I blushed, & received with pain all commendations even from you, that spring from that source; and though my command has been short & not marked with any very important military circumstances I shall embark with a firmer step, and more persuaded that the most experienced and distinguished officers of this army think it not impossible that I might have succeeded in this Command than when I disembark'd on the coast of Portugal about a month ago.

In all this matter, the kindness of the Commander in Chief [of the British army, the Duke of York] and L^t Co^l [James Willoughby] Gordon [the Duke's Military Secretary] affords a Cordial to my heart, whatever their opinions may be they have consulted the feelings of my Son and my own, and I feel some pleasure in the confident hope that I shall preserve a share of their esteem. I can have no desire to gain approbation where I feel nothing but Contempt. . . .

In a paper he later wrote on the Convention, Dalrymple complained:

. . . It is evident, that about the Time of my appointment, His Majesty's government expected that Junot would soon surrender under some Form of Capitulation or another; as it was therefore thought necessary, that His Majesty's Sentiments should be clearly understood, as to the impropriety and danger of the admission into Military Conventions of articles of a Description, which have been admitted into many if not most Treaties of the same sort, as the Declaration itself implies, it became the Duty of the Secretary of State to convey to me immediate, & explicit Instructions upon that head; and to the omission of that precaution, is I think to be attributed whatever ill consequences may have ensued . . .

Yet apparently Dalrymple himself did not give much prior thought to the details of a capitulation, although he fully realized that one was likely to occur. In a letter to Lieutenant-Colonel Gordon, written at Gibraltar on 9 August, he noted that since Junot had been cut off:

. . . he is sure when he thinks fit to capitulate that he will at least fall into safe hands[.] Ld Collingwood [the naval commander in the Mediterranean] thinks the French will immediately capitulate, & I hope it may prove so.

But where is the War to go next? it would be lamentable to wait for it again in Portugal, *in case of disaster befalling the Spanish Arms*, here my sentiment coincides most fully with yours. . . .

Similarly, Dalrymple subsequently claimed of his appointment that the 'ebb and flow of approbation and confidence was not satisfactory; and something seemed to lurk under this most complicated arrangement, which bore, I thought, a most unpromising aspect.'* But this does not tally with his correspondence at the time. He wrote to Castlereagh from Gibraltar on 8 August:

> In acknowledging the Honour of your Lordships Letter of the 15th July marked Private I beg to express my grateful acknowledgements for the very flattering terms in which your Lordship has been pleased to announce the high honour his Majesty has been pleased to confer on me by giving me the Command of the Forces destined to serve in Portugal and Spain, & I beg to assure your Lordship that it gives me a satisfaction I have not words to describe, to find that my late endeavours for the Publick Service [as Governor of Gibraltar since November 1806] have been honoured with Your Lordships approbation
>
> Your Lordship may be assured that the high character of Sir A. Wellesley & the confidence so justly reposed in him by His Majestys Gov.t would have induced me to avail myself of his talents & services as far as they could possibly be employed even without the suggestion your Lordships Letter contains. . . .

This fulsome acknowledgement also contrasts with the resentment towards the Government to be found in the letter that Dalrymple wrote in October 1826 to Lieutenant-Colonel William Napier, the historian of the Peninsular War:

> . . . I must now inform you (in reference to what you say about my appointment to the Command in Portugal,) that when I returned to England, I understood (from what I thought good authority) that Sir John Moore had said before he sailed to Portugal, that I had applied for that Command; – In that particular Sir John Moore had been misinform'd; it was never my object to place myself in a situation so

---

* H. Dalrymple, *Memoir written by General Sir Hew Dalrymple, Bart. of his Proceedings as connected with the Affairs of Spain, and the Commencement of the Peninsular War* (London, 1830), p. 52.

perilous, & under a Government of which I had already some Experience; the very terms upon which the Command was imposed upon me, were not flattering; – In short the Idea had never presented itself to my Imagination; but I was absent, & was order'd; I could not therefore expostulate & had nothing left but to obey. – It is true that about the beginning of May, the Enthousiasm of the moment induced me to intimate to the Commander in Chief [the Duke of York] (through his Secretary) my readiness to take the Command of any Auxiliary Force which might be destined to serve in Spain under the Command of General Castaños, I do not believe that either Sir John Moore or Sir Arthur Wellesley would have Envied me the appointment; perhaps this may have given rise to the Rumour I allude to [that he had applied for the command in Portugal]; though if so, the fact must have been much distorted, or misunderstood . . .

The Court of Enquiry concluded on 22 December that no further military proceedings were necessary, thus clearing all three generals. After a further sitting, the Court approved of the Convention by a majority of four to three. But Dalrymple did not escape censure altogether, for he was rebuked by the Duke of York on two political counts, namely the inclusion in the Convention of clauses affecting the interests of the Spaniards and Portuguese and the delay in sending the Government news of the armistice. Neither Dalrymple nor Burrard held another active command.

*

Meanwhile, on 25 September 1808, Moore had been appointed to command the army in the Peninsula. In the event, therefore, Wellesley's offer to him to press the British Government for his appointment had not been necessary. The success of the revolts in Spain, in forcing the French to evacuate most of the country, had inspired hopes that the Spanish armies, with British support, might inflict a devastating blow to Napoleon's Empire. In October, Moore therefore left 10,000 troops to defend Lisbon and took the other 20,000 into Spain. He would be reinforced by another contingent of over 10,000 men under Lieutenant-General Sir David Baird, which sailed from England on 9 October, and arrived four days later off Coruña on the north-western tip of Spain.

Lord Castlereagh, the Secretary of State for War and the Colonies, wrote a letter on 15 November which Moore received on 4 December:

... In entering upon Service in Spain, you will keep in mind that the British Army is sent by His Majesty as an Auxiliary Force, to support the Spanish Nation against the Attempts of Buonaparte to effect their subjugation. –

You will use your utmost Exertions to assist the Spanish Armies in subduing or expelling the Enemy from the Peninsula; and in the Conduct of your Command, you will conform to the Regulations hereafter stated with respect to the question of military Rank, and your Intercourse with the Government of Spain. –

In framing these Instructions, it is necessary distinctly to provide, first for the Case of the Spanish Government having entrusted the Command of their Armies to a Generalissimo or Commander in Chief; and secondly, for the Case which has hitherto existed, of distinct Armies, each commanded by it's own General. –

Should the Spanish Government appoint a Commander in Chief of all their Armies, (the necessity of which appointment every day's Experience appears to demonstrate,) you will consider yourself as placed under the Orders of that Officer.

If the Armies of Spain should remain as they have hitherto done, under their respective Chiefs, the Cooperation of the British Army must in that Case remain to be settled, as a matter of Concert by you with the Commanders of the respective Armies of Spain, in connection with whom you may be carrying on operations. –

When the Officers of the British and Spanish Armies meet on Service together, they must take Rank according to the Dates of their respective Commissions, without reference to the Powers from whence those Commissions are derived, provided such Commissions are at present acknowledged by the Supreme Government of Spain. –

You are to consider that the British Force under your Command is intended to act as a Field Army, to be kept together as far as the Circumstances of the War will permit; and that all Orders from the Commander in Chief proceeding either directly or through his Staff are to be given to the British Army through you, as it's immediate Commander, – that it is not to be separated into Detachments, nor any Detachment to be made from it, but with your entire Concurrence, and by your express order. – it is not to be employed in Garrisons, whereby a material Diminution would be made of its effective Strength in the Field, nor to be occupied in Sieges without your particular Consent. –

Whenever you shall have occasion to make any Communication to the Spanish Government, you are to correspond with it through the [British] Minister at Madrid; and all Communications from the Spanish Government are to be made to you through the same Channel; and altho' Communications either from the Spanish Government or the British Minister are not to be considered by you as in the nature of Orders, you will nevertheless receive such Requisitions or Representations upon all occasions with the utmost Deference and Attention; and in case you shall feel it your Duty to dissent from them, you will take care to represent in the fullest manner your Reasons for so doing as well as to the British Minister for the Information of the Spanish Government, as to the Government at home. –

You are also to keep up a constant and intimate Correspondence with the British Minister, and to cooperate in the most cordial manner with him in carrying on the Public Service. –

Should any difference of opinion arise on important military Subjects between you and the Spanish Commander in Chief, you are to consider it your Duty to pay obedience in the first instance to the orders you may receive. – But you will if you shall think it necessary make a Representation thereupon through the British Minister to the Supreme Government of Spain, as also to me for His Majesty's Information. –

As it is of peculiar Importance at the present moment that His Majesty's Government should receive early, regular, and detailed Reports of your Proceedings, I am to desire that you will make it a Rule to address a Dispatch to me at least once in every Week, or as much oftner as any occurrence of sufficient importance may arise; always being careful to send Duplicates of the preceding Dispatch by the subsequent Conveyance. –

It will be most grateful to His Majesty to find that the Intercourse between the British Army and the Spaniards has been invariably distinguished by marks of reciprocal Confidence and kindness. – His Majesty cannot doubt that the most exemplary Discipline will be observed; and His Majesty commands me particularly to enjoin that the utmost Respect and Deference should be shewn by His Troops upon all occasions towards the Manners and Customs of the Spanish Nation. – His Majesty trusts that the Example and Influence of the Officer's will be directed to inspire this Sentiment throughout every Branch of the Army.

On 13 November Moore reached the city of Salamanca, where he halted. He began to receive reports of a succession of disasters that had befallen the Spanish armies 250 km to the north-east, for Napoleon at the beginning of November had personally crossed the Pyrenees at the head of massive reinforcements in order to reconquer the Peninsula.

This unexpected development found Moore's army disunited, for he had sent his cavalry and guns under Lieutenant-General Sir John Hope by an easier route along the main road from Badajoz to Madrid and they had yet to arrive at Salamanca. Furthermore, Baird was delayed, for he had not been allowed to begin disembarking at Coruña until 26 October thanks to the obstinacy of the Spanish authorities, who wanted him to land at Santander, 370 km further east. They insisted that if he landed at Coruña he should do so in a succession of detachments which should advance immediately, supposedly so as not to overburden the local area. This posed problems as Baird had hoped to remain near Coruña until his force was fully equipped.

Baird's command included a cavalry brigade under Lieutenant-General Henry Lord Paget, later the second Earl of Uxbridge, consisting of the 7th, 10th and 15th Regiments of (Light) Dragoons (Hussars). The commander of the 7th, Lieutenant-Colonel Hussey Vivian, recorded his experiences of the campaign in his journal. His regiment disembarked at Coruña from 9 to 12 November:

> ... the first days disembarkation of the 7th was truly deplorable it rained torrents & from the Transports not being able to haul up to the quays, the Horses were slung into the water & most of them obliged to swim on shore – The poor men, most miserably soaked & having no place to go to but an open shed – many of them having lost their appointments & necessarys, & no man having a dry article to put on – add to all this the easy rate at which the men obtained wine & the consequent drunkeness, & the Confusion & misery [?] of the scene may be imagined – fortunately the following days were very fine & the Regt had an opportunity of getting into some sort of order. – but still from the distance to which it was necessary for them to go for procuring forage &c. nothing could possibly be more harassing than the duty of the soldier, who had scarcely an instant to himself from mo[rnin]g until night. With great exertions however on the part of both officers NC Officers & men the Regt was in a state to move on on the 15th Novb ...

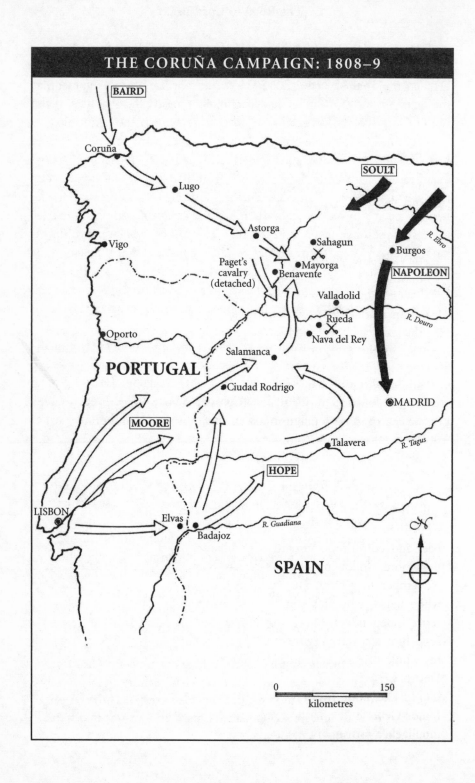

THE CORUÑA CAMPAIGN: 1808–9

BAIRD

Coruña

Lugo

Vigo

Astorga

SOULT

R. Ebro

Sahagun

Paget's
cavalry
(detached)

Mayorga

Benavente

Burgos

NAPOLEON

Valladolid

R. Douro

Rueda

Nava del Rey

Oporto

Salamanca

PORTUGAL

Ciudad Rodrigo

MOORE

MADRID

Talavera

R. Tagus

HOPE

LISBON

Elvas

Badajoz

R. Guadiana

SPAIN

N

0   150
kilometres

Sergeant Thomas of the 7th added further details in a letter that he wrote on 15 November to Adjutant William Shore in England:

... The accommodation for the men & Horses here is very miserable – worse than the Reg^t ever experienced before. – the boasted civility of the Spaniards to the English is to be found only in the English Papers, their conduct to us here is quite the reverse – they grossly impose upon us in the price of every article we want. – We have lost 12 Horses since Embarkation some were drowned in swiming [sic] them from the Vesels to the shore.

The men are in high spirits & the Horses in good condition considering the long & rough Voyage & the scanty & bad provision they are now allowed – the Ration for the Horse is 12^{lbs} Barly & 12 of Straw.

Our Route is from here to Astargo [Astorga] – abo^t 40 leagues Spanish which is 4½ miles English [per league] – I understand we shall march abo^t 3 or 4 hun^d miles thro a very barren Country before we join the Army & most of the Horses are in want of shoes before we begin the march – as there is no time to shoe the whole the first attention is p^d to the fore feet. –

Mr Kepple is very well – no material alteration in the Reg^t since we marched for Guildford. – Genl Baird went off yesterday & Lord Paget follows tomorrow. – the Reg^t has been much harrassed but all do their duty with cheerfulness.

As the 7th Hussars marched inland, Vivian noted how the horses quickly began to drop off, not only from the wretched forage but also from their forty-day confinement on board ship and from their having been moved off too soon after disembarkation.

Moore, following the disastrous Spanish defeats, decided on 28 November to retreat. He would withdraw from Salamanca to Lisbon, while Baird, who was still 160 km away to the north, was ordered to retire independently back to Coruña. Moore asked Baird if possible to send him a cavalry regiment. Paget persuaded Baird to let him go with his whole brigade and on 5 December set off southwards for the River Douro.

On the 28th Moore wrote a revealing letter from Salamanca to Major-General the Hon. John Broderick, who was at Coruña on an intelligence mission:

... It is impossible to say how far the success of the Enemy may carry them, if the same apathy continues amongst the Spaniards – you will probably have information of their movements along the coast – and if they approach you, you must take care that nothing falls into their hands. As little as possible, of stores &c should be kept on shore. He cannot come with heavy cannon, so you will always be able to embark, and be off – should such circumstance arise, you would aprize me of it – and sail for Lisbon with all that is with you – but I cannot help hoping that the Galicians will defend their mountains, and leave us the communication with Corunna open.

Within a week, Moore had reversed his decision to retreat. For Napoleon, being unaware of Moore's exact location, ignored him and advanced directly southwards on Madrid. Moore was joined by Hope's column on 4 December and the next day was informed that the people of Madrid were preparing to defend the city against the French.

Moore boldly decided to join Baird and strike eastwards against Napoleon's line of communications to disrupt his operations. He left Salamanca between 10 and 13 December and advanced north-eastwards in two columns, preceded by his cavalry, the 18th Hussars and 3rd Hussars of the King's German Legion, under Brigadier-General the Hon. Charles Stewart.

On the evening of the 12th, Stewart reached Nava del Rey, 16 km south of the River Douro, and learnt that a French detachment of about eighty men was just 13 km away at Rueda. That night, a squadron of the 18th Hussars made a surprise attack that was vividly described by Lieutenant-Colonel Loftus Otway (who held the regimental rank of major). His account reveals the unusual use of dismounted cavalry to attack a village:

... arrived at Naval [Nava del Rey] at 4 oclock. p.m. heard that a detachment of French Cavalry & Infantry were at Rueda. [Lieutenant-] Col [Oliver] Jones after feeding his horses, marchd with 100 men to the neighbourhood, to attack it, at 10 oclock I left Naval del Rey, with one Captain (Major) [Philip] Hay two Lieutenants (Conolly & Johnson) & joined Col Jones ½ a mile from Rueda about one oclock am. accompanied by B Gen[l] Stewart, who immediately arranged a plan for the attack. on a Hill close to the Town a picket of forty [French] Infantry and a few dragoons were posted, in the centre of the Town the remainder of the Infantry (about 30) were stationed, the Cavalry about 20 were distributed thro' the Town – the plan of attack was as follows –

forty of our Hussars were dismounted and ordered to attack the Infantry in the Town who were advantageously posted, being surrounded by houses in a small space, the entrance, so blocked up with bags of cotton that 2 men could with difficulty enter together, but nothing could long stop our brave fellows the French retired to their Guard house, the door was forced, the enemy fled by the back door[.] this attack was ably conducted by Col Jones. The attack of the picket on the Hill was entrusted to me, & this was made with so much celerity that we were in on the picket before they had time to form & we succeeded in capturing, dispersing & destroying it, only sustaining a loss of two Hussars wounded and two horses killed – the enemy lost on this occasion six killed & 26 taken & 12 horses, Colonel Jones in the attack conducted by him had one Hussars killed & two wounded, here the first blood was drawn in Spain, & our success obtained us 500 bags of Cotton value £30,000. . . .

Moore now knew that Madrid had fallen, but discovered on the 13th that a detached French corps, operating in northern Spain under Marshal Jean-de-Dieu Soult, would advance westwards against a Spanish army under the Marquess de La Romana. Moore saw that Soult would be dangerously isolated and decided to attack him. He accordingly shifted the direction of his advance more to the north, crossed the River Douro on the 15th and linked up with Baird on the 20th. His cavalry continued to screen his advance and took over 100 prisoners in a series of clashes with Soult's cavalry.

Lieutenant-Colonel Otway described one such action. He was sent by Brigadier-General Stewart towards Valladolid, 34 km north-east of Rueda. He commanded a detachment of the 18th Hussars and had obtained from Rueda a reinforcement of forty local men mounted on mules and asses. The French General Jean-Baptiste Franceschi-Delonne had 400 chasseurs à cheval and 100 infantrymen at Valladolid but pulled out a few hours before Otway arrived, leaving behind his sick. Otway occupied the city at 2.00 a.m. on 15 December and seven hours later set out back to Rueda, only to encounter a party of the 22nd Chasseurs à Cheval. These men were on their way from Madrid to join their regiment at Valladolid and were unaware that the city had been evacuated:

... About ½ mile or perhaps less from Valadolid on my return accompanied by many of the inhabitants, who now for the first time beheld british Hussars at that moment I heard them cry 'huy Jesus correr guevienen [?] los Franceses Oh Jesus, run, here come the French['], with screams & shrieks they all turned about & were soon in their houses – having come that road a few hours before & being well informd as to the patroles of the enemy I thought it a false alarm & I ordered an officer to reconnoitre, however he had not advanced many yards, before I was satisfied that I had fallen in with a detachment of the enemy Cavalry – I instantly resolved to attack supposing it was a party sent out to cut me off – drew swords formed line to the front (so as to fill the road.) – Gallop. March –

The enemy who had halted when first they saw us now got into motion & after a short advance, halted, to wheel about, we charged & after a few discharges of their pistols & carrabines, which did us no harm, they fled and then it was 'sauve qui peut' we soon gained upon them, & when the affair was over I found we had taken one Lt Col (Antignac) two Q^r Masters two Serg^{ts} and 22 rank & file all of the 22^d Reg^t of Chasseurs a cheval

We likewise captured two ladies one the mistress of the Lt Colonel the other wife to one of the Q^r Masters, My party consisted of one L^t one corporal & 26 Hussars that of the enemy 35 men and 100 Infantry, the latter from the impatience of the Colonel to arrive early at Valadolid were too far behind to be of any assistance to him[.] the Lieut. was with the Infantry that morning, so that he escaped, four were killed & the rest got off, I lost no time in collecting my men and prisoners and marched that day & part of the night, to Castronuva, [Castronuño?] distant forty four miles, being the quarters of the 18th and the outpost of the British army. . . .

On the 21st, Paget (who now commanded all of Moore's cavalry) brilliantly defeated a brigade of Soult's cavalry at Sahagun. But two days later, Moore learned that he had provoked Napoleon into advancing against him from Madrid. He instantly ordered a retreat for the safety of the Cantabrian mountains in the north-western corner of Spain. Napoleon, partly as a result of the British cavalry's successful screening operations, believed that Moore was further south than he in fact was and consequently failed to trap him in the open plains of Leon and Old Castille. But Moore escaped only at the cost of hard marching, which

took its toll on the discipline of his army. After reaching Benavente,
85 km north-west of Valladolid, he issued a General Order on 27 December
(the date entered erroneously in his General Order Book is the 7th):

The Commander of the Forces has observed with concern, the
extreme bad conduct of the Troops of late, at a moment when they
are about to enter into contact with the Enemy, and when the
greatest regularity and the best conduct are most requisite. – He is
the more concerned, as until lately the behaviour of that part of the
Army, at least which was under his own immediate command, was
so exemplary, and did them so much honor. – The misbehaviour of
the Troops, in the Column which marched by Valderas to this Place,
exceeds what he could have believed of British Soldiers: it is disgraceful to the Officers as it strongly marks their negligence and inatten-
tion: The Commander of the Forces refers to the General Orders of
the 25th October and 11th Nov[r]: He desires that they may again be
read at the head of every Company of the Army: He can add nothing
to them but his determination to execute them to the fullest extent.
– He can feel no mercy towards Officers who in times like these
neglect important duties – or towards Soldiers who disgrace their
Country by acts of Villainy towards the People they are sent to
protect.
     The Spanish Forces have been overpower'd and until such time
as they are reassembled and ready again to come forward the
situation of this Army must be arduous – and such as to call for the
exertion of qualities, the most rare and valuable in a military Body –
These are not bravery alone, but patience and constancy under
fatigue & Hardship – obedience to command, Sobriety and orderly
conduct, firmness and resolution in every difficult situation in which
they may be placed: it is by the display of such qualities alone that
the Army can expect to deserve the name of Soldiers – that they may
be able to withstand the Forces opposed to them, or to fulfill the
expectation of their Country. – It is impossible for the General to
explain to his Army the motives of the movements he directs – The
Commander of the Forces however can assure the Army that he has
made none since he left Salamanca which he did not foresee, and
which he was not prepared for, and as far as he is a judge they have
answered the purposes for which they were intended. – When he
thinks proper to fight a Battle he will do it, and he will chuse the

time and place he thinks fit –: in the mean time he begs the Officers
and men of the Army to attend diligently to discharge their parts,
and leave to him with the General Officers, the decision of measures
which belong to him alone: the Army may rest assured that he has
nothing more at heart than their honor and that of his Country.

Next day, Moore wrote a letter from Benavente to Major-General
Broderick at Coruña, in which he was more open about his plans:

> . . . we are continuing our march, I leave this [place] with the last of
> the Infantry tomorrow – As yet the Enemy's Infantry are not up –
> but are near – their Cavalry is becoming very numerous – It is not
> my wish to fight a battle – that, at present is not our game – which
> is rather to save this army, to protract, and give time to the Spaniards
> to rally, if they can – I may however be compelled to fight one, if
> much pressed.
>
> If once I enter the mountains, I fear the want of subsistence will
> compel me to go to the coast – at all events a reembarkation is a
> most probable event – and I wish you to give this information to the
> Admiral [Rear-Admiral de Courcy]. I, long ago, represented to L^d
> Castlereagh the necessity of sending Transports, for our reception
> and I desired [Lieutenant-General Sir John] Craddock [the com-
> mander of the British troops left behind in Portugal] after reserving
> the Transports necessary for the embarkation of the Troops from
> Portugal, to send the rest to Vigo, for us – the Admiral may perhaps
> enforce this – I shall write to you, in a day or two, at more leisure,
> in the mean time I give you this notice – the Force coming against
> me, is so superior, that if it presses me, I must retire – but otherwise
> I shall hold as long as I can

Paget with his cavalry was still at Benavente as the army's rearguard
on the morning of 29 December when about 600 cavalrymen of
Napoleon's Imperial Guard forded the River Esla under General Charles
Lefebvre-Desnouëttes. Lieutenant-Colonel Otway had spent the night
with a picket of the 18th Hussars and called in the other pickets when
he saw the French crossing. He retired from the river towards Benavente,
3 km away, skirmishing as he did so, until he arrived within 1 km of
the town. He now had about 130 men and began to advance against the
French:

... the enemy halted at this time one [French] squadron was somewhat in advance of the others, [I] thought it a favourable time to charge – [I] gave the word – the men cheered & rushed upon the enemy. The enemy's squadron was broke in an instant, tho composed of Buonaparte's best cavalry his Imperial Guards, after the charge [I] gave the word, to halt & form, but in vain[.] our men continued to pursue & whilst dispersed the 2ᵈ Squadron of the enemy advanced & on our left & took us in flank & rear[.] This brought our people to their recollection & in 2 minutes the french & we were completely intermixed when this moment had the French General advanced his reserve we should have been cut to pieces & he might have entered Benevente before the Cavalry could get to their alarm posts, – however we had better fortune for Genˡ Stuart [Charles Stewart] with a Squadron of the Germans [3rd Hussars of the King's German Legion] was approaching from the town, we rallied upon them & the enemy which took some moment to collect their scattered people & did not attempt to advance, we lost a good many men but not so many as the enemy, the Officer who commanded the advance was killed & I got his sword, when Genˡ Stuart had got us all in our places, he determined to attack the enemy who by that time had brought their force more together, tho' not in line, the Genˡ placed himself at the head of the Germans[.] I continued with the picquets & was about 50 yards to his right, & rather outflanked the French, in his advancing to the charge I gave similar orders to the Picquets, & from my position I kept the left squadron of the enemy in check whilst he broke the Squadron opposed to him, & by bringing the right shoulder forward, I came in contact with the right Squadron of the enemy who had wheeled to their left & had taken the General in the rear, thus were thay 2ᵈ time completely intermixed with the french, & both parties withdrew to collect a little when fatigued with the use of the sabre, in this attack I think, I may safely say the enemy fared the worse, as we took their General prisoner (le Febre) & they certainly did not shew so firm a countenance as before, the distance between us was not more [than] 130 or 150 yards & a constant fire was kept up on both sides whilst the men were regaining their places[.] in a few minutes, we were joined by more of the Germans, & the piquets were strengthened by the 50 men, I had sent for to the village, Lord Paget also came out to us & took the command, he soon put us in proper order for another attack, but would not allow

us to charge till the 10th Hussars & the 18th Hussars on their march
from the Town were near enough to act as a reserve, on seeing those
Regts advancing to our support, the French determined to retire, by
alternate Squadrons, but we were too close to them to allow them to
maneuvre, & Lord Paget led us on to the charge in gallant style, for
a little while they kept together, but we at length broke them took
about a 100 prisoners & drove the rest head formost into the river &
whilst they were swimming the river killed & wounded at least 100
of them with our pistols & carrabines. when they crossed the river
they formed & began to fire at us, but they were soon routed by two
[guns] of Captain [Thomas] Downman's Troops ['B' Troop, Royal
Horse Artillery] who destroyed several of them with shrapnel shells
& who just arrived as they formed on the other side.

It may be right here to observe, that the french did not in course
of this morning advance to the charge they always waited our attack
& I think to advantage except in the final instance when I attacked
them on hard ground, but all the other charges we made, were in
very deep ground (wheat land) the horses above fetlock deep, &
in consequence the horses always came up blown & feeble – . . .

Lieutenant-Colonel Vivian of the 7th Hussars added some interesting
remarks:

. . . this affair being over the 7th were ordered to remain on the
ground with two pieces of light artillery, the rest of the Cavalry
returned to Benevente – no movement of consequence took place on
the part of the enemy during our stay there – excepting that now and
then the head of a Column of Cavalry would make its appearance as
if intending to cross the water, when a cannon shot or two stopped
it. about the middle of the day a Gen[l] with a large suite made his
appearance on the hill immediately above us and reconnoitred our
position[.] from the number of attendants and more especially from
there being some Mamelukes of the party we had every reason to
suppose it was Bonaparte himself. The Officer Comm[g] the artillery
wished rather to have given him a shot – despising a war of outposts
I declined it[.] I afterwards rather regretted having done so when I
reflected that if it was Bonaparte and should a shot be successfull the
benefit that would have resulted to the world in general [would have
been great] – and I in consequence accused myself of having from
motives of humanity – avoided doing that which would have contrib-

uted so much to the happiness of mankind – An opportunity was afforded me during the time I remained in this post of seeing & conversing with several of the French officers having passed the water with a flag of truce respecting Genl LeFebres baggage &c – I saw Genl Danoruel [?] ADC to the Emperor – Co^l Count Grazinsky of the Polish Guards & several other officers of distinction[.] their dress was superb, & their appearance & manners altogether most perfectly that of gentlemen & their opinions most liberal – They freely abused the Spaniards & accused them of having deceived us – and spoke in the highest terms of the conduct of our men in the affair of the mo^{rg} – from passing the river I had an opportunity of judging of the difficulties the enemy must have encountered[.] I was mounted on an English Horse considerably stronger & larger than the best of theirs and in going I found it an operation of difficulty & several minutes in returning my Horse swam and was nearly carried down by the stream. Count Grazinsky afterwards came to my side of the water and would actually have been lost but for one of the men of the 7th who assisted him on shore. . . .

The bulk of Moore's army reached Astorga and the relative safety of the Cantabrian mountains on the same day as this action. Moore wrote to Major-General Broderick on 31 December:

> . . . Our affairs are come to that point which I had long forseen as the Spaniards were capable of doing nothing for themselves. The aid of such an army as this could not alone resist the great superiority of the French. I attempted a diversion, which has succeeded, for the whole disposable force is turned against us – in so doing, I have risked this Army to no purpose, for there is nothing in Spain to take advantage of it – all this I knew – but still a wish to do something, & to show that we were willing to aid the cause at all risks induced me to act as I have done – we have nothing left now but to march to the Coast as fast as we can – we want every thing, & shall arrive there in a very bad state – I hope we shall find sufficient Transports[.] Every thing will be on its march this day, by divisions – I shall follow this night or tomorrow morng with the Reserve & Cavalry, how far we shall be followed I cannot say but probably the difficulties which embarrass us, will prevent the French from passing Villafranca. . . .

Napoleon personally advanced no further than Astorga and on 1 January 1809 entrusted the pursuit to Soult before leaving for France five days later. He wanted to distance himself from the failure to trap Moore and was also concerned by both rumours of plots against his authority in Paris and reports that Austria, taking advantage of the situation in the Peninsula, was preparing for war in a bid to avenge her defeats of 1805.

Moore had the choice of two embarkation ports, Coruña and Vigo. Coruña was the easier to reach and offered good defensive positions on the hills south of the town. But it also had serious weaknesses, as Captain John Birch of the Royal Engineers had reported on 20 December:

> ... From what I have seen of this place, I may venture to say that it is an exceeding bad and improper one of the re-imbarkation of the Corps of an Army pursued by the Enemy – the fortifications of the Town are undefensible, and defenceless, and were the Town in the hands of an Enemy, the Citadel would be presently untenable, and it would be difficult if not impossible to embark from it
>
> The Bay is nearly commanded from all the shore around it, which might expose the Shipping to the Enemy's fire from thence, and the vessels might be detained in the harbour under it by a contrary wind – I think that from these circumstances it is not only an improper place for the re-imbarkation of an army, but also as a depôt of stores, which would of course be more exposed than the Troops to fall into the Enemy's hands.

He added on 21 December that some inconvenience might arise from Coruña being garrisoned by an armed bourgeoisie, among whom he understood were a great many foreigners, tradesmen, shopkeepers and intriguing and disaffected people:

> ... & I think it would be a disagreeable thing in the case of our army being obliged to retreat and embark here, for this operation to be any wise dependant on such people, which it might be, as our vessels and boats would be under the fire of the Cannon of their Citadel and Forts.

His reservations about the loyalty of the inhabitants in fact proved groundless.

Moore eventually decided in favour of Coruña, but detached

Brigadier-General Robert Craufurd's Light Brigade and a King's German Legion brigade and sent them westwards to embark separately at Vigo. They were not pursued, but encountered serious problems in finding supplies. Captain John Duffy of the 43rd (or the Monmouthshire) Regiment of Foot (Light Infantry) recorded on 11 January:

> . . . since the Army has passed we have constantly found the Country people in Arms and much inclined to insult our men this disposition has been in great measure brought on by the shamefull conduct of the Troops in their different Billets and the marauding of Stragglers who have fell in the rear of the Column under the pretence of indisposition – & as we have been without regular Provisions in most of the Country villages where we have been stationed for a night, it has been found necessary in several instances to press all the Bread, Wine & Bullocks requisite for the Troops for which only Receipts have been granted so that the Inhabitants are much enraged against us – . . .

Duffy reached Vigo on the 13th, but noted that stragglers were still arriving on the 22nd.

Meanwhile, Moore continued to retreat with the bulk of his army towards Coruña amid mounting disorder and suffering. He briefly turned at bay at Lugo on 6 January to try and rest his army and restore its discipline, but resumed the retreat two days later after some limited fighting. Ensign Augustus Dobree of the 14th (or the Bedfordshire) Regiment of Foot wrote in his journal:

> This day [the 8th] ended as yesterday the enemy still declining a gen[l] engagement, but late at night we rec[d] orders to retreat with the greatest silence which we effected leaving the enemy not a little astonished in the morning at our flight, a severe accident had like to have taken place it being pitch dark the left wing of our reg[t] (14[th] Foot) took a direct road over hills & ditches to a deep precip[ic]e & the whole fell down without any injury two or three men excepted.

Lieutenant-Colonel Vivian described the difficulties of driving on the stragglers:

> . . . Whenever they found straw, they rolled themselves up in it and altho our men rode in upon them they would not cry out – and we found the only means were to prick with our swords in order to

discover them & make them stir – the road presented a spectacle even more distressing – fine fellows willing and anxious to get on their feet bleeding for want of shoes, and totally incapable of keeping up – others whose spirit was better than their strength actually striving to the last to join their battallions, & several of this description perished in the attempt. I myself saw five dead on the road side & 2 women, whilst every now & then you met with a poor unfortunate woman perhaps with a child in her arms, without shoes or stockings, knee deep in mud, crying most piteously for that assistance which alas we could not afford her – . . .

Moore finally reached Coruña on 11 January, but was unable to embark his army until after his fleet of transports, delayed by contrary winds, arrived from Vigo on the afternoon of the 14th. By then, the French had arrived in strength. Moore hoped they would attack, so that he could defeat them on the hills outside Coruña and then embark in safety. He meanwhile evacuated his cavalry and all but eight of his guns, although Vivian later argued that it had been a mistake to deprive the army of the great advantage of superior artillery. Soult brought twenty guns into action, but his 3,300 cavalrymen were of limited use over the rugged terrain and he had available only 12,000 infantry against Moore's 15,000. The British also had the advantage of being able to obtain fresh ammunition and weapons from the magazines at Coruña to replace those lost or damaged during the retreat.

Soult attacked Moore's position on the Monte Mero, a ridge 3.5 km south of Coruña, on the afternoon of the 16th. His frontal assaults were repulsed after heavy fighting and his attempt to turn Moore's western flank was checked. Ensign Dobree of the 14th Regiment reveals how, on the morning of the 16th, a French soldier missed his own picquet and fell into British hands:

. . . he informed us that orders were issued by Marshal Soult to attack us at 2 O'Clock, when he should be reinforced by Gen[l] Junot with 12.000 Foot & 16 pieces of Cannon, accordingly we were prepar'd for them, at 12 O'Clock great to our surprise the enemy rec[d] the expected reinforcement, as we had not given the least credit to what the man had told us, a scene of bustle took place in their lines, their drums beating to arms & lines falling in[.] at ½ past 1 O'Clock, a most tremendous fire opened upon us of 20 pieces of canon besides

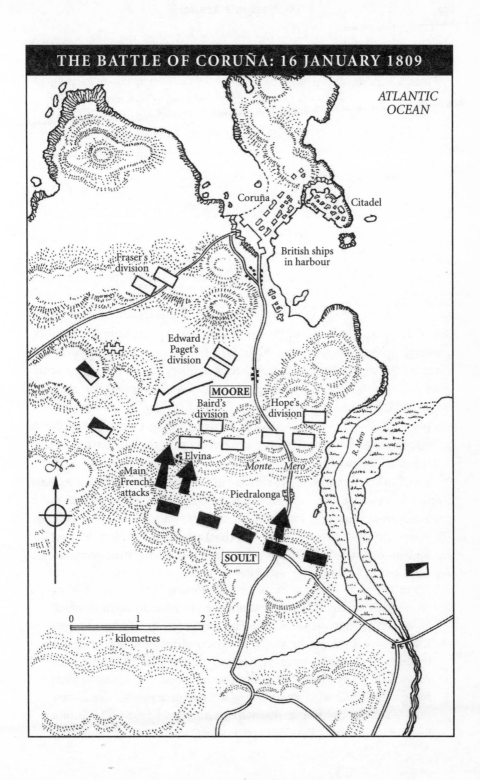

THE BATTLE OF CORUÑA: 16 JANUARY 1809

ATLANTIC OCEAN

Coruña

Citadel

Fraser's division

British ships in harbour

Edward Paget's division

MOORE

Baird's division

Hope's division

Main French attacks

Elvina

Monte Mero

R. Mero

Piedralonga

SOULT

N

0   1   2

kilometres

[howitzer] shells; the Enemy forming a Grand close column & reinforcing their picquets they rush'd down in the valley & began the attack with our out posts . . .

The brunt of this initial attack fell on the western end of the Monte Mero and was defeated. Dobree related that the French later assaulted his own, eastern, sector of the ridge:

. . . after they had been driven back from the centre, the threatening column on our left now descended as we supposed to the attack (consisting of [between] 2 & 3000 men) but their object was to take possession of a village [Piedralonga] situated on the great road to Madrid & Corunna which they effected & relieved their old Picquets, intending to maintain that situation till morning, that post being of the greatest consequence and as we could not have retreated into Corunna without their knowledge, Maj[r] Gen[l] [Rowland] Hill commanding our brigade, mentioned this in presence of L[t] Col. [Jasper] Nicholls 14th foot. he immediately volunteered to take his reg[t] & drive them out of the village, which Gen[l] Hill accepted, he took the right wing & made a detour to the right by which he gained an entrance to the village without being perceived while the left wing under Major Wood was to descend on a signal being given, down to the High road to support the right wing when the enemy might expect the attack the whole distance not being more than 200 yards from our line to the village, as we had 3 companies on picquet & afraid of coming in contact with them we were ordered to call in a low voice as we advanced 14th that they might answer us in return; the preconcerted signal being given the left wing descended rapidly, before the enemy had challenged us & cheering as we advanced into the village. Here Col[l] Nicholls labour'd under a very great disadvantage owing to the lane he came thro' being so very narrow & admitting him only to advance by files, consequently on gaining the high road he was obliged to halt the grenadiers to form up in company as they came up, the Grenadier & Light Comps having formed across the road; the enemy having gained knowledge of our advancing, retreated 20 or 30 paces in the village forming a close column & lining the houses, their was supposed to be 2800 men being the 70th or [?] chasseurs of the line of 3 Batt[s][.] Col. Nicols now advanced with the divisions that were formed, the others forming successively gave 3 cheers & cried out 14th which the enemy answered by also calling 14th, which occasioned us to halt, but a volunteer (now Ens' Stack[?]) advancing, ascertained the cheat & shot one of the enemies Sentries which was a sufficient signal for the Col[l] who ordered his men to fire & then charge, unfortunatly for us they [the French] fired previous to our discharge which did much execution, we now cheer'd & charged which struck consternation into the enemy (tho' it is supposed, they imagined it a general attack) who retreated precipitatly leaving a vast number of dead, wounded & a great many prisoners among which were many offrs but none of any note, The french off[rs] endeavoured to rally their men & with some difficulty effected it, but could not prevail on them to return to the village again, therefore we remained in quiet possession of it till we were recall'd; at 11 O'Clock orders were given to retreat into Corunna for the purpose of embarking[.] we retired in good order without being molested, the enemy not knowing of our retreat, but if they did it is doubtful if they would have made any movement to molest us, as they were not in motion next day untill between 9 & 10 in the morning . . .

Dobree's account throws new light on the report written by General Maximilien Foy, the commander of the French infantry brigade which attacked Piedralonga. Foy explained that after initially taking the village he posted skirmishers in the hollow lanes out in front, but claimed that these men suffered many casualties and used up their ammunition by the time the British counter-attacked. Foy admitted that the skirmishers in retreating carried away the head of their supporting column and that several of his officers were wounded, including two battalion commanders. But he portrayed a fiercer resistance than is suggested by Dobree and stated that the fighting involved the use of bayonets and firing at point-blank range. He also claimed that the confusion was only momentary and that after rallying his men he went back into the village at 8.00 p.m., leaving only one end of it in British hands.*

The British lost about 800 men during the battle, considerably fewer than the French. But Moore himself had been mortally wounded, as his Military Secretary, Major John Colborne, explained. Colborne wrote to his sister, Mrs Duke Yonge, after his return to England:

---

* M. Girod de l'Ain, *Vie Militaire du Général Foy* (Paris, 1900), p. 329.

... It seems a dream – I can scarcely believe that I am in England –
indeed this is the first day since the action I have had time to reflect
and lament my Friend [Moore], he was a noble fellow – had I not
seen him die I should have thought it impossible for the firmest
mind to have endured bodily pain, with such indifference with such
calm serenity – for although when in health and sound, one conceives
a possibility of bearing every ill, yet the stoutest hearts yield to nature
and sink under the pain of a mutilated body – ...

A cannonball had torn away Moore's left shoulder and mangled his
chest. Colborne remarked:

... from the profuse gushing out of the blood I should have thought
he would have instantly expired, his voice was rather hoarse, from
inward bleeding, when knocked off his horse he did not say any
thing, nor did [illegible] make him change countenance, he was
carried away in a blanket and spoke to every one as he passed – I
remained out until the action was over, and when dark rode to
Corunna. On my entering the room the General heard me and spoke
most kindly to me, and said Colborne have we beaten the French, I
replied yes we have repulsed them in every point, well says he that is
a satisfaction I hope my country will do me justice – he then said to
Col [Paul] Anderson [the acting Adjutant-General] – go to Colonel
Gordon [the Duke of York's Military Secretary] when you arrive in
England tell him it is my wish, *remember* I request that Colborne gets
a Lt Colonelcy – he then said remember me to Genl Paget – Genl
Edwd Paget – he is a fine fellow – he asked every one that came into
the room about the Enemy, and died in a moment after he had
spoken, without the least symptom of pain – ...

The army was able to embark in safety that night and the following
morning, although some temporary confusion occurred on the afternoon
of the 17th, when French artillery fired on the ships in the harbour and
caused several of them to collide or run aground. Moore was buried on
the morning of the 17th and the army's rearguard was evacuated the
next day from behind the cover of the citadel.

Captain Commissary John Charlton, of the Corps of Royal Artillery
Drivers, vividly described the aftermath of the battle. This extract from
his journal begins two days before the action:

Saturday 14th Jany The Fleet is arriving in very fast and preparations are making to Embark tomorrow morning understand the Horse Artillery and we are to take home 400 Horses, shot this day upwards of Two Hundred. Sunday 15th Jany Our intended Embarkation is delayed owing to the Enemy who no doubt knew the shiping had arrived and have all day kept out skirmishing parties and fired several Shot from the opposite heigths. I was with the advance about an hour during which time the firing on both sides was pretty smart; They have Artillery as several Shot fell near us, Capt [George] Skyring has fired several rounds and all day it has continued but I am of opinion it is not their wish for a General Engagement it is only to retard our Embarkation, indeed report says they have only Two Thousand men but in this I think they err as I could discern a considerable force on the opposite hills indeed I think more than that number altho' the day is rather hazy.

Monday 16th Jany Selected my Horses for Embarkation, during the whole of the morning the Boats were employed by the Horse Artillery in Embarking their Horses and it was not untill Twelve °Clock we could get the Boats, A very bad place to embark from, get my own Four Horses and Thirty Two Officers [horses] on Board and had sent One Boat of Troop Horses (7) on Board when a Heavy firing from the Enemy commenced and knowing should an engagement take place Ammunition would be immediately sent to the lines I ceased to embark more Horses and immediately gave orders to send every Horse I could muster to be employed taking Ammunition to the Field[.] at this time 3-°Clock P.M. the firing very heavy, went to Col^l [John] Harding [Moore's artillery commander] in the Citadel for Orders and was directed to use every endeavour to forward the Ammunition. Went towards the Action and met Major [James] Viney who ordered me to convey a message to Capt [Charles] Godby on the left of our line and on returning passed Sir John Moore who had been wounded about a quarter of an hour [before]. this must be nearly 4 °Clock in the Afternoon.

. . .

About 11 °Clock at night our Troops came in and commenced their Embarkation leaving Detachments on the Heights to keep on the Fires in order to deceive the Enemy. The night rather unfavourable the wind blowing very fresh which caused great Delay in the Troops embarking. At Day light on the morning of Tuesday the 17th

Jan[y] I got Orders to send round Capt[n] [Edward] Willmotts [Wilmot's] Eight Guns to the first sandy Beach behind the Citadel and if possible embark them and if not they were to be destroyed, and after taking them then to destroy all my Horses[.] for this duty I ordered Capt Humphreys who superintended the destruction of near Four Hundred Horses. After all had left the Citadel for the above purpose I repaired to the place of Embarkation and was here met by Major Viney who again Ordered me to the Barrier Gate with directions for Major [Robert] Thornhill who Commanded the Reserve of Artillery, on getting to the works could perceive the French Troops in the Street of S[t] Lucie [on] the outskirts of the Town, but a few Shots from the works soon cleared them, on Returning to the Rock from where the Troops Embarked met Capt Godby very anxiously demanding from the Commanding Officer of the Navy a Boat to take off Capt Willmotts 8 Guns sent to the shore as before mentioned, soon got a Boat in which he and myself went round to the beach where the Guns were and Capt Willmot with his Company[.] at this time the wind blew very fresh indeed and it was evident we could not embark the Guns we therefore were decidedly of opinion they must be destroyed which was accordingly done and with difficulty we got about 30 of his Company into the Boat the others with L[t] Sinclair were sent round to embark where the other Troops embarked, as did my men after destroying their Horses. We now endeavoured to pull into the Harbour Capt Willmot and Godby wishing to get to the Metcalf Transport and myself to the Nymph where my Horses and Servants were, after pulling upwards of Two Hours and the swell rather increasing, and the fire of the Enemy upon the Shiping the Lieu[t] of the Navy in the Boat stated the impossibility of our reaching the Ships we wanted and that he would according to his instructions put us on Board the first Ship he could make we were therefore all put on Board the Cambo an Ordnance Store Ship and Just as we got on Board the Signal was made to cut and get out of Harbour in doing this Twelve Transports got upon the Rocks and Eight were lost among which was the Nymph with my Servant and Horses on Board, afterwards learnt the men were all saved the Horses of course lost; Got out of the Harbour about 4 °Clock and lay off untill the next Afternoon Wednesday the 18 Jan[y] when we were Joined by all the Men of War which we understood had waited to bring off our Reserve which was effected[.]

the Spaniards in Corunna behaved in a very proper manner having defended the Town during the embarkation of our Reserve. Thus every thing considered we are a very fortunate people, had the wind not blown from the exact point it did not a vessell could have got out and from the position of the Enemys Guns we must all have been taken or Sunk, their possition being too heigh for the Men of Wars Guns to bear upon them . . .

*

Moore lost as many as 6,000 men during the Coruña campaign, with at least a third of them taken prisoner during the retreat. The survivors on their return to England were unfit for service for several months and their deplorable state shocked the inhabitants of the south coast and gave the impression of a disaster. Controversy immediately surrounded Moore's conduct of the campaign, particularly as the issue became politicized when the Whigs championed him in order to attack the Government. Yet despite the sudden collapse of the Spanish regular armies, Moore had successfully disrupted Napoleon's operations in Spain and diverted him into the north-west. This prevented the French from immediately occupying either Portugal or southern Spain and made it possible to continue the war in the Peninsula.

Wellesley during this time had resumed his duties as Chief Secretary for Ireland. Although keen to return to the Peninsula to serve under Moore, he had been prevented by the need to appear at the Court of Enquiry over the Cintra affair. He subsequently defended his conduct in the Commons when Parliament reassembled in January 1809 and received the thanks of both Houses for his victories at Roliça and Vimeiro. By now, the outcry against the Convention had largely died away and was eclipsed by a new scandal involving the Duke of York's former mistress, Mrs Mary Anne Clarke, who until the end of their relationship in 1806 had taken bribes in exchange for offering to use her influence to obtain the Duke's patronage. The Duke was acquitted of the charge of having sold commissions, but had to resign as Commander-in-Chief of the British army on 17 March and was not reinstated until 1811.

3

The Defence of Portugal

1809–10

Napoleon never returned to the Peninsula, but he left behind over 280,000 men. Portugal remained unoccupied, as did the south and much of the east of Spain, but the French found it impossible to concentrate an overwhelming force against any one point, partly for logistical reasons and partly because of the sheer size of the Peninsula. Most of the French troops were required to hold down the occupied regions, guard communications and contain the Spanish regular armies. The difficult terrain favoured guerrilla operations and helped isolate the French commanders, who were usually more concerned with their own local problems than with cooperating in joint ventures. The situation was worsened by Napoleon's attempts to direct the war from Paris, or indeed from further afield. He undermined the nominal authority of his brother, King Joseph of Spain, and often issued impossible orders by either not understanding or refusing to accept the reality of the local situation.

The effectiveness of the Spanish guerrillas has been exaggerated by propaganda. They had to live off the country and many of them were no more than brigands who feuded with each other and terrorized the local inhabitants. Yet the guerrillas were important in maintaining resistance to occupation and intercepting despatches as well as inflicting a relentless toll of casualties and undermining the morale and discipline of the French units. Atrocities were common on both sides. Many guerrilla bands increased the scale and effectiveness of their attacks over time, but were rarely able to inflict significant defeats except when cooperating closely with regular forces. When deprived of support, they were vulnerable to French counter-insurgency operations, which managed to pacify permanently occupied districts.

The Spanish regular armies had major handicaps including the absence until 1812 of a supreme commander, political pressure to take the offensive, inferior tactics and a crippling shortage of cavalry. The Spanish army had long been neglected and the country's dislocation made it difficult to pay, equip and supply the troops, many of whom were tempted to desert, often in order to join the guerrillas. Few of the senior officers were dynamic and many were political appointees. Yet the Spanish armies repeatedly re-formed after successive defeats and continued to operate in the periphery of the country. They maintained this relentless struggle for six years and were crucial in sustaining the guerrillas, supporting British operations and making possible the eventual liberation of the Peninsula.

The British still had 10,000 troops in Portugal under Lieutenant-General Sir John Cradock, who had arrived to take command at Lisbon on 14 December 1808. He complained in a letter to Moore, dated 26 December, about the paucity of information:

> ... as I have not heard from you since the 12th December, upon which all my arrangements so much depend, I have to say, that we remain the same at Lisbon, & are without Intelligence from any other Quarter. The [Spanish] Junta at Seville & the Superior authorities at Badajos &c have made most pressing solicitations for British & even Portuguese assistance. I am endeavouring as much as possible to procure the assembly of a Portuguese Force at [illegible] – but I cannot say I am sanguine upon the subject – & if ever effected, It will be but a wretched Composition – as to English Troops, I have neither the ability, or the authority to send any to the South of Spain, as requested – ...

Cradock kept the bulk of his force near Lisbon ready to embark, as a French invasion of Portugal appeared imminent. But the British government in the wake of the Coruña Campaign eventually decided to maintain its commitment to the Peninsula and to secure Portugal as a base for its operations. A British general, William Beresford, was seconded to the Portuguese army in February 1809 with the rank of marshal and began a thorough reform with the help of some British officers who entered the Portuguese service. The old Portuguese army had been unable to resist the French invasion in 1807 and had then been largely disbanded. Units had been re-formed following the uprisings against French occupation and it was hoped that the army could be rebuilt and trained until it could be integrated with the British forces in the field. Lieutenant-Colonel John Elley, Assistant Adjutant-General of the British cavalry, wrote on 4 April 1810:

> ... the Portuguese are numerous of good appearance and very tractable, if not too roughly handled at the onset. I really think they will fight – one Drawback however I must declare[.] The Native officers are despicable to a degree, and are despised by the men in toto, and with few Exceptions – are destitute of Principle – Honor, and consequently Courage – ...

In April 1809, Wellesley was appointed to command the British troops in Portugal and was sent with reinforcements to take over from Cradock. He resigned as Chief Secretary for Ireland and as a Member of Parliament and, although nearly shipwrecked in a storm, reached Lisbon on 22 April. The 23,000 British troops that he had available were inferior in quality to the army that Sir John Moore had commanded. Most of his units were understrength, home-service battalions, for Moore's formations had been put temporarily out of action by the Coruña Campaign. Of Wellesley's twenty-five battalions, only five had been with him at Vimeiro and another two had been formed from detachments of sick and stragglers left behind by Moore. He had only four complete cavalry regiments and had to contend with shortages of money, experienced commissaries and horses for his artillery.

Despite these difficulties, Wellesley quickly advanced against a French corps under Marshal Jean-de-Dieu Soult which had invaded northern Portugal and defeated it at Oporto by an audacious daylight crossing of the River Douro. Captain the Hon. Francis Hood of the 3rd Regiment of Foot Guards recorded in his diary on 12 May:

> Last night the French were within two Leagues of Oporto, still falling back, Severe skirmishing, this morning kept on, & expected to have had an action, but after heard that the French had retreated to Oporto in the night, & at three °Clock in the morning destroyed the Bridge across the Douro – About two °Clock we reached Villa Nova [the suburb of Oporto on the south bank], Gen¹ Stewarts Brigade crossing, a most beautiful sight, Light Corps engaged on the other side – Gen¹ [Edward] Paget wounded in the Boats, we crossed & marched thro' the Town, driving the French entirely out of it – The French retreated & took a position two Leagues off, it was determined

the army should not advance further that night, Picquets were placed[.] Maj [Felton] Hervey [14th (or The Duchess of York's Own) Regiment of (Light) Dragoons] wounded in the arm I saw him pass, when we were about to form Line, the 14th suffered much having only their advanced Guard [illegible] in the first instance – We were afterwards marched to the Town, & were quartered, dined with the Landlord, the Inhabitants, highly delighted, French had plundered them of every thing; the advanced Troops found money in almost every one of the Soldiers knapsacks the Baggage did not cross; Was a little tired, & slept well ordered to parade at 9 tomorrow if no further orders –

Soult was driven from Portugal and lost 4,000 men in retreating over the mountains. Wellesley then returned south to prepare for his next move. On 18 June, he organized his army for the first time into divisions. Hitherto, his battalions had simply been grouped into brigades, but his brigades in turn needed to be organized into permanent higher formations as his army expanded. Initially, Wellesley created four divisions, each of which had a strength of between 3,000 and 4,000 men, except for the 1st Division, which had 6,000. The Portuguese were still being trained, but their brigades were incorporated into the British divisions in February 1810, boosting a typical division's strength to between 5,500 and 5,800 men. The number of brigades in a division varied between two and four. As his army grew, Wellesley created another four divisions between February 1810 and March 1811. His cavalry was organized into a separate division, to which a second would be added in June 1811.

The divisional structure made it easier to control the army and gave it greater cohesion, flexibility and robustness. The divisions acquired their own identity and reputation and thus supplemented the regimental system in motivating the soldiers. Each division had its own staff officers and a powerful force of light infantry with which to counter the skirmishers that led the French attacks. As the war progressed, batteries of artillery were permanently attached to the divisions, along with other services such as engineer officers, ambulance wagons, medical personnel, mules and assistant-provost-marshals.

Wellesley on 11 June 1809 secured permission to operate inside Spain. It seemed a favourable moment, for Austria had invaded Bavaria,

Napoleon's ally in southern Germany, two months earlier. Despite initial defeats and the loss of Vienna, the Austrians had beaten Napoleon at Aspern–Essling in May and were not crushed until after the Battle of Wagram in July.

Wellesley could not obtain enough money to enable him to move until 27 June. He then advanced eastwards, intending in conjunction with the Spanish Army of Extremadura under General Don Gregorio de la Cuesta to defeat a French corps under Marshal Claude Victor and liberate Madrid. In fact, his plan was dangerously over-ambitious, especially as his Spanish allies were unable to supply him as they had promised, while another Spanish force, the Army of the Centre under General Francisco Venegas, would fail to pin down additional French forces and prevent them from reinforcing Victor.

On 3 July Wellesley entered Spain with over 19,000 British troops and advanced eastwards with Cuesta's 34,000 poorly disciplined and equipped Spaniards. On the 22nd, they reached the town of Talavera on the River Tagus, 110 km south-west of Madrid. Cuesta agreed to help attack Victor there on the 23rd, but at dawn refused to move and allowed him to escape. Wellesley furiously refused to advance further until he had an undertaking that the Spaniards would adequately supply his army. Despite these problems, Lieutenant William Coles of the 40th Regiment claimed in a letter of the 23rd:

> ... our Army are in high spirits which is almost incredible, consid-
> ering the fatiguing Marches & great Deprivations they have sufferd –
> on this account many Regts are ineffective, I believe the whole sick
> of the Army does not amount to less than between 5 & 6000 men. ...

Cuesta on the 24th decided to pursue Victor independently, but hurriedly retreated the next day as the French concentrated 46,000 men under King Joseph. Wellesley and Cuesta took up a defensive position at Talavera. The French attacked on the night of the 27th and seized the Medellin hill in the centre of the British sector before being thrown back. They renewed their assaults against the British on the 28th and were again repelled, but left Cuesta's strongly posted Spaniards in the south undisturbed. Wellesley, who was seriously outgunned and unable to find cover for all his troops, suffered heavy casualties. In a letter dated 29 July, Second Captain Eliot of the Royal Artillery revealed just how intense the fighting had been:

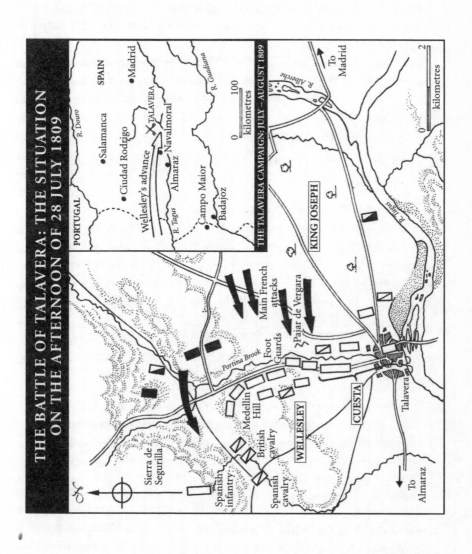

THE BATTLE OF TALAVERA: THE SITUATION
ON THE AFTERNOON OF 28 JULY 1809

PORTUGAL

SPAIN

R. Douro

•Salamanca

•Ciudad Rodrigo

•Madrid

X TALAVERA

Wellesley's advance

Navalmoral

R. Tagus

Almaraz

Campo Maior

R. Guadiana

•Badajoz

0   100
kilometres

THE TALAVERA CAMPAIGN: JULY – AUGUST 1809

To
Madrid

R. Alberche

KING JOSEPH

R. Tagus

0   2
kilometres

Sierra de Segurilla

Spanish
infantry

Spanish
cavalry

Medellin
Hill

British
cavalry

Portina Brook

Foot
Guards

Main French
attacks

Pajar de Vergara

WELLESLEY

CUESTA

Talavera

To
Almaraz

The time will only allow me to say that after the most sanguinary battle ever fought, I have again escaped without a wound, altho twice hit in my clothes, and my horse, also twice wounded[.] the Art[iller]y have suffered considerably. Capt [Henry] Baynes being early wounded I took command of his brigade with which I had being doing duty as a volunteer, a few moments after L^t [Henry] Wyatt was killed 2 men & 10 horses[.] the battle of Vimiero was a serious affair, but a mere skirmish to this which lasted 2 days and nights without intermission, without provisions, and never more than an hours rest. . . .

In a subsequent letter dated 19 August, Eliot revealed how during the night of the 27th:

. . . we slept this night at intervals if you could call it sleeping in our position and under our guns not having tasted any thing the day before. about 2 o Clock was another attack which lasted about half an hour and met the same fate as the former. when the sun rose in the morning [of the 28th] it discovered the two armies within almost 600 yards of each other the Ground between them covered with dead & dying. we now percieved the French had about twice our force and their Art[iller]y much more numerous and heavy. about 5 o Clock a most furious cannonade was opened on our line which we answered and an attack at the same time on the left by a very heavy column to regain the hill [Medellin] they had lost and so often attacked, here they were again beaten by the bayonet[.] this attack lasted with little intermission till twelve at noon when the firing ceased on both sides till about two when the French being reinforced by Sebastiani and 12.000 fresh troops commenced the attack on the right left and centre[.] on the left Joseph Buonaparte led the attack (and I had the honor of being opposed to this column and fired away the whole of my ammunition.) at night the firing ceased, and as before we remained all night in line totally exhausted from want of provisions and expecting a fresh attack in the morning we were agreeably surprised to find the Enemy was quite satisfied with our manner of handling him and had retreated during the night. . . .

Private George Woolger of the 16th (or The Queen's) Regiment of (Light) Dragoons wrote to his sister and brother-in-law on 26 October:

. . . as soon as Light Apeard on the 28th the Battle was Renewd with a most Tremendious Cannonade from the Contending arms, which

Continued for some hours without Intermission, our Infantry was sharply put to it our Reg^t sufferd much we Lost 8 men & 21 horses in about 15 minuets – bsides what we lost the Day before – about 2 P.M. the Battle became Dredfull all this Large Plaine was all in a smoake from Cannon & musketarey and when the french give way ther Dead & wounded Lay in almost whole Ranks – the french stormd the 2 hills 6 times & were as often Drove back with great Slaughter till both hill[s] were Coverd with killd & wounded – too much Praise Cant be given of the 29th 31st y^e [?] guards 48th foot – in short Everey Reg^t did ther Duty they stud like stone walls Disdaining to flinch Dispising there Num^r altho they were 3 to one & we had had scarcly any bread or water these two Trying days Excessive heate & hard fighting still I found none grumble[.] Provision Verey scarce as the french have layn here 7 month & made such havock with Everey thing round this Country – & they knew Every Inch of the Countrey for miles Round which was of great advantage to them in this battle, both sides fought hard –

. . .

it was shocking to see the killd & wounded on both sides some with both Legs of[f] others both arms or one arm of[f] in short wounded in all parts[;] men & horses lay together mangld in a shocking manner – all the houses in Tallavera are filld with English french & spanish wounded, maney die with loss of blood some with there wounds – . . .

Ensign William Walton of the Coldstream Regiment of Foot Guards likewise dwelt on the carnage in a letter to his mother on 29 July:

Sharp Work my Dear Mother the french only fell back on their Reinforcements & were here again on the 27th. We fought on that Day & the next – & King Joseph was with them – I have no time to mention particulars – we beat them – Our loss is great – I fear five thousand men[.] the Coldstream alone has lost *twelve* Officers, & near three hundred men killed & wounded – the Company in which I am, went into action 80 Strong – & had one officer, 3 Sergeants, & 35 Rank & file killed & Wounded – & you may suppose we did not play with each other. I have escaped without even a *Scratch – lucky Dog –*

Poor [Lieutenant-]Col. [John] Ross is killed – Jones was left at Abrantes unwell – therefore was not in the action – Charles I saw before the action well & I believe the 4th were not engaged – they say

the french have lost 8000 men – we have taken 19 Pieces of Cannon
– they are gone – I have not heard where – Excuse this I am writing
in the Fie[ld] on the grass – having nothing else to write on –

Captain the Hon. Francis Hood of the 3rd Foot Guards recorded his
experiences in his diary for 28 July:

> The Enemy soon after day break, attempted again to turn our Flanks,
> & at the same time Cannonaded the Center, we kept our Position;
> the Enemy were driven back, but firing continued the whole day;
> towards the afternoon, they attacked on every point, but were equally
> unsuccessful[.] The Brigade moved forward to the Charge, & com-
> pleatly routed the Enemy in their front, a most tremendous fire was
> kept upon both sides & the Brigade has suffered much both in
> officers & men –
>
> ...
>
> The fire was so heavy from a battery we were ordered to go to
> the right about, & after moving back, some yards to front again,
> by some of the Reg^t on our left moving to[o] close on us we were
> thrown into confusion, but after a little were in order again & took
> up our Position for the night, & the Enemy had at one time,
> threatened an advance again but afterwards retreated, & in the night
> moved still further –

Hood neglected to explain that the Guards were in fact driven back by
the French reserves after pursuing too far.

Although he won the battle, Wellesley lost a quarter of his troops
killed or wounded. Fortunately, reinforcements arrived on 29 July in the
shape of the Light Brigade under Brigadier-General Craufurd, which had
come out from England and made an epic march in a vain attempt to
arrive in time for the battle. The distance and duration of the march
have been disputed, but can be ascertained from the memoranda book
of Captain John Duffy of the 43rd Regiment. He recorded that on the
morning of 28 July he was at Navalmoral, 60 km west of Talavera:

> The Brigade moved off at 2 O Clock for Casada [La Calzada] – on
> the road we were met by a number of Spaniards with Baggage who
> gave us a vague account of an action having taken place – as we
> approached Casada the Road was filled with stragglers –
> Instead of halting at Casada in consequence of the Reported

action the Brigade moved on 2 more leagues to Orapesa [Oropesa] where we received information of the Enemy's attack from some of the British soldiers – Remained about 4 Hours during the heat of the Day at Orapesa and then continued our march till 11 at night when the men were allowed to rest for 3 Hours – The whole of the night wounded Officers & men with Baggage &c were passing us to the Rear – At 2 O Clock we pushed on for the Army who were on the position near Talavera in which they had fought the day before where we joined them about 5 O Clock in the morning[.]

[29 July:] The brigade marched 13 leagues since leaving Naval-moral at 2 O Clock yesterday morning a distance of upwards of 52 English miles –

Ordered forward to the Advanced Posts about 2 miles to the front of the Position – The Enemy had retired about 4 Hours previous to our joining and occupied their former position on the Hills accross the Alberche – The wounded & Dead were laying about in the Grove which the Brigade occupied – ...

Duffy's claim that he had marched fifty-two miles is inaccurate, for the distance was nearer forty. But it was an epic feat to cover this distance in twenty-seven hours, particularly in July.

Wellesley, who had now almost exhausted his provisions, discovered that his line of retreat was under threat. Soult had recovered from his recent defeat and was marching south with three corps. Wellesley retreated to the safety of the Portuguese frontier around Badajoz, where he could be supplied from Lisbon. Despite the failure of his intervention in Spain, he had boosted morale in Britain with his victories and was created Baron Douro of Wellesley and Viscount Wellington of Talavera and Wellington.

Unfortunately, the army's cantonments near Badajoz were in an area rife with malaria in the autumn. By 1 November, over 9,000 British soldiers, or 28 per cent of the total, were in hospital. Yet the demands of the pestilential Walcheren Expedition in Holland prevented any more medical officers from being sent to the Peninsula. Lieutenant Henry Booth of the 43rd Regiment complained in a letter from Campo Maior dated 24 November:

... I am now on the list of Convalescents from an attack of the ague, which came daily for 8 or 9 days, but I have now I hope completely got the better of it. I take a great deal of Exercise the Weather at present being very fine & wholesome. I am also plying myself with Bark [quinine] which is the only Remedy for the ague. I wonder how long these Ministers of England intend Keeping us here, we are in a perfect State of inactivity. The Army is wasting away from sickness, there are thousands of reports on the wing – some say we are to advance again into Spain that we only await the arrival of reinforcements from England. I hope at all Events this is not true, for it must be clear to every one of common sense that we can do no good in Spain. In the first place the Spaniards are not to be depended on & secondly Buonaparte (if Peace is signed with Austria) has only to march an immense reinforcement for the complete subjugation of the whole Peninsula: but the stupid Boobies are determined to risk every thing & when half the English Army is destroyed they gape & stare & wonder & debate how it happe[ned] but it is to be hoped before that happens the p[eople] of England will see the serious Necessity of recalling the Army. but alas! they are too much engaged with the Jubilee which affords a mighty plausible excuse for *stuffing & swilling with ox flesh & ale*, it w^d open their Eyes & their hearts too to witness the state of our hospitals here. But enough of this if I continue such dismal Strains you will be inclined to think I have lost all zeal for the *Sarvice* & dubt me the *Soldier tired* &c . . .

Napoleon, having secured a victorious peace with Austria at the Treaty of Schönbrunn on 14 October 1809, was free to send more troops to Spain. On 20 October, Wellington ordered the secret construction of fortifications to seal off an area of 1,300 km² around Lisbon in case the rest of Portugal was overrun. These fortifications, the so-called Lines of Torres Vedras, would be dotted across the hills from the Atlantic coast in the west to the estuary of the River Tagus in the east. The first line would lie 30 km north of Lisbon with a second about 8 km further south. They would take advantage of the rivers, rugged terrain and existing castles and would be strengthened by inundations. Communications within the Lines would be improved by new lateral roads and a semaphore telegraph system, while the Royal Navy would support either flank. A third and final fortified line would be constructed around a beach west of Lisbon to protect the evacuation of Wellington's army should that become necessary.

Despite inefficiency and some opposition, Wellington had effective control of Portugal's Council of Regency, and hence of the country's resources. Besides the Portuguese regular army, he could use the militia and in 1810 he also had the Regency call out the *Ordenança*, a levy of all remaining able-bodied men between sixteen and sixty. Both these second-line forces lacked the discipline or equipment to fight alongside the regulars, but could garrison fortresses, construct defensive works and harass French lines of communication. They would also destroy or remove provisions, transport and communication links such as roads, bridges and boats in the face of an invasion.

There were two main invasion routes across Portugal's mountainous frontier. Wellington believed that the French were most likely to use the northern corridor, which was guarded by the fortresses of Ciudad Rodrigo and Almeida. Early in December, he began to move the bulk of his army northwards from Badajoz to the area west of Ciudad Rodrigo. He left behind the 2nd Division and some attached units under the reliable Major-General Rowland Hill to watch the southern corridor, 200 km to the south, which was blocked by the twin fortresses of Badajoz and Elvas.

Wellington wrote from Badajoz on 9 December to Beresford, who was reforming the Portuguese army. His letter details the effect that his march north would have on the dispositions of the Portuguese troops on his route and indicates how he paid close personal attention to the staff work of his army, despite having the dependable Colonel George Murray as his Quartermaster-General:

> The Troops commenced their March this morning; but some time will elapse before we shall get them all off on account of the difficulty of relieving them of the Burthen of their sick. I don't believe (at least Murray does not believe) that we shall be of much inconvenience to you. We march necessarily in small Divisions, and I rather believe that we shall make our March without being obliged to obstruct you in any great degree. He writes however to [name illegible] upon the subject.
>
> We all pass the Tagus at Abrantes; which considering every thing, I think the best road for us.
>
> I omitted to tell you that I reviewed the other day the Troops of the Garrison of Elvas, and I shall do the same by all the Portuguese Troops I shall meet with. The 5th & 17th were really in better order than I expected to see any Portuguese Troops in; Their Tenue

[bearing] was very good; Cloathing Arms &c in good order; & their Field discipline & Manoevres by no means bad considering the defect of Instruction. As far as the Instructions have gone they are very good; and I would recommend to you as soon as possible to circulate the order for the formation & Exercise of a Battallion which has not yet been received by these Battallions. When they will be received I am convinced that as far as Parade Exercise goes, which is no inconsiderable point gained[,] these Battallions will be good.

They were weak under Arms, not much more than 800 Men out of the two reg^{ts}[.] But then they are weak even upon paper; & they had the Guards of the Garrison, of our Hospitals, & their own sick.

He added in a postcript:

Upon considering our Route, & your Cantonments we find that it will be necessary to move only the two Light Battallions from Punhete; & two of the 4 reg^{ts} from Thomar.

Unfortunately, the army's move north did not immediately improve its health and the sick rates fell significantly only by 1 March. The army tended to be healthiest in the spring, before it was assailed by malaria, diarrhoea and dysentery in the hot summer and early autumn. Winter favoured rheumatism and respiratory diseases and also encouraged outbreaks of typhus as the troops gathered together out of the cold. Venereal disease, fevers and leg ulcers were also common.

As a result of Beresford's reforms Wellington was able in February 1810 to integrate Portuguese brigades into his divisions and thus boost his numbers without undermining the effectiveness of his army. A typical division now had a strength of about 5,500 to 5,800 men. At the same time, Wellington created the crack Light Division by taking Craufurd's Light Brigade from the 3rd Division and reinforcing it with two Portuguese *caçador*, or rifle, battalions. The Light Division, placed out in front of the rest of the army across the 60 km wide entrance to the northern corridor, provided a highly responsive screen of outposts that prevented the French from gathering information on Wellington's dispositions.

Lieutenant William Coles, who had transferred to the 4th (or Queen's Own) Regiment of Dragoons, tried to assess the situation when he wrote to his brother on 19 February:

... It is impossible to know the Immediate Fate of Portugal as the Portugueze are as yet untried, if appearance should have any Weight in the Opinion of the Military Man we should be greatly prepossessd in their Favour, as their Battalions are very Respectable Disciplind by English Officers, the men seem to have a good deal of Esprit De Corps & in high spirits; therefore we may flatter ourselves that the first attack on Portugal may be effectively oppos'd & the French oblig'd to Retire ...

Coles's confidence was not universal either within the army or in Britain. He himself despaired of Portugal's long-term prospects even if the French should be repulsed in their initial offensive:

... But this will only procrastinate the Evil Day, & be the occasion of much Blood Shed; the Enemy must have it one Day or other, therefore why not Retire with our Shatterd Army & advise the People to make their Terms with the French untill a great change of Fortune takes place, and a Ray of the hope of Independence brightens their prospects, and animates them to Resist, But while Buonaparte has Spain Portugal must suffer the yoke; therefore the Easier they make it the Better, and the first plan of doing it, *is* by not Resisting – ...

*

The French did not immediately invade Portugal, for in January 1810 they instead overran the hitherto unoccupied south of Spain. Fortunately, the Spaniards managed to garrison the key naval base of Cadiz with 12,000 men just two days before the French arrived before it on 5 February. By May, the Spaniards had overcome their earlier reluctance and had allowed the garrison of Cadiz to be reinforced by sea by 8,000 British and Portuguese troops. Gunner Andrew Phillips of Captain Campbell's Company of the 2nd Battalion, Royal Artillery, wrote in a letter on 12 March:

... there is onely 4 regiments of the line and 3 Compnies Of Artillery but expct 14 thousand mor from England[.] Our tims in this place is verrey hard you may belive And lickley to be worce yet – evereything is verrey Dear in this place it is petful to sea the towns in this Countrey for I have sen a great maney Parts in it mor than I want to sea again[.] I have Lived on a nounce of bread a day and somtims

nothing For 2 or 3 days and 4 days but thank god we have[.] Now
we have plenty at the presant – . . .

Despite such hardships, Cadiz was in no real danger, although the
siege lasted for two and a half years until the French evacuation of
southern Spain in August 1812. Being surrounded by water on three
sides, it was practically impregnable given the size of the garrison and
the supremacy of the Royal Navy, which allowed it to be supplied by
sea. As the refuge of the Spanish Patriot Government, the city became a
symbol of Spanish defiance and a challenge to the legitimacy of King
Joseph's rule. The continued resistance of Cadiz, along with the activities
of the Spanish guerrillas and regular armies, also pinned down 70,000
French troops in southern Spain.

Meanwhile, Wellington with the bulk of his army continued to guard
the northern corridor into Portugal, with Hill's detachment of 12,000
men at Portalegre in the south, 65 km north-west of the Spanish-held
fortress of Badajoz. Hill was supporting a Spanish army under the
Marquess de La Romana, which was stationed around Badajoz. La
Romana's task was to watch the French II Corps, which had been
detached under General Jean Reynier and was posted 55 km to the east.
La Romana was one of the more cooperative Spanish commanders and
supplied Hill with valuable intelligence. This was exemplified by his
letter of 21 May, which was translated into English, apparently on
receipt:

> I have had the honour to request of you a small detachment of
> Cavalry in order to receive & transport the French deserters who
> wish to enter the British service & take the liberty to repeat that I
> think it of the utmost utility – The detachement will be furnished
> with everything able to make their stay at Badajoz agreable–
>   The enemy still continue in the positions of *Zafra* Head Quarters
> with two thousand men *Ayanchal Villa Sranca Almendralejo Villalha
> & Feria Merida* & subsequent –

Reynier was too weak to undertake anything more serious than feints
and diversions and moved to the north bank of the Tagus in July,
shadowed by Hill. On 11 August, Beresford wrote to Major-General
Henry Fane, who commanded Hill's cavalry, namely the 13th Regiment
of (Light) Dragoons and a Portuguese brigade. The Portuguese horsemen

had recently won some small but heartening successes against Reynier's cavalry:

> ... I really think that on all sides, in the little brushes the Portugueze have had, they have done very fairly, and given good Hopes of their future conduct[.]
>
> I think for some time you will have the most active Post with your Cavalry, and I was very glad to find you had crossed the Tagus. Ld Wellington means to attach to you half a Brigade of Horse Art^y that is now in Lisbon & I shall be glad to hear of it's getting to you, but this he will communicate himself. [Brigadier-]Genl [George] Madden's Brigade [of Portuguese cavalry] is to be attached to Romana as you have quitted that Part of the Country. We have nothing new here, nor does there appear any thing like a movement on the part of the Enemy − look well however to the 15th it is Bonaparté's Birthday − ...

On 10 September, Reynier again moved north, in order to join the invasion of Portugal, and Hill made a corresponding move to rejoin Wellington.

The situation in the north had developed significantly during the summer. Marshal André Massena had arrived in May to take command of the invasion force, the Army of Portugal. His first move was to besiege the fortress of Ciudad Rodrigo and its Spanish garrison, which had been isolated since 26 April. Wellington rightly refused to leave the safety of the mountains and advance into the plains to try and save it, for he was outnumbered, particularly in cavalry, and even if successful would merely cause Massena to resume the siege after bringing up more men. But his refusal was resented by many in his army. Captain Alexandre de Roverea was ADC to Major-General Lowry Cole, the commander of the 4th Division. He noted in a letter dated 17 July:

> ... During the whole of the month of May, & the first week in June, it was the general opinion in the army that Lord Wellington intended to fight an action for the Relief of Ciudad Rodrigo: − the preparations that were made, & the language of the Head Quarters seemed to warrant the conclusion which the public drew from them: − before Junot's [corps] having joined, we were if not superior, at least equal in numbers to the french near us: − it is not however a person of my very humble Rank, to presume to say we were wrong in not availing

ourselves of the opportunity: – I can only as an Individual, regret it
extremely, as besides causing the fall of Ciudad Rodrigo, it has
indubitably injured us much in the opinion of the Spaniards. – . . .

During the siege, the Light Division under Craufurd continued to
screen the army with its usual efficiency. Captain John Duffy of the 43rd
Regiment noted that deserters, chiefly Germans and Italians, arrived
every day from the enemy. He gave an example in his memoranda book
on 21 June of a French probe being repelled:

> Marched at 4 A.M. to Gallegos [17 km west of Ciudad Rodrigo] –
> Ordered on Piquet to the right Ford of Carpio – About 10 O Clock
> an Alarm was given of the Enemy being in motion – At 2 the Beacons
> were set fire too [sic] the Enemy's Cavalry soon after made their
> appearance on the Hill near Carpio skirmishing with our Hussars
> who were obliged to retire & cross the Azava – The Enemys
> Skirmishers approached the Ford – several dismounted and com-
> menced firing upon the advanced Party of my Company – after a
> short time finding them at a good distance & to prevent their
> reconnoitring the Ford the fire was returned which in a few minutes
> drove them back – The Picquet at Merialva on the Ciudad Road
> drove in by the Enemy – About 5 O Clock the Enemy's Cavalry
> moved up to the Hill near Carpio to the amount of a Thousand – in
> the Evening they retired & our Hussars occupied their former
> Position – Firing constantly the whole of the Day and at intervals
> during the night from Ciudad

Ciudad Rodrigo capitulated on 10 July, and eleven days later French
forces advanced westwards on its Portuguese twin, the fortress of
Almeida. Craufurd rashly delayed pulling back the Light Division and on
24 July was fortunate to escape across the River Coa in the face of a
heavy attack with only 300 casualties. Lieutenant Richard Brunton of the
43rd Regiment vividly described these perilous moments:

> . . . the Brigade was attacked by an overwhelming force. They were
> unsupported, and had in their rear a rapid River [the Coa] with
> steep, rocky and precipitous sides, and the heavy rain of the preceding
> night having rendered all the Fords impassible, their only retreat was
> by a Bridge of very few feet in width. – I had the honor to carry one
> of the Colours and the care of it when retiring, with the Regiment

1. Napoleon dominated the Continent, but his power ended at the coast. Here, he watches the British fleet guarding the Channel near Boulogne in 1805.

2. The landing of the British army at Mondego Bay in Portugal, 1–8 August 1808.

3. Robert Stewart, Viscount Castlereagh, one of Wellington's most important supporters in the British government.

4. Lieutenant-General Sir Hew Dalrymple, c. 1794.

5. Lieutenant-General Sir John Moore.

6. Major-General Robert Craufurd.

7. The audacious daylight crossing of the River Douro at Oporto on 12 May 1809.

8. The Battle of Talavera. The 40th (or the 2nd Somersetshire) Regiment of Foot, formed in line two ranks deep, counter-attacks a French infantry column in the afternoon of 28 July 1809.

9. The 3rd Division counter-attacks the French at the Battle of Busaco, 27 September 1810.

10. Marshal André Massena. He commanded the French invasion of Portugal in 1810, but was outgeneralled by Wellington.

11. Wellington in Portuguese Marshal-General's uniform, 1809.

12. Lieutenant-General Sir Stapleton Cotton, later Viscount Combermere, Wellington's cavalry commander for much of the Peninsular War.

13. Lieutenant-General Sir Rowland Hill, c. 1819.

14. Lieutenant-General the Hon. Sir Galbraith Lowry Cole, the commander of the 4th Division in the Peninsula.

15. Lieutenant-General Sir Thomas Picton.

16. The Battle of Fuentes de Oñoro, 5 May 1811. Captain Norman Ramsay of the Royal Horse Artillery gallops his two guns through French cavalry to safety.

17. Fuentes de Oñoro. Two British soldiers are carrying a stretcher, probably made from a blanket and two poles, while regimental surgeons tend the wounded. Note the battalion sitting down to rest on the right. Wellington's battalions often lay down in formation to shelter from artillery fire.

18. A bivouac near the village of Vila Velha de Ródão on the evening of 19 May 1811.

19. The 3rd Division crossing the River Tagus at Vila Velha, on the following day, 20 May. Note the infantry in boats and the rope ferry conveying artillery.

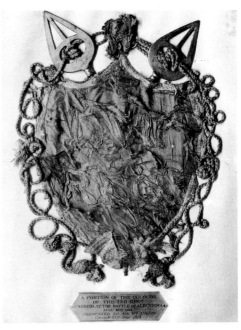

20. Lieutenant-Colonel William Inglis commanded the 57th (or the West Middlesex) Regiment of Foot at the Battle of Albuera, 16 May 1811.

21. Portion of the regimental colour of the 57th Regiment. The colour was riddled with twenty-one shots at Albuera and had its staff broken by French fire.

22. The 57th Regiment at Albuera. In the centre are the battalion's two colours and its commander, Lieutenant-Colonel Inglis, who has been wounded. The 57th won the nickname 'Die-hards' for its conduct in this desperately fought action.

broken up nearly into Skirmishing Order, by the difficult nature of the ground, and the necessity for repelling attacks in various directions; was a duty of no small anxiety, difficulty and exertion. – On being forced back in some disorder on the narrow and rocky road leading down to the Bridge, General Crawford came up to me, and the other Ensign and desired us to cross the Bridge, take up a conspicuous position on the opposite side as near the Bridge as possible, and display the Colours for the Regiment to rally on. – This was done and we remained standing under a tremendous fire of musquetry from the opposite side which was precipitous and well within range until the Regiment had passed the Bridge and rallied – I do not now exactly recollect, but I think there were 2 Officers and either 3 or 4 Serjeants killed and wounded with the Colours on that day. – I escaped unhurt, and in the evening I handed them over to Ensign [James] Considine (now a Major General in Africa [1838]), who had joined from England during the Action, and being then a Lieutenant, I was appointed to command a Company the Captain of which ([Ewen] Cameron) had been killed. – Our loss in Officers on that day (which I think was 16 killed and wounded) having left me the Senior for that duty. . . .

Wellington faced a crisis of confidence both within his army and at home. Lieutenant William Coles exemplified the mixed feelings of many when he wrote on 24 July:

... it would be a sin to express an Idea of seeing England, as confident [of] success seems to be the Motto of our General; perhaps He will find himself mistaken, tho He is a judge of Military Matters, & not deficient in foresight. The Portugueze like him very much and think him Invincible, which is a Good Idea for Soldiers to entertain, & is often the occasion of success, when they are fighting with inferior Numbers . . .

The confidence of the Portuguese people can be gauged by a letter written from Lisbon on 28 July by Lieutenant-Colonel John Elley:

You must pardon a hasty and almost unintelligible Scrawl – I did not find Lisbon quite what I left it – although a short Period only had elapsed, so short, that my Friends were astonished at the Expedition I had made –
  The French Party rears its Head, a Barometer of the Times, not

wholly to be disregarded – Civility to the English is on the wane –
and Despair, on the Countenance of the well disposed begins to
appear.

I regret to say recent Events, at the fore Posts, have made an
unfavorable Impression here – . . .

Elley was referring, in part, to Craufurd's scrape on the Coa. He
continued:

. . . These unpleasant Affairs have produced much conversation in
the Army, and also serious animadversions, from the Commr. of
the Forces. – Although the French have collected a very formidable
Force, to act on one Point I am persuaded the conquest of Portugal
is not immediately at Hand – The Country we have to retire through,
if obliged, is strong, and without supplies. . . .

At the front, Wellington carefully watched the French moves. He was
campaigning in friendly country and enjoyed plentiful intelligence from
secret correspondents and from guerrilla bands, who intercepted French
despatches. He also sent exploring officers to gather intelligence of
French numbers and dispositions and of physical features of the terrain,
such as the state of the roads. Existing maps of Portugal and Spain were
scarce and unreliable, but British staff officers gradually built up a wealth
of information by constantly reconnoitring and noting relevant military
details. More local knowledge was acquired through the army's outposts
and patrols and from inhabitants. In contrast, the French often knew
little of the situation beyond their outposts, for they had antagonized
most of the local people with looting and atrocities.

In addition, Wellington personally reconnoitred whenever possible.
The extent to which he went into detail and acted as his own chief of
intelligence is illustrated by his letters to Lieutenant-General Sir Stapleton
Cotton, who assumed command of his cavalry in June 1810. Cotton's
ability has been questioned. Many in Wellington's army favoured the
obvious alternative, Lieutenant-General Henry Lord Paget, later the
second Earl of Uxbridge, who had distinguished himself under Moore in
the Coruña campaign. Ensign George Percival of the Coldstream Guards
wrote on 11 July 1811:

. . . I yesterday heard for certain that Lord Paget was coming out to
this Country to take command of the Cavalry, he will be a great

acquisition *to the Cavalry*, as Sir Stapleton Cotton who now commands it, allows himself that he is not adequate to the command ...

But Uxbridge's suitability was undermined by the fact that he was senior until Wellington's promotion to field marshal in 1813; he had also eloped with Wellington's sister-in-law in 1809. Cotton, in contrast, had served with Wellington in India in 1799 and, whatever the limitations of his intellect, obeyed orders steadily and conscientiously and could be trusted not to get into scrapes by exceeding his authority.

Wellington's letters began 'My dear Cotton', ended 'Ever your's most sincerely' and tended to be no more than a page or two in length. They show how determined he was to avoid antagonizing the inhabitants. For example, he wrote to Cotton on 6 August:

> I wish to mention to you that I have received complaints from different quarters of the Conduct of the Hussars towards the Inhabitants of the Country; & their conduct has been so bad as to exasperate them exceedingly. It has gone so far as that they have enquired whether they might kill the Germans in our Service, as well as in the Service of the French when urged to resist the enterprizes of the latter.
>
> There is really no excuse for a Soldier in the Service of G^t Britain plundering; & I shall be obliged to you if you will talk seriously to [Lieutenant-Colonel Friedrich von] Arentschild[t] [the commander of the 1st Hussars, King's German Legion] upon the subject, & point out to him how unfortunate it would be, if this conduct which can be of advantage to nobody, should deprive his Reg^t of the Reputation which they have acquired.
>
> Write to Cocks upon it also; as well as to any other Officers who may Command detachments of Hussars.

Captain the Hon. Edward Somers Cocks was one of Wellington's best exploring officers and was with a party of cavalry observing French communications.

The lengths to which Wellington was determined to go in both gaining intelligence and denying it to the enemy are clear from his letter to Cotton dated 11 August:

> I beg that you will let me know the name of the Man you wish to have appointed Asst Provost & he shall be appointed.

Pay the Spies any thing you think they deserve. If you are certain that they go to Valverde, you should pay them very well; as it is a Service of much danger. Give them Rations as well as payment, which will probably encourage them more than money.

I write to Beresford about the Amm[unitio]^n for the Ordenanza. I cannot read the name of the Village which the people have not quitted; but let the Juiz de Fora [district magistrate] know that they may stay or not as they please, but that any Man who has any Communication with the Enemy shall be hanged.

This was not an idle threat. Captain John Duffy of the 43rd Regiment later recorded, on 7 March 1811, that Wellington had the district magistrate of Torres Novas imprisoned for having remained during the French occupation.

Almeida was invested by the French on 15 August, but hopes that it would significantly delay their advance were soon dashed. A massive explosion of the main magazine after a few hours of bombardment led to the Portuguese garrison's capitulation on the 28th. Massena made a limited attack on Wellington's outposts on 2 September, but could not begin a general advance from Almeida until he had gathered supplies. Wellington withdrew his infantry, leaving only cavalry at the front around Celorico and Guarda. He wrote to Cotton at 8.30 a.m. on the 3rd, ordering him to observe the enemy, but not to engage in any serious affair.

Wellington had previously destroyed sections of some roads to deny them to the enemy, including the Estrada Nova, which led from near Guarda south-westwards towards Abrantes in the direction of Lisbon. He hence expected Massena to advance in a more westerly direction along the River Mondego. He thought that Massena was likely to follow the main road on the south bank of the river, rather than the poor quality tracks on the opposite side, and he had therefore chosen a suitable defensive position behind a tributary, the River Alva, and had it strengthened with entrenchments.

Massena finally moved forward in earnest on 15 September. He was constantly observed by Wellington's cavalry, while his stragglers were picked off by Portuguese irregulars. By 4.40 p.m., Wellington at his headquarters at Gouveia, 23 km south-west of Celorico, had received a note from Cotton and had also heard from Cocks. He wrote to Cotton

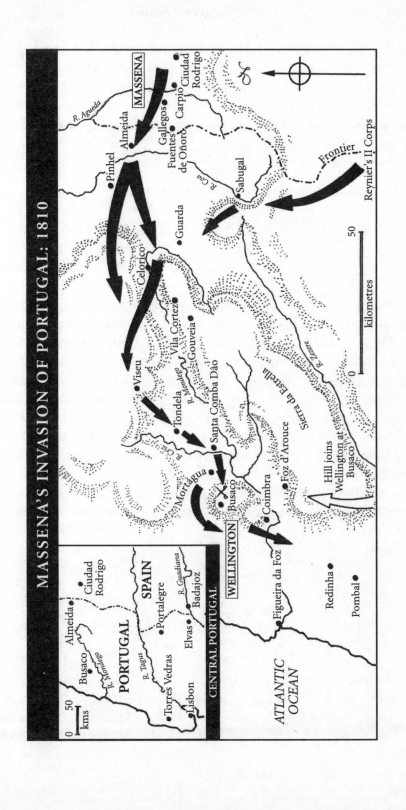

MASSENA'S INVASION OF PORTUGAL: 1810

at that hour, stating that he could depend on it that the movement was general and telling him to fall back at least as far as Celorico for the night, leaving only the 1st Hussars, King's German Legion in front in observation. This was reinforced by a subsequent letter sent at midnight, in which he added that there was some straw at Vila Cortez, almost 9 km north-east of Gouveia, that should be destroyed by the rear regiments. He wrote again to Cotton at 1.30 p.m. on the 16th:

> I fear that we shall knock up the Reg^{ts}, if we don't allow them to get to their ground; & the Hussars having observed the Enemy into Celorico should be allowed to retire to their Cantonments. We have a great deal of Work before us; & we must not knock up the Troops.
>
> I have received your note of 12 [noon] from Cortico [5 km south-west of Celorico].

Rather than advance along the south bank of the Mondego, Massena unexpectedly crossed to the north, where he followed the bad tracks on that side of the river. He had been misled by his unreliable maps and lacked the information on the terrain that Wellington had been so careful to gather. The presence of Portuguese irregulars prevented the French from reconnoitring except in strength. The way in which Massena's line of advance became clear can be traced in Wellington's letters to Cotton. At 8.30 a.m. on 17 September, he wrote from Sampayo, 3 km north of Gouveia, that the enemy did not seem to be moving in front, in other words on the south bank, but that they were certainly moving on the other side of the river. He stated that he could see a very heavy dust hanging over Mangualde, 18 km to the north-west. By 6.00 a.m. the next day, he was in no doubt:

> In case you should not have read Walters' [Lieutenant-Colonel John Waters, an exploring officer] reports I send them to you. It is obvious that the Enemy's arrangements are all directed to a movement upon the right [north] of the Mondego; but it is still desireable to have an eye upon their proceedings on the left [south] of the River. I think therefore that you should leave an Intelligent Officer with a party of Hussars in Goveia, who might keep a few Men in Sampayo.
>
> This is desireable as well to keep an eye upon what is passing on that Road, as to communicate with Walters at Fulzozinho [Fulgo-sinho, 7 km east of Gouveia].
>
> I beg you to write to him, & desire him to forward his Reports to

the Officer of Hussars at Goveia; & desire this Officer to send them
on to you.

On the morning of the 19th Wellington instructed Cotton to watch
the movements of the advanced guard of Reynier's II Corps, which
moved along the south bank as a diversion before crossing further down
the Mondego.

Wellington was delighted at Massena's line of advance. The rugged
tracks north of the river delayed the French, damaged their wheeled
transport and led to a superb defensive position on the ridge at Busaco.
Wellington revealed his intentions when he wrote to Cotton from the
Convent at Busaco at 9.15 p.m. on 21 September:

By the accounts which Lord Fitz Roy Somerset [ADC to Wellington]
brought of the Enemy from General Craufurd [of the Light Division],
I judge that the 6th Corps [under Marshal Ney] at least is assembled
on the left [east] bank of the Chris [Criz]; & I conclude that it did
not attempt to pass this day, because the other Corps were not ready.
It's first operation must be to drive in the Squadron of the Royals
which are on the Chris, in order to Repair the fords or the bridge; &
when this body is driven in you may be certain that the whole not
only of this Corps but of the others will advance in a few hours
afterwards. You should therefore have all your dispositions made to
retire the Troops in advance, when the Squadron of the Royals will
be obliged to quit the Chris.

I have not yet heard the result of the examination of the Ponte de
Vagia above the Bridge near Combado [Santa Comba Dão]. You
should observe this point, as it is the nearest to Tondella [Tondela];
& not only the Bridge exists but the banks of the River are more
practicable than they are lower down.

If you withdraw from Mortagua bring the whole of the Troops to
the villages on the fall of the Hill between this place [Busaco] & that.
I shall be with you in the morning.

We have an excellent position here in which I am strongly
tempted to give battle. Unfortunately Hill is one day later than I
expected; & there is a road upon our left by which we may be turned
& cut off from Coimbra. But I don't yet give up hopes of discovering
a Remedy for this last misfortune; & as for the former, the Enemy
will afford it to us if they don't cross the Chriss tomorrow.

The road that Wellington mentioned ran from Mortágua, 12 km east of Busaco, north-westwards through the village of Boialvo, thus outflanking the Busaco position. Wellington directed a force of Portuguese militia under Colonel Nicholas Trant to block the defiles on this track, but Trant through a misunderstanding arrived too late and in any case would have been able to impose only a limited delay with such second-rate troops against French regulars. More importantly, Wellington could simply draw Massena past the start of the track and directly towards Busaco by pulling back the Light Division at the right time.

The French II Corps under Reynier crossed the Criz on the 22nd, but was not followed immediately by the rest of the army, whose guns had been delayed by the poor state of the tracks. This gave Wellington the time he needed and he concentrated his divisions at Busaco between the 21st and the 26th.

Reynier advanced in force on the 25th and Wellington ordered the Light Division to retire. Massena's army deployed opposite the Busaco ridge on the 26th, but Wellington had his troops concealed on the reverse slopes and protected from artillery fire. He had also made a track behind the crest so that units could march quickly to reinforce any threatened sector, for he could not occupy the 14 km long position in strength everywhere. The steep slopes rendered cavalry superfluous, so the bulk of Cotton's men were in reserve 8 km west of Busaco.

Massena, unable to see Wellington's dispositions, did not realize how far southwards his line in fact extended. He planned to attack 4 km south of the main road at San Antonio de Cantara with Reynier's II Corps, which he mistakenly judged would turn Wellington's southern flank and then be in a position to advance northwards along the ridge crest. This would be the signal for Marshal Ney's VI Corps to launch the main attack in the north.

In fact, Reynier's assault at about 6.00 a.m. on the 27th came up against Major-General Thomas Picton's 3rd Division in the centre of Wellington's army. Reynier made three attacks, which were defeated one after the other, and Major-General James Leith brought up part of his 5th Division to help repel the third. Wellington was personally present in this area, but then rode north in time for the French main attack by Ney. This, too, was completely repulsed and Massena sensibly broke off the battle by midday.

Picton characteristically tried to deny any credit to his rival divisional commanders. In writing to his friend, Joseph Marryat, MP, on 31 October 1810, he brazenly claimed:

> ... I shall say nothing to you about the action of Busaco as you will have seen it in the Gazette, though not very clearly detailed. The serious attack was upon my Division on the right: that on the left being merely a feint. The attack was made with great impetuosity and en masse, but nothing could exceed the Determined Bravery of the Troops who repulsed them with the Bayonette. I had only Three British Regiments & three Portuguese Engaged with two Divisions and in the four different attacks they made upon different points of my position, the Enemy must have lost in killed and wounded nearly 4000.
>
> Massena appears to have got into a scrape, and in all probability will be obliged to yield up his Laurels to his more fortunate adversary. – He is in a most critical situation, without Provisions in an exhausted Country, with his Communica[tions] entirely cut off – another such an affair as that of Busacos will completely do him up. . . .

Picton's claim that he had only three British and three Portuguese regiments engaged is correct: these were the 45th, 74th and 88th Regiments of Foot and the Portuguese 8th, 9th and 21st Regiments. The 8th Portuguese were in fact part of Leith's 5th Division, but fought from the start of the action with Picton. Picton's other units were not seriously engaged, but he blatantly ignores the British 9th and 38th Regiments of Foot, which Leith brought up from the 5th Division further south to help repel the final assault.

Note, too, that Picton in his letter dismisses the defeat of Massena's main attack in the north by calling it a feint. Massena's total casualties in the entire battle were 4,600 and over half of them were in fact incurred by Ney's VI Corps in the north. Picton was clearly anxious to deny any credit for the victory to Craufurd, whose Light Division had repelled Ney. Picton's relations with Craufurd were notoriously prickly, for they were both ambitious and outspoken men.

Wellington by defeating Massena's attack at Busaco boosted morale both within his army and at home. He also gave his newly integrated Portuguese units some battle experience in a favourable situation and was gratified by their performance. Captain Alexandre de Roverea, who was with Major-General Lowry Cole's 4th Division immediately north of the Light Division, wrote in a letter dated 9 October:

> ... it is to be regretted the action was not more general: – we had upwards of 30000. men who did not fire a shot: – Genl Cole's Division was of that number: it fell to our lot to remain mere spectators. – The Portuguese behaved nobly, & have acquired the confidence as well as they deserve the admiration of their companions in arms. – their light troops suffered chiefly from the circumstances of their refusing to shelter themselves & persisting in chusing open ground....

Among the most distinguished of Wellington's regimental officers were the three Napier brothers, Charles, George and William. They all served with the Light Division and managed to collect wounds with distressing regularity. Wellington wrote to their mother on 30 September, three days after Busaco:

> I am concerned to be again the channel of conveying to you Intelligence of a distressing nature; but you received the last which I communicated to you in a manner so becoming yourself that I have less reluctance in writing to you than I had upon the former occasion, although the cause is more serious. The Army was engaged with the Enemy on the 27th Ins^t, & your Sons Charles & George were wounded. I saw the former after he was wounded & he was well & in good spirits, although he had a severe but not a dangerous wound in the Jaw. Charles [Wellington in fact meant George] is wounded in the hip but very slightly; & both are doing well. You will see the account of the action in which the Troops were engaged; & I hope it will be some consolation to you to reflect that your Sons received their Wounds upon an occasion in which the British Troops behaved so well.

This was but one in a series of similar letters. On 16 March 1811, Wellington wrote:

> I am sorry to have to inform you that your two Sons [William and George] were again wounded in an action with the Enemy the day before yesterday but neither of them I hope seriously....

He wrote again on 20 January 1812 to explain that George's right arm had been amputated following the storming of Ciudad Rodrigo:

> ... Having *such* Sons I am aware that you expect to hear of these misfortunes, which I have more than once had to communicate to you; & notwithstanding your affection for them you have so just a notion of the value of the distinction which they are daily acquiring for themselves by their Gallantry & good conduct, that their misfortunes do not make so great an Impression upon you. Under these circumstances I perform the task which I have taken upon myself with less reluctance; hoping at the same time that this will be the last occasion on which I shall have to address you on such a subject; and that your brave sons will be spared to you. . . .

Wellington had to retreat towards Lisbon on the evening of 28 September after discovering that Massena had belatedly begun to outflank Busaco to the north. The bulk of his army entered the Lines of Torres Vedras on 8 October. The actual fortifications were garrisoned by Portuguese militia, Spanish troops and British marines and artillerymen, leaving the field army free to respond to any French move. The existence of the lines had not in fact been totally concealed. As early as 10 April, Captain John Duffy of the 43rd Regiment had written, while on his way from Lisbon to join the army at the front:

> The Road to Villa franca lies along the River [Tagus] the Banks of which are well cultivated and stocked with Cat[t]le – on the left the Country is barren & mountainous – 4 leagues brought us to Villa franca a tolerable town built close to the River – on our Route to day we observed a Battery erected above the village of Alhamdra about a league from this – it is said that this work is the Right of a Position intended to be occupied in case of the Army's retrograding – it is almost inaccessible in flank or front as far as we could observe –

But Massena was taken aback when he reached these formidable fortifications on 14 October. He wisely declined to attack, but kept his ground since he could not cut his losses and abandon Portugal without massive loss of face. Wellington was keen to deny the French whatever provisions remained outside the lines. He wrote to Cotton from his headquarters at Pero Negro on 30 October:

I send you two reports & a letter shewing that the Enemy are getting large supplies on that side of the Country. I should think that General [George] Anson might continue to intercept these parties between Obidos & Cadaval; having Obidos occupied on one side of him; & Torres Vedras on the other; & it is really very desireable that these supplies should be intercepted.

Pray desire that an effort should be made.

Anson commanded a light cavalry brigade of the 16th Light Dragoons and 1st Hussars, King's German Legion. Obidos was 3 km from the Battlefield of Roliça near the Atlantic and Wellington added an encouraging postscript: 'The Enemy's force is but very small on that side, & they cannot do you any mischief'.

Lieutenant William Coles of the 4th Dragoons was already engaged in such harassment, as he revealed in a letter to his brother John dated 18 October:

... We have taken up a strong position & the Enemy has concentrated its whole force with in a League of us; the Heavy Brigade of Cavalry is still on the outside of the lines on the left of the position; & to the great annoyance of the French we send out partys continually to their Rear & intercept the provisions they collect in the Country; For some Days I have been honour'd with an Independent party, which is employ'd in the Sierra De la Junto, My Business is to make observation to the Enemys Movements, make reports on that Head, & if opportunity offers cut off Straggling Partys which are always to be found near a French Army, Respecting the latter concern, I have been rather fortunate, having during this Week taken 7 prisoners, besides prevented much Cattle being remov'd by the Enemy; as my Employment is observation, I return at Night to the Foot of a Mountain, where there is something better than a Cave, I here regale myself, & prepare my Petit Corps for the ensuing Day – You who are accustom'd to much Society would feel the loss of it. I myself think as a Soldier that He is never so well off as when his own Master, and does not mind the Sacrifice of a little trouble, to ensure that Sort of Independence which is attach'd to the Command of a Detachment; I am on one Side [of] the Mountain the French on the other; I am positive they do not much like the appearance of our position, as they have advanced to our Right twice, & Retird with a shrug of the shoulder; If they do not force the position soon they must Retire for want of Provisions, in that case they will suffer Desertion, & Every sort of Calamity Independent of the Difficultys that are oppos'd to them on account of the Recapture of Coimbra by Colnl Trent; I think the Cause brightens, and that Portugal will be English some time longer, Buonaparte must make another Sacrifice, as our Army tho small in Comparison to the Population of Spain, keeps him in more fear, & gives perpetual uneasiness to his Generals. . . .

Colonel Trant with 4,000 Portuguese militia had boldly attacked Coimbra on the River Mondego on 7 October. He had captured 4,500 French, including the wounded that they had left there, before withdrawing northwards with his prisoners.

Wellington lost no time in resting and reorganizing his troops within the lines. He ordered Cotton on 11 October to prepare three separate reports of the rearguard affairs that the cavalry had fought during the retreat, at Leiria, Alcoentre and Quinta da Torre on 5, 8 and 9 October, as these had all been highly creditable and he would be happy to have another opportunity of expressing how much the army was indebted to the cavalry. This is an interesting remark, given that Wellington is often accused of failing to give sufficient praise, particularly about his cavalry.

Morale in Wellington's army had already begun to improve. Ensign George Percival of the Coldstream Guards wrote to his aunt on 20 October from Lisbon:

> . . . The Portuguese in Lisbon appear very much down at the mouth at the French being so near them, but in my opinion the French will never succeed in getting here, as they must attack our position if they try to come, and by all accounts that is so strong – that Gibraltar is quite a joke to it, Massena is to great a General to attempt it, I dare say in England you expect to hear of a battle every day, here we have given up all thoughts of it, if there is the least chance of one (before the middle of next week) I shall certainly go up, which I can easily do in four hours as it is only three leagues and a half from hence. . . .

4

Stalemate

1811

On the night of 14 November 1810 Massena made a limited withdrawal of 45 km from before the Lines of Torres Vedras to an as yet unravaged area around Santarém. He settled down behind entrenchments to subsist as best he could, surrounded by Wellington's advanced units to the west, south and south-east and on the other sides by Portuguese second-line troops. Only on 5 March 1811 did he finally begin a full-scale retreat, having all but exhausted the available supplies. Next day, Captain John Duffy of the 43rd Regiment saw for himself the strength of his abandoned positions:

Called up at 4 this morning – informed that the Enemy had retired from the Causeway – went down to my Company on duty at it – 2 Serjeants had been down and found that the Sentry was still at his post – however on not observing him walking about they suspected he was asleep – went up and found that it was a uniform *stuffed with straw* – erect with a pole for a firelock –

Passed the Causeway about 5 O Clock, employed in cutting thro' the Enemy's Abbattis [line of felled trees] and removing a strong stockade – Passed on with the Picquets to Santarem, found another Abbattis in the Enemy's line of Defence – The tops of every Hill & rising ground masked with Bushes where Guns were formerly placed – Amazingly strong –

On arriving at Santarem the few half-starved Inhabitants that remained gathered about us with tears of joy – The Cavalry and Light Division arrived about 8 O Clock – moved on for Pournes [Pernes] – Found another Abbattis to the rear of the Town – The Hills to the Tagus and rear were in the same state of Defence as the front of the Position –

In 3 leagues from Santarem reached Pournes. The Enemy had

blown the Bridge this morning at 10 O Clock – The Inhabitants of this place had been cruelly used by the French having the whole of their Property plunder'd and not even the means of subsistence left – found several dead Peasants in the different out Houses – starved – Several Sheds filled with miserable Peasants lying unable to move from mere want – Party at work all the Evening making a bridge for the infantry to pass on –

Wellington pursued Massena and clashed with his rearguard at Pombal on 11 March. Captain William Stewart of the 30th (or the Cambridgeshire) Regiment of Foot arrived above the town in time to see the French driven back into it: '. . . From this place we saw the advance of most of the Divisions of our Army in every direction – It was one of the grandest Military Spectacles I had ever witnessed.'

The French retired during the night. Stewart passed through Pombal the following afternoon and saw indications of the hurried nature of their retreat: '. . . The Enemy left in & near the Town of Pombal a great number of their killed & wounded & it was distressing to see in the Streets of this dirty Town the mangled Remains of our Fellow Creatures bruised & blended with the Mud by the Trampling of Horses & Mules as well as the passage of Guns, Waggons &c over them, until those once valiant Heroes, could no longer be distinguished from the filth of the Road – . . .'

Next day, Wellington evicted Massena's rearguard from a new position at Redinha, 10 km to the north. Massena was unable to cross to the north bank of the River Mondego, where he had hoped to hold out using the more readily available supplies of that region. Instead, he was obliged to fall back north-eastwards, fighting limited actions on 14 and 15 March. But Wellington had outrun his supplies and would not compromise his army's discipline by pressing on regardless. Ensign George Percival of the Coldstream Guards wrote to his aunt on 21 March from Moita da Serra, 33 km east of Coimbra, where he had been halted for two days to allow provisions to catch up:

. . . On Monday last we took upward's of 500 prisoners besides a number of Bullocks and Sheep. The Country about this place is most beautiful, but the road's very bad, the River *Alva* is close upon our Rear, which makes it more pleasant being able to wash a weeks dirt off one's body we not having taken off our Clothes for that time.

. . .

Our reinforcements have joined us, which is a great relief to the
Light Division, as most of them are Light Infantry Regiments, which
generally have the most harassing work. It is really quite horrid to
see the number of Portuguese the French have put to death, for
having deserted their houses when they advanced. The other day two
of the Coldstream cut down from a tree three old men, two of which
were not then dead. . . .

Massena on nearing the Spanish border tried to save face by pushing
south to the River Tagus rather than retreating eastwards across the
frontier to Ciudad Rodrigo. He was forced to abandon the move through
lack of provisions and nearly lost his II Corps under General Reynier
when it was attacked on 3 April at Sabugal, 55 km south-west of Ciudad
Rodrigo. Wellington had intended the 3rd and 5th Divisions to engage
Reynier frontally from the west, while Major-General Sir William Erskine
with the Light Division and two cavalry brigades crossed the River
Coa 2.5 km to the south to attack his flank and rear. As a result of the
morning fog, the commanders of the 3rd and 5th Divisions sensibly
postponed their attack, but the lacklustre Erskine advanced anyway. The
Light Division crossed by the wrong ford. Its first brigade ran directly
into Reynier's main body, but was saved by its own fighting prowess and
the decision of the commander of the second brigade to disobey Erskine
and advance to its support.

Captain Duffy fought in this action as part of the Light Division. He
begins by describing the approach march prior to crossing the Coa:

... Halted for some time in a wood having found that we were
making too great a detour and altho it was wished that we might
cross the River if possible unperceived still it would have taken us
too far to the right had we continued this route and as the atmosphere was thick & constant Heavy showers – we moved to our left &
reached after about two miles march the River – Some few Cavalry
& Picquets of Infantry were all that we first perceived who did not
oppose our passage of the River tho' their side of the ground was
very Commanding – Our Cavalry had orders to follow except about
a Troop of Hussars & some of the 16th Lᵗ Dragoons who preceded
the Light Division – The 3ʳᵈ Cassadores who led (exceptᵍ two
Companies) moved direct up the Country with the Cavalry – The 5

Comp^{ys} of the 95th [Rifles] & the 43rd directed their march to the left
paralled [sic] with the River and about a mile from it – The ford was
about 3 feet deep, and our men were orderd to cross as quickly as
possible & to keep at the *step out* & when practicable the double
quick up the hill – About 12 the head of the Column gained the first
heights when the Companys of the 95th in front were commencing to
skirmish – shortly after when our Right wing had only gained the
line we were forming – we were orderd to move on, – The Enemy's
Guns [(]2 on our left and 1. 8 Pounder & 2. four Pounders with a
Howitzer on our Right) opened on us – but being rather coverd by
a ridge of Hill in front we did not suffer from it – About 200 yards
again halted to form, and being close to the ridge of Hill orderd to
lie [?] down but to be in readiness to charge as the Rifle[s] were
obliged to retire – on their passing thro' the line, moved on with a
Cheer & charge under a heavy fire of grape, musquetry & some shells
till we perceived the heads of 3 or 4 Columns of Infantry with a body
of Cavalry moving to support their front line which had taken post
behind some walls of an inclosure to our front – The ground from
the ridge of Hills gradually descended thro a wood for about 200
yards to the first part of the square Field that was surrounded by a
wall about 4 feet high but broken in many places & then ascended
for about 150 yards to a higher & more Commanding ridge of hills
on which the Enemys guns were placed, & from behind which, their
Columns of Infantry moved up occasionally to support or threaten
our flanks –

Finding that the Enemy were so numerous & well supported &
owing to a galling fire we fell back to the ridge again in line with
two 6 Pounders that had reached the Hill when we first charged –
we had scarcely got back – when I believe by mistake the Bugles
sounded the Advance and we again came to the Charge & cheerd –
upon which the Enemy's advanced line which were following us up
& cheering in return supposing we were retiring were again checked
& made to retire to their height & walls, at this moment a report
reached us that a strong Column was moving round our right flank
which was perfectly open – the Cassadores & Cavalry being a mile
& half if not more off – and we perceived some Cavalry already in
rear – We therefore fell gradually back – formed – ceased firing –
threw back the right Company in right angle to our line – to protect
the guns – Kneeled down & remained ready to charge again – all

this time the Enemy's guns were discharging showers of grape but fortunately too high to do much mischief – Two heavy Columns of the Enemy now moved to our Right to charge or break thro us and some other Columns opposite our left made their appearance on the ridge.

The Columns came on to within 30 yards of our guns & we expected every moment that their weight would press thro' our line – when at this critical moment the 52nd Reg^t (1st Batt^n) had just reached our Rear in good time and extended to our right – We then sprung up – cheerd again & charged & drove their Columns completely over the ridge to the right & got possession for an instant of the walls of the Field within 40 yards of the mouth of the Howitzers; – it was intended we should halt here, but the impetuosity of the Soldiers impelled them over the walls to secure the Howitzers (which had just been renderd immoveable) and thereby exposed them to the fire of the Enemy's Columns – their Cavalry seized the opportunity & charged right amongst us – luckily the 4 right Comp^{ys} of the 43rd and 2 or 3 of the left of the 52nd jumped the walls, took post behind them and opened a fire which upset most of the Cavalry complely [sic] preserved the flanks of both Reg^{ts} that were so broken as to be perfectly at the mercy of the Enemy – The flanks rallied again & the left of the 43^d formed line on the left of the wall – our skirmishers moved to the front and the Enemy finding that Pictons [3rd] Division had passed the Town [of Sabugal] moved off in confusion over the mountains towards Alfaites [Alfreites] – leaving about 300 Dead on the field & a number of Prisoners –

. . .

The constant haze & frequent heavy showers to day in great measure preserved our Reg^t for the Enemy's force by all acc^{ts} was at least 10 to one of our numbers & could they have well ascertained our strength surely they had the means of annihilating not only the Reg^t but the Division – Shot thro' the Great Coat

William Morris, Conductor of Stores in the Commissariat Department, visited the battlefield in September 1812 and revealed how the French had apparently used an unusual defence against cavalry:

. . . The other [eastern] side of Sabugal we came to some open Ground but rather hilly where the british & french Cavalry were engaged[.] a Grove of chesnut trees is near the spot[.] as we went

further we saw the bones & skeletons of a number of horses lie
bleaching in the sun[.] about half way to Nava de mar we came to a
number of fields almost cover'd with such heaps of stones which
gave it the appearance at a distance of an immense stone yard
number of __ of [sic] stones were as I was informd piled up by the
enemy as ramparts in order to protect them in their retreat from the
attacks of the british Cavalry . . .

Unfortunately, it has not been possible to find eyewitness evidence from
the actual battle to confirm Morris's second-hand account. A squadron
of the 16th Light Dragoons took part in the action, but otherwise
Wellington's cavalry was little engaged and only one squadron of the 1st
Hussars, King's German Legion attacked the French during the subsequent pursuit. However, the stone walls on the battlefield are known
to have been used by the British and French infantry for shelter during
the fighting.

By 11 April, Massena had been driven from Portugal, except for a
garrison left in the frontier fortress of Almeida. Wellington had won a
major victory, by starving Massena out, and in doing so he had secured
Portugal as a base for his future offensive operations. Massena during
the invasion had lost 25,000 men, of whom 8,000 were prisoners. Fewer
than 2,000 had died in battle; the rest had succumbed to starvation or
been picked off by guerrilla attacks. Equally serious damage had been
done to discipline and morale.

Portugal had been devastated by the invasion. But Wellington had
dramatically restored confidence within his army, in Portugal and also at
home. A letter from Ensign George Percival on 8 April indicates the
mood of the troops:

. . . The French are in Almeida not very strong; except the Garrison
that is left in that place, there is not a single Frenchman remaining
in Portugal, which I am extremely happy to say. Lord Wellington
deserves Kingdoms for his Military judgement in this advance[.] The
French is estimated to have lost upwards of Three Thousand and
that without a General engagement. Our Light Division found them
on the 4th [the 3rd] posted on a strong Hill near to Sabugal, they
attacked them and after having made three charges, at last succeeded
in gaining the Hill, with little lost on our side, the French loosing
nine Hundred men, the Light Division took two Colonels a Captain

an Eagle and a Howitzer. the Bravery of this Division is something wonderful. . . .

The Light Division did not in fact capture an eagle standard at Sabugal, although Portuguese peasants had found one that had been lost in the confusion of the action of Foz do Arouce on 15 March.

*

Meanwhile, the situation had changed elsewhere in the Peninsula. At Cadiz, part of the Anglo-Spanish garrison was taken by sea to land behind the French force under Marshal Claude Victor that was besieging the city. The incompetent Spanish commander, General Manuel La Peña, threw away the opportunity to crush Victor and refused to give any support when the British contingent under Lieutenant-General Thomas Graham was attacked by superior numbers in the Battle of Barossa on 5 March. Graham defeated the French, but lost almost a quarter of his men and subsequently returned to Cadiz. One of the casualties was Ensign William Cameron of the First Regiment of Foot Guards, who wrote to his father on the 8th:

> As I flatter myself it would give yourself & my Dear Mother as well as all friends at home great satisfaction to receive a few lines from myself after the severe action we have been engaged in, it shall not be neglected – the loss of the Brigade has been great, but none have suffered that yourselves are acquainted with – I must candidly confess to you my own situation – less [lest] it should be rendered worse than it really is by reports from this place & my name be confounded with others – as it is indeed to be lamented that many of our officers are killed or wound[ed] – my own wound is nothing alarming altho' severe – my medical attendant tells me every sympton [sic] is as favorable as can be expected. I have only to regret I fell early in the action & did not therefore [see] all our operations; nothing could exceed the good conduct of the Brigade[;] the loss of the french has [sic] treble our own[.] I beg you will not suffer yourself to be deceived with regard to my situation by any other acc^t whatever – I have been struck in the upper part of the thigh by a musket ball, which still remains in the wound but will in the course of time find its way out again without any injury to body – I have entered thus into particulars that you may rely upon my account. . . .

One result of Barossa was to minimize a threat to southern Portugal. Marshal Soult had advanced with 20,000 men from the French army in southern Spain and received the surrender of the Spanish fortress of Badajoz on 11 March. But he returned to Andalusia as a result of Barossa, leaving only 11,000 troops in Extremadura. Wellington detached Beresford with 18,000 men to this region.

On 25 March Beresford reached Campo Maior, 18 km north-west of Badajoz. The French after capturing the town five days earlier had left 2,400 men, who were destroying the defences prior to falling back on Badajoz. What followed was one of the most controversial cavalry actions of the Peninsular War. Beresford, seeing the French withdraw on his approach, sent his cavalry commander, Brigadier-General Robert Long, round Campo Maior to the east to delay the French until his infantry and artillery could come up. Long had a brigade of British heavy cavalry, two and a half squadrons of the 13th Light Dragoons and five weak squadrons of Portuguese cavalry.

Despite being outnumbered by at least two to one, the 13th Light Dragoons brilliantly charged and routed the French 26th Dragoons. The 13th then rallied and, supported by two Portuguese squadrons sent by Long, pursued the broken French horsemen for 16 km up to Badajoz. During this orderly pursuit, they took a convoy of stores and 16 heavy guns. But then, as they returned, they discovered to their surprise that they had been left unsupported by the heavy cavalry. The 13th were too weak on their own to tackle the rest of the French column retreating from Campo Maior and had to abandon their captured guns and head off northwards across country.

Long, after seeing the 13th disappear over the undulating ground, had wanted to use the Heavy Cavalry Brigade against the French column. He still had three Portuguese squadrons in hand, but they were of limited value and he had to rally them when they were panicked into a flight. He then found that Beresford had stopped the Heavy Brigade after being misinformed that the whole of the 13th had been captured. Beresford had been warned by Wellington five days earlier to retain tight control over his cavalry and to keep it massed in reserve ready for a decisive blow. Unnerved at the apparent fate of the 13th, he allowed the French to escape unhindered.

When Wellington learnt of the missed opportunity, he jumped to the wrong conclusion and reprimanded the 13th, obviously being unaware

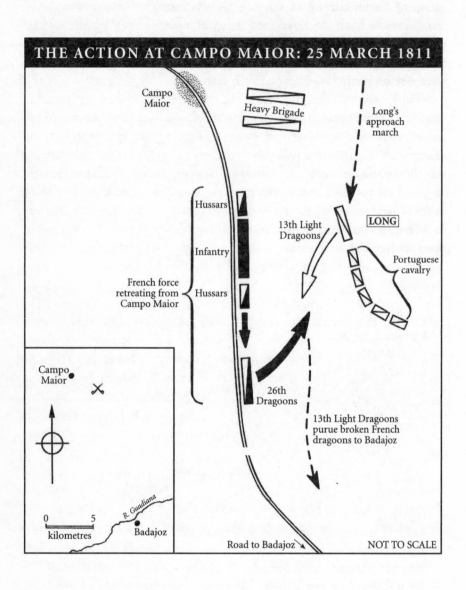

THE ACTION AT CAMPO MAIOR: 25 MARCH 1811

Campo Maior

Heavy Brigade

Long's approach march

Hussars

Infantry

13th Light Dragoons

LONG

Portuguese cavalry

French force retreating from Campo Maior

Hussars

26th Dragoons

13th Light Dragoons purue broken French dragoons to Badajoz

Campo Maior

R. Guadiana

0   5

kilometres

Badajoz

Road to Badajoz

NOT TO SCALE

of the full facts. He saw the problem as one of British cavalrymen galloping out of control. A few notorious mishaps, such as a disastrous charge by the 20th Regiment of (Light) Dragoons at Vimeiro, contributed to his failure to appreciate the full potential of his cavalry. In fact, the fiasco arose not because the 13th pursued too far, but because they were not supported as they ought to have been. The regiment's officers duly protested. Wellington apparently accepted their explanation in private, but characteristically refused to alter his published reprimand and this has led most historians to portray Campo Maior as a notorious example of the British cavalry's supposed indiscipline. The real culprit was Beresford, who lacked the nerve for an independent command, as he confirmed two months later at the Battle of Albuera. Long, who unfairly received much of the blame for Campo Maior, made this clear in a letter to his brother on 28 March. He first described the charge by the 13th and how he subsequently sent Captain Doyle of the Quarter-master General's Department to order the immediate advance of the Heavy Brigade:

> ... For the first time I learned from Capt Doyle that Marshal Beresford himself was with the Brigade of Heavy Cavalry, & had himself halted them in the situation I have described – I had nothing further to say! Soon after I saw them in motion at a very slow pace in two lines keeping to the right of the road on which the Enemy were retreating – at length they approached the right flank of the Enemys Column, indicating an apparent intention to attack, bringing up at the same time 2 pieces of artillery which no earthly obstacle prevented firing into the french Column at such distance as they chose – I hung upon their left flank with my valiant runaways [the three Portuguese squadrons], the Country was beautifully open & favorable for the movement both of artillery & Cavalry, the Enemy had still several miles to go to their point of retreat, & between them & that point was interposed the 4 Squadrons of British & Portuguese who had pursued their adversaries to the bridge of Badajox taking all the artillery they had with them, & had employed at the siege of Campo Major – about 12 or 15 Pieces [in fact, 16] – In such a state of things I did not conceive it possible for the Enemy to exist 10 minutes longer, & I really am convinced that had they been summoned an immediate surrender would have taken place – after parading & escorting them in this manner for two or three miles,

judge my *astonishment* at seeing all the Troops, artillery &c *halted*, &
the Enemy permitted to retire without molestation before us, taking
with them all the Prisoners they had made from us, retaking their
guns, & absolutely threatening the safety of the [13th Light] Dragoons
in advance & who were then returning from their pursuit, tho' their
exact situation was unknown, &, to speak the truth I augered but ill
of their fate from the unsupported manner in which they had pushed
forward, & which, tho' displaying great gallantry, was a sad proof of
want of order & discipline in both officers & men. . . .

It is clear that at this stage Long himself was unaware of the orderly
nature of the 13th's pursuit. He continued:

. . . The Heavy Brigade by some improper, tho' perhaps well-meant
interference had left me to myself, & the subsequent retreat of my 3
[Portuguese] Squadrons with the loss sustained, obliged me to leave
the others almost to their fate, but the defeat of the Enemys Column
[would have] ensured safety to the whole, & would have wound up
as brilliant a little field day as Fortune could have delighted my heart
with – Had Marshal Beresford not interfered, you may rely upon it,
I should have accomplished it (not merely *attempted*) but positively
accomplished, for it was impossible they could resist the force of 11
Squadrons which I sh[d] have had at my disposal to bring against them
– It was only necessary to charge beat, & throw into confusion the
Cavalry at their head & rear, & which if British Dragoons could not
do they have no business here, & the object was accomplished – But
I am convinced that had a determination to annihilate them been
shown, & steps taken accordingly, they would have surrendered at
the first summons!

Such is my decided opinion, &, I believe, (with the exception,
perhaps of Marshal Beresford) that of every officer present on the
occasion – The motives of his conduct were I dare to say excellent,
but sure I am that Lord W. himself would never have conferred such
an Honor on the Enemy & entailed such a disgrace on his own
Troops as to suffer 2 Batt[ns] of Infantry & 2 Squadrons of Cavalry to
bid defiance to & retreat in safety before 8 Squadrons of British &
3 Squadrons of Portuguese Cavalry, 2 pieces of artillery, & a large
Column of Infantry that were following the same road, & were within
a couple of miles of the scene of action – & this too in a Country
so favorable to the operations of Cavalry, & after the whole of the

Enemy's covering force of Cavalry had been charged, broken, & pursued for nearly 9 miles! The *thing* speaks for itself, therefore I shall say no more. After keeping away from me above ½ my force (& that of the best quality too) upon which I relied, & founded all my intended operations, because I could not exactly inform him what might, under the existing circumstances, be the fate of the Dragoons who had so improperly pursued, without adequate support, & against my order, His Excellency, I say, was pleased to remark that I had made a bad business of it – First of all under the circumstances, I think it was a brilliant day for the small Corps with which the attack was made, & the killing the Col^l of the 26th Reg^t of Cavalry, Count Chamorez [Chamorin], with many of their men & horses, taking 15 pieces of artillery & several ammunition waggons, the bringing away of all which depended upon the mere ipse dixit or will of the Marshal himself, the beating & cowing of two of their best Cavalry Corps, are in my opinion, no symptoms of a bad business even tho our loss in Prisoners by the flight of the Portuguese has been considerable, the retaking of whom, however, likewise depended upon the Marshal. But suffering 2 battalions & Squadrons to escape from before a Field Marshal with 11 Squadrons at his disposal 2 pieces of artillery & a column of Infantry in the rear, is in my opinion as bad a performance as ever disgraced a theatre of War & with this remark I shall conclude, namely, that if Marshal Beresford had known the powers of Cavalry as he certainly does those of the Infantry, I think he would not have lost so favorable an opportunity of striking a severe blow with a very paltry sacrifice of men, & had he heard the remarks of the Private Dragoons as I did, on their inglorious return, he would have regretted the extreme care he took of their bodies in preference to their credit. . . .

Despite the controversy, Campo Maior established the British cavalry's moral superiority for the rest of the war. The French had hitherto underestimated the British cavalry, but revised their opinion following the success of the 13th Light Dragoons in defeating twice their number of opponents.

*

Wellington's immediate objective, now that he had driven Massena from Portugal, was to take the frontier fortresses that guarded the two main invasion routes between Portugal and Spain. Badajoz in the south would be besieged by Beresford. In the north, French garrisons held both Almeida in Portugal and its Spanish twin, Ciudad Rodrigo.

Massena restored his army with the help of reinforcements and within three weeks resumed the offensive in a bid to relieve Almeida. Wellington had isolated the fortress, intending to starve it into surrender. He occupied a defensive position on the frontier near the village of Fuentes de Oñoro to prevent Almeida from being resupplied. Massena attacked on 3 May and was beaten off, but two days later turned Wellington's southern flank. Wellington pulled back his southern wing to a stronger and more compact position immediately south of Fuentes de Oñoro and at right angles to his original front line. Despite their superior numbers of cavalry, the French failed to inflict significant damage during this 3 km retreat. It was covered by the Light Division, gallantly supported by the outnumbered British cavalry and a troop of the Royal Horse Artillery.

John Insley of the 1st (or Royal) Regiment of Dragoons reveals how the French skilfully supported their cavalry by boldly pushing forward their guns:

> ... On the 5th the Enemy began at ½ past 3 °Clock in the Morning and advanced and took about 200 of ours before they could clear the Town [Pozo Bello?] I had my Horse Wounded – our Regiment fell back and the French Cavalry charged our Guns and then 2 Squadrons of our Regiment charged their Cavalry and killed and took about 200 and saved our Guns – The Cavalry moved their station a little further back and their Guns & skirmishers advanced very fast – our Reg[t] charged their Guns and skirmishers and saved our Guns again which played upon them greatly and killed 500 of their Cavalry – their Guns & skirmishers came on again – We again charged – our Artillery was forced to creep under their Guns – – Lord Wellington gave us great praise and said we had saved 6 Thousand men – our Guns and all the Spiritual Shot [sic] – – Our left Flank was greatly Engaged all Day but they could not come at our lines – they lost 6 Thousand Men that Day we still kept our Position – Our Regiment had 19 Horses killed and 10 Wounded besides General Slades and our Colonels Horse was wounded. ...

Captain William Stewart of the 30th Regiment added:

... The Action continued with various successes on each side, (but chiefly on ours) during the Day, & the brilliant conduct of many of our Reg^ts could not be surpass'd –

Our Cavalry consisted of about *900* whilst the Enemy brought into action more that [sic] *4,000!!* our Infantry however ably assisted in bringing down a few of the Enemy by well directed Vollies; & none more so, than the *Chasseurs = Brittaniques* – at night all firing ceased –

This is an illuminating comment, given the Chasseurs' mixed reputation. The regiment had originally been composed of French émigrés, or royalist exiles, but had subsequently been diluted by the addition of enemy prisoners of war of various nationalities. Many of these men volunteered simply to have an opportunity to desert back to French lines, which meant that the regiment could not be trusted on outpost duty. But the Chasseurs proved their worth in battle, largely owing to the leadership of their officers, who were often highly motivated French royalists. The regiment at Fuentes de Oñoro belonged to the 7th Division and defeated an outflanking attempt by a brigade of French dragoons by firing a devastating volley from the cover of a stone wall.

Captain John Duffy of the 43rd Regiment explained that at the end of the day, after the French had been checked:

... Our Brigade [was] orderd at sunset to occupy & defend the Village of Fuentes – relieved the 79th Reg^t and Flank Companies – found the Roads, Streets & Lanes about the place coverd with Dead & Wounded – The Enemy requested permission to remove some of their wounded & Dead from the Streets which was granted, in consequence of which soldiers of both Parties were mingled together in the streets for near an hour –

During the night employed in strengthening part of the walls near the Church & demolishing others that gave the Enemy cover in advancing

Lieutenant John Ford of the 79th Regiment of Foot (or Cameron Highlanders) recorded:

When the Bugles sounded on both sides to cease firing on the Evening of the 5th May – A Frenchman started up from behind a dyke and calling to our men in very good English, said – 'If you don't fire upon us we will bring in some of your wounded' – Without waiting for any orders, our Grenadiers cheered him, and a mutual exchange of wounded men took place on the Right of the Regiment. –

. . .

After the Enemy had retired from the field, I visited the ground on which their cavalry had attacked the Picquets of the 1st British Division (which were obliged to form a Square to meet the attack) and as a Battery not seen by the Enemy opened an unexpected fire upon them, they were defeated with great loss. – This Battery was commanded by Capt [Robert] Bull – The *Trous de loups* [pits] around it formed an admirable defence, and the Earth having been removed, they were quite invisible to the Enemy –

I found that during the night, they had returned to the ground, and with knives cut all the flesh from about 40 of the Cavalry Horses for food, leaving nothing but the skeletons but whether from choice or necessity, I never could learn though I should rather think the former, as they had so recently advanced from Ciudad Rodrigo for the relief of *Almeida* and could not have been without supplies – and besides it was not the only instance that came to our knowledge of a similar practice. –

Wellington rarely used field fortifications as they tended to immobilize troops and encourage a passive defence. But he made an exception at Fuentes de Oñoro in order to strengthen his new position and neutralize the superior numbers of French cavalry.

Massena finally conceded defeat and withdrew on the 10th. The isolated garrison of Almeida broke out that night and despite considerable loss managed to escape. Massena was relieved of command of the Army of Portugal and replaced by Marshal Auguste Marmont.

Meanwhile, in the south Beresford had begun to besiege Badajoz. The French governor of the city, General Armand Philippon, was an energetic and experienced soldier. He wrote to Soult on 20 May:

The enemy on the 4th of this month appeared before the fortress and blockaded the city on the left bank of the Guadiana. On the 8th, about 3,000 men appeared on the right bank, the garrison disputed the heights of San Cristobal with them foot by foot. On the 9th in the night, the siege works were begun and a battery was erected above San Cristobal to batter this fort. On the 10th, I had a sortie made which cost the enemy 900 wounded; the number of dead is unknown. I had some dead and about a hundred wounded. [The besiegers in fact lost only about 400 men.]

On the 11th, the fire of San Cristobal and that of the Castle silenced the enemy battery. On the 11th, the siege works were entirely stopped and the enemy camps emptied.

On the 12th, Marshal Bellesford [Beresford] summoned the fortress to surrender. I replied to him that I was resolved to defend the fortress to the bitter end. Nothing new happened on the 13th and 14th.

On the 15th, the enemy took away all his guns. In the evening, I had my cavalry go out and they made a charge on the advanced posts, killing or capturing them all without losing a man wounded or killed. On the 16th, the siege was raised and I immediately had all the enemy's works destroyed.

Yesterday, the 19th, the enemy reappeared before the fortress on the left bank of the Guadiana. He did not seem to want to undertake anything. . . .

The siege had been raised in response to Soult's approach from southern Spain with a relief force of 24,000 men. Between 13 and 16 May Beresford concentrated 35,000 British, Portuguese and Spanish troops at Albuera, 21 km south-east of Badajoz. Beresford was attacked here on the 16th, outflanked in the south and suffered heavy casualties in confused fighting. The 2nd Division suffered a disaster when one of its brigades was massacred by French lancers and Beresford himself had to grapple with a lancer and hurl him to the ground with his bare hands.

The situation was saved by the intervention from reserve of the 4th Division under Major-General Lowry Cole. Major Henry Hardinge, the Deputy Quartermaster-General of the Portuguese army, urged Cole to advance without waiting for orders from Beresford. Such a move had apparently already occurred to Cole, who undertook it after consulting with the cavalry commander, Major-General William Lumley, who would support his advance. The day ended in a French retreat. Albuera had been a soldiers' battle, won more by the courage and steadiness of the rank and file than by skilled generalship. Beresford had lost over 5,900 men and wrote a despatch so dispirited in tone that Wellington had to edit it before sending it on to England. Beresford's conduct of the battle was widely criticized, but sometimes excessively so. The

near-defeat to a large extent had been due to the disobedience of one
of his Spanish subordinates, General Joachim Blake, and the tactical
mishandling of the 2nd Division by Major-General William Stewart.

Brigadier-General Robert Long's letters shed light on the battle's
controversies. His relations with Beresford had been tense since Campo
Maior and worsened when he was replaced in command of Beresford's
cavalry on the morning of the battle. His replacement, Lumley, was
sufficiently senior to prevent any of the Spanish officers with Beresford's
army from claiming the command of the cavalry. Long wrote to his
brother on 22 May:

> Our situation does not permit me to enter into those details of our
> late interesting proceedings which led to the battle of Albuera on
> the 16th Inst – a battle which we ought to have lost but which the
> unconquerable spirit of the Troops secured to their fortunate com-
> mander – The fault committed by us was not occupying the *proper*
> position, & what indeed was the key of it – The french saw our error
> – took advantage of it, & we had to recover by deadly exertion the
> ground which, if disputed originally as it ought to have been done,
> would have cost our Enemies rivers of blood & saved our own.
> However, as it was, enough has been shed –
>
> . . .
>
> Had the whole Army been put in motion to follow up the victory
> I can have no hesitation in asserting that the greater part of Soults
> Corps must have been destroyed, all his wounded & Prisoners taken,
> his Artillery & baggage, & in short every thing which constitutes an
> Army – but it has been deemed more prudent to offer him the
> golden bridge to retreat by, & our Troops have resumed the invest-
> ment of Badajox –
>
> Their Cavalry was so much superior to ours both in quality &
> numbers, that our Services during the day of action were limited to
> keeping them in check, & counteracting their attempt to gain our
> flanks, & deprive the Infantry of our Support – We only came in
> contact with them, partially, twice, but our Artillery made consider-
> able havoc among them – I never, in any instance in my life, saw
> such a scene of Carnage in the same space of ground. The field of
> battle was a human slaughter house. In consequence of the union
> of the spanish Cavalry, & to prevent disputes about rank, General
> Beresford directed Majr Genl Lumley to take the Command of the

whole of the Cavalry, &, in my opinion, rather indelicately, permitted this Command to be assumed after the action had commenced & whilst I was manoeuvring the Troops – *This* I can never forgive & thus has fortune deprived me again of what I am free to think & hope might have been my hard-earned reward – tho' deeply hurt, I did not abate my zeal & endeavours to promote the Marshal's [Beresford's] glory & my perfect knowledge of the ground which I had reconnoitred the night before, enabled me, I believe, to be of assistance to the officer who thus superceded me.

It is odd enough that the evening before the action I pointed out to the Adj^t General the defect of our position as then taken up, & foretold the consequences & had I obeyed the orders I rec^d in the morning to move with all the Cavalry to the position intended for us in rear of the British line, the consequences might have been fatal. The Q^r Mr General had himself marched off with one of the Reg^{ts} & not half an hour afterwards down came a strong Column of Cavalry opposite the ground they had occupied, & endeavoured to force the passage of the River [Albuera] which a portion of them actually accomplished but were driven back by a charge of the 3^d D^n G^{ds} which Reg^t & the 13th Drag^{ns} (foreseeing the danger) I had detained near the Village of Albuera to counteract any such attempt – Had my advice been followed as to a further part of the disposition I think the fatal advantage taken of our Inf^y by the french Cavalry, would not have occurred – I pointed out the certainty of this happening, recommended a Reg^t to be placed in column on the very spot where it happened, & even placed a Spanish Corps in reserve there, but which Corps, when the french attack upon our Infantry by their Cavalry took place, never moved one yard in advance to their assistance. The only difference in what afterwards happened between what General Lumley did, and I sh^d have done, was his not availing himself of a favorable opportunity to attack the Enemy's Cavalry during their retreat, & at a time when their Infantry were flying in all directions – by shaking *their covering* force at such a moment we sh^d have been put in a situation to cut off a great part of the run-aways – The events of this battle rested entirely on the Cavalry preserving their ground – had they been beaten, the Infantry would have been annihilated – but tho' dreadfully weakened by separation on different points, our countenance was so firm and imposing, that the whole french force (upwards of 3000) attempted, and appeared to wish, but dared not carry into effect the *duty* of attacking us – . . .

Long wrote another letter to his brother on 9 July, in which he justified himself further and claimed that the battle had in its conse-quences been a victory to the French. But he contradicted himself in a letter to his father on 20 August:

> . . . But à propos of Victories I must not allow you to call the action at Albuera 'a drawn battle' & still less upon the ground that Soult *also* claimed the Victory –. Now the better way to distinguish on such an occasion is to say that Soult tho' *completely beaten in the field*, gained partially nevertheless, the *object* he had in view of interrupting *the siege of Badajox* –. But I think I may venture to say that had *we* been beaten on that day in the degree he *was*, this army would never again have crossed the Guadiana – & my opinion still is that if we, instead of returning to Badajox, had followed up the routed french army, they never could or would have recovered [from] the blow, & the whole of Andalusia might, at this moment, have been ours – No! that the battle of Albuera was not a *drawn* one I promise you –
>
>   . . .
>
> So little did they, the french, consider it a drawn battle, *they* had no idea or *hope*, at the time, of saving Badajox – The morning they went off they bade us 'Adieu Messieurs' adding thereto 'Badajoz est à vous' [Badajoz is yours] – . . . .

Beresford was relieved on 27 May. A correspondent who wrote from Lisbon to Colonel Loftus Otway in England on 4 October revealed:

> . . . The Marshal is confin'd to his bed by a *severe fever* – poor man he has not philosophy to bear up against the Buffets of Military Critics who attack on all quarters – You know not the severity with which he is treated – I have the honor to know some of our generals intimately, & do assure you they treat his name more lightly than you you [sic] are aware of – this gives me no pain – for God knows I have no reason to be obliged to him having refus'd the every favor however trifling, that I have ask'd of him – . . .

The 57th (or the West Middlesex) Regiment of Foot won the nickname 'Die-hards' at Albuera, for that is what Lieutenant-Colonel William Inglis reputedly called on his men to do after he fell wounded.

The regiment lost more than 66 per cent of its strength in killed or wounded. Inglis returned home to recover and subsequently received a letter from the Duke of York's Military Secretary dated 11 September:

> In reference to the Conversation I had the pleasure of holding with you relative to the mistake which occurred when you presented yourself at the Com^r in Chiefs Audience, I feel it to be incumbent upon me now to acquaint you that I have taken an opportunity of again mentioning to HRH^s the apprehension you entertained that from His not having known you, He might have been unmindful of your recently distinguished Conduct at the Head of your Reg^t.
>
> I have the pleasure to assure you that HRH^s has expressed Himself to me, to have been possessed of a full knowledge of your very long and meritorious Services – and any other feeling could not possibly have been apparent except under the mistake of the Officer who anounced *you*; & from whom HRH^s did not hear your name.
>
> You may be convinced that no person can more highly appreciate the Conduct of the 57th Reg^t than His Royal Highness.

Wellington personally arrived in Extremadura on 19 May and also ordered reinforcements down from the north for a renewed attempt to take Badajoz. He had inadequate equipment and minimal numbers of trained specialist personnel, so that ordinary infantrymen had to undertake the siege work such as digging trenches, which they did reluctantly. Wellington also had to use antiquated Portuguese and Spanish guns to bombard the fortress. Yet expectations of a quick success were surprisingly high. Major Thomas Downman of the Royal Horse Artillery wrote to his wife on 4 June:

> ... Since my last long letter to William *dated 29th May* we have had little change here; indeed the siege of Badajos has been the subject of our conversation and anxiety, as the plans of the Campaign must then shew themselves – the Batteries opened against [Badajoz] on the night of the 2nd[.] they were mounted with Fifty pieces of heavy artillery and we hope by tomorrow Evening, it will surrender. if so, the Vessels which conveys this, will carry home the dispatches respecting it, and which will be welcome news I am sure –
>
> ...
>
> at present we are all quiet and in good quarters and when or where we may move no one *here* can say – His Lordship keeps his

plans very snug – He is still at Elvas & will remain until Badajos falls – . . .

Unfortunately, Wellington was badly served by his engineers, who advised him to assail Badajoz on the northern side, concentrating on the Castle and the outlying fort of San Cristóbal. These were in fact the most formidable points of the defences and two attempts to storm San Cristóbal failed bloodily on the nights of 6 and 9 June. Inside Badajoz, Philippon instructed his company commanders on 13 June that if they had incorporated any English deserters into their units, they should not allow them to change their red jackets. This was presumably intended to ensure that they fought well in the knowledge that they would be executed as deserters if captured in their old uniform.

But Wellington decided on the 10th that he would have to abandon the siege, as the French field armies were concentrating against him. The young and energetic Marshal Marmont was hastening with the Army of Portugal to link up with Soult in the south and produce a joint force of 60,000 men. Wellington on 17 June retreated about 15 km north-westwards to a strong position along the River Caia, between Elvas, Campo Maior and Ouguela, where he was able to field 54,000 men. Soult and Marmont despite their advantage of numbers declined to attack Wellington in a position of his own choosing. By 15 July, they had both been forced to withdraw and disperse to find supplies. Wellington had won the stand-off, for he had been able to keep his army concentrated as a result of his meticulously organized logistics.

Despite being forced to retire, the French had managed to reprovision Badajoz. Rather than resume the siege, Wellington turned his attention to Ciudad Rodrigo in the north. He blockaded the fortress, but was obliged to withdraw when the French again concentrated two of their armies. This time, Marmont's Army of Portugal united on 23 September with the Army of the North, commanded by General Jean Dorsenne. Wellington fell back and concentrated at Fuenteguinaldo, 22 km south-west of Ciudad Rodrigo, before withdrawing to a stronger position near the River Coa. Marmont again decided not to risk an attack and shortly withdrew, leaving Wellington to resume the blockade of Ciudad Rodrigo.

Wellington had left a detached force of 16,000 men under Hill in Extremadura. On 28 October, Hill surprised an isolated French division under General Jean-Baptiste Girard at the village of Arroyo Molinos de

Montanchez, 80 km north-east of Badajoz (the battle honour is known as Arroyo dos Molinos). The assault, which followed a determined pursuit, established Hill's reputation as a bold and capable general, which was strangely belied by the mild, generous and good-humoured nature which endeared him to all in the army. He attacked the village frontally with one brigade and turned it to the south with the other to try and cut Girard's line of retreat. One of Girard's brigades had already marched off, but the other was defeated and its remnants forced to flee over the range of mountains that overlooked the village to the east.

Captain Richard Brunton took part in the subsequent pursuit. He had initially served in the Peninsula in the 43rd Regiment, but transferred in February 1811 to command a company of the Portuguese 6th Caçadores. He claimed that nothing could exceed the suffering during Hill's arduous marches in the days before the successful attack:

> ... Daybreak on the morning of the 28th repaid us for all our hardships, we followed close on the heels of the Enemy's Picquets as they retired, and came upon them quite unprepared to see us, 'tho they were ready formed in close columns to commence their march, which they immediately did on perceiving us, but our movements had been too rapid, we marched for some time in open column parallel with them and within Pistol shot without a shot being fired on either side, they having the Sierra de Montanches on their left flank and we striving to reach the Merida road before them; at length finding we were heading them, they broke and rushed up the Sierra to their left. – After this the warfare became very irregular, my Battalion exerted themselves in the pursuit, but they [the French] had the advantage of us, as every few yards of the Sierra presented a defensible position and they having thrown off their knapsacks and all incumbrances got away from us the moment there was a chance of our getting at them. – We however continued following them all day taking many Prisoners, and when we arrived at the extreme point of the Sierra nearest Truxillo [Trujillo], had the mortification of seeing the remnant of them under the command of General Gerard [Girard] at a very short distance formed in mass, and retiring across the plain to Truxillo. – I was with [the brigade commander, Briga-dier-]General [Charles] Ashworth and we used our utmost exertions to collect a few men to follow them, but in vain. We could only get together a few stragglers, and they so completely knocked up that

they could go no further. – At this time the Marquis of Tweedale [of the Quartermaster-General's Department] came up to us, and said he could muster (I think it was) 16 Dragoons with which he would attack them, if we would support him. We made fresh exertions, but it was all in vain, and we reluctantly saw about 500 men who by that time must have expended all their ammunition, walk unmolested away from us. – the glorious results of the enterprise are however known and appreciated. . . .

Hill took 1,300 prisoners at a cost of 71 casualties and returned to his former positions on the frontier for the winter.

5

Triumph and Disaster

1812

Despite Wellington's liberation of Portugal, the French had made progress in 1811 in conquering the remaining parts of unoccupied Spain. The Spanish regular armies had suffered heavy losses of men and equipment and the reduction of territory undermined the prestige and resources of the Patriot Government at Cadiz.

But at the same time, the French were becoming overstretched. They had to control the vast territories that they had now overrun and needed further reinforcements to complete the conquest of Spain before turning on Wellington. But Napoleon's relations with Tsar Alexander I had broken down since July 1807 and by the beginning of 1812 he was preparing a massive invasion of Russia with over half a million men. The French armies in the Peninsula could no longer count on reinforcements and, indeed, were reduced by 27,000 men. Despite this, Napoleon insisted on his forces maintaining the offensive and ordered Marmont to detach 10,000 troops to help Marshal Louis Suchet conquer Valencia on the eastern coast of Spain. He also extended Marmont's area of responsibility to take over some of the territory hitherto occupied by the Army of the North, which after being weakened by the removal of two divisions for the invasion of Russia was drawn back eastwards into the regions between the city of Burgos and the Pyrenees. These were fatal mistakes, as they reduced the numbers of troops directly opposed to Wellington and thus broke the stalemate of 1811. Marmont could not concentrate so readily should Wellington take the offensive and even after doing so could not count on numerical superiority.

Wellington in preparation for an offensive into Spain needed to take the border fortresses of Ciudad Rodrigo and Badajoz and had to act quickly before the French field armies could concentrate against him as they had done the year before. He now had available a proper siege train, but was still short of trained personnel. The British army was simply not equipped to conduct sieges in Europe without the assistance of a Continental ally: it had relied on the Austrians while operating in Flanders in 1793, but in the Peninsula was thrown on to its own resources.

Marmont did not expect serious operations to resume before spring and was taken aback when Wellington advanced and reinvested Ciudad Rodrigo on 8 January. Six days of bombardment breached the walls in two places. The Great Breach, on the north-western face of the fortress, would be stormed by Picton's 3rd Division, while the Lesser Breach in the north-east was allocated to Craufurd's Light Division. The assault was ordered for the night of the 19th.

Captain George Call was serving on the staff of Major-General Henry Mackinnon, whose brigade spearheaded the attack on the Great Breach:

... at 10 minutes before 7. the attack began – the Enemy threw shells hand Grenades & kept up a smart firing of musketry[.] At 7. the Brigade rushed out of the Trenches and leaping into the Ditch, into which the Sappers had previously thrown woolsacks, & planted three ladders – ascended the breach – on reaching the summit of which – the Enemy sprung their mine, a little opposition was made – but the Forlorn Hope & Storming party, consisting of the Grenadiers of the 45th & 88th who both volunteered their Services with Lt Mackie 88th and [illegible] of the 45th to lead the Forlorn hope – soon drove them back – the Enemy retired into the houses and kept up a brisk fire – they had also cut off the breach from the place, which caused much delay, during which, the column suffered very much – the different parties had by this entered the Fort and the enemy were retiring from the walls in all directions – a few minutes after the head of the column had gained the Top of the breach & directed itself to the Left to join Major Manners [who had made a subsidiary attack] – another mine or quantity of loose Powder Shells, hand Grenades &c &c, took fire and blew up Majr Genl MacKinnon & Lt [John] Beresford 88th who had just got over a work which had been thrown up to cut off the breach – a minute later would have saved them both – the obstacles on the Right being surmounted, the Brigade rushed forward to the interior of the Fort – where it is joined by the other Brigade, Light Division &c the houses were searched and the Enemy laid down their arms – by 8 o'Clock the Fort was in our possession –

about 1500 prisoners were taken, and also their cowardly Governor
– The Troops now began to plunder & destroy, the houses were set
on fire in many places – and not till 3 of the next afternoon, was the
Town quiet – the plunder was very great – horses, silks, watches,
plate &c, &c, wines, Brandies &c &c. –

Captain Duffy took part in the Light Division's assault on the Lesser
Breach:

... A little after 7 O Clock as our Batteries slackened fire – the
Enemy we suppose had some suspicion of our intention as they
threw a fire Ball on the Glacis which fortunately burst but gave light
enough to shew some of our men – About half past seven we moved
from behind the Convent – a Party with Ladders preceded – the
volunteers followed & then part of the [Portuguese] Cassadores with
Bags of Wool & Hay – some Companies of the Rifle[s] to line the
Glacis & keep up a good fire at the Embrasures – then the 43rd &
52nd Regts in contiguous Columns of 3 men to the front.

The attack at the Great Breach began too soon as it was intended
that our Division was to have commenced it – The Enemy opened a
Heavy fire of Grape & musquetry which swept the Glacis as we past
– owing to some mistake a stop took place at the counterscarp of
some Companies of Rifle[s] not extending as directed and Genl
Craufurd called out for the 43rd to disengage to the right & lead in –
which was complied with by myself & part of the Company – the
rest by mistake kept in the Column & I believe the Caçadores with
the Bags of Hay impeded their progress – We were therefore obliged
to sound the Bugle to advance & then rush on – We descended the
Counterscarp about 9 feet – then ascended the fosse braye [sic] and
down to the ditch – The Breach was perfectly practicable & we
ascended with but little opposition about 40 feet – The Enemy
seemed to have given all their attention to the Great breach and the
3rd Division suffered in proportion

As soon however as our people had gained the Ramparts the
Enemy fled in every direction and were followed thro' the first Streets
by parties – The Governor was found in the Castle on the walls and
the Soldiers hid themselves in different Houses

The Town was on fire in several places and two or three
explosions took place owing to the careless manner their powder was

placed in – one of them was fatal to several of our people just after we had formed on the Rampart.

Left on duty all night at the Breach to keep out plunderers & extinguish fires –

It is impossible to describe the Scene of pillage that followed – but as there were but few Inhabitants in the City the loss sustained was chiefly French

Our loss was considerable . . . –

Lieutenant William Staveley of the Royal Staff Corps volunteered to guide the Light Division's assault and was one of the first to reach the top of the breach. He wrote to his mother the next day:

. . . The Trenches had been open eleven days and two breaches effected through which we attacked, other parties scaling the walls at the same time – Major [George] Napier Brother to the one of whom you have heard so much led one of the storming parties, he has lost an arm being wounded as he reached the top of the Rampart, I was with him at the moment and soon after stunned by the explosion of a mine from which I received no other injury than the loss of my hat, sword, and part of my Coat, and a few slight Bruises in the legs, the latter of so little importance that I have been walking about the City all the morning – Gen¹ McKinnon was killed by the same explosion and several others were literally blown to pieces – The scene after the affair was over was dreadful the dead lay so thick on the Ramparts that it was difficult to pass along – but this is a disquieting subject, I shall drop it – . . .

The siege had been surprisingly quick and successful, but had cost Wellington over 1,100 casualties, including Major-General Craufurd, whose death from a mortal wound was a particularly severe blow. Major Thomas Peacocke of the 4th Division wrote in a letter of 21 January:

. . . You will no doubt have heard of the Capture of Ciudad Rodrigo – It was stormed about 2 hours after Sunset by the Light & 3ᵈ Divisions, & the Brigade of Portuguese commanded by B. General [Denis] Pack – Curiosity led me to accompany the storming Party of the 52ᵈ [Regiment] and I had an opportunity of witnessing the gallantry of the British Soldier, and the still more distinguished Conduct of the officers – We had effected two practicable Breaches which were assaulted simultaneously, and the Place carried in great

Style. our loss was severe owing to one of the Breaches being mined – M Gen¹ McKinnon was literally blown to atoms [in fact, his body was recovered] – General Crauford, whose Gallantry was highly conspicuous [was] dangerously wounded – M General [John] Vandeleur slightly – Lᵗ Colonel [John] Colborne – Major [George] Napier – & several other officers were hit, which added to 250 R[ank] & F[ile] killed & wounded in the assault renders the Price of our Success fully, if not more than the equivalent to the object . . .

Within a week Wellington was sending troops southwards to tackle Badajoz, the second and stronger of the two keys to Spain. The governor of the city, General Philippon, was soon aware of the gathering threat. On 12 March he wrote to Marshal Soult to inform him that on the previous evening Wellington had reached the nearby fortress of Elvas. He explained that no guns had been fired to mark his arrival, but that the town had been illuminated and that this had been clearly visible from Badajoz.

Wellington had invested Badajoz by 17 March. A French sortie on the 19th caused little damage, but bad weather flooded the trenches and delayed the opening of the bombardment by at least three days. It is interesting to note that the French soldiers shared the distaste for siege work of their British counterparts. Philippon issued an order on 23 March:

> The Governor General finds himself compelled to complain of the lack of zeal that the soldiers of the garrison apply to the siege works. The circumstances in which they are placed should on the contrary oblige them to redouble their efforts in order to oppose new obstacles to the enemy every day; it is tiresome to see that they are not convinced of this truth.
>
> . . .
>
> It is truly hard to see that soldiers who receive the full ration, and brandy twice a day, do not make more effort and are not more convinced that it is for their own defence and their liberty that they are working. . . .

Philippon ordered the Colonel of Engineers to have the works carefully supervised and warned of very severe measures if there was no improvement:

... At this moment, every soldier forming part of the garrison must apply himself with all his strength in cooperating in a vigorous resistance and must also become convinced that in a besieged fortress it is the works and the obstacles that are opposed to the enemy that save the garrison. . . .

Wellington's guns finally opened fire on the 25th and that night 500 men stormed an outwork called Fort Picurina. Philippon in an order the next day blamed its fall on the lack of coolness of its defenders. He reminded his men that although the garrison of Badajoz would be saved, energy, courage and goodwill were needed. The garrison would then cover itself with glory, honour the French army and would avoid being exposed to a slavery a thousand times worse than death. He urged those of his men who had previously been prisoners of the English to tell their comrades of the sufferings that they had endured.

Wellington ordered Badajoz to be stormed on the night of 6/7 April after three breaches had been made in the walls on the south-eastern side of the city. These would be assaulted by the 4th and Light Divisions, while the 5th Division attacked the San Vincente bastion in the north-west and Picton's 3rd Division attacked the castle in the north-eastern corner of the city.

Dr James McGrigor had reached the Peninsula in January to take over as Inspector-General of Hospitals, the army's principal medical officer. He explained that:

The Engineers having reported the main breach practicable on the 6th of April, it was known to Lord Wellington's Staff that the Fortress would be assaulted that night. I dined on the 6th with Marshal Beresford in his Tent near Lord Wellington's. – The Company consisted mostly of the Marshal's Staff. There was little conversation at table, for every one appeared impressed with the anticipation of the terrible and most momentous struggle so near at hand. A young officer present did not much exhilirate the tone of the general feeling by exclaiming 'I wonder how many of us will be alive tomorrow.' The Marshal gave him a look of disapprobation and there was a dead silence and immediately after dinner the party broke up. . . .

The main assaults, on the breaches, were bloodily repulsed. Dr McGrigor had decided to attend Wellington personally so that he could afford him professional assistance if necessary and receive immediately

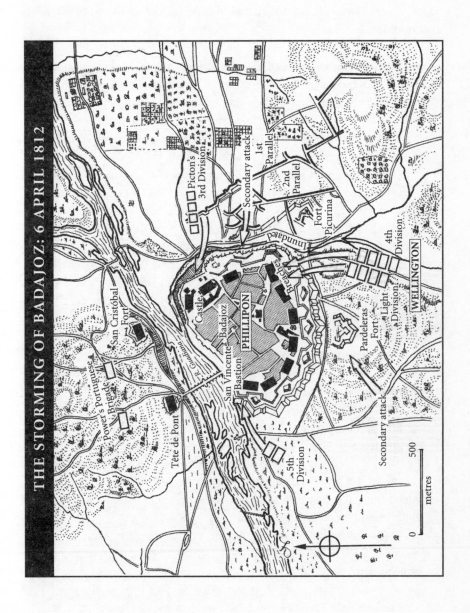

THE STORMING OF BADAJOZ: 6 APRIL 1812

Picton's 3rd Division

Secondary attack

1st Parallel

2nd Parallel

Fort Picurina

Inundated

San Cristóbal Fort

Power's Portuguese Brigade

Tête de Pont

R. Guadiana

Castle

San Vincente Bastion

Badajoz

PHILLIPON

Breaches

Inundated

Pardeleras Fort

4th Division

Light Division

WELLINGTON

5th Division

Secondary attack

0   500
metres

any orders that might be necessary. His description of Wellington during these tense hours belies the usual image of the cold, imperturbable commander:

... by the time we reached a slight elevation on the glacis near the main breach where Lord Wellington was standing, the storming parties had advanced, and the firing of shot shells musketry grenades powder barrels &ᶜ &ᶜ was terrible. Blue lights were frequently thrown out by the Garrison, which clearly showed the red masses of troops in the ditch advancing to the breach and illuminated all around.

Lord Wellington was attended only by two of his Aides-de-Camp – the Prince of Orange, and Lord March now the Duke of Richmond both very young men, soon after myself and sir Charles Forbes [a surgeon] came up an officer arrived with a most unfavourable account of the contest at the main breach[.] [Lieutenant-]Colonel [Charles] Mᶜ Leod [of the 43rd Regiment] and several officers had been killed and heaps of the dead and wounded men choked the approach to the breach – At this time the group was so near the ramparts that we could distinctly hear the shouts of the combatants in the momentary intervals of the firing; and were distressed to find, that the sounds from the assailants became fainter and those from the ramparts, louder every moment mixed with oaths and execrations, – 'Avancez, sacres b__s Angloises[!] Avancez [illegible] In a short time another officer came up with a still more unfavorable report. At this moment I cast my eyes on the countenance of Lord Wellington with the light of the torch held by Lord March upon it. I never can forget it to the last moment of my life, and I could now sketch it. The jaw had fallen, and the face was of unusual length, whilst the torch cast over it a lurid coloring – more shade than light, still the expression was very firm.

In an instant after, turning to me and putting his hand on my shoulder Lord Wellington said 'Go immediately to Picton and tell him he must succeed at the Castle.' I replied 'My Lord, I have no horse, but I will go on foot as fast as I can; and I know the way.['] The answer was 'No, No, – I beg your pardon, I thought it was [Lieutenant-Colonel William] Delanc[e]y' [the Acting Quartermaster-General] – I then repeated my offer to go to General Picton, but His Lordship would not hear of it. This moment appears to have been the crisis of the great Commander[']s agony during this awful night – after a short but dreadful suspense, a horseman was heard approaching; who shouted 'Where is Lord Wellington?['] – 'Here, here.' every one exclaimed. Then when he had come up, he cried out 'My Lord the Castle is your own.' . . .

For the secondary attacks had been more successful than the main assaults on the breaches. Once lodgements had been secured within Badajoz, French resistance collapsed.

Philippon fled the city and crossed the River Guadiana to take refuge in the outlying fort of San Cristóbal, where he surrendered on the morning of 7 April. Lieutenant-Colonel William Warre was among those who received his surrender. He was serving as ADC to Marshal Beresford, who was present at the siege without being actively involved. Warre wrote to his father later on the 7th:

> . . . I was sent before daybreak as soon as our men were in the town to endeavour to establish a communication across the Bridge & tête de Pont [bridgehead] with [Brigadier-]Gen¹ [Manley] Power [the commander of a Portuguese brigade] who was on that side, I met Lord Fitzroy Somerset, who was going on nearly the same duty & in the tête de Pont we found an officer & 40 men & in fort Sᵗ Christopher, whither we heard he had retreated, the Governor, Gen¹ Philipon, General Weyland [Veilande] & a great many officers, all of whom surrendered immediately on our summoning them & the Ch[i]efs we conducted to Lord Wellington. . . .

Major Lord Fitzroy Somerset was Wellington's Military Secretary and forty-two years later, as Lord Raglan, commanded the British army in the Crimean War (1854–6). He was furious at Warre's interference and explained the full story in a letter to the historian Colonel William Napier in 1834:

> It is certainly true that Colonel Warre was present when the Governor of Badajoz surrendered in front of San Christoval and that he was senior to me in the rank we then respectively held, but in my opinion the circumstance of his presence or seniority does not affect the question at issue . . .

Somerset explained how he crossed the river to summon San Cristóbal:

... In a short time the Governor General Philippon and the Lt Governor Veillande came out; and on it's being announced to them that the Town was in our hands, they said, they had no knowledge of the fact, and could not surender until they should be acquainted with it; but they were willing to go to Lord Wellington's Camp to arrange the terms of capitulation. A warm discussion ensued in which Colonel Warre and myself took part, he, if I recollect right, being disposed to agree to their proposition. I on the other hand being violently opposed to it and declaring that they should not stir from the Fort otherwise than as Prisoners. In the end they agreed to surrender.

. . .

I cannot say precisely when Colonel Warre announced to me that he as Senior Officer should take possession of the Swords of the Officers; but if I mistake not, it was immediately before the Governor and Lt Governor came out to the conference. I at once protested against his having the smallest claim to the Swords or any right to interfere in the operation, which I had undertaken as one of the Staff of The Commd^r of the Forces and I appealed to Sir Alex Dickson [the artillery commander during the siege], who coincided with me – Colonel Warre however got possession of the Swords which he delivered to Lord Wellington.

. . .

I never mentioned the subject to Marshal Beresford, but as a proof that he viewed the question in the same light as I did, I beg to state that he sent Colonel [Robert] Arbuthnot [of his staff] to me the following day to say that he was very sorry to find that his Aide de Camp Colonel Warre had interfered with me, and that he entirely disapproved of his conduct. . . .

Dr McGrigor entered Badajoz soon after first light on the 7th to estimate the number of wounded and provide accommodation for them. He described how:

... In one street I met General Phillipon the French Governor of Badajoz between his two daughters, holding each by the hand, and endeavouring to convey them out of the Town, to Camp where they were sure to find an Asylum. Two British officers with drawn swords escorted them, and had some difficulty in making their way through the drunken ruffians who sought to do them violence. I joined in their protection and seeing some of the 88th amongst the assailants

I told them they were a disgrace to their Corps, but two of them hearing this, presented their muskets at me and if I had not cried out, 'What! shoot one of your own Officers? – I was once in the 88' they would most probably have murdered me, but hearing this exclamation they lowered their muskets. . . .

The sack of Badajoz by the crazed survivors lasted at least forty-eight hours and indelibly blotted the reputation of Wellington's Peninsular army. But in fact, the city had already suffered considerable looting by the French garrison. As recently as 3 April, Philippon had issued an order stating: '. . . Complaints are daily brought by inhabitants of the city against several soldiers of the garrison who loot the inhabited houses as well as the churches, this dreadful disorder deserving an exemplary punishment for those who commit it. . . .' He ordered occasional patrols to be made to prevent this brigandage and instructed that every soldier caught while looting should be brought before a council of war and shot.

Lieutenant Dugald MacGibbon of the Portuguese service explained to his father in a letter of 7 April that while the inhabitants suffered severely after the storming, the French garrison were treated astonishingly well:

Badajoz is ours. The contest has been a hard but glorious one. – The assault was made at ten oClock last night and after four hours of the hardest fighting I have ever seen we became masters of the place.

The 4th and Light Divisions were directed against the breaches whilst the 3rd and 5th Divisions attacked by Escalade – The former against the Castle and the latter against the western body of the Garrison near the Guadiana. – nothing but the most gallant and determined conduct on the part of our Troops could have brought the business to a favorable issue, opposed to the almost unparalleled resistance made by the Garrison – The most consumate skill has been shown by the Enemy in their defensive works and retrenchments in the points breached, indeed so excellent and formidable were their works in those points that but for the success attending the Escalades particularly that against the Castle it was next to impossible that we should have carried the place. – The Scene of horror after our entrance beggars all description. – The place was given up to plunder

and the excesses of Soldiers enfuriated by their labours and the loss
of their companions cannot be judged by any one who has not
witnessed such scenes –

The tenderness shown by the Soldiers to the French who fell into
their power is unaccountable – I do not believe a Single French man
was put to death in cool blood. – whilst the whole wrath of our
people seemed to be directed against the Spaniards who remained in
the Garrison. – Philippon the Governor is prisoner. – It is impossible
to say what number of prisoners have been made as we have been all
day collecting them from their hiding places – . . .

MacGibbon's account is supported by Lieutenant-Colonel Warre:
'. . . It is most extraordinary that notwithstanding the obstinate defence
& causes of animosity which our men had, & all their previous determi-
nations they gave quarter to almost every frenchman . . .'

Lieutenant-General Sir Thomas Graham had been covering the siege
to the south-east with 19,000 men and had driven back a French
detached force of 12,000 under General Jean-Baptiste Drouet, Count
d'Erlon. Marshal Soult, commanding the Army of the South in Andalusia, had marched from Seville on 30 March with another 13,000 men,
intending to relieve Badajoz in conjunction with Marshal Marmont's
Army of Portugal. But Napoleon had ordered Marmont to threaten
northern Portugal rather than march on Badajoz. Soult on his own was
too weak to raise the siege, for Graham was joined on 6 April by another
12,000 men under Hill.

At 8.30 a.m. on the 7th Graham was at Santa Marta, 42 km south-
east of Badajoz. He wrote to Sir Stapleton Cotton, who was further in
advance with Graham's cavalry:

I must begin by telling you that Badajos is taken – by escalade both
of the Castle & the town by the 3ᵈ & 5ᵗʰ Divⁿˢ the the [sic] Lᵗ & 4ᵗʰ
being repuls'd from the Breaches & having suffer'd much – Col.
Macleod 43ᵈ killd & several Genˡˢ wounded
    the attack began at 10 at night & it was 2 hours before the Castle
was carried –
    I recᵈ your letter of yesterday 1 p.m. at 4 this mornᵍ & I have got
yours of 2 this morᵍ an hour ago w[i]ᵗʰ Soults [intercepted] note –
when the men come I will send them all on to Lᵈ Wellⁿ
    It is an odd reflection in such a communication 'du moins il en

est grandement tems [?] &c' calculated for *effect*, if it fell into our hands – if not so intended –

I don't know at all what L^d W^{ns} plan will be – He has orderd G^l Hill back by Lobon –

Soult at first will not believe the reports [of Badajoz's fall] & will probably come on wch may give us an opportunity of striking a Blow agst him –

Soult's advanced guard arrived that day at Fuente del Maestre, 18 km south-east of Santa Marta. But he then hurriedly fell back after learning on the 8th of Badajoz's fate, particularly as Spanish regular forces were threatening Seville in his rear.

Wellington lost 4,670 men during the siege of Badajoz and was sickened by the slaughter. He urged the immediate formation of a corps of sappers and miners to shorten future sieges and avoid such great losses. His pleas were heeded and from 1813 he had 300 properly trained men of the Royal Sappers and Miners.

Another problem was the absence of ambulances and a body of stretcher-bearers dedicated to removing casualties from the battlefield. Instead, the wounded had to be carried to aid posts and regimental hospitals by either bandsmen or comrades. Spring wagons were available to reduce the discomfort of those wounded who had to be transported to the general hospital at Elvas, 15 km to the west, and Dr McGrigor also set up a hospital in Badajoz itself.

Lieutenant James Gairdner had joined the 1st Battalion of the 95th Regiment of Foot (Riflemen) in the Peninsula in January 1812 and took part in the storming of Badajoz. He was, in fact, an American, having been born in Charleston in 1792. His father had emigrated from Scotland and owned a large plantation in Georgia. Lieutenant Gairdner described the arrangements for the care of the wounded:

... The defense of the Garrisson is universally allowed to have been very good – I received three wounds early in the attack Viz one in the right leg very slight – one in the left arm – and one in the chin – and after lying on the ground was at last helped off by a Serj^t of our Company and with the assistance of some of the 52nd [Regiment's] band who were coming with bearers carried to the hospital tent where my wounds were dressed and I was then put into a tent for the reception of wounded officers – The firing continued for a long time after I was carried off . . .

In the afternoon of the 8th, Lieutenant Gairdner was taken to a newly established hospital in Badajoz. On the 15th, he was removed in a spring wagon to Elvas and gradually recovered. A month later, on 18 May, he set out with two wounded comrades, in accordance with an order that all the sick and wounded should go to the general hospital at Estremoz, a further 38 km to the west, as soon as fit to do so. They arrived on the 19th and the following day attended a medical board, which gave Gairdner three weeks of local leave.

The Medical Department acquired valuable experience and developed important surgical techniques during the prolonged war. Some of the practices of the time, such as bleeding patients, were misguided, and the quality of the surgeons could vary widely. But the Department saved countless lives despite the absence of anaesthetics and the high risk of infection in such dirty and overcrowded conditions. It had to contend with makeshift accommodation, blunt instruments, inadequate medical supplies and insufficient numbers of surgeons to handle the thousands of casualties after a battle. The Peninsular War boosted the standing of the Department, for Dr McGrigor persuaded Wellington to mention the Medical Officers in his despatch on the capture of Badajoz:

. . . I then said – Nothing would be a greater reward or more powerful incentive to future good conduct, than a notice of their behavior in your Lordship's Despatches. Lord Wellington thought a moment and eyeing me keenly asked 'Is that usual'[.] I replied the exigency of the case has never been equalled, and the very meritorious services of these Gentlemen give them a claim on your Lordship for a favorable notice; and, doubtless this will be most beneficial to the Service hereafter. His Lordship was in good humour and said smiling 'I have finished my Despatches but I will mention the Doctors in a Postscript.' When the Gazette appeared the Medical Officers at home were gratified to see that the merits of their brethren in the Peninsula had been publicly acknowledged, in the same manner as the Military Officers. This was the first instance of such justice having been done them and the example has been followed since both in the Navy and Army.

*

Wellington planned to second his forthcoming advance into Spain with diversionary attacks around the Peninsula to help the guerrillas tie down as many French troops as possible on the periphery. The year before, over 1,100 British troops had been detached from Cadiz under Colonel John Skerrett and sent by sea to the besieged city of Tarragona on the eastern coast of Spain. Skerrett had arrived off Tarragona on 26 June 1811, but had realized that it was untenable. He had orders not to land unless he could evacuate his troops in the event of the city falling. He therefore refused to reinforce the Spanish garrison directly, but agreed to land further along the coast to join a Spanish relief army. Unfortunately, the departure of his force undermined Spanish morale. The French stormed the city on the evening of the 28th and conducted a brutal massacre. Gunner Andrew Phillips of the 2nd Battalion of the Royal Artillery vividly described this dismal episode:

> ... Our Companey imbarked at Cadiz in June With a Small Divison Consisting of the ninth regement and 47th Regement under Command of Cornel Scirrit Bound for a place called taragona about five hundred mils above Gibraltar we arrived in taragona bay on the 27th of Jun the french seing a few british Shippind Coming with trupes Ceapt a verry hevy fir with Shot and Shells and musqutry untill the[y] got Clos up to the Wals of the town the french forced open the geats and Entred the town and Drove the Spanish Solgers and Inhabations Out of the town to the fields of Slaughter Which it was a pitefil Sight to sea them putt man woman And Children to the eage of the Sword and burnt the town to ashes wich I Sa with my eyes but having the good forting [fortune] not to be on shore. ...

Spanish resistance in Catalonia was thus crushed: Skerrett's force had simply been too weak to intervene effectively.

Wellington hoped to produce more of an impact in 1812. Spanish regular armies in southern and north-western Spain became more active. Commodore Sir Home Popham with a naval squadron and two battalions of Royal Marines caused alarm by attacking French strongpoints on the northern coast of Spain in conjunction with local guerrillas. Similarly, the threat of a major seaborne landing by an Anglo-Sicilian force tied down a French army on the eastern coast.

Wellington also struck at French communications. He ordered Hill to lead part of his detached force from Extremadura in the south to destroy the French pontoon bridge on the River Tagus at Almaraz, 150 km north-east of Badajoz. The French had erected two forts to cover the bridge and had placed a garrison 8 km to the south-west in the Castle of Mirabete. Hill feinted at Mirabete and successfully attacked Almaraz on 19 May, as Captain Richard Brunton of the 6th Caçadores described:

> ... We arrived there [Mirabete] in the night of the 17th but owing to the darkness and extreme difficulty of the ground day broke just as we hoped to accomplish our object. – We were discovered, and our purpose of taking them by surprise frustrated. We bivouacked on the ground during the 18th, and in the afternoon Lord Hill made his arrangements for the attack, which were that His columns should advance by a rather circuitous and very difficult pass through the mountains [to Almaraz], whilst their object was to be covered, and the attention of the Enemy diverted from it, by a prior attack on the Castle of Miraveté which was a fortified Tower enclosed by works, situated on a very lofty and almost inaccessible peak of the mountain, completely commanding the main pass; and overlooking all our operations. – The Light Companies of the 28th & 34th were selected for this duty, and 100 picked men of the Caçadores were called for, of which I volunteered to take the command, – the whole under the orders of Captn [James Harrison] Baker of the 34th – Accordingly at dusk we moved, with scaling ladders, as far as was thought necessary, up the mountain, and lay down until the proper time arrived for our advancing. – In the middle of the night however we got orders that ours was only to be a feint, but to be conducted with such vigour as to deceive the Enemy into a supposition that a real attack was intended. – This was entirely confided to me, and accordingly at the proper time before daybreak I commenced climbing the Height. – I had with me a Section of the 34th or 28th (I am not sure which) and my Caçadores, the others remained in reserve. We had the greatest difficulties to encounter in getting up in the dark, but arrived silently and tolerably well closed up, exactly at the proper moment on the French Picquet who challenged, and immediately after fired a volley on us and retired – We rushed after them and our road was made clear by the Tower &c becoming a blaze of light. – We took up our Stations as well as we could amongst the rocks and stones close around it, too close as I afterwards proved, for some of my men had

actually got under cover of their outward defences. – We kept up as heavy a fire as we could, which was returned, and all the effects produced on lookers on at a distance of a real attack, and it appears that it distracted the attention of the Enemy at the Forts, exactly as was intended. – Sometime after day-light I received orders to retire; and the question now became, How was it to be done, without the loss of many lives, as, when leaving their hiding places close to the wall the men must fall a prey to the murderous fire of those within, who were of course anxiously watching their opportunity. – I therefore determined to remain, and wait for a favorable moment, and not very long afterwards it occurred, for as if by an interposition of Providence, the whole Peak became enveloped in a dense cloud. – I immediately sounded the Retreat, and got my men off, with the loss only of one Officer and two men wounded. – In the Evening I received officially, through Captain Baker, the thanks of Lord Hill for my conduct. . . .

Hill then withdrew, having cut direct communications between Soult's Army of the South and Marmont's Army of Portugal.

At the same time Wellington strove to improve his own communications. One of the most outstanding achievements of his engineers during the war was the temporary repair of the broken bridge at Alcantara near the Portuguese border with a portable suspension bridge. Lieutenant William Staveley of the Royal Staff Corps explained to his mother in a letter of 2 August:

. . . You have heard of the Famous Roman Bridge of Alcantara an arch of which was blown up about 4 years ago – Lord Wellington wished to have it render'd passable to facilitate the Communication of his army with that under General Hill: it had hitherto been deemed impossible without building it up with masonry at an enormous expence – but Col [Robert] Sturgeon and Capt Tod undertook it, and constructed a Bridge of *Ropes* the strength of which was proved by passing over it the 24 pounder battering Train & 50 or 60 waggons going from Badajos to Salamanca. What renders the thing more complete is, that the bridge can be taken on and off, so as to deprive the Enemy of deriving any advantage from it – I had a very good description of it lately in a letter from Captain Tod. . . .

On 13 June Wellington advanced against Marmont and occupied the city of Salamanca four days later. Marmont could be expected after concentrating the bulk of his army to march to the relief of three forts on the western outskirts of the city. These were besieged by the 6th Division, which was covered by the rest of the army posted on the hills of San Cristóbal to the north-east. Lieutenant John Massey of the 3rd (or King's Own) Regiment of Dragoons in a letter dated 19 June commented: '. . . Lord W is very close you will hear Generals talking of affairs with as great uncertainty as Subalterns – he reviewed two brigades of Cavalry on the banks of the Agueda – he looked remarkably well – . . .'

Marmont advanced up to the San Cristóbal hills on the evening of the 20th, but hesitated to assault Wellington's compact position as he had not yet concentrated the whole of his army and was significantly outnumbered. Wellington was disappointed, but also declined to attack without a more comfortable advantage. The stand-off lasted two days, until Marmont withdrew on the night of the 22nd.

The besieged forts finally fell on 27 June. An unidentified officer of the Royal Horse Artillery, who apparently belonged to 'I' Troop, revealed in a letter of 31 July that they turned out to be more formidable than had been supposed:

> . . . The Army took up a position on the heights above the City to cover it & the 6th Division remained to carry on the Seige [of the forts] – 4. 18[prs] with 100 rounds p[r] gun was all we brought up supposing the forts of little strength. [Captain John] Elijes [Eligé's] Brigade of long 6 p[rs] was placed in a convent & 4 Brigade How[itzer][s] to [illegible] their fire whilst the battery was forming, & they suffered so much from the fire of the Place that on the 2[d] Day they were obliged to withdraw them, not however before Elije was killed & about 30 of his Comp[y] disabled. on the 28th [actually, 18 June] at night the battery was ready & open'd the following morn[g] in order to knock down the gable end of a large convent projecting over the wall of the Fort, which it was supposed they would do in 6 or 7 hours & thereby open a passage for an assault. The guns did their part in 3 Hours, but it was then found that the interior of the convent (as might have been supposed) was strengthe[d] more than the outside, so that we only opened a more formidable opposition, notwithstanding this an assault was attempted at night & failed in which we suffered severely, & [Major-]General [Barnard] Bowes was

killed. The only reason for this attempt was our having but little ammun^n left. The next day the Battery was nearly destroyed by their fire & the guns were withdrawn to wait for more amm^n which with 4 H[eav]^y Iron Howitzers arrived on the 24th[.] The Battery for them & then for the 18 p^{rs} were constructed during the night of the 25th & open'd on the morn^g of the 26th[.] after breaching one of the smaller Forts, we fired red hot shot into the old convent which succeeded in setting it on fire, & on the morn^g of the 27th The smaller Fort was assaulted at the Breach, when they made but little resistance, & the other two fell by capitulation immediately after. up to this moment their defence was vigorous & decisive & our loss nearly am[oun]^{td} to 500 men. what made them surrender I know not, as the defences of the larger Fort were entire, & I do not think we could have retained the smaller, they were well supplied with every thing & the interior defences of the works astonished us. They had cost the French 2½ years labour & an immense expence, & were built on the ruins of convents & Houses which they had thrown down for the purpose & had ingeniously work'd in many of the arches & strong walls of the former – Their foundations from this circumstance were so solid that mining was impracticable. To open their fire they had thrown down as I said ¼ of the City – and had they had time to have completed their plan the noble Cathedral was to have shared the same fate, as from its Dome you could see into the works. The Forts themselves also were not completed, but in their then state, they were very much superior in point of strength to the Fortress of Ciudad Rodrigo & when we went thro' them we congratulated ourselves on getting them so cheaply. (we have since totally destroyed them) . . .

Marmont withdrew behind the River Douro, 70 km to the north-east, and remained there until 16 July, when he became active again after being reinforced to a total of nearly 50,000. Wellington, who had followed him from Salamanca, had 52,000 men on the south bank of the Douro. A week of manoeuvring ensued as Wellington withdrew back to Salamanca. King Joseph collected 15,000 men from the Army of the Centre and on 21 July set off from Madrid to reinforce Marmont. But the interception of Joseph's despatches by Spanish guerrillas apparently left Marmont unaware of this move, while Wellington knew that he would have to retreat to Portugal rather than fight the combined forces of Marmont and Joseph.

Marmont on 22 July continued to manoeuvre as he sought to turn Wellington's right flank in the rolling countryside 8 km south-east of Salamanca. Wellington knew that Marmont was seeking to cut his line of retreat and, having already sent his baggage to the rear, was ready to order a retreat. But then Marmont in his eagerness to outflank Wellington allowed his army to become overextended. Wellington immediately launched a devastating counter-attack, with his divisions attacking in succession from west to east. These onslaughts, which began in the middle of the afternoon, opened the Battle of Salamanca. An unidentified soldier of the 38th (or the 1st Staffordshire) Regiment of Foot described the attack of the 5th Division under Lieutenant-General James Leith. The regiment had been advanced to under the brow of a hill:

> ... But we had not been long there before Some of our Officers went up to the top of the Hill to See in What position the French wass In[.] But in doing so the French Saw them and Began to throw the Cannon Shot abought Us as Quick as possible So that we where forced To move agane[.] we then ran in duble quick time For A great distance by the Side of A Hill So That we where Covered from the Enemys fire And As soon as we got to the end of the Hill We where ordred to drop down instantly we did So And in A few Secconds Gen¹ Leath Came up Waveing his Hat and Shouting Now my Lads this Is the day for England[.] thay would play at long Ball with us from Morning untill Night But we Will Soon give them Something else[.] So as soon As he got to the right of the Line the Bugle Sounded to Stand to Our Harms and to Charge Them Immediately[.] As soon as we rose up there wass 3 Cannons fireing upon us which we soon took but We passd by them and left them for our rear Lines to Secure and passd on untill we came to A Small Villidge [Arapiles] but we had to go through It Left in front and in going through there Came A Shower of grape Shot and knocked down 4 Men at my Left hand But when we got through The Villidge the French had got over an hill out Of our of our [sic] Sight except their rifles [skirmishers] But we drove Them in and advanced up the hill after them as Soon as we got to the top the French wear in A [illegible] Square not more than 200 yards from us[.] as soon As we Saw them we gave A shout hopned A tremendeous Fire and ran into them directly So that that Line wass in A few Minets killed and taken Prisners[.] We then

Atacked their rear lines and After we had engaged them Some time we where Chargeing them I received A Ball in my right Foot . . .

Wellington's cavalry under Sir Stapleton Cotton advanced on Leith's western flank, led by Major-General John Le Marchant's brigade of heavy dragoons, which crushed eight battalions in some of the finest charges of the war. Le Marchant was shot dead. Lieutenant-Colonel John Cameron, the commander of the 9th (or the East Norfolk) Regiment of Foot, explained in a letter of 1827 to Lieutenant-Colonel William Napier:

> . . . I can give you the particulars of General Le Marchant's death, described as having taken place in a charge of cavalry. When halted under the enemy's artillery, as I before told you, a Serjeant of the 9th [Foot] came to me from the left of the battalion, with the General's watch and sword, sent to me by the surgeon of the Regiment. I directed that his body should be immediately removed to the nearest village. A party accordingly conveyed him: preceeded by the Serjeant, who at the entrance of the village met Captain Le Marchant, his son and aide de camp. Being informed that they were bringing in the body of a General Officer, Captain Le Marchant said 'It is impossible that it can be my Father, for I have just left him': on going up to the body, however, with the Serjeant, he discovered it to be too true. The General was killed by a musquet ball, which passed through his sash into the abdomen, and he breathed his last a few moments after the surgeon found him: He was lying a few yards to our left, his sword was firmly grasped in his right hand, the knot round his wrist, and the edge very much hacked. . . .

Le Marchant was one of the most brilliant officers in the British army. He had designed a new sabre, which had formed the basis for the famous 1796 light cavalry pattern, and had also produced a manual, issued officially in December 1796 as *Rules and Regulations for the Sword Exercise of Cavalry*. Even more importantly, he had played a key role in the establishment of the Royal Military College, which was located at Sandhurst from 1812. It offered professional instruction to cadets and had a Senior Department that trained officers in staff duties.

Another casualty of the Battle of Salamanca was Marshal Marmont, who was wounded in the early stages. The French managed to launch a major counter-attack in the centre, but were routed by dusk. Wellington for the loss of 4,700 men inflicted about 14,000 casualties and temporarily dispersed at least another 10,000 troops. He had won the British army's greatest victory since the Battle of Blenheim in 1704 and had raised himself in the eyes of many to the level of the Duke of Marlborough. In doing so, he had conclusively destroyed the myth that he was solely a master of the defensive. An unidentified British officer noted in a letter of 27 July:

> ... But the great novelty of the day was the keeping the troops so well in hand, and stopping their headlong impetuosity after each succeeding attack – The 3 divisions wheel'd round as a single company would, & the long lines were preserved most beauti- fully – ...

However:

> ... The effort appeared to be too much for the Portuguese who did not I think distinguish themselves tho' they generally kept together – The Portuguese Cavalry however who were with the 3^d division charged very gallantly & did every thing that was required of them. – ...

William Morris, a Conductor of Stores in the Commissariat, did not take part in the battle. But when he visited the battlefield on 5 October, he recorded an anecdote showing Wellington's concern for the wounded. He also suggested that a desire to preserve access to drinking water may have contributed to the bitterness with which the French fought in the evening:

> ... I went on Monday Morning to look at the field of Battle which took place n^r Salamanca[.] as you enter the Town from Ciudad Rodrigo it is about 2 Miles to the right of the Town[.] it must have been witnessd from the lofty buildings of the Place[.] it still presents a shocking Spectacle great numbers remain on the ground some partly buried with thier bones scatterd about sculls & Teeth – the effluvia arising from it is very offensive[.] Various kind[s of] accou- trement lie scatterd in every direction with Cartridge papers which had been fir'd of[f.] I did not go so far as the hills w[h]ere the principal force of the french was stationed and the battle raged with the greatest violence[.] our men repatedly charging them with the bayonet here[.] I am told the slaughter was dreadful[.] a Sergeant who was present told me about 7 °Clock in the evening [it was] so

tremendious that the hills appeard as if they were on fire and the Elements of heaven let loose at once at [sic] this grand struggle took place over some water which the french had possesion of and they wanted to keep but nothing could withstand the undaunted bravery of the british who carried every thing before them with the bayonet[.] I was told an Anecdote of Lord Wellington that during the engagement as he passd by his wounded men he exclaimd now do my brave fellows those that can hold up your heads & see what a precious beating we are giving them[.] this I had from [a] Soldier who was wounded in the battle, his Ldship is spoke of by the Soldier in Terms of the greates[t] admiration for his ability as a commander and cool determind bravery . . .

Yet Wellington's order of thanks to his army on 23 July read more like a reprimand:

G.O [General Order] July [23] – The Commd[r] of the Forces returns his thanks to the General Officers Officers & Troops for their conduct in the action with the Enemy of the 22[n] Ins[t] of which he will not fail to make to H.R.H. The Prince Regent the favourable Report which it deserves.

He trusts that the Events of yesterday have impressed all with a conviction that Military success depends upon the Troops obeying the orders which they receive, & the order of their formation in Action; and that upon no occasion will they ever allow themselves to depart from it for one moment –

Col. The Hon[ble] W[m] Ponsonby is appointed as Col. on the Staff till the pleasure of H.R.H. The Prince Regent is known & is to command the Brigade of Cavalry Commanded by the late M Gen[l] Le Marchant.

This original version differs in minor details from that published in Wellington's *General Orders*. Ponsonby, who was given command of Le Marchant's brigade, had hitherto led the 5th (or Princess Charlotte of Wales's) Regiment of Dragoon Guards.

The anonymous soldier of the 38th Regiment wrote a fascinating account of his sufferings after being wounded at Salamanca. He had previously undergone a religious conversion:

. . . I lay in the Field 4 or 5 howers After I wass wounded before I wass taken away And While I lay my Spirits Failed me so that I wass filled with doupts and fear and began To think I Should be Seperated from my few Pious Comrades and I Should not have one pious Frend to Converse with but provedance had ordred It otherwise for when I wass picked up thay Took and lade me in A Churchyard for both the Church And the yard where as full of wounded men as thay Could be but it wass so dark that I Could not see So as to know aney person that lay near me except One that lay Close by me and I should not [have] known Him but when I heard him grone I knew his Voice[.] I Called him by Name and Asked him if he wass Hurt mutch he told me his Thy [thigh] wass Shattered All to peices by A Cannon Shot verey soon after The Docters came and Ordred him to be taken to Another place to have the Limb taken off And When thay took hold of him he told them to be Carefull of him for he wass badly hurt and In three Minutes after he expired[.] after that I lay in the Churchyard abought an hour[.] I think it wass abought 11 O Clock at Night when thay Came and Carried me and all that Could be found Of our reg^t to A Large Stable where we Stopt 3 or 4 Days then we wass taken into the Town of Salemanco And when they Carried me from the Carr thay Set me down just within the Convent That we had for an Hospital and then there came A pious Man Belonging to the 5 reg^t of Foot that I had been Aquinted with in Ireland he wass Wounded in the Harm [arm] And mine being in the Foot It Confined me to my room So he had used to come And Stopt with me 2 or 3 hours most days and I often Felt it A refreshing Seson to my Soul . . .

Wellington pursued the remnants of the Army of Portugal north-eastwards, but was unable to advance further than Valladolid, 110 km from Salamanca, without straining his logistics. He also had to watch his flank, as King Joseph had the 17,000 men of the Army of the Centre at Madrid, 160 km south-east of Valladolid. Wellington later explained his quandary, and his decision to march on Madrid, in a letter to Sir Stapleton Cotton on 13 August. Cotton had been accidentally shot and wounded after ignoring a Portuguese sentry's challenge on the night after Salamanca and was recovering in hospital in that city:

I have long intended to write to you, but I have really not had time to write to any body. I was much concerned to learn that you were so unwell; and I hope that you will soon be better, as I am very anxious to have you again with the Army.

Our operations since you left us have been as follows. We followed Marmont as closely as we could to the Douro; but he marched at such a Rate, & our Troops were so much fatigued that after the first day we did him but little mischief. After driving him from Valladolid it appeared that he & the King [Joseph] who had returned from this side [Madrid] & Segovia, had thoughts of joining at Aranda de Douro [85 km east of Valladolid]; and I moved our Right to Cuellar [45 km south-east of Valladolid]. I there gave the Troops a day's halt upon finding the King retired upon Madrid; & afterwards I thought that upon the whole the best thing I could do would be to move upon the King, & fight him or force him from Madrid; which I have carried into execution. I could not go farther North without great inconvenience; and I could at that moment do nothing else. I have left Anson's Brigade [of light dragoons] on the Douro to observe Marmont; & [Major-General Henry] Clinton's [6th] Division & all the new Infantry [five battalions recently arrived from England] at Cuellar to support, & keep the Communication with him. The King has retired [southwards] upon Aranjuez & Toledo [on the Tagus]; leaving a Garrison in the Retiro [the citadel of Madrid].

We had a Devil of an Affair on the evening of the 11th [at Majalahonda, 11 km north-west of Madrid]. The French 2000 cavalry moved upon the Portuguese Cavalry; D Urban ordered them to charge the advanced Squadrons which charge they did not execute as they ought; & they ran off leaving our Guns (Capt [Robert] Mc Donald's ['E'] Troop). They ran in upon the German Cavalry [1st and 2nd Dragoons, King's German Legion] half a mile or more in their Rear; where they were brought up; but they would not charge on the left of the Germans. These charged & stopped the Enemy but Col. De Jonquiere was taken; and we have lost a good many of these fine fellows. There are 20 killed, & about as many wounded & Prisoners. We likewise lost 3 Guns of Mc Donald's Troop in the Portuguese flight; but the French left them behind.

If Elley is recovered I wish you would desire him to have an eye to the sick & wounded Horses & Men of the Cavalry, particularly of Ponsonby's Brigade which are at Salamanca. The 5th Dn Gds are very weak. I have written to England about Horses; but I am sadly apprehensive that our Horses will fall off terribly before the Campaign will be over. They are now however in as good condition (the

Germans in better) as they have been during the Campaign. But the
Wear & tear in these constant Marches & Skirmishes must wear them
out.

I have desired the Lt Dragoons & Hussars to mount some of their
dismounted men upon French & Spanish Captured Horses. I think
that the Heavy Cavalry also might do something of the same kind.
That is they might mount upon French Horses the Men who attend
the Baggage, & [illegible] all the Effective English Horses into the
Ranks. I wish you could turn this suggestion over in your Mind.

A postscript suggests that Wellington expected the Retiro to hold out for
some time: 'I'll make every body shoe up while we shall be engaged in
the Siege of the Retiro.'

Wellington rode triumphantly into Madrid on 12 August. Private
William Stephenson of the 3rd Dragoons recorded: 'Entred the Citty of
Madrid cappital of Spain, amidst the rejoicings of the Inhabitants, and
Halted some Days for Orders, the Citty was Illuminated three nights
during our stay in celebration of the arrival of the English Army. – The
Inhabitants behaved exceeding well to the Army.'

The forts of the Retiro in fact soon surrendered and were found to
contain a mass of stores. Wellington remained in Madrid for a fortnight,
but was then obliged to take action to secure his position before the
French could unite their armies against him. General Bertrand Clausel
had rallied the Army of Portugal following its defeat at Salamanca and
returned to Valladolid on 13 August. Wellington had left a brigade of
light dragoons under Major-General George Anson in observation on
the River Douro. On the 18th, one of Clausel's infantry divisions and
800 cavalry crossed the river at Tudela and pushed Anson back a few
kilometres to the south-east. Lieutenant William Smith of the 11th
Regiment of (Light) Dragoons noted:

The French came on about 9 oclk, which gave us time to unload our
Baggage (which was always loaded when we turned out) and was just
going to breakfast when an orderly came in to say the Enemy was
coming on[.] wishing to make good the little time I had, commenced
runing a stone caught my foot and down I came however I made a
tolerable Breakfast[.] we retired across the Douro to the Artillery
and supported them[.] Poor [Lieutenant John] Lindsell was killed
charging on the bridge with his party by a musket ball, we lost a

great many Artillery men by the Enemy firing from the windows &
roofs of the houses; retired at night to Parilla [8 km south-east of
Tudela.] Bivouac –

This was only a probe: the French pulled back to the Douro that same
evening and Anson reoccupied Tudela on the 20th.

But Wellington decided to go north. He left four divisions to cover
Madrid and ordered Hill to join them with his detached force from
Extremadura. Hill would be free to make this move because Soult had
been ordered to evacuate southern Spain, where his position had become
untenable in the wake of Salamanca. Wellington himself advanced from
Madrid with the rest of his army, but found that Clausel retired north-
eastwards from Valladolid without a fight. Wellington on 23 August
wrote to his brother Henry, the British Ambassador at Cadiz, expressing
concern about the enormity of his task and its outcome. But he seems
to have intended this message to galvanize the Spaniards into giving him
more support and probably revealed his true feelings more accurately
when he wrote to Cotton from Valladolid on 9 September. After
discussing recommendations of officers for promotion, he commented:

> . . . I wish you were well. Matters are going on famously. Hill's Corps
> will soon be across the Tagus, & I shall have the whole Army either
> together, or in close communication. The Blockade of Cadiz is raised;
> Seville evacuated & Soult retiring through Andalusia. I am about to
> join here with the [Spanish] Galician Army & to push the French as
> far as I can, & then return with some of the troops particularly the
> Heavy Cavalry towards Madrid. . . .

Wellington followed Clausel north-eastwards for about 160 km, but
did not pursue vigorously; nor did Clausel make a stand. Wellington
entered the city of Burgos on 18 September, but found that the Castle
overlooking the city was held by a French garrison of 2,200 men. He
knew that in his hands, Burgos could block a renewed offensive by the
Army of Portugal and permit him to return south to join Hill should
Soult and Joseph advance on Madrid. It would also effectively block the
main French supply route into Spain and jeopardize their occupation of
the country. Yet Wellington seriously underestimated the difficulties
of taking the Castle. Despite its weak defences, it occupied a naturally
strong position. Moreover, the only effective siege artillery that he had

with his army were three 18pdrs; he also lacked sufficient engineers and ammunition.

Wellington's first attack, on an outlying hornwork, succeeded on the night of 19 September, though at heavy cost. A subsequent assault on the Castle's outer wall failed, largely as it was undertaken with too small a force. A letter from Ensign John Blackman of the Coldstream Guards to his parents on 28 September offers a clue to Wellington's confidence at this stage:

> The siege is going on pretty well & I believe our batteries will open very soon; our men are busy mining &c. &c. – Captain [Charles Mackenzie] Fraser, a very fine young man of our Regiment was wounded severely the other night, when we were trying to make a Lodgement in the Castle, which I am sorry to add through misman-agement did not succeed. – Yesterday being the anniversary of the Battle of Busaco, the Marquis [Wellington] gave a grand dinner. [Lieutenant-Colonel] Sir H. Sullivan of our Regiment was there, he says the Noble Marquis was in high spirits, & discoursed on the late battle, but that he did not mention a word about the Siege, which I fear is rather a fish bone to him at present – The weather continues fine. – Ensign [James] Bradshaw of our regiment retires after the siege is over which will give me a step – Poor [Ensign William] Grimstead continues very unwell, the best thing he can do is to go out. I believe his Father thinks so too – as for myself thank God I never was in better health, and am much stouter than when I left England. – ...

After two more assaults Wellington gained the outer wall on 4 October. Progress was then checked by two French sorties and by heavy rain, which set in after the 7th. The troops were dispirited and, with some exceptions, did their duty reluctantly. A final assault on the 18th failed bloodily, partly as it was made by too few troops in a misguided attempt to limit casualties.

On 21 October, Wellington learnt that Soult and Joseph had united and were marching on Madrid with 60,000 men. To resist them, Hill had only 36,000 and he was over 250 km south of Burgos. In the north, the Army of Portugal, now under General Joseph Souham, was becoming increasingly active.

Wellington, who had lost 2,000 men during the siege, retreated on the night of the 21st. Some 1,300 British and King's German Legion cavalry provided the rearguard with the help of some Spanish irregulars. Lieutenant William Smith of the 11th Light Dragoons marched early on the morning of the 22nd and frankly admitted the indiscipline and confusion that quickly ensued:

Withdrew my vidette at 3 oclock unperceived by the Enemy and marched to Villa Toro where I came up with the Reg^t[.] halted here for some time for Bullock Cars &c to pass[.] the scene between Villa Toro and the high road was shocking. the number of men lying in the mud drunk, some dead, others dying, Bisket and Rum, casks broken, dead horses, oxen, and mules, together with the two 18 Pounders, far exceeded whatever before I could conceive, soon after we arrived on the high road, the Enemy advanced from Burgos indulged us with a cannonade which obliged us to retreat farther than was intended and we got under cover considerably after dark –

Lieutenant Smith added that on the 23rd:

The Enemy came up with us at day break[.] a Cannonading for some time they then charged our skirmishers and pressed us so hard that one Squadron of the 16 L^t D^{rgs} and our Reg^t were obliged to charge in front of Celada-del Camino some confusion and retired behind the Hormasa on which were placed L Col^l Ackett's [Halkett's two light battalions of King's German Legion] Infantry when we again got in order and retreated a Squadron occasionally charging

The German Brigade [of heavy dragoons] joined us near Venta del Pozo they charged came back in disorder[.] our Brigade also charged got intermixed and the confusion all together not to be described[.] had the Enemy behaved well that day they must have played the devil with us

Major William Clowes of the 3rd Dragoons was similarly hard-pressed on the 24th:

March^d in rear of two divisions of the Spaniards by which we were so much retarded as to be in danger of being surrounded by the Enemy – The rear guard of the right Division were roughly handled by the Enemy's Cavalry & [rank and name illegible] was taken Prisoner & halted at 11 P.M & encamp^d on the Hill near the Arlanzon –

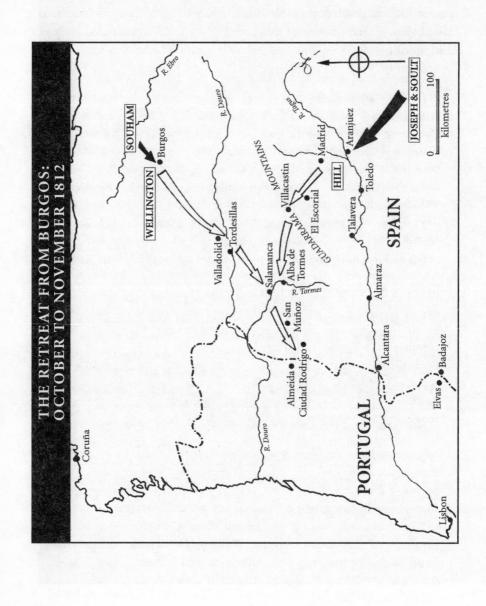

THE RETREAT FROM BURGOS:
OCTOBER TO NOVEMBER 1812

Wellington fell back to the south bank of the Douro, where he intended to rest his troops and contain Souham for as long as he could. Ensign Blackman wrote to his parents on 31 October from near Tordesillas:

... Thank God I got well & safe from the Siege of Burgos, after besieging that Fort for one month, storming &c. &c. The French army advanced in order to relieve the Garrison, & Marquis Wellington thought proper to retire; we have since been marching parallel with the French army who are themselves in the town of Tordesillas, while we are now occupying the ground on this side of the river; the retreat, as I suppose I must call it, has as yet been conducted very well, we shall in all probability remain in our present position 2 or 3 days. I do not recollect having ever heard my dear Grandfather say whether he has ever been employed in a siege, but no doubt he is perfectly acquainted with the nature of that employment, and I dare say will agree with me when I pronounce it, the most harrassing & unpleasant duty in the British service, and attended with no small degree of danger; however I thank God I am as well now as I was before the siege, and have only to lament the death of my friends & companions in arms. First then I must mention poor [Ensign John] Buckeridge, he died nobly whilst doing his duty in the Trenches, and I relieved him instantly in the very place where he received his death. I wrote concerning this unfortunate event, to Mrs Swanton, requesting her to break it gently to the Family. he was a most worthy fellow and I bitterly lament his loss. – Captain [Edward] Harvey who commanded the company I am in, received his death by a musket shot in an advanced part of the Trenches, a few days afterwards, he was a worthy Officer, I was also in the Trenches that day with some other Officers, that evening about 4 Oclock we were ordered to storm, in doing which poor [Ensign Wentworth] Burgess received his death, & Captains [the Hon. William] Croften and [the Hon. John] Walpole were wounded, myself escaped unhurt: Ensign Bradshaw has given in his resignation, and is gone home – I have now only 5 Ensigns before me. – In these events you behold La fortune de guerre [the fortune of war] – ...

Assistant-Surgeon Thomas Maynard of the Coldstream Guards had joined Wellington's army about a week before. He added a few lines to Blackman's letter:

... John and I soon met, and I found him looking much better than ever I saw him do in England which is rather fortunate considering how many have suffered from the wet and the perils of the Trenches at Burgos[.] all that have escaped have escaped at a hair's breadth – You have no idea of the life we lead nor can description give it you; nothing but the trial of it can convince you – ...

Hill now began a corresponding retreat with his part of the army from the River Tagus south of Madrid. One of his men was William Paterson, who had arrived from England that autumn and was a clerk in the Commissariat under Deputy Commissary-General Randal Isham Routh. He was posted at Aranjuez, 43 km south of Madrid, before the retreat began. Paterson admired Routh as a gentleman, but did not get on with the other two men in the office. Routh later wrote his recollections and argued that a commissary should personally know everyone, of whatever rank, who might be attached to him, so that he would be served from personal as well as public motives: 'there is no loss of rank or dignity in carrying out this principle. It is a maxim applicable to all bodies of men called upon to act together, and who never can act in concert if they are strangers to each other. It is a duty still more essential to the Commissary-General, who acquires thereby not only a knowledge of the particular talents and ability, but obtains the good will and co-operation of his Department.'*

These principles certainly helped endear him to Paterson:

... During our few weeks residence in Aranjuez I so far obtained the approbation and confidence of Mr Routh that he gave to my care & management the whole business of the Office, sending to the rear for the purpose of making up some old accounts those two Gentlemen, one a Portuguese and the other an Englishman, whose society was so uncomfortable to me; and with the assistance of only a Portuguese Boy I was left to all the duties of the office which at that time considering my little experience on the Commissariat were sufficiently arduous; I did not however regret the many laborious hours which these duties occasioned to me as I had every reason to believe

---

* R. Routh, *Observations on Commissariat Field Service and Home Defences* (London, 1852), 2nd ed., pp. 28–9.

that my exertions would not be unobserved by a Gentleman like M[r] R. so capable of discriminating –

During this period of quiet at Aranjuez nobody seemd to think of the french army more than if they had been beyond the Pyrenees; Parties were daily making up for Madrid and I believe almost every english officer [words missing] had the satisfaction of spending a few days at that time in this celebrated city, and certainly I also with much pleasure would have visited the Capital of Spain had not I been deterred by the idea of the dreadful expences which were incurred by a few days residence there, which I was neither prepared nor inclined to expend. I was consequently induced to remain at home contenting myself with the idea that my duty would perhaps call me there before the end of the campaign –

This state of tranquillity on which w[e] [word missing] ourselves was towards the end of October very materially disturbed by the approach of the french army under Soult in a force very superior I believe to what General Hill had expected, and who I believe was not well aware of their advance untill within Six or Eight leagues of his Head Quarters, about the 26[h] of October we received an order suddenly to leave Aranjuez, and on the 28[h] all our Troops had crossed the Temporary bridge which had been erected over the Tagus there & which was immediately burned by our Engineers to prevent the French Troops from following us; Another Bridge however was very rapidly erected by the Enemy & in two Days after our crossing the Tagus they were in a situation perfectly capable of following us; in consequence of which orders were issued by Gen[l] Hill to retreat from Bayona the village in which Head Quarters were, and to cross the Harama [Jarama] a river of considerable magnitude [word missing] which falls into the Tagus a little above Aranjuez; Over this River w[as] a large & beautiful bridge [the Puente Larga, 3 km from Aranjuez] which it was the intention of our General [Hill] to blow up in order to prevent the french from harassing our retreat; Orders were in consequence given out at Ten o clock in the evening that every person should pass before Day break in the morning as the Bridge would at that hour be destroyed. This order by omission was not communicated to me before five o clock on the morning appointed for our march, when my Portuguese servant brought the unwelcome intelligence as I was soundly sleeping in a comfortable bed; and in the terror which the information had occasioned he led me to believe that all our Troops had left the village that the french were close upon us and that the Bridge was already, very probably, in Ruins

Well aware however by this time of the cowardly timidity of the Portuguese character I was by no means so much alarmed as the import of the News would have sanctioned. I immediately dressed got my Baggage loaded & after ascertaining the truth of the reports which my servant had not however greatly exaggerated, I proceeded on my march and had the satisfaction of passing the Bridge in perfect safety. In the course of that day or next morning the bridge was however actually attempted to be destroyed but from its extreme solidity and strength it unfortunately withstood the shock of the Gunpowder which only destroyed the walls on each side leaving the arch entire, our brave Troops on this failure of the explosion presented themselves upon the bridge & resultely for a considerable time opposed the advance of the french; the rising grounds however on the opposite banks of the river affording an advantage to the french artillery and a protection to their soldiers they were in consequence enabled to destroy with grape shot many of our men who defended the Bridge till after losing about 150 men we were obliged to retreat into the wood adjoining where the Enemy did not think it safe to follow us . . .

The bridge was defended by Major-General Skerrett's brigade, which was acting as Hill's rearguard. Skerrett in fact lost only about 63 men killed and wounded and retired after dark. French cavalry pursued on 31 October and captured 300 drunken stragglers. But Soult suspended the pursuit after hearing falsely that Wellington was expected at Madrid to fight a battle with his whole army. Hill in fact was never seriously harassed as he fell back.

The abandonment of Madrid resulted in Spanish refugees taking to the roads, for many of the citizens had openly committed themselves to the Allied cause. Hill retreated north-westwards to El Escorial on the southern slopes of the Guadarrama mountains. Paterson on his arrival there noted how badly the retreat had undermined discipline:

. . . [The] Army was now in full retreat every one pressing on in the best manner they could, and as the Escurial is a Town of no great extent it was not of course capable of containing the immense number of British Spanish and Portuguese Troops which that evening entered it, Every hour was bringing in hundreds & the confusion for Quarters consequently every moment increased till at last all order and authority seemd to be at an end & every one availed himself of his own personal power to place himself in the best Quarter he could find.

I obtained no less than [word missing] or four Billets, & by superior force was turned out of every one of them till at last tired & exhausted I was glad to go into a wood adjoining with a Spaniard who pitched a tent and afforded me a part of it

During the whole of the night nothing but noise and Confusion was in the Town of Escurial, & even in our Distant retreat in the wood we heard Doors & windows breaking open attended with every other appalling Circumstance which may be Conceived to follow the regardless actions of retreating Troops.

On the day preceeding, the melancholy effects of a retreat were also worthy of remark particularly on our march from Cunpazuelas [Ciempozuelos] to Madrid where the road was Completely Covered with the flying Inhabitants.

Horses Mules & asses were every where in crowding the highway, some conveying women & children others the most Valuable of the poor creatures effects & others Led by Boys were bearing Grey Headed men who hardly were enabled to support themselves on the backs of the Animals and whose lives seemed so nearly worn to the last extremity that flying from the French Army seemed only to be the means of shortening their few Days by the fatigue of a march which their exhausted frames seemd incapable of supporting ...

Between 1 and 3 November, Hill crossed the Guadarramas. Paterson revealed that:

... On our march to this place [El Espinar, 18 km north-west of El Escorial] we passed over the famous pass of the Guadarama which in some places is so narrow & the rocks on each side of the road so steep and so rugged that more than Six or eight men Could not go over abreast and as there is no other passable road for many leagues round it becomes a place of the utmost importance to a army, particularly on a retreat, as it enables them, with a very small proportion of men, to defend the Narrow passage against any army however numerous. At this moment our Troops were in full retreat

& the whole extent of the pass as far as the Eye could carry was covered with soldiers & as we were nearly in the rear it was some hours untill we could obtain the height of the Gaudarama mountains, so slow was the progress of the Troops in this Narrow and confined way. . . .

On 4 November Hill concentrated his force at Villacastin. Wellington was still on the Douro, 85 km to the north-west, so that they each covered each other's rear. They intended to unite near Salamanca, 80 km to the west.

Wellington at the end of October had noted that he might be unable to hold on along the Douro and had ordered Hill to be prepared to retreat by a more southerly route, along the valley of the Tagus. But Hill would no longer require this route, or the provisions stockpiled along it. Paterson reveals that after reaching El Espinar, he and Routh were ordered immediately to remove the large stores deposited at Talavera and Truxillo to the safety of Badajoz. If this could not be accomplished before the French came up, the provisions were to be destroyed.

While Paterson successfully removed these stores, Hill continued his retreat and by 8 November had linked up with Wellington near Salamanca. Wellington now had 70,000 British, Portuguese and Spanish troops in hand. The French armies could field a combined total of 90,000 men. But Soult, who had taken overall command, hesitated to make a general attack and instead decided to outflank Wellington and threaten his line of communications with Portugal. On 14 November, he crossed the River Tormes 25 km to the south of Salamanca. Wellington shifted his army southwards in response to this move. He personally arrived before the French bridgehead towards noon and seems to have hesitated whether to attack, but decided not to risk it. At dusk, he fell back to his old battlefield at Salamanca, where he took up a strong position, apparently being ready to accept a defensive battle should the French make the mistake of attacking him frontally.

But Soult on the 15th outflanked Wellington to the south and forced him to retreat without a fight on Ciudad Rodrigo, 85 km to the south-west. The baggage and stores had already been evacuated from Salamanca. Unfortunately, they were sent by Colonel James Willoughby Gordon, Wellington's Quartermaster-General, by a northerly route that was more secure but too far from the troops, who were left without provisions. The result was a breakdown of discipline as Wellington retreated on 15–19 November. The situation was worsened by torrential rain.

First Lieutenant George Belson of 'A' Troop, Royal Horse Artillery sheds a new light on Wellington's supposedly harsh character. His diary entry for 16 November reads:

> ... [Second Captain Alexander] Macdonald was sent back this morning (his division [two guns] being the rear one) by an order from Lord Wellington with one gun, to bring on a drunken man upon it, whom his Lordship in passing had mistaken for a sick, & knocked up man. – He went back about a mile to the camp for him. – There was a great deal of musquetry last night throughout from about 8 p.m., & was at one time so heavy, that we supposed it was skirmishing, but Lᵗ Col [Charles] Rowan the A.A.G. [Assistant Adjutant-General] Lᵗ division rode out some distance to our rear and found it was the soldiers shooting pigs, whom they saw in the woods, feeding on acorns, the men being without rations. – Hd. qrs. were last night in the little village in front of the bivouac. – The whole column moving on this road had halted in this same wood close at the skirt of it, & from their leaving no space at the extremity of the wood, the Light division, & ourselves, were obliged to bivouac in the centre of the column, on the left side of the road. Owing to this firing last night, the 7ᵗʰ divⁿ sounded their bugles, & stood to their arms for some time, untill it was known that all was quiet, and a false alarm. – ...

Wellington retreated in three columns to ease congestion, but on the 17th his centre column was left without a cavalry rearguard, apparently through another error by Colonel Gordon. It was attacked near San Muñoz on the River Huebra, 38 km north-east of Ciudad Rodrigo. Major William Clowes of the 3rd Dragoons commented:

> The army retir'd as before but after commencing its march part of the Cavalry were ordered to join the Centre & left Columns & on their march thereto received counter orders – This was a day of great confusion, & which with the delay occasion'd there by & the fatigued state of the Troops our losses must have been very great – ...

The Light Division provided the rearguard of the centre column. In its ranks was Lieutenant Gairdner of the 95th Rifles, who in his account of the 17th criticized Lieutenant-General Sir William Erskine, the notoriously erratic commander of the 2nd Cavalry Division:

The baggage was ordered off some time before the column moved[.] The column moved at ab^t ½ past 7. the roads as they were yesterday miserably bad the weather very cold – we had not moved on far before we were halted that is to say the 1st brigade the Compys equallized to be ready to form a square* our Compy was sent to the front to look out – after ab^t half an hour we moved on again for ab^t a mile and made another halt for nearly an hour. all this time the enemies Cavalry were skirmishing with ours – we then moved on[.] after some time the enemies Cavalry and ours still skirmishing in our rear, we percieved some of the enemies Cavalry on our left flank part of our Compy was out as a flank patrole they fired some shots at the Cavalry – some of their Cavalry rode in upon the column of the 7th Div^n which was just on our front & fired into them they having no flank patroles[.] They also charged some sick and baggage who were between us and the 7th Div^n and took several, Lieut Cameron of our 2nd batt^n [95th Rifles] who was in charge of the sick was taken they rifled his Pockets took away his horse & shoes & let him go again. Lieut: Genl Sir A [Edward] Paget who was 2nd in command to L^{ord} Wellington was taken prisoner ab^t the same time – soon after Genl Erskine told [Major-]Genl [Charles] Alten [the commander of the Light Division] that it was necessary one brigade of the Light Division should halt to cover the retreat of his cavalry across the river Huebra which was just in our front – our brigade was accordingly halted and while Genl Alten was remonstrating with Erskine Ld Wellington very luckily for us came up and ordered us to retire immediately, we were hard enough pushed as it was if we had retired 5 minutes later, God knows what would have been the consequence – at this time we thought that they had nothing up but cavalry they however pushed on their infantry just as we approached the river – The ground on the immediate bank of the river is quite flat, but there is a ridge of very commanding heights on the right bank of the river on which

---

* The companies of a battalion had to have similar numbers of men to ensure that the sides of its square were equal.

the enemy planted their artillery immediately on our quitting them and commenced cannonading us as we crossed the ford, they killed and wounded some of our men – we found the artillery of our Division drawn up on the left bank of the river returning the enemies fire, also our the [sic] rest of our Division & the 7th Division drawn up in columns –

They continued shelling and cannonading our columns & they sent a great quantity of infantry to our left and down towards the river, 2 Compys of the 1st battn [95th] Viz Grey's & MacNamara's were sent out to skirmish down to the bank of the river the other four Compys of the 1st Battn were sent down towards the river and formed in line[.] some of the 52nd [Regiment's] Compys were out skirmishing & Poor [Captain Henry] Dawson (whose Compy was one) was killed – [Lieutenant George] Ridout of the 43rd was wounded by a cannon shot which was thrown into the column there were several other officers of the Divn wounded but none of our Regt. We continued cannonading and skirmishing untill dark – we lay all night on the ground on which we formed line the 2 Compys remaining in front (where they had been skirmishing) as a Piquet – it rained very hard all night we of course had no baggage; there was a little beef issued – by great good luck I got [Captain Jonathan] Leach to carry my boat cloak when the baggage was sent off this morning, otherwise I should have had nothing to lye in; independent of the rain it was a bitter cold night –

I am convinced that if we had not made those 2 long halts at the commencement of the march we should have crossed the ford without interruption. –

First Lieutenant George Belson, who commanded two guns of 'A' Troop, Royal Horse Artillery, offered a different perspective of the same action in his diary. He described how the Light Division's two brigades retired alternately to cover each other, but noted that they were impeded by the slow marching of the preceding divisions, which would explain the halts of which Gairdner was so critical. The Light Division near San Muñoz was in danger of being outflanked by the French cavalry and its regiments formed squares before retreating across the River Huebra. Lieutenant Belson decribed how:

... Previous to their moving off each front rank knelt & loaded as if expecting an attack from the enemy, at which moment I was ordered off by M. [Major Hew Dalrymple] Ross [the commander of 'A' Troop] with the 2 guns down yᵉ main road, & across the ford near San Munoz, & to make the best of my way when I shortly overtook [Second Captain Alexander] Macdonald with 1 gun & [Second Captain George] Jenkinson when we turned off to the left in a very deep ploughed field on the side & half way down the hill in front of San Munõz to which M. Genˡ [John] Slade's brigade of heavy Cavalry (Royˡˢ & 3ʳᵈ Dⁿ Gds.) & some few Portuguese had recrossed from the opposite side of the stream. – We had not remained here many minutes when we retired, the brigade of Cavalry with us, & just as we entered the ford the enemy's first gun opened from above the height we had last quitted, whose shot pitched close to the ford, & the dragoons galloped thro' the ford at the same time as the 3 guns passed, headed by the M. Genˡ.

. . .

As soon as we had crossed the ford we found Capt. [George] Lefebure's (D) troop under [Second Captain Edward] Whinyates, & Major [Robert] Macdonald's (E) troop engaged with the enemy's Artillery the former on the side of the road nearest San Munõz & the latter on the left of the road. – The enemy shewed no Infʸ whatever, so that our cannonade was solely confined against their Artillery. – The enemy had at first only 4 guns on the height above San Munõz, but he soon afterwards brought up two others on the height to the right of the other 4, & against Major M's troop principally. Major M. was here wounded on the thigh with a shell, which laid it open to the bone, & both troops lost some few men in killed, & wounded. – Marshal Soult & staff were witnessing the cannonade to the left of the enemy's 4 guns (all 4 prs, but one 6 inch howitzer) just above the village. – The cannonade on both sides lasted till quite dusk, & the 20ᵗʰ Portuguese regᵗ under Lᵗ Col. Pryer formed in line, (& recently posted to the light division since their junction with the Army at Madrid from Cadiz.) immediately in rear of Major Macdonald's guns as a support during the whole time, & behaved admirably steady. – The remᵍ regᵗˢ of the light division were lower down the stream skirmishing with the Enemy's Infʸ, who endeavoured to cross it, but were driven back. – Capt [Henry] Dawson of the 52ⁿᵈ was here shot dead, Capt [Thomas] Fuller d[itt]o. [i.e. 52nd] badly wounded in the right knee pan & [Lieutenant George] Ridout 43ʳᵈ badly wounded in the ancle, & since dead at Ciudad Rodrigo. The light division lost about 150 men killed & wounded throughout the affair. – The rain fell in torrents the whole of this afternoon, & night, particularly just as the action commenced. – Lord Wellington determined on maintaining his ground here for the night, (as he had previously fixed upon it as the day's halt,) & we bivouaced in a wood with the whole army contiguous to us, & just across that stream for the night, on a small rise just above it. . . .

Wellington withdrew the next day, 18 November. The French had also suffered during the last few days and now discontinued the pursuit. Wellington's army had reached cantonments and regular supplies by the end of the 19th. The retreat was over, but it had cost nearly 5,000 men. The drunkenness and straggling of the final four days after leaving Salamanca accounted for a disproportionate share of this loss. In addition, 36 per cent of Wellington's British troops were listed as sick on 29 November.

William Morris on 13 December was at Pinhel, 50 km north-west of Ciudad Rodrigo:

this day a most unpleasant one it raind almost incessantly the whole of ye Day[.] our rains in England are little more than dews compared with the rains which fall in this country no Garments except Oil cases seem proof against its effects[.] I think it may be attributed in a great measure to the wetness of the season the Ague & fevers so prevalent at this time of year[.] it is astonishing the number of sick troops which pass thro here . . .

Wellington faced some bitter criticism from within his army as a result of the siege of Burgos and the subsequent retreat. Ensign John Blackman had written to his parents from near Salamanca on 11 November:

. . . if not the most brilliant I think you will allow it [the 1812 campaign] to have been the most active campaign we have experienced in the Peninsula: it would undoubtedly have received an additional brilliancy, had we succeeded in the capture of the Castle of Burgos, but that siege will serve as a lesson to the Noble Marquis not to proceed in future *so hastily* to a place of that kind, without sufficient cannon for batteries, thereby thinking *light* of it, and sacrificing his men, without being able to gain the proposed end – . . .

Wellington for his part issued a memorandum to his senior subordinates on 28 November, harshly criticizing the disgraces that had occurred during the retreat. The contents soon became common knowledge and caused considerable discontent. In fact, his criticisms were to a large extent justified. Major-General Long, for example, thought that the conduct of the troops throughout the retreat had been most vandalic and that not even the enemy could have behaved worse or done more mischief to the inhabitants and their dwellings. But Wellington in moments of anger generally failed to target his reprimands sufficiently at those responsible and instead issued blanket condemnations. Lieutenant George Woodberry of the 18th Hussars, newly arrived in the Peninsula, noted the consequences on 3 February 1813:

> ... a Lieut. Wallis 52nd Regt. refused this day after dinner to drink Lord Wellingtons health. – I find he [Wellington] is very much disliked by all the officers who have come from the army: – he was at Lisbon last week – He made a grand Entry into the Town and nothing but Viva de Granda Lord – was heard from every Portuguese. . . .

Yet the 1812 campaign, despite the bitter disappointment of its final phase, had dramatically altered the balance in the Peninsula. The French had permanently abandoned southern Spain, were demoralized and, as a result of Napoleon's disastrous invasion of Russia that year, could not count on any reinforcements. In contrast, the Spanish guerrillas were bolder than ever and the keys to Spain – Ciudad Rodrigo and Badajoz – remained firmly in Wellington's hands. The tide had finally turned against the French.

6

Wellington and his Peninsular Army

Major-General Robert Long explained in a letter to his brother on 14
March 1812 that he had never been a soldier at heart:

> ... I dislike butchery in all its shapes & forms, & of all kinds of
> butchery that of the human species is to me the most odious – No
> ambition, no love of reputation can conquer this feeling – A Profes-
> sion that is at constant war with one's feelings cannot be an agreeable
> one – Lord W. talks of *expending* such & such Battalions in such &
> such affairs, as you would talk of expending so much shot & powder
> on the 1ˢᵗ Sepᵗ. To him War must have every charm that can fascinate
> a man's heart – He is a *thorough-bred* Soldier – I make a distinction
> between the duty that summons every man to the field to defend his
> own country & rights – but Armies which are formed for other
> purposes, (& all of them are) shᵈ be made up of Volunteers; those
> who adopt the profession from preference & predilection – who love
> War as a trade in all its forms & features, & follow what they like –
> I say honestly that *I* have no business among *this* class of men, for I
> dislike the thing & always have. . . .

Wellington in fact felt the butchery of battle deeply, particularly
after Talavera, Badajoz and Vitoria and he broke down and wept after
Waterloo. But, as Long's letter shows, he successfully hid his innermost
feelings from those under his command in order to project an imperturbable image.

Lieutenant George Woodberry of the 18th Hussars gives a fascinating
glimpse of the great man in his journal on 14 May 1813:

> ... Freneida [Freinada], the Headquarters of the British Army is
> within 3 leagues of this place [Freixedas], it is much such another
> village as this & Marquis Wellington is quarter'd in a Wretched
> House, his room of audiance is so low that Colonel Grant [a tall

man] could hardly stand upright in it. he hunts every other morning. his dress yesterday was, Blue Coat White Waiscoat White [illegible] & Grey Overals & round Hat – he is an Extraordinary man for the following morning after the famous retreat from the neighbourhood of Burgos to his present cantonments he order'd the Hounds out & was acturely hunting himself – his dress is always very plain & he swears like a Trooper at any thing that does not please him he's remarkably fond of the Portugueses & listens to any complaint made to him against the English but never any made by the English agt. them: –

Wellington for his part had no illusions about his soldiers. He claimed that they were 'the very scum of the earth' and that it was really 'wonderful that we should have made them the fine fellows they are'.* Since there was no conscription into the British regular army it depended on volunteers and few men joined if they had an alternative. Military service was brutal and the army widely resented as a result of its role in enforcing law and order. Many men enlisted simply to escape unemployment, starvation or a hard master. As soldiers, they were paid less than farm labourers, but had at least secure employment while the wars lasted. Many recruits were irresistibly tempted by the cash bounty, which could be equivalent to four months of a farm labourer's wages. It was only later that they discovered that a deduction was made for necessary items of equipment. Wellington himself ridiculed the notion that recruits enlisted for patriotic reasons and claimed that some joined after fathering illegitimate children and many more for alcohol. A few were fugitives from justice. Each battalion had a hard core of perhaps fifty criminals who were responsible for much of the desertion and looting that Wellington was so keen to control. Discipline had to be strict and included the use of flogging. Sentences of as many as 300 lashes were commonplace.

Recruiting parties on their own were unable to supply the necessary manpower. The Government therefore looked to the Militia, which was permanently embodied in wartime for home defence. Militiamen provided about half the regular army's recruits: they often volunteered for

* Earl Stanhope, *Notes of Conversations with the Duke of Wellington 1831–1851* (London, 1938), p. 18.

better motives, such as a desire for adventure, and had already received a year's drill, discipline and training.

An anonymous soldier of the 38th Regiment explained how he joined the army. He had been for some years in mental turmoil about his sinful state and had left home at the age of ten to become an apprentice:

> ... I felt assured that real happiness Could not be enjoyed in this world without real Religion in that agatated and perplexed State I Lived untill I had attained to 16 years of Age[.] I Then formed this resolution in my own mind To run away from my apprentiship and go To Leicester and if I Could get into Work I would form no acquintance with ane one But keep from all Company and Strive to Live A better Life[.] But I soon found all my Promeses being made in my own Strength To be weak as Water for when the first Sabbath Came after I got to Leicester I felt Enclined to go to Chappell I set off with that Intent but as I wass going the Enemy of souls Beset me with these thoughts you have no Place to go to sit and you are A stranger all The people will be looking at you and youl Feel so much Ashamed these thoughts did So oporate upon my mind and over pourred me So much that I beleive I only went twice to A descinting [Dissenting] place of Worship while I stayed in Leicester[.] when I wass 17 I engaged as A Soldier in The 38 reg^t of foot I then began to think I might give Up all thoughts of religion for I should have so much to Occupy my mind that it would be imposible for me To attend to that So I began to try to Stifle my Convictions By giving way to all kind of Enoquitey and O the Wonderfull Goodness and mercy of God that I wass not Left to fill up the measure of my Enoquitey and perish Which I Carred on to sutch Lengths as to astonish those Arround me indeed I was so much adicted to that I felt Myself Completly mesirable when I had any time to Spare if I Could not be Either at a Publick house Singing Songs or at the Card table. ...

An anonymous soldier of the 71st Regiment joined the army in July 1806 after quarrelling with his parents about his determination on a career in the theatre and subsequently being overcome with stage fright. He met a recruiting party, but being an educated man from a respectable family did not like army life:

... Now I begun to drink the cup of bitterness[.] How different was my situation from what it had been! Forced from bed at five O Clock each morning, to get ready for drill; then drilled for three hours with the most unfeeling vigour, and often beat by the Sergeant for the faults of others. I, who had never been crossed at home – I, who never knew fatigue, was now fainting under it. this I bore without a murmur as I had looked to it in my engagement. My greatest sufferings were where I had not expected them.

I could not associate with the common soldiers their habits made me shudder. I feared and [sic] oath – they never spoke without one: I could not drink – they loved liquor: they gamed I knew nothing of play. thus was I a solitary individual among hundreds . . .

In describing the retreat to Coruña, he supported Wellington's claim that soldiers enlisted for drink:

... the great fault of our soldiers, at this time, was an inordinate desire for Spirits of any kind.

. . .

So great was their propensity to drown their misery in liquor, that we were often exposed to cold and rain, for a whole night, in order that we might be kept from the wine stores of a neighbouring town . . .

Whatever their faults, the rank and file were long-service professionals. A limited service scheme was introduced in 1806, under which recruits could join for a limited initial period. In the infantry, for example, this was seven years. But most recruits still signed up for life.

Infantry regiments usually had territorial titles as well as numbers, but were rarely composed predominantly of men from their local districts. This was partly because recruiting parties could not afford to restrict their activities to local areas and partly as volunteers from the Militia were not directed into joining their local regiments. In fact, at least a fifth of the soldiers in the vast majority of English regiments were Irishmen. A good example is provided by an account book showing the income and expenditure of Lieutenant George Cocke's recruiting party of the 2nd Battalion, 57th Regiment between December 1808 and November 1809. The 57th's territorial designation was West Middlesex, but Lieutenant Cocke himself had joined as a volunteer from the West Essex Militia. Furthermore, his account book records his recruiting party marching between Haverhill in Suffolk and Maidstone in Kent. It was not unusual for parties to recruit even further afield, particularly in the great cities such as London, Edinburgh, Glasgow, Liverpool and Birmingham. A return of the 859 NCOs and men of the 1st Battalion, 57th Regiment on 9 May 1809 showed that only sixty per cent were English. Thirty-four per cent were Irish, four per cent Scottish and the other two per cent were foreigners.* The majority of the Highland and Irish Regiments were exceptional in being recruited predominantly from their local region.

The sort of persuasion used to entice recruits is shown by a recruitment poster of the 7th Hussars, which was printed in 1809 soon after the Regiment's return from Coruña. The 7th needed to replace both the casualties it had suffered on campaign and the seventy men lost on the way home when a troopship had been wrecked off the Cornish coast:

THE OLD SAUCY
SEVENTH,

Or Queen's Own Regt. of
Lt. Dragoons.

COMMANDED BY THAT GALLANT AND WELL KNOWN HERO
Lieut. General
HENRY LORD PAGET.

YOUNG Fellows whose hearts beat high to tread the paths of Glory, could not have a better opportunity than now offers. Come forward then, and Enrol yourselves in a Regiment that stands unrivalled, and where the kind treatment, the Men ever experienced is well known throughout the whole Kingdom.

*Each Young Hero on being approved, will receive
the largest Bounty allowed by Government.*

*A few smart Young Lads, will be taken at Sixteen Years of Age,
5 Feet 2 Inches, but they must be active, and well limbed.
Apply to SERJEANT HOOPER, at [left blank]*

―――――――

*N.B. This Regiment is mounted on Blood Horses, and being lately
returned from SPAIN, and the Horses Young, the Men will not be
allowed to HUNT during the next Season, more than once a week*

―――――――

―――――――

* H. Woollright, *History of the Fifty-Seventh (West Middlesex) Regiment of Foot 1755–1881* (London, 1893), p. 399.

The Regimental Letter Book offers a more realistic insight into a soldier's life and suggests an additional reason why the 7th needed recruits following Coruña. On 15 February, Lieutenant-Colonel Hussey Vivian wrote from Guildford Barracks to inform the Inspector-General of Hospitals of the result of the fever that had been afflicting the regiment since its return from Spain:

> I think it absolutely necessary to report to you the the [sic] State of the 7ᵗʰ Regiment of Hussars, we have at present in the Hospital 110 men Sick – and the number daily Encreasing – I have every reason to beleive that the utmost possible attention is paid by the Surgeon, but still I think the Case so alarming that some other steps should be taken, and if possible an Inspector of Hospitals sent to Examine into it.

New recruits had to be taken before a magistrate or justice of the peace to swear an oath of loyalty to the King and attest that they were fit and legally entitled to enlist. They could reverse their decision, by paying within twenty-four hours any money that they had received and a fine, called smart money.

A printed General Order issued on 27 August 1813 by the Adjutant-General, Lieutenant-General Sir Harry Calvert, indicates the intensity of the competition for recruits:

> There is reason to believe that certain Persons employed on the Recruiting Service, have advanced Money to Recruits engaged with other Parties to enable them to pay the Smart Money with a view to their afterwards enlisting in the Regiments to which they themselves belong: – Any Person who may hereafter be guilty of this practice, which is highly injurious to the Public Service, will be considered as guilty of disobedience of Orders and will be punished in the most exemplary manner.

The pressure to obtain recruits sometimes led to unsatisfactory results. On 23 May 1808, for example, Lieutenant-Colonel Vivian requested the Duke of York to order the disposal of twenty-five-year-old Martin Pearson, who had been enlisted by a recruiting party on 4 May. Under 'Cause of objection', Vivian noted: 'Too heavy & clumsy for a Light Dragoon. Weighs 14ˢᵗᵒⁿᵉ 2ˡᵇˢ'.

Another potential problem was highlighted by a letter of complaint

from Captain Drake of the 56th (or the West Essex) Regiment of Foot
to Major Edward Hodge of the 7th Hussars, written from Reading on 24
July 1814:

> I am extremely sorry to be under the necessity of reporting to you
> the disgraceful, and unsoldierlike conduct, of Serg^t York belonging
> to the 7th Hussars, who was ordered to march with his party yester-
> day for Romford, according to Route, and sent a Serg^t of mine to
> see them out of Town, to my great astonishment found that Serg^t
> York had returned last night and had been in a state of extreme
> intoxication, and living with a Vile Prostitute whom he has taken
> to the Reg^t with him, he has contracted several Debts which sums
> I have enclos'd for your perusal, and at the same time beg leave to
> recommend to your notice, acting Corp^l Wm Robson Private Ab^m
> Atkins & John Harbor for their general good conduct, while under
> my command

The British army had traditionally boosted its manpower with foreigners, particularly German mercenaries, and despite Napoleon's occupation of Europe was able to maintain a number of foreign units. The
most outstanding of them was the King's German Legion, whose
regiments in the Peninsula established a reputation for courage and
professionalism. Wellington also had the less reliable Brunswick Corps
and Chasseurs Britanniques, which both suffered from high desertion
rates. In addition, he had incorporated Portuguese formations into his
army and throughout the war benefited from the cooperation of Spanish
regular and guerrilla forces. In 1812, he even used Spanish recruits to fill
the ranks of depleted British regiments, as Lieutenant-Colonel Warre
described in a letter to his father on 28 May:

> ... Lord Wellington has adopted a new plan in order to derive a
> more effectual assistance from the Spaniards[.] Each *British* Regi-
> ment, except the Guards & Dragoons are allowed to enlist 10 men p^r
> Comp^y of a certain stature, 5f. 6. Inches who are to be in every
> respect treated as British soldiers, to serve as long as the army
> remains in the Peninsula and then to have a months pay to take
> them to their homes, I think it a most excellent plan, and I have very
> little doubt we shall very soon get the whole number 5000. & they
> will make excellent recruits, for in point of activity & fineness of
> appearance, the Spanish Peasantry are certainly inferior to none, and

this measure may hereafter serve as a foundation for a more regular Spanish army. and Napoleon will be greatly annoyed at our having adopted this means of filling up our casualties, without draining England, & with recruits little inferior to our own in appearance or Phisycal strength . . .

Private Edward Costello of the 95th Rifles recorded that his battalion towards the end of 1812 sent out recruiting parties to nearby villages and soon had ten or twelve recruits for each company. The Spaniards explained that their only alternatives were to enter the British service, join Don Julian Sanchez's guerrillas or be hanged. 'Many of them were made corporals, and, indeed, proved themselves worthy of their new comrades, whom they rivalled in every undertaking of courage and determination.'*

The Battle of Vitoria in June 1813 was one of the British army's greatest victories. But only about half of Wellington's men at that battle had actually been born in the British Isles.

*

Wellington's regimental officers were more capable than is often supposed. Only a small minority were aristocrats or landed gentry. Most came from the professional classes and many were the sons of officers. The purchase system, whereby infantry and cavalry officers had opportunities to purchase ranks up to lieutenant-colonel, was limited and its worst abuses had been checked by the Duke of York as Commander-in-Chief. In particular, officers had to serve in each rank for a minimum period before becoming eligible for promotion. During the Peninsular War, only 20 per cent of promotions went by purchase, the vast majority instead being decided by seniority. The result was an officer corps that was more experienced and professional than is often thought.

Officers in the Royal Artillery and Royal Engineers were promoted solely by seniority and received formal training. Most infantry and cavalry officers, in contrast, joined their regiments without any prior military education. A small proportion were taught as cadets at the newly established Royal Military College; others transferred from the Militia and some served in the ranks of the regular army as volunteers

---

* E. Costello, *Adventures of a Soldier* (London, 1852), pp. 145–6.

until a vacancy arose for an ensign. But most learned their duties while performing them.

Ensign William Cameron was among those who had professional instruction after joining his regiment. He joined the 1st Foot Guards in 1809 at the age of seventeen and wrote to his mother from London on 30 August:

> As this is the first letter I have had an opportunity of writing you since entering on my military career I have yet to express how much I feel sensible of your kindness in having thus readily yielded your consent to a measure which has so much promoted my present happiness & leads me to entertain most pleasing prospects of the future – In fact I have now every wish gratifyed; Every step which could have been, certainly has been taken on the part of my Dearest parents to ensure my welfare & on myself alone does all hereafter depend –
>
> The being situated in Town [London] too gives me, independent of many other advantages, the opportunity of pursuing those studies connected with a military profession & which are indispensably necessary to any future success. This another situation would probably by no means admit of, certainly not with equal facility – The temptations here to deviate from a prescribed line of good conduct are no doubt very many; but, they are every where to be met with sufficiently numerous & in almost an equal variety of forms to lead to every excess, when once the disposition is inclined to yield – These temptations indisputably require a certain degree of resolution to overcome, as many are seen to be drawn away by them but aided by the advice of my Dear Parents & Friends & with some resolution on my own part I hope myself to make a successful opposition –
>
> . . .
>
> Amongst other reformations in my system I have adopted that of more early rising & am generally up at 7 o'Clock never later than half past. I study regularly six hours in the day & my watch before me regulates the time I allow for each study, by this I would mean those studies for which I have Masters, viz Fortification French & Perspective Drawing – The Evening after Dinner is employed in reading different military Books. The above-mentioned masters attend me twice a week, all of them on Tuesdays & Saturdays, that I may have

time to digest the information I receive & otherwise prepare for them
between each visit. The Gentleman in *Perspective*, (you must know
the *boy* attends me in the absence of the master from Town) is with
me at seven in the morning. The Frenchman at 9 & the Fortifying
Gentleman at 12 – Amongst my instructors I forgot to mention the
noble Sergeant, who has been drilling me every morning from 11 till
12 since Thursday last & tells me a few more lessons will enable me
to go thro' the requisite Duties – I shall therefore soon become an
efficient member of the Battalion, which is now quartered in Portman
Street Barracks here to remain for six months to come, which makes
it extremely convenient to me – . . .

Courage and the willingness to lead by example were the most
important qualities in subaltern officers. Cases of cowardice were rare,
the most notorious being that of Lieutenant-Colonel Sir Nathaniel
Peacocke of the 71st Regiment at St Pierre in December 1813, when he
ordered his battalion to retire and galloped to the rear, where he was
found beating some Portuguese ammunition-carriers. More common
were officers who overstayed their leave in Lisbon, neglected their routine
duties or were guilty of financial or other irregularities. But the majority
were brave, capable and imbued with a strong sense of personal and
regimental honour.

Wellington was insistent that officers should not carry their private
baggage on wheeled transport, as this would have impeded the army
unacceptably. He also tried to limit the number of baggage animals that
they could have according to their rank. Officers would usually buy the
necessary beasts on arrival in Portugal and would hire Portuguese or
Spanish servants, often of dubious honesty, to look after them.

Ensign John Blackman of the Coldstream Guards reached the Peninsula in March 1812 and acquired two mules, one for riding and the
other to carry his baggage. He set off inland to join Wellington's army,
but on his first day's march, the baggage mule collapsed under the
weight, forcing him to share the load with the other animal and walk on
foot. He then obtained an ass, on which he could ride, but he explained
to his father on 24 May:

. . . I had not been in camp with them 2 days or rather 2 nights
before I lost my baggage mule, a thing that *frequently* happens in
camp, as the inhabitants seize every possible opportunity of stealing

them away; and every thing being new to me I could not be supposed to manage so well as those older in the service . . .

Since he had to march the next day, he bought a mule, but it turned out to be so weak that he had to sell it after one day's march at a loss of seventy-five dollars. He walked for the next three or four days before buying a fine mule from a Coldstream Guards captain. He sold his ass, which had become exhausted, for the price he had paid for it and bought a baggage pony, so that he was finally equipped with a riding mule, a baggage mule and a baggage pony.

Assistant-Surgeon Thomas Maynard of the Coldstream Guards wrote on 3 May 1813 to Blackman's father to allay fears that his young friend had been extravagant:

> . . . the fact is this that beasts do absolutely run away with all our money; they are in the hands of men who care not how they use them, & for all the comfort we are to enjoy we are compelled to look to our horses & mules, – we must therefore have them, and feed them. The Ensigns are particularly badly off in point of forage & Corn, they are allowed but for half a beast & they must have three at least the consequence is that food must be purchased and that at a most exorbitant rate. Now add to all this the wear & tear & their turning out ill adds much to what one might reasonably calculate upon.
>
> . . .
>
> There is one thing which he tells me you have recommended him to do, that is to sell his riding pony: this I have taken the liberty decidedly to oppose my veto: health is a consideration paramount to every thing, and the climate the roads & the service all require the help of a riding animal. Every serjeant keeps a beast of some kind, who can, and I would throw away half my baggage before I would part with my riding pony – Our marches sometimes lie through plains almost entirely under water and through for[ds] up to a man's breast & these so frequently occu[r] as to try one's strength & constitution. Besides an officer's duty is not done when the march is over, he has to go on picquet, or some more active duty perhaps, on legs that would require other usage than standing or running all night. No, let him keep his riding horse at all events. . . .

Each regiment's camp followers included not only twenty to thirty servants with the baggage, but also women and children. Four or six soldiers' wives were allowed to accompany each of an infantry battalion's ten companies from England and a similar proportion was set for the cavalry. Limits on their numbers were strictly enforced. Lieutenant George Simmons of the 95th Rifles landed at Ostend on 27 April 1815:

... Previous to leaving England, the Colonel had issued a most stringent order to the 6 Companies that no Soldier's wife would be allowed to accompany her husband on service under any pretence whatever. – You may guess his astonishment, standing on the wharf to see the Companies land, he observed Corporal Pitt with his wife leaning on his arm, he said, Corporal, you have disobeyed my order, put your wife on board the vessel instantly, or I will bring you to a Court Martial. Sir, my wife was separated from me when I went to the Peninsular War, & I had rather die than be parted from her again. Very well then, take the consequences, the woman was put in charge of a party & taken on board. – A Drum-head Court Martial was held on the spot, the Corporal was reduced to a Private soldier & sentenced to receive *300 lashes*. – The Companies that had arrived were formed to witness the punishment, we were all very sorry for the Corporal as he was a good & brave soldier. I knew him well, he had been in a great many actions in the Peninsula with me but there was no help for it, orders must be obeyed. Accidentally the two Doctors had not yet landed [n]or was their vessel in sight, & the man was tied up to receive his punishment the Colonel in this dilemma observed me, George Simmons you see how disagreeably I am placed with you, act as surgeon (it flashed across me that by doing so I could abridge the number of lashes) so I agreed to do it & stepped forward to superintend it. After the man had received 100. lashes I said, stop, I addressed the Colonel saying it is my opinion the man has had enough. Do you say so, I do Sir! then take him down. I think at the moment, I gave pleasure to every man present, for they knew well that if the surgeon had been there he would not have dared to do so. Some short time after the Colonel said George Simmons you are a good fellow, you did exactly what I wished you to do. I was very sorry to be compelled to punish that man, but for the force of example & landing in a Foreign country I had no other alternative, although I dislike flogging as much as any man. ...

Soldiers' wives, together with women collected locally while on campaign, were a mixed blessing. They often straggled or impeded the army, particularly during a retreat, and were as notorious for plundering as were the men. Ensign Edward Macready of the 30th Regiment called them 'the most callous and insensible creatures in existence.' But theirs was a hard existence; they received half-rations but were unpaid except for what they could earn by cleaning and mending clothes for the men of their battalions. Widows usually remarried quickly from necessity, but many women were fiercely devoted to their husbands. During Hill's retreat from Madrid in 1812, Mrs Biddy Skiddy saved her husband by carrying him on her back for 2–3 km, along with his musket and knapsack. At the end of the Peninsular War, Wellington issued a General Order on 26 April 1814 that all the Spanish and Portuguese women with his army should be sent back to their homes unless they were legitimately married to a soldier. This led to terrible scenes and some men deserted rather than abandon their women.

A few officers' wives also accompanied their husbands on campaign, most famously Juana, the beautiful young Spanish wife of Captain Harry Smith of the Light Division, who rescued her during the sack of Badajoz in April 1812. Visiting convents was a favourite pastime of young officers. Lieutenant Woodberry of the 18th Hussars was at Olite, south of Pamplona, on 3 July 1813:

> ... Opposite to my quarters is a Convent and in it 22 Nunns. I was talking to several last Evening thro' a thin partition of Wood. – This morng I was allow'd to see them thro' a Grate. There were several young Women amongst them but none Handsome: one who have been in the convent 32 years, was the most engaging of the whole, she Enterd it very young, and her countenance bespeaks she was once beautiful. I asked them if they would like to live in a Caza, instead of the convent, which was answer'd immediately by the Lady abbess in the negative: they appear'd particular happy in the sight of an Englishman, and thro' [sic] I could not talk much to them, I made them comprehend that I was an Hussar, and that in England we are the pride of the fair sex: which they were not at all astonish'd at: They said, they liked us better than those they had seen from their Windows in red coats: – ...

*

Wellington was determined to keep his army as disciplined and efficient as possible and to avoid antagonizing the local people as the French had done with their marauding and atrocities.

Most of the Peninsula was too infertile to support an army and this made British seapower vital for the successful prosecution of the war. Supplies were landed at ports and then shifted to the front through depots, using river transport, carts and mules. The scale of the task is indicated by a table of statistics for the 7th Division, which on 18 December 1813 consisted of 5,867 men and 244 horses. It also had 268 regimental mules to carry equipment and baggage. To collect supplies for these men and animals from the depots, it possessed 246 commissariat mules and 113 muleteers.*

Bullock carts were used as well as mules, but could cover at most 3 km per hour, carried limited loads and were less suited to difficult terrain. Lieutenant Woodberry explained on 18 February 1813:

... Our daily Rations arrives every morning from Lisbon and is deliver'd out to the Regiment about Mid-day – my Rations are as follows – one pound of Bread (rather brown but very good) ¾ lb Beef (generally killed a few hours before) 6 pounds of Hay 8 pounds of Corn and 9 pounds of Wood [?] – for which I am charg'd *three pence:* – an Officer may live very well indeed in Portugal on his pay: – particular[ly] after he gets up the Country: –

An illconstructed Cart are [sic] employ'd drawn by two Bullocks driven or rather led by a stout fellow who walk in front of the animals, he has a stick with a small spike at the extremity to goad them occasionlly, this vehicle being extremely low, narrow and clumsy will carry from Six to Eight hundred weight & as the Portuguezis have no idea of greasing the axletree – when loaded they send forth a horrible noise: – twenty to thirty of those Carts bring our Rations daily: – ...

The army initially obtained most of its supplies through contractors. A manuscript note dated 25 August 1808 records that Mr Deputy Commissary-General Pipon contracted with Mr James Walsh to supply 25,000lb of beef daily to the troops north of the Tagus. Walsh bound himself in a bond of £2,000 for the performance of the contract. Mr

* NAM. 1975–12–124.

Pipon was permitted to cancel the agreement by giving a fortnight's notice.

Some contractors provided poor-quality supplies, but others were themselves badly treated. Urniza & Co. and F. Heath & Co. claimed in July 1825 for money outstanding from supplying Wellington's army in the Peninsula:

> Claim estimated at £30.000, being for the balance due for Supplies furnished to the British Forces in Spain during the Years 1813 & 1814, arising chiefly from sundry Bills paid on Account having been calculated at an erroneous Exchange, decidedly contrary to the express conditions of the various Contracts. . . .

The claim was apparently still unsettled in March 1829.

The army could not always rely on contractors and found that transporting supplies became progressively more inefficient the further it moved from its depots. Thus commissaries regularly purchased food locally or, if they lacked ready cash, requisitioned supplies by issuing receipts for future payment. Wellington insisted that everything should be paid for, but the inhabitants in practice had problems exchanging their receipts and often had to sell them to dealers below their face value. Even when they were paid by commissaries in cash, they found it difficult to find enough food for themselves given the exhausted state of the country. Lieutenant Woodberry made this clear in his journal on 15 May 1813 as he advanced through Portugal:

> . . . The nearer we draw to the frontiers, the more distressed are the Inhabitant[s]. The wretched state of misery & starvation they are subject to beggars all discription. The longer we stay in our present quarters the worse it will be for them, we are now acturely oblig'd to send near 2 leagues for green Forage the whole produce of the fields near us have already been consumed by the 15th [Hussars] & us, those very fields of Corn, Barley &c was their principal support for the Summer. – We are daily assail'd by the Women & Children with Tears & Mourns, begging us to leave them a little to subsist upon: – . . .

Banditry became a serious problem, as William Morris revealed on 31 March 1813:

... the accounts which arrive almost daily of robberies & murders
are truly alarming in every direction the roads are infested with them
so that it becomes unsafe to travel except in large parties[.] a british
soldier took up a villain a few days ago who has confessd to having
robbd & murderd twenty persons within the space of a month[.] the
rascal is a spaniard[.] he told the soldier if he would let him escape
he would shew him where there was 30 thousand dollars conceald in
10 minutes but the soldier was not to be manouverd that way[.] he
took him to head Quarters where no doubt he will meet with that
punishment his crimes so justly merits[.] I am informd that several
british officers have been robbd & murderd on their way to Lisbon[.]
I think some strong measures should be taken to extirpate these
villains or no person can travel with any kind of security or comfort
for fear of falling a sacrifice to these diabolical wretches –

Major John Duffy of the 43rd Regiment claimed on 19 January 1813
that British deserters were among the culprits:

Halted [at Abrantes] – a Banditti of Deserters from the Spanish,
Portuguese & English Armies have committed depredations for some
time past in the Alentejo and on the road to Niza – Several murders
have likewise taken place of Passengers.

Lieutenant John Ford of the 79th Regiment noted that Wellington
was not always able to prevent local inhabitants from being plundered
by his troops:

... The Towns and Villages which suffered most by being occupied
by British Troops, were those on the line of march by which the
Detachments [drafts of reinforcements from the depots] joined the
army, Being composed of men of different Regiments, and not always
under the command of their own Officers, best acquainted with their
characters, they were not in every case under the same control and
command. – I was much shocked to see the state of the little Village
of *Pinhanços*, which when we marched through it in pursuit of the
Enemy [when Massena retreated from Portugal in the spring of 1811]
had sustained but little damage, but the next time I saw it, it was in
a complete state of delapidation, though the inhabitants had returned
to it, and not an Enemys Soldier had been there. –
    In some Towns in France [in 1813–14], where the Inhabitants
were misled by false reports of our character, and left their Houses

on our approach without taking a single article with them but what they had on their backs, it required [the] great and unceasing exertion of the British Officers to keep the Troops from the Wine Cellars and from unnecessarily destroying property, if they were fatigued by a long march and without a sufficient supply of food and fuel, or long delay in the issue of Provisions. – Whatever loss of Property may have been sustained, no lives were unnecessarily or wantonly taken by British Soldiers.

They suffered great privations. – In the Division I belonged to in the South of France there were *Sixty barefooted men* marched every day under charge of an Officer. – each man carrying his knapsack containing his kit – a musquet weighing [about 10] lbs a Blanket and Great Coat, a Canteen with water, a Haversack containing what provisions he had (sometimes three days rations were issued at one time) his Cartouch Box containing Sixty rounds of Ball Cartridges – a Tin and cover, and sometimes (in his turn) a Cooking kettle and Billhook. – This was a severe trial for them in an Enemys Country. – . . .

The total weight carried by an infantry soldier could be as much as 70–80lb. Infantrymen usually carried either a greatcoat or a blanket rather than both, for an anonymous writer noted in the *United Service Journal* in 1831 that a 'soldier's blanket and greatcoat are more than he can carry. The Duke of Wellington tried it in the year that his army entered France [1813], but it distressed the troops greatly.'

One of the improvements Wellington introduced before the 1813 Campaign was the issue of a light tin kettle and bill-hook to every six infantrymen. This could be carried by the men themselves, whereas hitherto heavy and inefficient iron kettles had to be carried on a mule and sometimes arrived at camp long after the men. Lieutenant Ford continued:

. . . Soldiers look well on parade in England and from their healthy state appear fit for any duty but two or three campaigns in a foreign country put their strength to the proof – many have constitutional diseases, which do not appear 'till they are tried in this way, others sink under the load they have to carry, with long marches and bad food. – of a Regiment composed of a Thousand men (and leaving out of the calculation the killed and wounded (say none)[)] Two or three Campaigns will only leave about *Five hundred men present,* but those men will be fit for any duty. – as a proof of this I can mention one instance, – a Regiment joined our Division in the Peninsula from England, and on the first long march, *One hundred of their men dropped down and were left on the road,* while at Roll call after the march, we had *not a man missing.* –

That kind of life which Soldiers lead on Home Service is not calculated to make them bear much fatigue, or change of food – They also suffer from the diseases incidental to the climates they visit and from neglect and bad management –

. . .

When in pursuit of the Enemy through an exhausted country, the Troops frequently outmarched the Commissariat supplies and suffered much from Hunger – The Biscuits called by Seamen *Blow and Bite* were very often issued to us, Rye flour &c &c &c – (These Biscuits were sent from England which is a proof of the Scarcity of food. – Rye flower always disagreed with the men[)]. –

As the Enemy always destroyed the Bridges on their retreat, we were obliged to go through such Rivers are [as] were fordable. – The Officers *not mounted* were then worse off than the mounted Officers or *the Soldiers* if the Baggage was in the rear (which was frequently the case for days and sometimes weeks together) they had not a change, and the first two or three Campaigns in the Peninsula being made without any Tents or covering, the Troops were much exposed to the weather. –

On the [left blank] 1811 we forded three Rivers in one day, indeed we passed through the third, a very rapid one *at night,* and were detained some time in the middle of it, as they could not get the artillery up the bank on the opposite side which impeded our passage, and created great confusion – We remained for the night on a Wet common without any covering or change of clothing. – These are trifling and common occurrences which Soldiers must expect to meet with. – But they will account for the *great wear and tear of Shoes.*

*

Wellington recognized the importance of good roads and communications and actively sought to increase the speed with which he could reinforce any sector of his front. For example, Lieutenant Gairdner of

23. A recruiting party of the 33rd (or the 1st Yorkshire West Riding) Regiment of Foot, c. 1814. The recruiting sergeant has a havercake (a West Riding oatcake) on his sword to encourage recruits in believing that they would have plenty to eat if they enlisted.

24. The deserter apprehended, c. 1815. Desertion was common immediately after enlisting and some recruits made a habit of accepting the bounty money, deserting and repeating the process with another regiment. Desertion was also a problem for Wellington's army on active service.

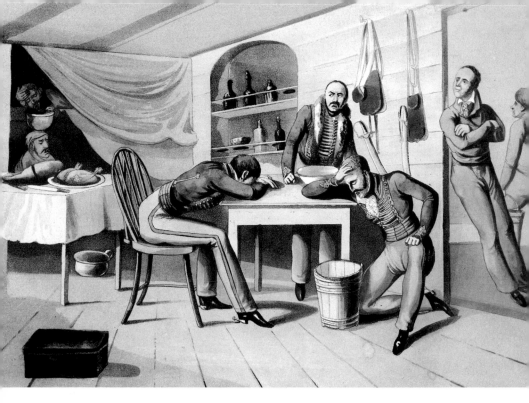

25. Military discoveries, or the miseries of campaigning (from a series of seven plates, being hints to young officers, published in 1819). Seasick officers on board a transport.

26. 'On getting into a love affair, you DISCOVER that the numerous part of the family assisted by some professional gentlemen are determined to revenge the supposed injury . . .'

27. A group of British hussars inside a church in the Peninsula, c. 1808. Note the two Spanish or Portuguese servants.

28. A popular pastime: British officers in Portugal visiting a nunnery.

29. Wellington first besieged Badajoz in May and June 1811. He had to raise the siege as the French concentrated their field armies against him, but undertook another siege in March 1812 and finally stormed Badajoz on 6 April.

30. Lieutenant-General Sir William Carr Beresford KB, c. 1812.

31. Major John Scott Lillie. He served in the Peninsula, initially with the 6th (or the 1st Warwickshire) Regiment of Foot. He was attached to the Portuguese army in December 1808 and subsequently commanded the 7th Caçadores.

32. Ciudad Rodrigo the day after it was stormed. The great breach is on the right and the lesser breach on the left. Watercolour by Cornet Thomas Livingstone Mitchell of the 95th Rifles.

33. Wellington triumphantly enters Madrid on 12 August 1812, after his great victory at Salamanca. Unusually, he is wearing uniform rather than civilian clothes.

34. Caricature of the scene after the Battle of Vitoria, published on 10 July 1813. Wellington is on horseback on the left. Note the box and sacks of plunder in the right foreground.

35. Lieutenant-General Robert Ballard Long, c. 1821. He commanded a cavalry brigade in the Peninsula as a major-general, but was recalled in July 1813.

36. Lieutenant-General (later General) Thomas Graham, the victor at the Battle of Barossa, near Cadiz, on 5 March 1811. He is seen here in c. 1820 and is wearing a fur-lined coat over a general officer's uniform.

37. The storming of San Sebastian, 31 August 1813. Note the castle in the background.

38. Wellington with some of his senior officers before the Battle of the Nivelle in November 1813. He is talking to Sir Stapleton Cotton, who wears the uniform of a general officer of hussars.

39. The Battle of Toulouse, 10 April 1814. Wellington (second from left in the group of four officers in the right foreground) watches the 6th Division attack the Calvinet Heights. The city of Toulouse lies on the other side of the heights.

40. The French city of Bayonne, looking south from the village of St Etienne, with the Pyrenees in the background. This sketch was drawn by Ensign Robert Batty of the First Regiment of Foot Guards on 13 April 1814, the day before the French sortie.

the 95th Rifles recorded that on 22 December 1813 he went on a working party to make lateral roads behind Wellington's position near Arbonne, supervised by the Royal Staff Corps. Accurate information about roads was equally vital. Lieutenant-Colonel the Hon. Alexander Abercrombie, an Assistant Quartermaster-General attached to the 7th Division, obtained detailed intelligence in March 1814 about the roads in the French Department of Les Landes from Monsieur Garrillon of Mont de Marsan. This included responses to questions about the system used to repair roads; the classification of roads into byroads, Routes Départmentales and the three classes of Routes Impériales; and sources of information on the roads in the neighbouring Departments of the Gironde, Gers and Lot et Garonne.*

The army's system of postal communications, both within the Peninsula and with England, was grafted onto the existing civilian arrangements. A weekly packet service brought mail from Falmouth to the British Post Office at Lisbon, where it was handled by a packet agent. The army then distributed its mail within the Peninsula. From April 1809, it had one, later two, NCOs serving as Postmasters and attached to the Quartermaster-General's Department. In Portugal, there were two main civilian postal routes, running to the north and the east of Lisbon and using mules and dismounted messengers. At the Commissariat's expense Wellington extended some of the routes and increased the frequency of the post between his headquarters and Lisbon to a daily service.

The communications system became more complicated as Wellington's army grew in size and operated further inland. For example, a supplementary line of military communication was established after April 1811 to link Wellington's headquarters at Freinada in the north with Hill's detachment near Elvas in the south. The mail on these additional routes was carried by letter-parties, each consisting of one NCO and about six men detached from cavalry regiments.

Messages within the army which were urgent or addressed to a location beyond the normal routes were carried by orderlies or by the Corps of Mounted Guides. Sir George Scovell wrote a memorandum in 1854 to advise on the formation of a Staff Corps for the Crimean War. He explained that in the Peninsula, he had superintended the formation

* NAM. 1985-10-38-19.

of the Mounted Guides in 1808, using deserters from the French army
as it embarked following the Convention of Cintra. They were mainly
Italians and generally from the infantry, were mounted on captured
horses and even had to be taught how to saddle their horses. They were
initially used as interpreters, as they spoke French and considerable
Spanish and Portuguese. They also helped to procure local guides, who
would be given rations and made to deposit their cloaks to ensure they
did not abscond. These guides would afterwards be rewarded with a
dollar and, if they wished, dismissed. When Sir John Moore's army
advanced into Spain, some thirty Spaniards were added to the Mounted
Guides. The Corps's Italians were evacuated from Coruña, but those of
its Spaniards not in uniform were discharged.

Scovell added that after Wellesley returned to the Peninsula in April
1809:

> ... at the request of Sir George Murray [the Quartermaster-General]
> & against my own wishes, I was persuaded to undertake to form
> another Corps of Guides on the nucleus of the men of the old Corps
> who had been sent out from England – Ten or twelve young
> gentlemen, students at Coimbra who spoke French were added to
> this corps, which at first consisted of only some thirty men – these
> officers were also of the greatest use in all our communications with
> the inhabitants – The corps was by degrees augmented and was at
> last upwards of 200 strong – The officers had the pay of officers
> of cavalry and were [illegible] as Subalterns in the Portuguese Regi-
> ments of Infantry – the men had also the pay of our cavalry. The
> uniform of the whole was the same as that of our Lᵗ Dragoons, but
> the color of the clothing brown, to distinguish them from the other
> men – These men kept up the communications of the army between
> Frenada & Lord Hills Command in front [south] of the army, by
> regular stages of some ten and twelve miles each – The orderlies had
> printed bills which were checked by N.C. officers at each station, &
> returned to Head Quarters – *There was no instance of any of these
> deserters betraying his trust* – ...

In August 1811, Scovell was entrusted with the superintendence of the
whole of the army's communications and he remained in charge until
April 1813.

Attempts to enforce systematic procedures on the handling of the mail in the Peninsula had limited success. In May 1812, commanding officers were ordered to compile lists of the letters that they were forwarding from their regiments for sending home. The postage would then be paid to the Packet Agent by the army's Deputy Paymaster-General on Scovell's directions. But such directions were often unheeded. In fact, the system worked better for the soldiers than for the Post Office, for the biggest problem was the difficulty in collecting payment and large sums were left outstanding.

While advancing across Spain in 1813 Wellington switched his main supply base from Lisbon to Pasajes on the northern coast. The army's mail was handled by the Packet Agent there, Charles Sevright, who later moved to San Sebastian, where he had more adequate resources. He unsuccessfully pressed for mail to be carried by the Royal Navy rather than the packet ships to ease the burden on the Post Office. In June 1814, following the end of the war, an Army Post Office was opened at Bordeaux, where it remained until Wellington's army had left France.

As a result of an Act of Parliament in 1795, soldiers, NCOs and sailors serving overseas had the right to send or receive letters weighing under a quarter of an ounce at a one penny concessionary rate. This fee was payable in advance, not on delivery, and the outside of the letter had to bear the soldier's name, rank and unit and the signature of his commanding officer. The measure was in fact introduced primarily for economic reasons as hitherto soldiers had often been unable to pay on receipt the postage for letters that had been sent to them. The penny rate was first used by soldiers on campaign during the Duke of York's Expedition to Holland in 1799. The privilege was extended to the Peninsula on 31 October 1808 and the penny rate remained constant despite increases in domestic rates.

The postal system worked reasonably well and was crucial in main-taining morale. For example, Major-General Long wrote to his brother on 10 January 1813:

Yesterdays post brought me your letter of the 20th Ult – never was any thing more beautifully regular than our mails, nor was motto ever more correct than 'une lettre adoucit les peines de l'absence' ['a letter softens the sorrows of absence'] – The packet however to which we look with peculiar anxiety is the one destined to convey to us the expected Brevet [promotion] of 1813, & the winding up of the

Russian Campaign [of Napoleon] – In the former I am not at all
interested, upon the latter point I am all anxiety – ...

But other accounts indicate letters being lost or delayed. Major Warre,
for example, complained about the post in a letter to his father dated
11 September 1809. He was serving as Beresford's ADC and was based
at Lisbon rather than inland with Wellington's army:

> I have been most truely vexed at not receiving your very affectionate
> letters of 5th July & 2 August annexed with my Dear Mothers of 10
> July till yesterday late in the Evening, the stupid clerks in the Army
> post office sent them up to Lord Wellingtons Army. I have for some
> time past been very figgety at not hearing and the three last Packets
> do not bring me a line from any one or they also are gone to the
> English Army, while I am in Lisbon. ...

Such problems increased when the army was on the move. The
growth in its size and area of operations in 1813–14 also had an adverse
effect. Sergeant William Simonds of the 7th Hussars complained to his
brother Richard on 5 May 1814:

> I suppose you will be much pleased at the great & Glorious News of
> the Termination of a long and destructive War[.] I have written to
> you before but the uncertainty of our letters reaching their desti-
> nation is owing to our being continualy on the march and the letters
> frequently thrown aside[.] we expect to be in England in the Course
> of a month or six weeks and I hope never to leave it more, of all
> the Countrys I have seen the old Spot is the best[.] France is a fine
> Country much beyond Spain – Thank my good God that he has
> preserved me from several dangerous Engagements that we have met
> with since we left England ...

Lieutenant-Colonel the Hon. Henry Murray of the 18th Hussars also
experienced problems. On 9 August 1813, he wrote to his wife:

> ... Though your last letter gave me happiness enough to last for a
> month, I yet cannot help being anxious to hear from you – dont
> imagine I say this by way of reproach for I know very well how
> frequently you write but by some mismanagement here, the letters
> do not often reach me. ...

Murray was recovering from an injury at a hospital in Palencia at the time and the fact that he was over 250 km in the army's rear contributed to these problems. He claimed in a letter of 2 July that he heard less about the army at Palencia than his wife did in England. He informed her on the 24th that when he got up to the army, he trusted their correspondence would be regular as the army was near the port from where the packets sailed.

Many letters were written on the spur of the moment as officers had just heard that a packet was due to leave for England in the next day or so. Formal notice that mail was being made up was apparently not given from 1809 onwards as it would have been impossible to spare enough mules to carry the number of letters that would have resulted.

The army's morale was better served by the postal service than by its chaplains. Regimental chaplains had been replaced in 1796 by clergymen from the new Army Chaplains' Department, who served an army as a whole while it was on overseas service. But the chaplains were few in number and rarely commanded respect. Lieutenant William Coles of the 4th Dragoons wrote from Lisbon on 14 January 1810: '. . . We have some Chaplains with the army: were I to detail their mode of living, you'd be a little Surpriz'd: to be sure They preach, but dont ever make the appearance of following Their doctrine . . .'

Religion was not a preoccupation for most of Wellington's army, but those who did seek spiritual reassurance often turned to Nonconformism, despite some ridicule from their comrades. Wellington recognized that Methodist meetings were more beneficial than most alternative off-duty occupations, but was concerned by their potential to undermine discipline and subordination. He could hardly approve, for example, of privates preaching sermons to officers and NCOs. He therefore urged that more suitable chaplains should be sent from home, but at the end of the Peninsular War still had only sixteen with his army.

The anonymous soldier of the 38th Regiment offers a valuable insight into the influence of Methodism. As a boy, he had listened to Methodist preaching and attended Dissenting places of worship. He had been in some anxiety for his soul since childhood, but was unable to reform, despite thinking that he led a sinful life. He described what happened one day while stationed in Ireland after returning from the Walcheren Expedition of 1809:

... there came A man into the Barrack room that I wass in and Told us there wass a brother Soldier going to preach At the Methodist Chapel that night and wished For as maney as Could to Come and hear him[.] I told Him I would be there he sade he hoped I would Strive to bring as maney more with me as I Could[.] After the man wass gon thay in the room asked Me if I ment to go I told them I did thay began To Laughf at me and sade I wass going to be A Methodist But I thought I wished I wass A real Christian[.] when Night Came I whent and maney More and While I sat under the word I wass wishing I Could feel it So to afflict my heart as to Caus[e] in me a thorow reform in my whole Life and Conduct[.] After the Service wass over the preacher Said He hoped that all that felt aney Concern Abought the Salvation of their Souls whould Stay after the rest where gon and there Where 14 that gave in their names to join The Society[.] as Soon as I got into my room One of the Men had heard of it and asked Me if I had given mine I told him I had Not he Said I wass in the right of it For he wass Sure those that had did not Know what they where doing for He wass sure that before aney one gave Their Name to join aney religious society Thay ought Seriously to Consider what Thay were abought to do For he said He did not beleive there wass aney thing Of real religion in aney of them ...

The anonymous soldier attended meetings regularly, but otherwise continued his sinful ways and was rebuked by a fellow soldier. After a period of mental turmoil:

... the Lord wass pleased again to shine Upon my Soul it wass then and not Till then that I Could sing in The Spirit those Buteful Lines this is The way I Long have sought and [illegible] Because I found it not My grief A Burden Long [h]as been because I Could not cease From Sin[.] From that time I felt sutch A Love and Affection for the people of God with Whomb I Conversed from time to time that it Far Surpased all that I had ever felt for my Nearest relatives on earth it wass now that I began To Know what real happiness Consisted in[.] But in The Situation I wass in I knew that I should have Maney difucultes to encounter and maney Crosses to Take up ...

*

The experiences of prisoners of war constitute another less familiar aspect of the struggle in the Peninsula. The French waged a bitter war with the Spaniards and Portuguese in which atrocities were common, but enjoyed more civilized relations with their British enemies. It was in Napoleon's interests to treat his British prisoners better than those of other nationalities as they were valuable bargaining counters given the larger number of French prisoners in British hands. Negotiations were undertaken in 1810 for a comprehensive exchange of prisoners of all nationalities, but foundered on the simple fact that Napoleon could not be trusted. As a result, officer exchanges had to be arranged piecemeal and were mostly for the higher ranks.

Captured officers were generally treated correctly and enjoyed certain freedoms in return for giving their parole not to try to escape. The men, in contrast, were imprisoned and sometimes endured harsh treatment. The anonymous soldier of the 38th Regiment vividly described the traumatic seventeen months that he spent in captivity. He had been wounded at the Battle of Salamanca and was subsequently taken prisoner when Wellington's army retreated from Burgos in the autumn of 1812:

> . . . as soon as Thay [the British] heard in Salamanco that our Armey wass Retreating thay began to send the worst of the Cases away to Lisbon and all that thay Could Get Conveyances for wass sent but my wound had Just healed up So I wass laft untill our Armey came Down and then I wass Ordred to join the reg^t[.] I Marched But it wass with Verey great pane Abough^t A Mile and A half[.] But when I got to the reg^t I wass so much spent that I wass forced to ly down I had not lay long before I wass Ceased [sic] with A Verey Strong fit of the Ague [apparently a renewed bout of Walcheren Fever] I was verey ill and Had to ly on the Cold ground all the Night the Next Morning I wass taken and put into one of [the] Sick Waggons[.] I wass taken 3 days in the Waggons But when the 4th Morning came the French Came upon Us so quick that those Who where Able to get Into the Waggon did But I had the Ague so bad every Day and wass So Weak that I Could not get in of Myself So I wass Left Laying on the ground and Wass taken Prisoner[.] When I wass Captured I felt assured That I must use every exersion in my power to preserve My Life for if I had not tryed to march I should Either have been put to death instantly or left to die Upon the ground So I throwed all away that I could And whent through the French Lines about the Distance of A Mile

then I got into A Field Where there wass maney more prisners that
Where taken there thay kindled A fire the Night wass verey whet and
Cold and I had nothing But the few Clothes that I stood in for while
I was going through the French Lines one of them Stept out of his
rank and Came to me and took My Big Cote and every thing I had
except some Books which he gave me Back again[.] on account of
The Whetness of the Night we did not attempt To Lay ourselves down
untill A verey late hour So the Fire wass kept Burning Untill the Rane
Ceased And then thay put it out[.] But Seeing me So verey ill they
lade me on the place Where the fire had been that I might get what
nurishment I Could from the warmth of the ground and the rest Of
the Men Lay round me[.] in the Morning the french Guard came and
Colected us together and Marched us Off But there where maney
more among us that wass Sick and as soon as we began to march the
French Put maney to death that Could not keep up But Most of them
that where killed where Portugase and Spanyards and I expectd everry
minute it would Be my Lot to Suffer the Same fate[.] But in that Case
the Lord wass pleased to show mercy unto Me in Causeing one of the
Sergants belonging to The French guard to take pitey on me So that
When I Could not keep up he whould Stay for Mee[.] We did not go
more than one Legue or 3 miles That day and that Night we where
put into a place Under Cover and had Some Straw to ly upon[.] the
Next Morning we marched again but we did not go mutch more than
2 Miles and there where Several put to death that day also the third
day We Marched[.] we marched abought five mile and I believe that
there where 36 put to death that day And one of them wass A Man
belonging to the Same Reg^t as myself[.] But when the forth Morning
Came we had the longest days March to go to get Into Sallemanco
And I felt So ill that I expected That it would be my Lot to Suffer the
Same Fate that So maney of my fellow prisners had Met with But
when the forth Morning Came we march^d And we had A young
Officer that had the Command of the Guard and he seemed to be A
Verey feeling man which Made the Whole of the guard seem to put
on A difrent Feeling toward us so that thay treated us with more
Kindness than thay did before So that when aney of Us got far behind
thay would halt and let us rest As mutch as posible thay Could so
that on that on that [sic] Day there wass but one put to death And I
beleive it Whould not have been Onley for A Circumstance that We
Saw on the roade[.] But the Spanyards where cruell People and if

thay Could ever light [sic] of aney one or Two of the French alone thay whould Murder them In the Most Cruell manner that thay could so as we wher[e] Marching we saw one of the French Soldiers that had Been Murdred laying in the most Shamefull and Dissgracefull manner that he Could be left in so When the guard saw it thay Began to swear and Said thay whould have Sattisfaction before thay got Into the Town So there wass one poor Man with us That wass verey ill indeed his Legs where so swelled That he could not keep up wether he wass A spaniya[rd] Or A port[ugu]eze I did not know for their dress wass so near Alike that I Could not tell them asunder but we Had not gon far from the place where the dead man Lay before one of the guard came to the poor sick Man and ran [h]is Ba[yo]nnet through him and left Him there to die[.] So that wass the Sattisfaction Thay had for the death of their fellow Soldier But we Continued our march untill we got into The Town [of Salamanca] . . .

The anonymous soldier remained in Salamanca for six or seven weeks before being taken in the winter into France. Being too weak to march, he was carried on baggage cars. His feet were so frozen on one occasion that it was three days before he could detect any feeling in them again and he shortly afterwards lost his toenails. At nights he was lodged in prisons and he suffered agonies from rheumatism in his left knee and shoulders. He eventually arrived at Givet, in north-eastern France, where he remained for nearly five months and gradually recovered.

Many of the prison depots were in fortresses near the northern and eastern frontiers of France and were threatened by the advance of the Allied armies as Napoleon's empire collapsed. The British prisoners were evacuated because of their importance as bargaining pieces and among them was the anonymous soldier, who was moved at the end of 1813, apparently to the south of France. His fellow prisoners were in a terrible state, but received little help from the inhabitants, who could not count on any payment given the impending downfall of Napoleon's regime. On 14 April 1814, the prisoners finally learnt to their delight that peace had been made and after hearing the next day that it was not true, they received confirmation of the news on the 16th. They embarked on a British warship on 6 May and after a two-month voyage via Minorca arrived at Plymouth. The anonymous soldier had to remain in quarantine for another fortnight before being permitted to land.

Some prisoners managed to escape. The fact that Wellington was campaigning in friendly countries increased the likelihood of escapees managing to return to the army. Ensign George Percival of the Coldstream Guards wrote to his aunt on 2 June 1811:

> ... I perfectly agree with you that the Portuguese deserve all the support they have met with and I have no doubt that their Neighbours may equally profit if they do not cut their own throats. In one instance the Spaniards have always behaved most friendly to the English Soldier, which is in assisting them (as much as is in their power) to make their escape if taken prisoners by the French if they are fortunate enough in getting off, the Spaniards always escort them over the Mountains and feed them. ...

News of a soldier's fate was often sparse or inaccurate. Major Charles Napier of the 50th (or the West Kent) Regiment of Foot was wounded and captured at Coruña on 16 January 1809, but initial reports at home indicated that he had been killed. His aunt, Lady Emily Leinster, wrote an undated letter to her daughter Lucy:

> if you happen to hear any of the various reports about poor Dear Charles Napier not being dead but a Prisoner don't let yourself go to any hope about it as there is certainly no grounds to give room for it as all speak from conjecture, no Body has seen his poor Body either Dead or alive since the fatal Day ...

On the urging of Napier's family, the French were contacted to ascertain his fate. Marshal Ney learnt that Napier's mother was a blind widow and released him on 20 March, on his parole not to serve again until exchanged for a French prisoner of similar rank.

Similarly, it took time for the fate of Major Thomas Brotherton of the 14th Light Dragoons to become apparent after he was wounded and captured while charging French cavalry at the village of Hasparren on 12 December 1813. The War Office wrote to Mrs Brotherton a month later, on 17 January 1814, and did its best to reassure her:

> I would have written to you ere now had I been able to learn any thing further of Major B. but some time must necessarily elapse before Returns of the Prisoners are received from France. – There is yet a hope that he may have escaped, but you must not indulge it too much – The Report of his having been wounded does not in my opinion deserve any credit – The next Returns from the Regiment, I

expect will be received in a week or two, and then I shall be able to learn exactly the circumstances attending his capture –

If you wish particularly to write to him I will forward your letter to the Minister of War at Paris by whom it will be transmitted to the Major whereever he may have been ordered.

Major Brotherton sent his wife a brief letter that was undated but postmarked 25 January 1814, to let her know he had been wounded and captured and that he had not been able to inform her before of his misfortune. A subsequent letter, dated 29 December 1813 from Tarbes in southern France, was postmarked 31 January 1814:

> My exchange has not taken place & I am sent into the interior of France but I am well & still entertain hopes of seeing you soon – my wounds which were slight are nearly well and I have been well treated – I trust you are well

In fact, Brotherton had narrowly survived, having surrendered just as a Frenchman was about to blow his brains out with a pistol. He was saved from eight thrusts by a buffalo-leather cuirass he had made for himself after being run through the body at the Battle of Salamanca. Another thrust would probably have cut a vital artery in his thigh, had it not been for some letters in his pocket that he had received that morning.

Captain Lemonnier-Delafosse, ADC to Marshal Soult's brother, recorded in his memoirs, published in 1850, that following Major Brotherton's capture, the French 13th Chasseurs à Cheval ribbed the 14th Light Dragoons by sending them letters addressed 'to the Buffalo Cuirassiers'. He claimed that Brotherton was ashamed at the discovery of his hidden cuirass and wanted nothing better than to leave the scene of his misfortune. He was ordered to escort him, and the lieutenant who had been captured at the same time, into France. Lemonnier-Delafosse did his best on the way to make them forget their humiliation and to leave them with a better opinion of French officers, especially those on the staff.*

*

Wellington's army recovered in health, morale and discipline during the winter following the retreat from Burgos. It never had a longer period of

---

* M. Lemonnier-Delafosse, *Campagnes de 1810 à 1815: Souvenirs Militaires* (Havre, 1850), pp. 250–1.

rest during the entire war. Reinforcements arrived from England. Units were drilled. Tents were issued for all the infantry, so that they would be able to sleep under cover on campaign: as a result, they were less heavily burdened, for they no longer had to carry greatcoats.

The army's principal medical officer, Dr James McGrigor, was an outstanding administrator and significantly improved standards of medical care. He advocated the treatment of wounded wherever possible in the divisional and regimental hospitals, for transporting the injured to general hospitals in the rear reduced their chances of recovery, helped spread disease and discouraged men in the more comfortable bases such as Lisbon from returning to their units. Furthermore, the general hospitals were often insanitary, poorly ventilated and staffed by inexperienced hospital mates. Wellington accepted McGrigor's arguments at the end of 1812, despite having reservations that his army's mobility might suffer from the extra transport needed to move each regiment's hospital equipment. McGrigor also persuaded him to obtain portable wooden hospitals that could be erected close to where they were needed.

A Staff Corps of Cavalry was established in March 1813 with combined courier and military police duties. Wellington wrote to the Duke of York from Freinada on 21 April 1813:

> I have the Honor of writing to Your Royal Highness a Return of the Number of Men from each Reg^t of Cavalry in this Country transfered to the Staff Corps.
>
> I considered it most consistent with Your Royal Highness' Intentions that the Men should be allowed to volunteer their Services for this Corps; and I arranged accordingly; taking from no Reg^t any Men that had not volunteered, & confining the numbers taken from the Reg^{ts} who were to remain in the Service in this Country to ten Privates. The King's Heavy German Dragoons nor the Light Hussars did not furnish any.

Thus was established the first organized body of British military police. Sir George Scovell commented in 1854:

> ... a Staff corps of Cavalry was formed, and I left the Corps of [Mounted] Guides to take charge of it – Lieut Co^{ln} Sturgeon succeeded me in the Guides and was shortly after killed at Vic Bigoure [Vic-en-Bigorre, 19 March 1814] – This corps consisted of two Squadrons, and was composed of the best men from all the

Cavalry Reg[ts] in the army – Cavalry officers were also sent with the men, but a great mistake was made in the selection – They were generally speaking excellent soldiers, but very few of them knew any language but their own –

This error was corrected when I had the reforming of this Corps after the battle of Waterloo, when one of the conditions of the officers appointment was that he should speak French. . . .

Wellington from the end of 1812 also had a judge-advocate-general, Francis Larpent, to help enforce discipline.

It was on his infantry that Wellington most relied, for unlike Napoleon he used his artillery and cavalry merely as supporting units and not as powerful arms in their own right. His infantry deservedly had the reputation of being the best in Europe.

In the British army, the infantry regiment was an administrative concept rather than a battle formation. Most had at least two battalions, with one acting as a depot, or home-battalion. This would recruit, train and periodically send out drafts to reinforce its sister battalion overseas. The account of the anonymous soldier of the 38th Regiment offers a case in point. He was originally in the 2nd Battalion, but volunteered to join a draft of men to strengthen the 1st Battalion, with which he landed in Portugal in August 1808. The 1st Battalion took part in the Coruña campaign, but on arriving home was unfit to return immediately to the Peninsula with Wellesley in April 1809. It instead took part in the expedition to the Dutch island of Walcheren that July. The expedition was intended to strike at the Scheldt Estuary and the Port of Antwerp, but achieved little and had to be evacuated later that year as almost one in ten of the troops was killed by fever, apparently a deadly combination of malaria and more common infections such as typhus.* The anonymous soldier fell ill three months after arriving at Walcheren and was sent home:

> . . . But most part of the few that did enjoy their Health in the Cuntry took bad and died as soon as Thay Came home And After I had Been A few weaks At Shoranclift [Shorncliffe, near Sandgate] I wass taken Very Ill of the Ague and Fever And I had it so verey Bad that

---

* M. Howard, *Wellington's Doctors: The British Army Medical Services in the Napoleonic Wars* (Staplehurst, 2002), pp. 174–5.

As soon as The Ague fit wass gon off me I had the Fever come on
directly and used to Continue untill The Ague came on again and so
heavely Afflicted Wass I that in A Short time I wass not much In
Appearance But Skin and bone I wass given Up by all the Doctors
that Saw me and in my Hown v[i]ew [?] I thought it wass imposible
that I Could Continue long . . .

The 1st Battalion after Walcheren was in no state for foreign service and
returned to Ireland to recover. It was therefore the 2nd Battalion of the
38th that went out to reinforce Wellington in the Peninsula in April
1810. The 1st Battalion did not follow until two years later. The
anonymous soldier recorded that he embarked at Cork, sailed to Lisbon
and joined Wellington's army just in time for the Battle of Salamanca
on 22 July 1812. After the retreat from Burgos, the 2nd Battalion was
ordered home and left the Peninsula in December 1812, after drafting
those of its men who were still fit into the 1st Battalion. One of them
was needed to replace the anonymous soldier, who had been captured
during the retreat from Burgos. He might have escaped had he not been
rendered too weak to get in a wagon by an attack of the ague. For
Walcheren Fever had a lasting effect, so much so that Wellington
requested that he should not be sent any more battalions that had served
there.

A battalion had ten companies, including an elite company of
grenadiers and a light company of men particularly suited to act as
skirmishers. Theoretical strength was 100 men per company, but a
battalion on campaign often had no more than 550 men. Battalions of
the Foot Guards, in contrast, were unusually strong.

The infantryman's basic weapon was the flintlock musket, nicknamed
'Brown Bess'. It fired when a flint struck the steel frizzen and produced
a spark that ignited the black powder charge. Misfirings were common,
especially in damp weather, and repeated firing fouled the inside of the
barrel. As the weapons were muzzle-loaders, they could fire no more
than four shots a minute. They had no rifling and were accurate to only
70 metres, although they could fire balls powerfully enough to take effect
up to about 300 metres. Soldiers fired in volleys in closely packed ranks
to compensate for the inaccuracy of individual muskets and were soon
so enveloped in smoke that they found it difficult to tell what was
happening except in their immediate vicinity. A bayonet could be fixed

around the muzzle of the musket to form a pike and this proved particularly effective when a battalion formed a hollow square formation as an all-round defence against cavalry. A number of light infantry units, notably the 95th Rifles, were armed with the Baker rifle, which had an accurate range at least double that of the musket, but was slower to load.

Wellington built up his artillery from an initially weak force and fielded significant numbers of guns only after 1811. Moreover, it was only in May 1813, with the appointment of Lieutenant-Colonel Alexander Dickson, that he found an artillery commander in whom he had full confidence, for promotion in the Royal Artillery and Royal Engineers went solely by seniority and resulted in too many senior officers being old and incapable. His batteries each had six guns, one of which was a howitzer for firing explosive shells at high angles. The British, uniquely, also used shrapnel shells designed to burst in flight and shower enemy troops below with lead balls and shell fragments. In the Royal Foot Artillery, batteries of guns were known as brigades and their personnel as companies. The Royal Horse Artillery, formed in 1793, had more mobile batteries, called troops, in which every gunner was mounted on either a horse or a limber.

One of the improvements that Wellington made was to increase the number of heavy-calibre guns. Major-General William Borthwick, one of his early Commanders Royal Artillery, wrote on 14 March 1812 to Major Thomas Downman, the commander of the Royal Horse Artillery:

> Have you ever thought of the Troops of Horse Artillery in this Country, having Guns of a larger Calibre? – my reason for asking this question is, – that Lord Wellington seems to think very unfavorably of the Light 6 p^{rs} and not withstanding the great Service, that has on many occasions been performed with them, His Lordship has now on three times spoken in such strong terms against them and in favour of 9 p^{rs} that I am inclined to wish the Troops had 9 p^{rs} –
>
> . . .
>
> Lord Wellington has *ordered another 9 p^r Brigade to be equipped* and brought into the Field as soon as possible.

The letter is annotated, presumably by Downman, in March 1813:

> Maj^r Genl Bo[r]thwick is kind enough to ask the opinion of the Comm^g officer of Horse Artillery, on a change likely to take place in

the Establishment of that Troops. L^t Co^l [George] Fisher [one of
Borthwick's successors] does not even mention it to him[.] Capt
[James] Webber Smiths Troop to have 9 p^{rs}

Since about 1750 the British Army had preferred to use 3pdrs and
6pdrs, which were more mobile and better suited to colonial campaigns.
But it reintroduced 9pdrs in 1808 as a response to the superiority of the
French 8pdr and 12pdr cannon to the British 6pdrs. Although the larger
calibre guns were less mobile, they fired heavier roundshot, which had
greater momentum and destructive power and also a longer effective
range. The range of the British 9pdr at 1° elevation and with a charge of
3lb was about 604 metres. A light 6pdr to reach the same range would
require an elevation of 1⅜°. Greater elevation decreased both accuracy
and the effectiveness of richochet fire, in which a cannonball was
bounced along the ground to tear through files of troops. Artillery also
used case-shot, or canister, consisting of a tin can filled with lead balls.
These scythed down enemy troops at close range when the can burst on
the gun being fired. Larger calibre guns fired case-shot containing more
and heavier balls. For the 1813 campaign, Wellington had thirteen British
batteries, seven of which had 9pdrs.

The British also possessed the primitive Congreve rocket, consisting
of a warhead attached to a long stabilizing stick. Wellington had a Rocket
Troop in the Peninsula from 1813 onwards, but had little faith in the
weapon, which was notoriously inaccurate.

As with his artillery, Wellington only had significant numbers of
cavalrymen in the second half of 1811, when he was able to field two
divisions of them. Obtaining enough horses was a particularly serious
problem, and was a recurrent theme in his letters to Sir Stapleton
Cotton. One of his favourite threats when a cavalry regiment misbehaved
was to dismount it and return the men to England. For example, he
wrote to Cotton on 9 November 1811:

> ... I am very much concerned to hear such bad accounts of the
> 11th Lt Dragoons. It is difficult enough God knows to find forage for
> a Reg^t of Cavalry anywhere, but it is not impossible as the Officers
> of other Reg^{ts} have proved. All depends upon the diligence & atten-
> tion to their duty of the Officers; and I can only say that if any
> circumstances exist in the 11th Reg^t to make them less efficient than
> other Reg^{ts} I must take their Horses from them; & give them to other

Reg^ts^ who will take care of them; & send the Reg^t^ to Lisbon to do duty there; & eventually to England.

I shall be sorry to be obliged to adopt these measures by a Reg^t^ of which I have reason to entertain a good opinion; but dragoons are worse than useless if their Horses & appointments are not taken care of; & we must get rid of all of this description.

A cavalry regiment on campaign would leave a squadron at home as a depot and would rarely field more than 450 men. Regiments of light dragoons or hussars were particularly suited to reconnaissance and outpost duties. They were armed principally with the 1796 light cavalry sword, a superbly effective slashing weapon. The heavy cavalry, namely the Household Cavalry, dragoons and dragoon guards, carried a less efficient long, straight-bladed sword that was effective only in chopping strokes. None of the British cavalry carried lances until their introduction after Waterloo.

Wellington took the field in 1813 with about 8,000 cavalry. One of the newly arrived regiments from England was the 18th Hussars, which sailed from England in January as part of the Hussar Brigade. It had last served in the Peninsula during the Coruña Campaign and had serious internal problems. Lieutenant Woodberry recorded on 8 February:

> . . . no one can detest corporal punishment more than I do but – subordination must be kept up or we shall all soon go to the dogs: I am very much afraid some of our men will get themselves into serious trouble when we join Lord Wellingtons Army [at the front] – for if they go on with any of their drunken tricks there Lord W. may perhaps shoot some of them which I should be extreemly sorry for: – I look forward with pleasure for the Regiment to go into action am confident they will not disgrace themselves and return home, whenever we may: it will be with Laurels: – . . .

He added on the 19th that most of the men were discovered to have sold their horses' corn daily. Discipline seems hardly to have improved by 16 April, when he complained:

> . . . I am plagued to death with the Troop the men are going on very bad: – Two men were punish'd this morning by their Comrades, and I was compell'd to send another (George Carr) to Cartaxo, to be

tried by a Court Martial; I am now determin'd to work them right & left till I bring the fellows to a true sence of duty. . . .

Woodberry blamed the situation on the ignorance of his commanding officer, Lieutenant-Colonel the Hon. Henry Murray. Naturally, Murray himself took a different view. On 25 April 1814, he wrote:

> . . . [Henry] Duperier is in my highest favor, but the men behave past endurance ill.
> The Officers are idle with some few exceptions & the men the worst in the army.
> I do not dislike Capt [James] Grant, he is either stark staring mad, or might as well be so, he is for ever in a paroxysm of rage or good humour, invective or smiles, he is either excessively angry or excessively pleased he has much volubility some cleverness & the loudest voice that ever shook a Cathedral or hailed a prize. . . .

Yet the Regiment's flaws were belied by its appearance when Wellington reviewed the Hussar Brigade on 18 May 1813. Wellington is often accused of failing to give sufficient praise, but Woodberry recorded that: '. . . he express'd himself highly pleased at our Appearance, what he said will never be forgotten by any one belonging to the Brigade and I have the vanity to think he did not flatter us when he said, "The Brigade is the finest body of Cavalry I ever saw in my life, and I feel no hesitation in saying I think it not equall'd in Europe." . . .'

On 7 April 1813 Wellington wrote to Cotton, who had returned to England on leave in December, about various cavalry matters. His letter sheds particular light on the problems he faced in obtaining reliable generals. He also had to send four cavalry regiments home as they had become too depleted in men or horses:

> I think it probable that you will arrive at Lisbon nearly about the time that this letter will reach that place; and as I propose to take the field as soon as the appearance of the green forage will secure the food of our Horses, I lose no time in acquainting you with the situation of your Cavalry; & in requesting to know your wishes upon some points relating to it. You will have heard in England that in consequence of orders from Home I have drafted the Horses from the 4th D^n G^{ds} 9 & 11th L^t D^{ns} and that I have orders & have it in contemplation to draft the Horses from the 2^d Hussars [King's

German Legion]. By sending to the AG [Adjutant-General] at Lisbon you will get a copy of the orders of the [left blank]; in which you will see the distribution made of the Horses drafted. Excepting the first & second Heavy Germans all the Reg^{ts} will have as many Horses as they can mount, I preferred to draft the Horses from the 11th to drafting them from the 13th; as the Men of the 11th were very sickly; & I found that by keeping the 13th I should have more mounted Dragoons than by keeping the 11th

I propose that the whole Cavalry of the Army should be in one Div^n under your Command; & that the Cavalry duty of any Detachments that should be made from the main body shall be done by Detachments of Brigades or other subdivision, from that Division. This will simplify the Concern very considerably.

Private & confidential
I have received discretionary orders to send to England General [John] Slade, General [Victor] Alten & Genl Long; & General [George] Anson has asked to be appointed to the Staff in England. General Fane is coming out. I have not sent home any of these Officers because I am not quite certain what your wishes & opinions are; & because I doubt whether you could mend matters very materially by their removal. The Hussar Brigade is vacant; & is at present commanded by Col. Grant of the 15th

One of the Generals above mentioned must go at at [sic] all events, as I conclude that you will wish to put the 13th Lt Dragoons in the Brigade with the 12th & 16th, or with the 1st Hussars [King's German Legion] & 14th if the 2^d Hussars should be drafted; and I beg to know which of these three you wish should go.

You will recall that General [John] Vandeleur [a brigade commander in the Light Division] has had a claim to a Command in the Cavalry and if he is to have one, you must fix upon the second who is to go. If he is not to have a Command, the Senior Colonel is Sir Granby Calcraft; & I acknowledge that I don't see that the Service will derive much advantage from sending to England any one of these Genl Officers above mentioned in order that Sir Granby may Command a Brigade. The next to Sir Granby is Lord Edward Somerset; & he can have a Brigade only by sending home the three General Officers above mentioned; & not taking Vandeleur from the Infantry.

I wish to have your opinion upon all these points as soon as possible; & likewise that you will let me know what Reg^{ts} you wish should be in each Brigade & what General Officer at the Head of each Brigade.

I must observe to you however that the English Hussar Brigade having come out as a Brigade I don't think we can with propriety break it up.

There is no General Officer at present in the Household Brigade; but I understand that [Major-General Terence] OLoghlin is coming out; & in the mean time *according to the principles of the Guards* they must be commanded by an Officer of their own Corps.

I hope that your wound is entirely healed & that you are in good health.

Orders were issued on 21 April for the amalgamation of the cavalry into a single division. But Cotton did not in fact rejoin until 25 June, his place apparently being taken in the meantime by Major-General Eberhardt von Bock. Nor did this united division ever see action as such, for Wellington continued to employ its brigades individually or in small groups, partly as he lacked sufficient confidence in his cavalry and its commanders to use it in mass and partly as the terrain was rarely suitable.

Cotton's return to the Peninsula was apparently delayed by the issue of who would assume command of the army if Wellington became a casualty. Wellington viewed Beresford, with his political and administrative experience, as the most suitable candidate. But Cotton was one of the three lieutenant-generals in the Peninsula who were senior to Beresford in the British service, despite the fact that Beresford had a claim to seniority as a Portuguese marshal. Cotton reluctantly accepted the arrangement. He was also disappointed by the failure of his attempts to secure a peerage: he would not become Baron Combermere until May 1814, after the end of the war.

Major-General Long commented in a letter to his brother dated 25 January 1813:

> ... Sir Stapleton Cotton is now in England but expected back again – the truth is, the old Cavalry Generals, like their native oaks, bid defiance to age & weather, & will not die off – They bend but they will not break – One concession now on their part, would give Sir Stapleton a Reg^t – This obtained he will retire, look out for another wife, & the rest of his campaigns will be confined to her Boudoir & St Stevens Chapel – tho' I do not believe the Gallant General is much

of an orator – In this case Sir William Erskine would become the Senior Cavalry General, but as he is as blind as a beetle I fear he would lead us into many a ditch – . . .

Erskine had repeatedly blundered in the past and in fact his sanity was in some doubt. In any case, he died after jumping from a window in Lisbon in February 1813. Cotton became engaged to his second wife, Caroline, while on leave and married her in June 1814.

All three generals listed by Wellington in fact returned home in 1813. Slade was the first to go, on 23 April, being replaced by Fane. Anson followed, his brigade being given to Vandeleur on 2 July. Finally, Long was recalled by a letter from the Horse Guards dated 22 July. He wrote an undated narrative to explain the circumstances, including Wellington's less than forthright explanation:

> . . . On receiving the notification of his recal M General Long of course waited upon the Marquis of Wellington, and expressed a hope that no disapprobation of his conduct, on the part of his Lordship, had caused a measure so unexpected and distressing – Lord W. disavowed all personal implication in the proceeding – declared that the arrangement had originated at *Home*, & that M General Long must fight his own battle in England as well as he could that such circumstances were, of course, distressing to himself, but he washed his hands of all participation in the arrangement – . . .

Long had already written himself a mock epitaph in a letter to his brother on 9 July 1811:

Thanks of his Country

To

Robert Long –

Major General & Cabbage Planter

Who had luck enough to do his public duty,

Sense enough to know when he had done it – and

Wisdom enough to prefer – Cabbage-planting

to

Dependence upon Princes or Powers,

for

more substantial happiness!

Bello finito

Requiescat in pace!

The shortage of capable generals was one of Wellington's greatest problems and helps explain his insistence on seeing to as much as possible in person. 'Really,' he wrote scathingly in 1810, 'when I reflect upon the characters and attainments of some of the General officers of this army ... on whom I am to rely ... I tremble: and, as Lord Chesterfield said of the Generals of his day, "I only hope that when the enemy reads the list of their names he trembles as I do." '*

The most common fault was a lack of self-confidence, which imposed a ceiling on otherwise capable generals. Wellington remarked that they were really heroes when he was on the spot to direct them, but that when he was obliged to leave them they were children. Picton and Cole, for example, were both good divisional commanders whose physical bravery was never in doubt, but in July 1813 they lost their nerve when operating in the Pyrenees outside Wellington's immediate supervision. Only Hill and Graham could be wholly trusted with an independent command and they won outstanding victories in the Peninsula in their own right while commanding detached forces.

Several of Wellington's more capable subordinates returned from leave in the spring of 1813, including Graham and Major-General George Murray, his trusted Quartermaster-General. Wellington had used the lull to bring his army towards a peak of efficiency in readiness for the coming campaign.

Captain Alexandre de Roverea, Cole's ADC, wrote confidently on 20 April:

> ... For the last three Days, there has been, at last, much talk of our moving: – Lord Wellington said *at Dinner* we should march on the 1st May, which, by the bye, is his Lordship's Birth Day; – with any other person but him, such Dinner conversation, would not be paid much attention to: – but he has, more than once, already, taken in friends & foes, by the very publicity of his measures. – We shall take the Field with little short of 70.000 effective Rank & file, of which number, about 42000. I believe, will be British, & 28000. Portuguese: – & at no former Period of the war, has our army been in a fitter

---

* Second Duke of Wellington, ed., *Supplementary Despatches, Correspondence, and Memoranda of Field Marshal Arthur Duke of Wellington, K.G.* (London, 1858–64), v. 6, p. 582.

state for the field than it will be at the opening of this campaign: our men are mostly old soldiers, & with few Exceptions, we are composed of Regiments which have already tried the climate of the Country, & the fatigues of long marching, for two or three years. – . . .

7

The Great Offensive

January to June 1813

In January 1813 Wellington received confirmation that Napoleon had suffered a disaster in Russia. He realized that Napoleon was likely to withdraw some troops from the Peninsula to rebuild his army in central Europe, where Prussia would join Russia in the field in March, followed by Austria in August. Even so, 200,000 French soldiers would be left in Spain. Wellington himself would take the field with 80,000 British and Portuguese troops, plus over 21,000 Spaniards directly attached to his army following his appointment as *generalissimo* of the Spanish armed forces.

The French had abandoned southern Spain, but still had to hold large areas of the north, east and centre of the country against Spanish regular armies and the increasingly active guerrillas. The Army of Aragon under Marshal Suchet and the Army of Catalonia were both tied down on the east coast. The Army of the North under General Clausel was trying to regain control in northern Spain between the River Ebro and the Pyrenees, where insurrections threatened communications with France. That left three armies directly opposed to Wellington, those of the South, the Centre and Portugal. They were under the overall command of King Joseph and his Chief-of-Staff, Marshal Jourdan, and were widely dispersed, with most of their divisions lying between Madrid and the River Douro, a distance of 150 km. Furthermore, Napoleon ordered the bulk of the Army of Portugal to be detached to reinforce the Army of the North. This reduced Joseph's strength to between 70,000 and 80,000 men.

Joseph would be able to check or seriously delay a frontal advance by concentrating on the north bank of the River Douro, which was a formidable obstacle at this time of year. Wellington before the start of his offensive therefore intended to push the bulk of his army in secret across the Douro within Portugal. He would do this by sending it through the remote and mountainous region of Trás-os-Montes in the north-eastern corner of Portugal, which the French mistakenly believed to be impassable for an army. He would thereby turn Joseph's northern flank and could then thrust across northern Spain, relentlessly outflanking any positions he tried to adopt. He judged that if he moved fast enough, the widely scattered French units would not have time to concentrate sufficient troops to check him.

Wellington would start his offensive by feinting frontally with a third of his army under Hill along the road that he had used the year before, from Ciudad Rodrigo to Salamanca. He would then unleash the other two-thirds under Graham from the Trás-os-Montes along the north bank of the Douro. He was forced to postpone the start of his advance from 1 May, partly as he encountered problems in transporting his pontoon train across the mountainous country and partly as he had expected forage to become available earlier than it in fact did. Major Duffy of the 43rd Regiment recorded on 27 April that it had rained seriously the previous night for the first time of the season and that the grass had been more delayed by the dryness than the inhabitants could recollect for thirty years.

In the middle of May, Graham's units began to move from their winter quarters up to the north-eastern frontier of Portugal ready for the start of the offensive. Major-General Andrew Hay, commanding a brigade of the 5th Division, noted in his usual execrable handwriting on 21 May:

> ... The *Duke* [Wellington was a Spanish and a Portuguese duke] is bringing us onto our [illegible] gradually as our marches have been short & this is the second halting day since we left Lamego which has the best effect, as it enables the men who were lately dismissed the hospitals to recover their strength & wind & gets rid of the loose flesh acquired by the healthy ones in their long winter quarter, & considerable use of Douro wine which they consumed during their stay it is astonishing the quantity [illegible] of wine the Division have drank yet there have been no outrages committed & scarcely a drunken guard & they are looking healthy & brown as gipsys ...

Also in Graham's command was Picton's 3rd Division, which included one of the most famous units in Wellington's army, the

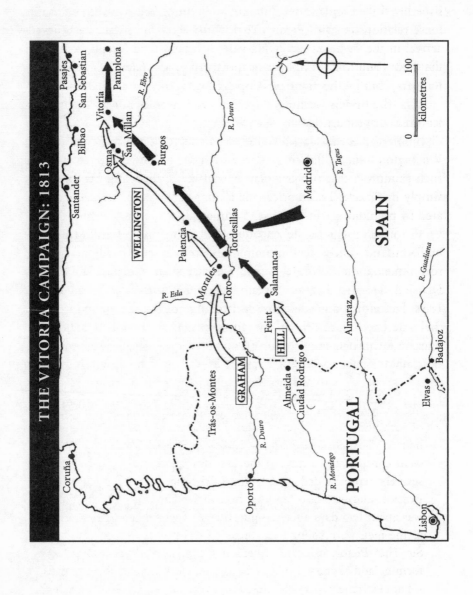

1st Battalion of the 88th Regiment of Foot (Connaught Rangers). It was superbly drilled and enjoyed a fearsome reputation in battle, but had a tense relationship with Picton. The feud dated from soon after Picton's arrival in the Peninsula in January 1810, when he had sarcastically told the 88th: 'You are not known in the army by the name of "Connaught Rangers", but by the name of "Connaught *footpads!*" '

It is true that in Wellington's army as a whole, men with Irish names featured disproportionately in general courts-martial. But the 88th's disciplinary record was no worse than that of many other units and Wellington's claim that he hanged and shot more of its men for crimes such as murder and robbery than he did of all the rest of the army was simply incorrect.* Its notoriety for looting seems to have been exaggerated by prejudice against an Irish regiment.

Picton accepted publicly that he had been misinformed about the 88th, but no officer of the regiment was ever promoted through his recommendation during the four years that he commanded the 3rd Division. Despite this, as Captain James Oates revealed in a letter of 1831, Picton had a grudging respect for the men and a real concern for their welfare. The 88th at the time of the following incident were marching through the mountains of northern Portugal, with Major R. Barclay McPherson in acting command:

> ... In order to facilitate the movements of the [3rd] Div^n we were ordered to proceed by single regiments, and the commanding officer of each, directed to procure a guide for himself to where we were to halt on the first days march – Major McPherson by some mistake went considerably astray on the first days march, for which he was severely reprimanded by Sir Thos Brisbane who commanded the Brigade, and who also reported him to Sir Thos Picton,[.] I think it was about two days after at some village of which I forget the name, as the men were falling in at break of day preparatory to marching Sir Thos Picton came up where my company (Gr[enadier]s) was forming and addressed [us] as far as I recollect in the following terms – I am extremely sorry 88th that a regt who has so often distinguished itself when properly commanded should now be so unnessarily

---

* H. Jourdain and E. Fraser, *The Connaught Rangers: 1st Battalion, formerly 88th Foot* (London, 1924), p. 43; C. Oman, *Wellington's Army 1809–14* (reissued London, 1993), p. 214.

harrassed through the ignorance and unfitness for command of your present commanding officer, but I'll take care he never shall command you again if I can prevent it. –

Some little time after Sir Tho⁵ Picton accosted me and said he was surprised that I as second in command did not interfere and prevent *that man* from destroying the regt, as he knew they were marched twelve miles at least further than they should have been, which was the cause of one of the men dropping dead –

I of course gave the usual excuse of not commanding being simply a Captain at the head of my Company – Well Sir, he replied you will now take the command of the regt, as I have put Major McPherson in arrest, and I have no doubt you will do your duty, or words to that effect – I was in command about three days, when through the strong intercession of Sir Tho⁵ Brisbane who commanded the Brigade Major McPherson was restored to the command – however I firmly believe Sir Tho⁵ Pictons aversion continued during the whole campaign – . . .

As planned, Wellington diverted French attention from Graham's impending offensive. He advanced frontally on 20 May with the third of his army under Hill and occupied the city of Salamanca six days later. A division of French infantry that had been posted at the city hurriedly retreated, pursued by two brigades of Hill's cavalry. It escaped after repelling several charges, but lost its ammunition train. John Insley of the 1st Dragoons explained how:

. . . our squdron charged a Solid square of them – they gave us a Volley which caused us to fall back again – we had 2 men wounded – The Major & Adjutants Horses were killed – 2 Troop Horses killed & 9 wounded We took 130 Prisoners and killed 100. they were mostly all Drunk – they had 12 Days Rations with them – . . .

William Paterson, a clerk in the Commissariat, wrote that:

. . . we accordingly prepared to proceed to this famous City which we entered on the morning of the 26th with the Royal Horse Guards amidst the blessings and aclamations of the inhabitants who with sincere delight seemed to welcome our arrival, exclaiming in every corner *Viva los Ingleses*, & inviting us to enter their Houses and become their Guests, the appearance of our troops on this morning was truly flattering to every Englishman & seemed the astonishment of every Spaniard;

The Royal Horse Guards are so well known & so remarkable, even in England, for the superiority of their appearance that any description of the Gigantic figures of the men or the noble appearance of the Horses seems here unnecessary. So different did they appear to the astonished Inhabitants from their own diminitive Horses and their degenerated Soldiers, that they seemed to look upon these noble Troops as more than mortal, and really I may myself confess that I never saw any thing before so much resembling the figures which the enthusiasm of the mind draws when warmed with the descriptions of Homer or of Virgil of the warriors of Greece & Troy

By the end of the 26th Wellington had 30,000 men under Hill in position north and east of Salamanca, where they waited for the next six days.

Wellington left Hill and rode north to join Graham for the main thrust from the Trás-os-Montes. On 31 May, the Hussar Brigade under Colonel Colquhoun Grant seized the ford of Almendra across the River Esla, 20 km east of the Portuguese frontier. Several men and horses were lost in the swift current, but most of the hussars made it across with infantrymen hanging on to their stirrups. The French picquet watching this sector had negligently withdrawn and Lieutenant Woodberry of the 18th Hussars wrote:

At last I have seen a skirmish – The Brigade passed the Ford of Almandra supported by the 7th & 8th [6th?] Divisons of the Army & Boltons Squadron of Flying Artillery – we passed about 2 oCk then very dark, the Enemy did not expect us so early was taken by surprise and out of about sixty men, that formed the Squadron, in charge of the Heights & Ford not more than 10 Escaped. The officer commandg the piquet was shaving himself at the time [and was] took prisoner, some of the men made great resistance but was most horribly cut & hacked about by the men of the 15th Hussars who had the honor of passing over first & was thereby oblig'd to act. – Captn [Robert] Carew & the Veternary Surgeon saw a party of the flying Enemy enter the village [of] Almandra gallop'd there immediately & took five men & four Horses – I was order'd to return to our Camp &

bring the Baggage of the Brigade over the River – by the time I arrived with it the Pontoon Bridge was put accross the River which I passed over; it was made with 9 Boats with Boards &c accross them. – when the Baggage Mules &c had advanced about 2 miles on the Road to this place [Yeneste] from the Ford, an Orderly man from a Piquet under Captn Grammont, of 10th Hussars, came Gallopping past & inform'd us that Two Squadrons of the Enemies Draggoons was advancing towards us, – I halted the whole & desired an officer of the [15th] Kings Hussars who had charge of their Baggage to remain with the whole while I went forward & reconnitred – On my return I observed all the Baggage Mules &c &c flying back as fast as they were able. – I was just able to stop by the swiftness of my Horse about half of them, & proceed immediately here. – The Enemy who was really advancing but turned about & retreated immediately on observing our Piquett. – – The Alarm was given thro' this Orderly & before I had proceeded half a mile heard the Bugles sounding in all directions & the Infantry who had taken their Cantonments for the day was oblig'd to march near 2 Leagues further. – This was certainly the most fatiguing march I have experienced since I have been in the Army, – Lord Wellington employs himself reconnitg & arrainging every thing on the march and appears very confident that we shall drive the Enemy out of the Country; – ...

The Hussar Brigade subsequently pushed eastwards along the north bank of the Douro. The French had a dragoon division in this sector under General Alexandre Digeon, but it withdrew. On the morning of 2 June, the Hussar Brigade expelled a reconnaissance party of about 200 French dragoons from the town of Toro, 45 km east of the Esla. The 10th Hussars pursued, followed by the 18th, but encountered Digeon's division nearly 8 km to the east near the village of Morales de Toro. Woodberry explained how they came across the foremost French brigade on the plain before the village:

... Two Squadron's of the Enemy's 16th Dragoons – was drawn up: & appear'd determin'd to oppose us. – The 10th Hussars & 18th immediately formed up in squadrons & advanced towards them; I was out in front commanding the Skirmishers – & had much trouble in keeping my men from advancing upon their body: – The Flying Artillery [two guns of the Royal Horse Artillery] now came up & I was call'd in, they immediately fired twice & the Enemy then broke

& moved towards this place [Morales], we now discover'd 2 more Squadrons of their dragoons formed on the left of this Town:– The 10ᵗʰ Hussars now charg'd those retreating when they turned round & charg'd them, in high stile, all was now bustle & confusion. the French tried to make their best way off while the 10ᵗʰ was hacking & cutting them about in all directions – . . .

The right squadron of the 18th Hussars joined the action by pushing round to the south of Morales and caused the French brigade to panic by appearing on its flank. The pursuit continued for 3 km up to the end of the plain, where Digeon's second brigade of dragoons was posted, supported by infantry and artillery on the heights above:

. . . it was impossible to distinguish the Enemy from our own Hussars such was the confusion. The whole plain in 10 minutes presented a dreadful scene dead, Wounded and Prisoners in all direction [sic] for as fast as our men could get up with them they were cut down and out of the four squadrons a very few made their Escape to the Hills in front of this plain where the Enemy had Eight squadrons more & a Column of Infantry with artillery those never came from the Hills but upon our closing upon them and being in the act of following them up the hill they fired their Artillery at us. it was here our Centre squadron came up with the remains of their flying force, & comm-enc'd the Carnage: I had a cut at one man myself who made point at me which I parried: I spoild his beauty, if I did not take his life for I gave a most severe cut across the Eyes & cheek & must have cut them out. however in the scene of confusion, when the Enemy fired their first shot, he and many other prisoners made their escape – The Bullet [cannonball] from their second fire fell within a foot of my horse and nearly smother'd me with dust: But as the saying is, every bullet has its billet: – we in our turn was oblig'd to retreat back out of the range of their Artillery which after firing about a Dozen times & throwing two bombs they retreated. The country over the Hills, being so much in their favor and our horses being much blown, we took up our quarters in this village & trusts to morrow we shall again come up with them . . .

The Hussar Brigade, according to Woodberry, lost 16 men and captured 239 Frenchmen and 181 horses.

Lieutenant-Colonel Murray, the commander of the 18th Hussars, also described Morales, in a letter to his wife on 23 June:

We crossed the Esla the day after I wrote to you. Some of the Infantry crossed at the same time as we did. The enemy most obligingly made no opposition, but the passage of the river from its deepness & impetuosity cost us several of the Infantry. There was a little skirmishing between a squadron of the 15th and some of the enemy's cavalry. Two days after there was a brilliant affair near Moralez. The 10th overwhelmed some of the enemy's cavalry with a degree of brilliancy that might be expected from the best Regt in our service. Young Somerset's behaviour on this occasion was *noble*.

Our right squadron under [Major James] Hughes came up with the enemy & behaved very well. The rest of the Regiment merely supported the 10th & had no other share of the honours of the day than being cannonaded a little. Col¹ Grant distinguished himself so much that the French asked Capt. [James] Lloyd of the 10th whom they took but afterwards gave leave to go away, 'who that great black fellow in a cocked Hat was?['] . . .

Grant's nickname was the 'Black Giant', while his red-headed Brigade-Major was dubbed the 'Red Dwarf'. Murray continued:

. . . We had a very long gallop indeed after the Enemy all the way from Toro to a bridge beyond Moralez. The Troopers were quite done, & [illegible] had pretty near enough of it when we halted. Col Grant's orders of the day paid a very great tribute to the brilliancy of the conduct of the 10th & then said 'the steady support given by the 18th Hrs under the Hon. L.C. M.[urray] & the determined bravery of that part of it that came actually in contact with the enemy kept up the high character of that distinguished corps.' To give the devil his due Hughes is a very brave little fellow & dont vapour about his courage. I had been with the right squadron, but had gone to the left for as they had put us for I know not what reason on the right of the 10th the left squadron was the one that it was probable would be the first brought into action.

I am here [Palencia] laid up from the effects of an accident but dont be in the least uneasy for I am doing quite well. Tho my recovery may be tedious I am doing very well I assure you. In coming out of the Esla Fabian's [Murray's horse] feet slipped from under him & he fell with my knee against some sharp rocks. I rode for three or four days afterwards until my knee became too harmful for it to be in my power to ride. The kindness of General G. Murray [the Quartermaster-General] & Lord Dalhousie [commander of the 7th Division] having provided me with a spring waggon I kept up with the army until the surgeons said I must not go on. I stopped two days at Villa Diego & from thence came back to this place where there is a permanent Hospital Station. I am attended by a good & attentive [illegible] tho' I dont know his name. He says I am very patient & so I think I am for except against the drivers of the waggon when they took me over morasses rocks &c. by way of short cuts shaking the very soul out of my body I have not uttered anything like a murmur since my accident. I never in my life experienced more kindness than I have from every body. Since I have been obliged to march in a waggon I have not seen my own Brigade. But that did not signify every body seemed to outdo the other in giving me assistance. . . .

Hill's diversion at Salamanca had now fulfilled its purpose and on Wellington's orders he joined Graham on the north bank of the Douro. Major Duffy of the 43rd Regiment crossed the river on 3 June by the broken bridge at Toro:

The [Light] Division commenced crossing at 3 this Morng – The Bridge not being repaired and the space between the Arches being filled up by the Explosion – Ladders were placed & the Division descended one ruin of an arch & ascended another by the same means – The Baggage Artillery &c passed the Ford – the only accident that happened was two children who fell off mules being drowned –

. . .

One of the Soldiers was bit by either a Viper or a scorpion a few nights ago in the neck. his head & neck swelled a good deal next day & he was sent back to the Hospital at Salamanca where he died in the course of 36 Hours from the time of the bite – he was asleep at the moment the accident happened and the pain did not wake him – . . .

Wellington thus united his army north of the Douro, leaving only garrisons and some Spanish cavalry to the south. As a result, Joseph was outflanked and had to withdraw north-eastwards along the main road to

Burgos. Wellington advanced in four columns to the north of this road in order to continue to turn his flank. He was determined to maintain his momentum. Lieutenant Woodberry recorded on 6 June: '... The English Mail arrived the day before yesterday. Lord Wellington only allow'd the Letters to be deliver'd to the officers reserving the newspapers till a future time thinking if the officers got them now they would be reading the news instead of attending to their duties: – ...'

On 9 June, Joseph deployed his available forces west of Burgos. Wellington was now 150 km from Portugal. After reconnoitring, he decided to attack the foremost French units, two divisions of the Army of Portugal, on the 12th, as he realized that they could be outflanked to the north and that their nearest support was 8 km to the rear. He deployed part of his southernmost column under Hill for a frontal attack and sent the rest of it, two cavalry brigades supported by the Light Division, to turn the French flank. Brigadier-General Charles Ashworth commanded a brigade of Portuguese infantry, which as part of the 2nd Division was intended to join the frontal assault. But he described in his journal how the French withdrew so promptly that Hill's infantry was not engaged:

> Marched at ½ past three oClock in the morning past Castroxeres [Castroxeriz] & through Bario [Barrio de Santa Marta] a short distance from which I was joined by the 3d Brigade & two of the *Best* Guns (one 9 Pounders [sic], & a Howitzer) of the Brigade of our Artillery of the 2d Division, which formed the center Column of attack made upon the Enemy, who were formed on the Heights above [the] Hormaza, some skirmishing took place between the Cavalry about eleven oClock, when we gained the heights we saw five Batns formed in Line at some distance who seemed inclined to wait for us, Lord Wellington sent me orders to form the troops under my Command into Line, which when the enemy observed instantly commenced his retreat, in squares of Battns our Cavalry pressing them & the Horse Artillery firing on them occassionally, we could not get after them in time & they escaped across a small river near the high Burgos road where the quarter part of their Army was formed – One Gun was taken by the Cavalry & a few Prisoners. After the enemy crossed the river nothing further was attempted, their Columns moved off towards Burgos 2 leagues off & we returned & encamped at the village of Rosamaza –

The French had insufficient supplies to remain at Burgos for more than a few days and retreated that night, abandoning the city and blowing up its castle on the morning of the 13th. They intended to concentrate in greater strength behind the River Ebro, 70 km to the north-east. But Wellington veered more to the north and pressed on, crossing the Ebro between the 14th and 16th well to the north-west of the French. Lieutenant Woodberry noted on 15 June:

> ... I took a sheep from a flock on the hill side, kill'd him in the Hussar stile – with my sword and divided him with M[r] [Lieutenant Edward] Barrett of 15th Hussars. – I dined off a part and think I never enjoy'd a dinner more in my life. – My heart aches for the unfortunate Infantry who I saw to day on the march such numbers laying on the Roadside unable to stir a step further, it is impossible for the poor fellows to march 35 to 40 miles two days running: but Lord Wellington was anxious to cross the Ebro to day. God only knows what may be done to morrow: – ...

The French belatedly realized that Wellington had outflanked their positions on the Ebro, but concluded that he was heading for the port of Bilbao on the Biscay coast, in order to execute a wide turning movement in the far north. Consequently, on the 18th they sent the three infantry divisions of General Honoré Reille's Army of Portugal northwards to cover Bilbao. But Wellington in fact intended a more limited outflanking movement and after crossing the Ebro had inclined to the east. His columns collided on the 18th with Reille's units at San Millan and Osma, 40 km south of Bilbao. Captain Henry Booth of the 43rd Regiment described in a letter to his sister two days later how the Light Division mauled one of Reille's divisions at San Millan:

> ... In winding thro' these Vallies; and just as the head of our division began to dèbouche into a more open Space, we found we had been marching parallel to a french division commanded by Genl Maucune; but this Circumstance had been concealed from us by the high hills which divided our line of march between them – The french were also coming out of the Mountains into the same open Space thro' which was also their line of March; but as the head of their Column was more advanced on the line of March than ours', part of this division made its Escape from us – We succeeded however in cutting off one Brigade which dispersed itself into the Mountains on their

right. The 52[d] and 95th with some Portuguese light Troops forming the 2[d] Brigade of our division pursued them took about 300 prisoners besides killing a great number by their fire – captured all their Baggage, and a few only of *this* unfortunate brigade made their escape by taking refuge in the Mountains – our loss was very trifling, nothing to speak of – ...

Following these actions, Reille retreated 20 km to the east, where he took up a position behind the River Bayas near the village of Morillas. He was ordered to delay Wellington for as long as possible here in order to cover the retreat of the Armies of the South and Centre as they fell back past Reille's southern flank towards the city of Vitoria. Otherwise, Wellington could check them by blocking the main road at the Puebla Pass to the south-east of Reille's positions.

The action that ensued with Reille on the Bayas on 19 June offers an insight into Wellington's command methods. First, the Quartermaster-General, Major-General George Murray, issued a movement order entitled 'Arrangements for the ulterior movements of the army on the 19th June'. It directed the army's advance in several columns. In the centre were the Light and 4th Divisions, each preceded by a cavalry brigade:

> ... The movement of these two columns are to be combined and they will as far as circumstances permit keep up a constant communication with each other and favour each other's advance in case of opposition on the part of the Enemy. ...

This was not always easy, as Captain Booth explained. Since the 18th, he wrote:

> ... some part of the army has been skirmishing with them [the French] every day. We often hear the roar of Cannon, with Musquetry, on our line of march, in the Mountains, the Echo of which is *tremendous* and *sublime*; and at the same time quite ignorant what division is engaged, or what is going on, so entirely are we separated by the Mountains from each other – altho' every division of the army is marching *parallel* & *close to* each other. – ...

It was midday on the 19th before Wellington's leading divisions had closed up on the Bayas. He then sought to prise Reille out of his position by attacking him frontally at the village of Morillas with the 4th Division, while he turned his southern flank near Póbes, 2.5 km away, with the Light Division. The 4th Division took Morillas and, supported by the fire of some guns, continued its advance. The French offered little resistance, being more intent on delaying Wellington than checking him, so few men were lost on either side during this skirmishing.

The progress of the action can be followed in three characteristically precise notes that Wellington sent in succession to Lieutenant-General Sir Lowry Cole, the commander of the 4th Division. They were written in ink on small leaves of paper apparently cut from a notebook with a knife and they show how Wellington exercised a close, personal command style. The first read:

> On the heighths near Podes [Póbes] June 19th 1813 ½ past 12 at Noon. –
> I have ordered the Light Division to cross the River, & to get possession of the Ridge on the Enemy's left; and you will advance, & cannonade them in front, & push your Light Infantry across supporting it by Cavalry & Heavy Infantry. –
> There is a Bridge at the Village, & I understand several fords. Wellington
> I understand that the Enemy have no Cannon; and I have seen none –

The paucity of good, detailed maps meant that orders often referred to descriptions of the terrain rather than to place names. Wellington followed up his initial order one and a quarter hours later by a second message as the action progressed:

> I will make the Light Division continue its march till the Ridge on your right ends; & do you follow them up the valley to the same point
> Wellington
> ¼ before two P.M
> Let the Cavalry go with you

A third and final order reached Cole shortly afterwards:

> 2 P M. June 19th
> Since I wrote to you a quarter of an hour ago I have heard that the Enemy are in strength on the great Road; you had better therefore

halt when you will have crossed the River; & taken up such Posts as you may think proper – Wellington

The enemy forces in strength on the great road, 7 km to the south-east, were the Armies of the Centre and South retiring towards Vitoria under the cover of Reille's delaying action. Wellington had evidently decided not to risk a general engagement since he did not have all his columns in position; it was also raining and late in the day.

Major Duffy, who was in the Light Division, described the fighting on the Bayas:

> Our Route this morning was to our right towards the High road from Frias to Vitoria – passed near Espejo – and through the Village of Salines [Salinas de Añana] – a very strong pass – the last of the Enemys Column had left it only a few hours previous – in about a league halted – found a Divⁿ of the Enemy posted on a wooddy mountain to our left – soon after heard our 4th Division engaged with them – the Affair lasted all the afternoon – The Light Division moved to the rear of the mountain to attack but were halted by order as it appeared that two other French Divisions were on the High Road to our right – Rain all day – The men no Bread for two days

Lieutenant James Gairdner of the 95th Rifles contributes more detail. As part of the Light Division, he passed through the village of Salinas and, about 3 km beyond it:

> ... we halted for some time soon after moved on a little[.] the 4 Divn were all this time engaged at a pass near[by.] some of the Cacadores of our Divn were sent up a mountain above it & killed a great number[.] encamped on this ground – very rainy –

Reille, prised out of his position on the Bayas, retreated eastwards, having assured the safe withdrawal of the French behind the River Zadorra and into an extensive valley containing the city of Vitoria. Wellington's leading divisions spent the night along the Bayas. The next day, Lieutenant Gairdner described how he was:

> Halted here all day[.] our Compy was sent to the Front on Piquet – The Place we are in now is a valley we are encamped at one side Close at the foot of a Ridge of very high mountains, the 2nd Battⁿ [95th] & 1st Caçadores are on the top of the mountain & to the left

of the rest of the Div^n[.] I rode up to their encampment today the view from it is most beautiful, the ascent of the mountain is steep on this side but on the other side it is quite Perpendicular & between it & another ridge is a narrow valley with a small river running thro it[.] in this valley are the 4th Divn encamped and thro this valley the enemy retreated yesterday when the 4th Div^n forced the pass[.] Ab^t a league & ½ in front I saw Vittoria & on this side of it the enemy encamped[.] The view from this is very extensive – . . .

Wellington spent the 20th reconnoitring and planning his moves for the battle that he hoped to fight the next day. The valley in which the French lay was contained by mountains on three sides, being open only at the eastern end, near the city of Vitoria. It extended for 16 km from west to east and 9 from north to south. Except in the east, it consisted of uneven terrain broken by hills and dotted with villages. The River Zadorra meandered its way along the northern side of the valley before turning to the south-west and flowing out of it through the Puebla Pass, which formed its western entrance. The French, expecting an attack from the west, had arrayed their armies one behind the other across the valley, but had neglected to guard their northern flank along the Zadorra River or to destroy its numerous bridges.

Wellington could field 79,000 troops against the 66,000 that Joseph had at Vitoria. He intended not simply to defeat the French, but to cut their line of retreat, the main road which led from Vitoria to the north-east. To do this, he would fall on Joseph's open northern flank by advancing from his start line, the River Bayas, and swinging round to the right through the mountains to reach the northern side of the valley. The attack would be made in four prongs, starting with a diversionary assault in the west at the Puebla Pass and developing eastwards as the prongs came successively into action.

The diversion would be made by Hill with the 2nd Division and its attached units. Its task was to secure the western entrance to the valley by seizing the heights on the southern flank of the Puebla Pass. This would distract the French commanders and absorb their reserves. The next prong, the 4th and Light Divisions, would second this assault immediately to the north. Then, further to the north-east, the 3rd and 7th Divisions would sweep out the mountains and plunge across the River Zadorra into the French flank. The final prong, under Graham, would attack the French rear near the city of Vitoria, 8 km to the east, and cut their line of retreat.

Hill began at about 8.00 a.m. by pushing a Spanish division under General Pablo Morillo up the Puebla Heights. He subsequently supported Morillo with Lieutenant-Colonel the Hon. Henry Cadogan's brigade of British infantry. In the course of hard fighting, these troops drew French reinforcements onto the heights, weakening their position in the valley and distracting their attention. Hill meanwhile pushed the rest of his command, including Brigadier-General Ashworth's Portuguese infantry brigade, into the valley immediately to the north of the Puebla Heights. Ashworth described in his journal how he was sent to support Cadogan:

> . . . all arrangements for our attacking the left of their line were soon made, the first Brigade took to the right up the mountains & soon drove the enemy from them in capital style, Colonel Cadogan who commanded the Brigade fell early in the action, having received a mortal wound of which he died a few hours afterwards, my Brigade advanced some distance upon the main road & then formed in column on the right of it on some rising ground, soon afterwards moved to occupy other heights in advance & so on, while the centre & left of our army was advancing to the attack, in the mean time the 71st Regt on the heights had advanced rather too far, & without support, & were charged by a very superior force of the enemy & driven from a hill which they had got possession of, with very considerable loss, in consequence I was ordered up to support the 1st Brigade with the 18th Regt & took the command there. the enemy were very strong opposite to us but did not venture to advance any further, the attack on the center took place in the valley & their Army was completely routed, we saw them flying in all directions in the greatest confusion. The Troops opposed to us seeing their second line below giving way, immediately retired, & we followed them, but the country was so difficult & hilly we could not hope even to come up with them, & we marched by a flank movement on the right to the city of Vitoria – . . .

Meanwhile, Wellington's second and third prongs had crossed the River Zadorra to assail the French northern flank. The French were unable to establish a proper line of defence, particularly after 3.00 p.m.

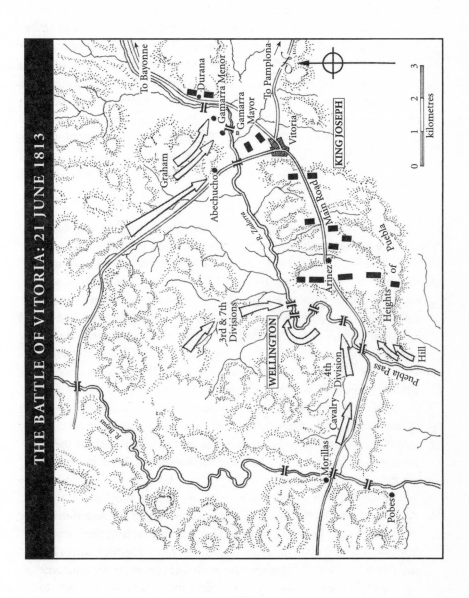

THE BATTLE OF VITORIA: 21 JUNE 1813

To Bayonne

Durana

Gamarra Menor

Gamarra Mayor

To Pamplona

KING JOSEPH

Vitoria

Graham

Abechucho

R. Zadorra

Main Road

Puebla

3rd & 7th
Divisions

Arinez

WELLINGTON

Heights

of

4th
Division

Puebla Pass

Hill

Cavalry

R. Bayas

Morillas

Pobes

kilometres
0   1   2   3

when Picton's 3rd Division breached their positions by storming the hill and village of Arinez. Wellington pressed home the attack and drove the French back along the valley to the city of Vitoria. Major Duffy of the 43rd Regiment described the Light Division's role during this fighting:

At 5 O Clock [in the morning] the Division moved off its ground and turned to the left leaving the direct road to Vitoria and the mountain to our right – passed the 4th Division[.] The Enemy were seen yesterday in position in front of Vitoria, but it was doubtful whether he would retain his position & wait our attack – Our Division halted about 7 O Clock and as the Mist & Rain cleared up had a distinct view of the Enemy's Position to our front[.] His right appeared to rest on a high Sugarloaf Sand Hill [the hill of Arinez] having two lines extending to a high ridge of mountains where his left rested – the great road from Miranda leading through the Centre of his Position which was defended by two Batteries of 10 Cannon in position – we could not see to the right further than the sand hill but when the attack commenced it appear'd as if he had given a front resting his right upon Vitoria and his Centre behind the Sand Hill –

About 10 O Clock we moved to our left and crossed the Zadorra River by a Bridge which the Enemy had very fortunately left unprotected and behind a round hill the Division formed without opposition – 2 Field Pieces that the Enemy had on our left at another Bridge opened upon us a few shot without effect – The 3rd Division [under Picton] soon after appeared and passed the Bridge to our left which at first the Enemy seemed determined to dispute – however a few rounds from our Field Pieces cleared away the Enemy and the 3rd Div[n] passed –

    . . .

As soon as the 3rd Div[n] had crossed about 11 O Clock we moved on and the Battle became general – The Enemy withdrew the Troops they had on the plain in front of where we crossed immediately and the Guns they had commanding the great road as we directed our attack on their right flank and rather to the rear of it[.]

The Enemy allowed us to gain the high ground without opposition but opened a tremendous fire from behind a Village [Arinez] on the top of it which brought us to a momentary check – the Village however was carried by part of the Rifle Reg[t] and some of the 3 Div[n] and we then moved on without a halt for the remainder of the day –

Having rec^d a slight wound in my head at this moment I left the Brigade – . . .

It was during the attack on Arinez that Picton reopened the festering wound in his relations with the 88th Regiment. Captain James Oates explained:

> . . . With regard to the abuse of Sir Thos Picton to the regt (if it can be called by that name) it was this – as we were advancing to attack a village in the possession of the Enemy we were halted by Sir Thos Brisbane [the brigade commander] when he saw we were so much exposed and unsupported on our left, at this moment Sir Thos Picton came up and said why dont you go on, I think to the best of my recollection, that the reply was from Sir Thos Brisbane you see how exposed we are on our left, Sir Thos Picton repeated *go on* upon which the whole Brigade with Sir Thos Brisbane at its head instantly moved forward, and before it was possible to see who were first or last Sir Thos Picton said in the same breadth, *there 74th, shew the 88th the way* – this was the whole of what passed by way of abuse – we rapidly advanced drove the Enemy out of the village and formed line on the other side, gave them a volley, charged, and drove the Enemy till they got into complete route and confusion through the Town of Vittoria – . . .

The 88th remonstrated to Wellington after the battle, as a result of which Picton wrote a letter expressing regret that so distinguished a regiment should have been offended by words spoken in haste.

By now, Wellington's fourth prong under Graham should have been in a position to cut the French off. Graham had 20,000 men, namely the 1st and 5th Divisions, two independent brigades of Portuguese infantry, two cavalry brigades and four battalions of Spanish infantry under Colonel Francisco Longa. Wellington had been obliged to give him considerable discretion in view of the distances involved. Graham's main task was to outflank the French to the east and cut the main road, but he had to regulate his advance by the progress of the other prongs.

Graham would be opposed by the Army of Portugal under General Honoré Reille, but both Wellington and Graham overestimated its strength. Reille in fact had only two infantry divisions present and Graham might have been bolder had he known this. As it was, his conduct of the action was hesitant and unimaginative. Reille withdrew his troops to the south bank of the Zadorra on Graham's approach towards noon, but left garrisons in the villages of Abechucho, Gamarra Mayor and Gamarra Menor on the north bank to cover the three bridges that spanned the river in this sector.

Longa's Spaniards took Gamarra Menor, the easternmost village, and subsequently stormed the nearby bridge at Durana, thus severing the main road. His further progress was checked, but the French now had only a poor quality road to Pamplona as a line of retreat.

Major-General Frederick Robinson meanwhile stormed the village of Gamarra Mayor with his British brigade of the 5th Division. But when his troops assailed the adjacent bridge, they were massacred by French guns. Major-General John Oswald, the commander of the 5th Division, reinforced Robinson with Major-General Andrew Hay's brigade, composed of the British 1st, 9th and 38th Regiments of Foot. At 8.30 p.m. that same evening, Hay wrote a fascinating letter in which he described his role and also that of his son and ADC, Captain George Hay. When Sir Charles Oman wrote his definitive, seven-volume *History of the Peninsular War* early in the twentieth century, he had available only one good account of the fighting in Graham's sector, by Sergeant James Hale of the 9th Regiment. Hay's letter now sheds new light on the action and reveals, for example, the role of the 38th Regiment, about which Oman in the absence of any primary evidence could say only that it must have been minimal given its low casualty figures:

> ... I have totally escaped untouched, where we my Brigade were mostly engaged today was in the attack of a village [Gamarra Mayor] on the Enemys Right which G¹ Robinsons brigade were ordered to attack, the [5th] Division having this day marched left in front, the Enemy were very numerous & strongly posted & tho' Robinsons people attacked them in the most gallant stile the fire was so severe & his loss heavy that I was obliged to go down *Double quick* to support him, I do not remember a more warm job & George who was every where & the admiration of every one for his cool gallantry & *inteligence* after we were in the village was wounded in the lower part of the back but the ball has been extracted & he is sent to a village with a number of others & is doing well & pronounced out of danger. You may judge of my feelings, tho in the heat of action, when I saw him helped off his horse the grey & the poor animal at the same time pinned with balls he [the horse] died soon after.

I shall never forget Georges placid countenance when he told me after I had put him behind a house where I thought he would be safe from further injury, he saw as the business is so severe & the enemy are in such force they may force the bridge & I may be taken prisoner, as the fate of the day at this time was very uncertain, their people are supposed to have had 75 thousand[.] I then immediately had him carried off by his favourite 9th [Regiment] this I hope with dry Eyes though I thought him in great danger but when a young Surgeon of the 9th some time afterwards came & told me he had extracted the ball & that he was *out of danger* as his spine was safe had the perfect use of his legs & was sent off in a Spring waggon with [Lieutenant-]Col [Colin] Campbell Royal [Scots] & another officer, then & not till then I burst with tears of Joy & certainly never was more thankful to God or went back with more zeal to direct some guns to be pointed at one of the Enemys Columns. every private was anxious to know how he was going on both English & Portuguese & I assure you they would have stormed any thing to revenge him; as we are still in pursuit, tho now halted for want of light which alone put an end to the conflict I can not by any means give you at present particulars except that this will be as proud a day for Englands troops as any she has seen. . . .

In fact, Captain Hay's wound proved mortal and he died on the 24th aged twenty-four. The day afterwards, a grief-stricken Major-General Hay informed his daughter Mary:

. . . There is every prospect of a speedy termination to this ever memorable & Glorious Campaign which has been as rapid as lightning & without a check[.] Such a brilliant succession of events was not to be expected without heartrending losses & many a promising young soldier has given his life on this occasion for his Country[.] I am afraid little do many of our people at home surrounded with luxurys consider how much they owe to their sailers & soldiers to keep [?] the *seat of war* from their fire sides [illegible.] 24 hours of the scenes, privations Dangers we are accustomed to would make them think very differently . . .

In a letter of the 23rd, he had added more details of the fighting. He described how Robinson 'went on in the most gallant stile & had his hat & clothes torn but his skin not touched' and how he himself brought down the 9th in line so that they were less exposed to the French cannonade and how he was able to put the 38th under a degree of cover:

> ... I was leading the centre along this road leading in to the village when I never in my life met with a more tremendous fire of musqutry & cannon so much so that the bachelor whom I rode tho [illegible] leaped about as if he had been going over hedges & ditchs[.] I did not see the Royal [Scots] but George told me the stile they dashed at & across the bridge with their bayonettes exceeded all praise[.] the 38th followed me double quick & came to Robinsons aid when very hard pressed indeed, when G¹ Oswald get us all in he would have defied the whole french army, yet the post was [(]the main road to [illegible]) of such consequence that they persevered for more than two hours, when they began to retire, my Brigade being comparatively fresh I volunteered to pursue which Oswald agreed to I soon met Sir Thomas [Graham] who approved much of what I had done[.] I kept moving on the left of the Cavalry to support them who every now & then when the ground permitted gave them a charge I galloped on with [Lieutenant-Colonel] George Berkeley [of the Adjutant-General's Department] with the Cavalry & it certainly was the grandest sight I ever saw [Second Captain William Norman] Ramsays 3 guns going every now & then at full gallop in the midst of heavy & light cavalry every now & then battery [sic] & giving them some case shot & so forward again till darkness put an end to the pursuit – ...

Hay highlighted a puzzling question about Graham's handling of the action:

> ... our worthy friends the heavy Germans & guards [of the 1st Division] who ought to have supported us were nether [sic] seen & unless [except] Halkets brigade of light Germans who were detached & behaved admirably the rest of the 1ˢᵗ Divⁿ did not fire a shot nor could I even see them, no doubt this will be explained but you will observe in Sir Thomas Grahams thanks that he does not even mention them ...

In fact, Graham made no progress until Reille was forced to abandon his defensive positions by the advance of the remainder of Wellington's army across the valley from the west. Of the 1st Division, only the two light infantry battalions of the King's German Legion saw action when

Graham, after receiving an order from Wellington towards 2.00 p.m. to press his attack harder, had belatedly attacked the village of Abechuco, 2.5 km to the west of Gamarra Mayor. But although he cleared the village easily, he made no attempt to storm the bridge further south and thus bypass the bloody stalemate at Gamarra Mayor.

Graham's unusually lacklustre performance was overshadowed by the conduct of many of Wellington's troops, who stopped to loot the vast French baggage trains as they passed the city of Vitoria instead of relentlessly prosecuting the pursuit. One such unit was the 18th Hussars. Lieutenant Woodberry explained:

> ... Joseph [Bonaparte, King of Spain] had a body guard of about one Hundred Hussars and I think [Captain Arthur] Kennedy's troop would have taken him had they kept together but they run after a set of fellows and Plunder and did not support their Captain who was very near being taken prisoner being oblig'd to dismount off his horse and leap over a ditch to save himself. Captn Bolton and Burk did not give him either that support they ought, and for which I hope they will suffer....

Wellington lost 5,100 men at Vitoria, but won a decisive victory, inflicting over 8,000 casualties and capturing all but two of Joseph's 153 guns, along with a vast amount of treasure and military supplies. The French field armies now retreated from the whole of Spain except Catalonia on the east coast. The Battle of Vitoria finally destroyed Joseph's claim to be King of Spain. He left the country for good on 28 June and formally abdicated on 11 December. He spent most of his remaining years in exile in the United States and died, aged seventy-six, in the Italian city of Florence in 1844.

Wellington has been accused of caution in exploiting his victory, but he faced serious logistical problems. Major Duffy noted on 28 June:

> ... The [Light] Division reduced by constant marching & privation to nearly one half of their original numbers at leaving Gallegos [17 km west of Ciudad Rodrigo] – Yesterday was the first full delivery of Bread we have had for Eight days and during which by receiving it 5 & 6 Ounces at a time in all it has not amounted to more than two pounds p^r man of Bread & Biscuit – We have had a little flour & the Soldiers have been allowed to collect beans from the Fields ...

Ashworth encountered a similar situation on 22 June when he marched his Brigade eastwards by Salvetierra:

... The whole road [was] strewed with French Tombrils, Carts, Papers & [illegible] & some dead Bodys – Dreadful heavy rain all this night, & no Baggage arrived, nothing can be more miserable than we all are not a bit to eat, the men also starving –

Two days later, he added:

The [2nd] Division moved about ten oClock, the roads in the most dreadful state from the heavy rains, & to mend the matter Gen¹ Stewart took the Troops by a mountain pass, between three & four oClock there came on a most tremendous thunder storm & the heaviest rain I ever recollect seeing, ¼ after Five oClock a Flash of Lightining struck the column just at the head of my Brigade, knocked the breath out of my body & rendered me insensible for a few seconds, killed Lᵗ [W. Thomas] Masterman 34ᵗʰ Regᵗ & his horse who was riding close to me, struck my Brigade Major on the head & knocked down about 20 Soldiers, fortunately no more lives were lost, which appears unaccountable – ...

The defeated French were pushed back into the Pyrenees and a lull followed. The 18th Hussars were now disgraced following their conduct at Vitoria. Lieutenant Woodberry had been sent on the morning of 22 June to put the regiment's sick and wounded in the hospital at Vitoria and caught up only on the morning of the 24th:

... Soon after my arrival I was called out to Parade; it was for the men to deliver up their plunder & be searched; a great deal was found on them, which of course was took, to be equally divided amongst the Regiment, on one man was found Seven Hundred & Forty quarter Doubloons: – ...

Two days later, near Pamplona:

... Colonel Grant order'd the officers before him to day and inform'd us, he had Lord Wellingtons authority to inform us that his Lor[d]ship was very much displeased with the insubordination of the Regiment, particularly of the conduct of the men in Vitoria, on the 21ˢᵗ Insᵗ numbers of them he saw plundering in the streets. he was likewise very much displeased with several of our officers, who was there likewise, instead of being in the field: and to finish he had to inform us that his Lordship was determined if he heard any complaint against the Regiment, he would immediately dismount us, and march the Regiment to the nearest sea port-Town, and Embark us for England, and at the same time, send the Commander in Chief [the Duke of York] his remarks on the subject: – O God is it come to this? I want language to express the grief I feel on the Occasion, to think I should have come out with a Regiment, who have contrary to all expectation acted so differently: – . . .

Wellington's threat was not an idle one. He wrote on 29 June to Earl Bathurst, the Secretary of State for War and the Colonies, that the 18th were a disgrace to the name of soldier, both in action and elsewhere. He added that he would take their horses from them and send the men back to England, if he could not get the better of them in any other manner.

Woodberry himself had not taken part in the looting during the battle, but had afterwards appropriated some of King Joseph's baggage from a mule lying in a ditch. He recorded on 27 June:

. . . I shew'd my good Hostess the Coat I have of Buonaparte's, who immediately bro^t half the Inhabitants of the Town to see it; and I am very much afraid I shall lose it for if Lord Wellington should hear I have it I shall sure to be oblig'd to give it up: –

The Hussar Brigade was now quartered in reserve around Olite, 37 km south of Pamplona, for there was little scope for cavalry in the forthcoming operations in the Pyrenees. On 2 July Woodberry added further details of the developing furore:

. . . a subject that [h]as made a great noise here, amongst the Brigade I have forbear before to notice in this book: – the day of the Victory of Vitoria, after the 18th & 10th Hussars had charg'd the Enemy thro' the Town, Major Hughes, directed Mr Dolbel to take charge of 20 men, who were placed Centry over the Carriages Baggage &c (of the nobility & french officers.) – he immediately, so is the report commenced plundering. – Many of the prisioners & persons of rank belonging to the Enemy dined with Lord Wellington, at Dinner in course of conversation Madam Genzl [?] say'd that if it had not been for a Private Hussar an Officer of Hussars would have plunder'd her of every thing. That after she had deliver'd up her Husband Sword

to him and likewise a Beautiful double' barrelld Gun he took by force
off her finger a ring: Lord Wellington was in a great rage & swore he
would sacrifise him immediately, he sent for Colonel Grant the next
morning and reported it to him at the same time desired him to
make immediate inquiry that he might bring Mr Dolbel (whose name
he had learnt[)] to a Court Martial. – Mr Dolbel wrote a justification
to Lord Wellington & to the officers of the Brigade & utterlly denies
the ring business but owns that he took the Gun & sword: here the
matter stands at present: –

On 3 July Woodberry recorded news of a major reorganization of
the cavalry. Sir Stapleton Cotton had finally rejoined the army from
England a few days after Vitoria and was able to put in place the new
arrangements that Wellington had previously raised with him in
correspondence:

> . . . I am very happy to understand the Hussar Brigade will be broke
> up, immediately, by Lord Wellington who is not at all pleased with
> Colonel Grants manuvering at the Battle of Vitoria, they all allow
> this officer to be Possess'd of Courage and resolution, but all say he
> wants judgement: The 10th & 15th are to be Brigaded together & Lord
> Fitzroy [in fact Edward] Somerset will command it: – The 18th will
> be Brigaded with the [1st] German Hussars, under General Bock [in
> fact, under Victor Alten]. The whole of the Cavalry Brigades will
> likewise be broke up [and re-organized.] . . .

Lieutenant-Colonel Murray also approved of the new arrangements
when he wrote to his wife on 16 July:

> . . . I am very sorry to be away from my friends the 10th [Hussars]
> but perhaps we shall learn more by being with the Germans, & that
> Regt in particular for they are first rate & always keep their horses in
> the highest condition when others are starving, they are also perfect
> masters of outpost duty, & much may be learnt from them if the 18th
> could believe that they did not know every thing better than any
> body else when in fact they are more deficient than any body. . . .

On 6 July, Woodberry recorded with glee:

Colonel Grant, who have had the finest command in the world The
Hussar Brigade, is superceded in the Command by [Major-General]
Lord Edward Somerset. Grant went to Lord Welington to remon-

strate with him and Lord W. gave him leave to go back to England immediately which Grant accepted, all his Horses & finery is to be disposed off this day and he sets out for St Ander [Santander] to morrow. – God be thank'd we have got rid of the Black Giant. The red Dwarf [Grant's brigade major] stays with the Brigade: – . . .

Woodberry's views were echoed by his colonel. For Murray on 17 July sent his wife more details of the Battle of Vitoria, which he had just heard at second-hand at Palencia:

. . . The Brigade (this man of ours said) took 106 pieces of cannon a quantity of plate & three carriages. King Joseph had scarcely time to get on his horse and make his escape. The Brigade attacked in the same order we did at Moralez viz. the 10th. leading the 18th on the right & the *15th. in reserve.* He also said that the same error was committed at Vitoria that was likewise done at Moralez getting entangled with some marshy ground which gave the enemy the advantage of ground. He also said that Lord Wellington being on the spot reprimanded Colonel Grant for leading on the Brigade so rashly. . . .

Murray was delighted at the appointment of Somerset, whom he thought of as a good officer and a pleasant man, and stated that it would be a change for the brigade. But Grant retired only to the northern coast of Spain, where he met Sir Stapleton Cotton and was dissuaded from going home. He then obtained permission from Wellington to remain until he had received a reply to a communication he had sent to England about his situation. Major-General Long claimed that the very next mail brought news of his own removal from his new command of a brigade formed by the 13th and 14th Light Dragoons. Grant on 6 September was appointed to take over Long's brigade, although he was again replaced on 24 November and served no more in the Peninsula. Long resented his replacement by Grant, who was junior to him, and believed that Grant's status as a Royal ADC lay behind the move.

Meanwhile, the 18th's bad conduct at Vitoria continued to come to light. Woodberry recorded on 14 July:

. . . now half the officers are implicated (so I was inform'd last night) in an unfortunate affair respecting the Plunder & remaining in the Town of Vitoria and will be oblig'd to Exchange Resign or perhaps

before either can be done they may be Cashier'd: – There names are
Major Hughes Captn Bolton & Burk, Lieu^t Connolly & Dolbel & Adj^t
Waldie. Those are the men whom Lord Wellington [h]as on the
Black List: The whole may not suffer but I think it likely the whole
will leave. That brute of a Fellow Dolbel [h]as charges ag^t Bolton &
Burk, which would [enable him to] superceed them[;] no one yet
knows how he will act: – The Regiment it is plainly to be seen is
gone to the devil: God send I was out of it, but I must now stop, and
see the end of it. I feel more than happy, when I think of that day
and of my not going into the Town, during the plunder: – I dined
with [Captain] Kennedy yesterday he, poor fellow is very unwell,
fearful his name may be bro^t in question with the above I think is
the occasion of his illness: – reports in the Regiment intimate that he
got a prize: – Burk gave up the Diamond Cross which is supposed to
be worth about a Thousand Pounds: – One of the men made me a
present to day of a Peice of French Calico which I will get made into
Shirts & sheets, tho' its to fine for either, yet its the only way I can
smugle it home: – . . .

On 25 July Woodberry blamed the regiment's insubordinate state on
the want of a good adjutant; but on 7 September, he wrote:

. . . Every Subaltern officer of the Regiment, that is out here, seems
anxious to leave the service all disappointed – I may say disgusted,
having entered the Service in a Regiment that all Ireland [the 18th
was an Irish regiment] & England look'd too for something great by
which means we become the Envy of the Army, but all would have
been well, had we had, another Colonel, in the place of that great ass,
Col. M[urray]. – who knows no more how to command a Regiment
than I do: – we are beholding to him for every misfortune or disgrace
attached to the Regiment: – . . .

Major Hughes had an interview with Wellington at the beginning of
September after discovering that Colonel Grant had not forwarded to
him Lieutenant Dolbel's justification of his conduct. Yet the 18th, unlike
the other two regiments in the Hussar Brigade, never received Vitoria as
a battle honour and recovered its reputation only in April 1814.

*

Equally undistinguished was the direction of a sideshow on the eastern coast of Spain. As part of his strategy for 1813, Wellington had wanted to distract the French Army of Aragon under Marshal Suchet and prevent it from detaching reinforcements to King Joseph. The guerrillas were neither formidable nor particularly active in this region of Spain. Wellington therefore looked primarily to an Anglo-Sicilian army based at the port of Alicante and to the local Spanish regular forces.

Sicily had been a British base since the French had overrun southern Italy in 1806. British troops stationed on the island had helped protect it from the threat of invasion and had also been detached on expeditions within the Mediterranean. The army now based at Alicante was one of these detached forces. It consisted by January 1813 of about 14,000 men, but contained a mixture of British, Sicilian and other foreign units and the ranks of many of the latter were filled with enemy deserters or prisoners of war.

Command of the Anglo-Sicilian army changed hands five times between 1 October 1812 and 25 February 1813, when the post was assumed by Lieutenant-General Sir John Murray. A fleet was available to transfer the army by sea, but insufficient transport curtailed mobility on land. Another problem was highlighted in a letter from Major-General William Clinton to the Duke of York, which was drafted on 9 November 1812:

> ... I observe that M. Gen[l] [John] Mackenzie who I found in the temporary command here wrote to Col Torrens [the Military Sec-retary, at the Horse Guards] on the 22[d] U[t] giving an account of a reconnaissance the Enemy had made on the 8th of the month – This I am convinced was made to see what our cavalry was – the French Gen[l] had I understand 8 or 900 cavalry with him on that occasion – In this arm we are deficient indeed – having but *200* upon whom any reliance can be had – of 160 spaniards of M. Gen. Whittinghams Corps – their only service to be looked for is patroling – however the General is exerting himself to bring them as forward as possible – ...

Suchet took the offensive in April 1813, but was checked at Castalla, 30 km north-west of Alicante. Wellington then produced an imaginative plan for Murray to go by sea to attack the city of Tarragona 250 km behind Suchet's position on the River Júcar. He hoped that this would enable the Spanish regular armies to break through frontally and seize the city of Valencia, 25 km north of the Júcar. Murray, a notably timid and indecisive commander, landed on 2 June and besieged Tarragona, but panicked at the reported advance of relief forces and re-embarked, abandoning his siege artillery. He was replaced in mid-June by Lieutenant-General Lord William Bentinck and later court-martialled.

Suchet after Wellington's victory at Vitoria to the north-west withdrew along the coast into Catalonia. The allied pursuit was slow. Thomas Pickstock, who was attached to the Commissariat Department, noted on 18 August that near the ruined village of Hospitalet, south-west of Tarragona:

> ... There are no resources to be had in this neighbourhood, & we do not even meet with 'paisanos' [peasants] that was it not for our 'Depôt-afloat' [the fleet] we would be much inconvenienced, we procure Water for 'man & beast' from Wells we have dug along the sea, it is brackish, but we have no other means of procuring better, the river over which there is a neat bridge being dried up; in the rock of Balaguer, our Engineers are excavating the mountains, where a spring has been discovered, and a Cistern is being built on the spot, to secure Water, and it is in a pretty state of forwardness, its conjectured from the pains taken, that Lord W[m] Bentinck, must have determined on keeping the Army quartered here, his Lordship transacts his plans of the new Campaign in a 'Venta' [inn] some few yards in the Fields, in sight of the whole Allied Forces. ...

In September Bentinck advanced on Barcelona, but retreated to Tarragona after his advanced guard was surprised and defeated at Ordal on the 13th. Subsequent operations were unremarkable and petered out. Lieutenant-General William Clinton, who replaced Bentinck on 22 September, explained in a memorandum:

> Lord W[m] Bentinck embarked for Sicily he having early in that month, & on one or two intermediate occasions, intimated to me his intention of returning to Sicily but leaving me no further instructions in handing over the command of the Army to me than a reference to Lord Wellingtons dispatches & a suggestion as to continue the just then commenced repairs of the Works of Tarragona.
>
>   ...
>
> With respect to the state of efficiency of the Anglo-Sicilian troops at this time, they could be moved from 30 to 40 miles from the

Depot (viz Tarragona) but it could not have been practicable without a very great additional outlay to have provisioned those troops at this time, at a greater distance, had even the circumstances of the moment rendered such a measure advisable . . .

Clinton stressed that it was not simply a question of numbers of troops, but how far they could be moved or depended upon. He also noted that the Spanish 1st and 2nd Armies, which had been considered under Bentinck's command, now acted independently. He added:

> . . . It was no small addition to the difficulties & inconveniences to which the Anglo-Sicilian army was exposed *at this time*, that the Ports of *Gibraltar*, & *Malta* were shut: The first, on account of the contagious Fever, which had broke[n] out there & Malta on account of the Plague which had shewn itself there. Upon these Ports the Army on the East Coast very much depended for supplies of Provisions of all kinds, & for money & stores. At this time too, the troops were very much in arrears of Pay, & so low was the state of the public purse, that there was scarcely sufficient to meet in prospect the expences of the current month. Add to this the small stock of *salt-provisions* in hand, which by a Return of the Commissary General made not many days after Lord William Bentinck's departure, shewed only seventeen days '*Remain*' of this Article . . .

The exhausted state of Catalonia undermined attempts to save the salt provisions, for it was found impossible to provide the troops with fresh meat more than twice a week.

Fortunately, Suchet had serious problems of his own. He was severely limited by the depletion of his numbers, resulting both from the garrisons that he had unwisely left behind in fortresses and from Napoleon's demands for more troops in northern Europe. He remained on the coast rather than join the French forces directly opposed to Wellington.

8

The End in the Peninsula

July 1813 to April 1814

After his stunning victory at Vitoria Wellington sought to consolidate his position by taking the fortresses of San Sebastian and Pamplona in north-eastern Spain. The French Armies of the North, Centre, South and Portugal had been driven back through the Pyrenees into France and were being reorganized on Napoleon's orders as a single army under Marshal Soult. The French enjoyed better lateral communications on their side of the Pyrenees and had available three suitable routes through the mountains should they switch to the offensive. To watch these avenues of approach Wellington had to disperse his army over a front of 65 km. He also had to position his divisions in considerable depth so they could delay a thrust until reinforced from other sectors.

Soult took the offensive on the morning of 25 July, within a fortnight of assuming command. Wellington had previously received indications of French movements, but believed that if Soult came at all, he would come in the north to try and relieve San Sebastian, the defences of which had been breached by the besieging force. Instead, Soult attacked 55 km to the south-east towards Pamplona. His main assault came through the pass at Roncesvalles, with a secondary thrust directed through the Maya Pass 28 km to the north-west.

Captain Charles Forrest of the 3rd (or the East Kent) Regiment of Foot, or The Buffs was serving as a Deputy-Assistant Quartermaster-General with the 2nd Division and was stationed at Roncesvalles. The Pass was defended by a Spanish division and by a brigade of British infantry under Major-General John Byng from the 2nd Division. Lieutenant-General Sir Lowry Cole's 4th Division was in support to the rear. Forrest recorded in his journal that Byng received an anonymous letter in Spanish on 24 July informing him that his post would be attacked the following morning by a large French force. Every disposition

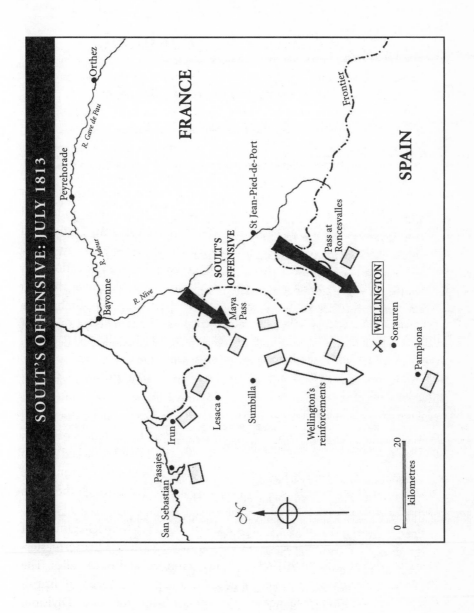

SOULT'S OFFENSIVE: JULY 1813

was made to be ready at dawn and 500 light infantrymen were posted in advance of Byng's main position on a spur on the eastern side of the Pass. Captain Forrest described how:

> The Enemy came on at day break, by the great Road from St Jean Pie[d] de Port, and appeared surprised to find us all ready posted to receive them. – they drove in our advance to within about 600 yards of our Post, & there they halted to collect. – As day light came on we could distinguish immense columns of them moving up both on the high road, and also by the heights to our left of it. As they successively came up they halted & piled arms; this continued 'till about 6 o'Clock by which time about 12,000 men had collected in our front. – About 8 oClock they made a shew of attacking, sending down skirmishers, and moving a small body round to our Right. – Our [one Spanish] gun however, and the Lt Companies effectually checked the former, whilst the latter were gallantly repulsed by the Lt Comp^y of the Spanish Batt^n of Union – This attack however was evidently only to amuse us whilst some more serious one was in contemplation at another point. All firing ceased about 11 a.m. and both parties continued looking at each other in suspense. – . . .

Another strong French force was advancing along another spur to the west, but Cole was bringing up his 4th Division to check it. The French attacked there at 1.00 p.m.:

> . . . no sooner had the attack commenced upon the left than the Enemy made their grand one to force our Pass, with two immense Columns covered by a large body of Light troops, & supported by three guns. – Our Troops with their brave allies the Spaniards & Morillo at their head behaved like Heroes and withstood the immense superiority of numbers for above half an hour; but the Enemy overpowered us by his hosts, and we were compelled to retire, not however before we had made the Enemy pay dearly the price of his conquest. He losing in killed & wounded full 800 – Our loss did not exceed *120* and to our credit be it said we scarcely left a wounded man behind. Our retreat was slow, and at ½ a mile from our first we took up our Second Position determined again to stand. – The Enemy however appeared satisfied with having forced our Position & halted perhaps to wait the result of his attack on our left, where during all this time he had made desperate

attempts to force the 4ᵗʰ Div. but without success, altho his force was at least 12,000 men. – Between 3 and 4 °Clock an Extreme thick Fog came on, & the contending armies were entirely hidden from each other. About this time too came an order to retire, but ere the whole of the Troops were in motion, it was countermanded & we were desired to hold our ground if possible. – The Enemy pushed on a Small Patrole of Cavalry to feel where we were, they soon found this by a Volley of musquetry with which the Spanish Picquet saluted them & which sent them back faster than they came. – They soon after sent on a Serjeant and Private of Infantry the former was killed, the latter wounded & taken. – After this they were quiet. –

Altho we had repulsed the Enemy on the left, and checked him in a certain degree upon the Right, yet it was Evident our position was not tenable against his immense superiority of numbers. – Orders to retire were therefore given, & leaving a small rear guard and under cover of the Fog we slipped off unperceived . . .

The fog was in fact low cloud which had descended on the battlefield and put an end to the fighting. Cole had orders from Wellington to defend the pass to the utmost against any direct attack and to ignore any wider turning movement to the east. But he became alarmed at the possibility of being outflanked under the cover of the fog and ordered a retreat.

Wellington initially was unsure whether Soult's offensive was a feint, but in the evening of the 26th received a message from Cole informing him of the extent of his retreat towards Pamplona. Picton had already been ordered to support Cole with the 3rd Division, but likewise lost his nerve and fell back with Cole to Sorauren, just 6 km north-east of Pamplona.

Wellington personally arrived at Sorauren at 11.00 a.m. on the 27th and sent orders for additional units to join him. His presence boosted the morale of his men, who burst into cheering, and apparently induced Soult to postpone an attack until the 28th. The action that ensued became known as the First Battle of Sorauren. Wellington had occupied a steep ridge just 2.5 km long, short enough to be held in strength, and protected by a river on either flank. Wellington had 10,000 men on his ridge, including Cole's 4th Division, Byng's British brigade from the 2nd Division and a Portuguese brigade, and had additional troops in support 3 km to the rear. He had not yet been able to bring up artillery because of the difficult terrain, but was reinforced on his western flank by the 6th Division towards 11.00 a.m. Soult, who had occupied a parallel ridge 1 km to the north, attacked at noon with 20,000 infantry but was repulsed after hard fighting. Wellington lost 2,600 men, but inflicted even heavier casualties and a complete check on the French. Captain Forrest recorded that day:

> ... Lord Wellington passed along on his return to Villalba [a village immediately south of the battlefield] about dusk, & was cheered by Every Batt^n as he passed with the most enthusiastic huzzas, how gratifying a conclusion to such a day. – never did [a] Comm^r in Chief enjoy so fully the Confidence of his Troops, for none so well deserved it. –

Both armies remained quietly in their positions on the 29th. Wellington managed to have a battery of six guns hauled to the top of his ridge and had another battery posted on high ground to the west of the River Ulzama. Soult realized that he had failed in his bid to relieve Pamplona, but to save face resolved not to retreat the way he had come and early on the morning of the 30th set off north-westwards. Wellington attacked Soult's army as it moved across his front and smashed it in the Second Battle of Sorauren. Captain Forrest vividly described the day's events in his journal:

> We had yesterday got up our Canteens, a Tent, and our bedding from the rear, and were enjoying a comfortable nap, when about 2 °Clock in the morning we were awoke by a sharp firing at the outposts, & several shots within the Camp, together with a confused noise and bustle in the whole of the Troops getting under arms. – Before I perfectly awoke I thought nothing less than that the Enemy had surprized & passed our Picquets & that all was over with us; however when I got myself quite awake & found the firing had subsided, I concluded it was what it afterwards proved to be a false alarm, occasioned by some musquet going off, which was immediately taken up on our left, & the Troops fired without knowing at what. Every thing was soon quiet, but it had the confounded effect of cutting short our two hours sleep, which in these times we could ill afford to lose. – and at 4 °Clock we were as ordered all under arms. – Daylight shewed us the Enemy as yesterday. – They were

however now to pay for their attack on us on the 28th and to feel us as assailants as well as Defendants. Lord Wellington had in the course of yesterday got up a Brigade of 9 Prs on his Position, these commenced their fire upon the Enemy about 5 °Clock, & they evidently had a great effect. These guns were served with the greatest accuracy, every shot told, & fell almost invariably in the center of their Columns, they appeared to be in great disorder and to waver very much now ascending, then again descending moving now to the Rt & now to the left, – they continued thus for two hours our artillery doing dreadful execution among them – about 10 °Clock the Bde of the 4th Divn which had all along occupied the hill on the Right, advanced and drove the Enemy from the Ridge in its front, & then ascending the face of the hill on the left of the Enemy drove them from it, and about ½ p. 11 we saw the British Standard flying on its Summit. – . . .

The French still held the village of Sorauren in strength in the west, opposite to which was posted Byng's brigade. Captain Forrest was sent to Sir Lowry Cole to say that Byng thought he could drive the French from the village. Cole replied that Byng was to risk nothing, but simply to feel and keep close to the enemy when he thought he could do so. Forrest added:

. . . By this time the guns on our left had with their shells made the Village rather warm, & the Enemy began to retire from it – Genl Byng immedy moved down with the Lt Companies & Provisional Battn & a Company of Detachments under Lt Law 71st which latter had been sharply engaged since the morning at the Chapel with the Enemy's Sharpshooters & had behaved extremely well – with this force the Enemy were soon dislodged from the Ravines in our front, and the 42d [part of the 6th Division] at this moment charged into & drove the Enemy from the Village in great Style. – and but a short time before we saw the 7th Divn which were on our left at some distance ascend, and drive the Enemy from the height to our left, & opposite side of the river. Their turning their Right flank, as the 4th Divn had before turned their left. – The Third Division in the mean time was moving directly upon the great road to Roncesvalles. By noon every part of the Enemys Line was carried & they in full retreat. . . .

Over the next three days, Wellington pursued Soult back into France.
On 2 August, Major John Duffy of the 43rd Regiment described a
typically exhausting day:

> ... marched about 5 (a vast number of men not come up from
> yesterdays dreadful march – some men reported dead of Fatigue –)
> on the road to our old Encampment at the Puente de Saco [?] – The
> 4th Divn followed us till they came to the road leading to Echelar
> where they turned off – the whole road they came from Sunbrilla for
> a league cover'd with the Enemy's Baggage left last night[.]
>
> Orderd with 5 Companies up to the heights of St Barbara opposite
> to the French Position above Vera – shortly afterwards observed &
> reported the Enemy to be in possession of the heights in my rear
> leading to the Puerto de Echelar – when the fog cleared up he
> appeared to have about 15 Thousand men on the different heights –
> about 12 he was attacked by the 4th & 7th Divns and was driven
> successively from hill to hill 'till about 4 O Clock when he made a
> stand in front of the Puerto –
>
> At this time he had possession of a high rocky mountain to our
> right that looks down upon this ridge which our Brigade was orderd
> to attack – it was seldom clear of [illegible] rain all day and in the
> afternoon quite thick – The 1st & 3rd Battns of the Rifle[s] ordered
> to lead the attack – they soon got within fire of the Enemy up a
> perpendicular rock & in less than an hour drove him from his strong
> hold although the Enemy had a Thousand men on the top of the
> mountain – part of the Rifle[s] reached some of the Enemy's huts in
> the fog before they were perceived and were actually pushed back by
> the butts of the Frenchman's firelocks over the rocks and by the bad
> footing broke their necks – It was a most daring gallant attack –
>
> At Dark the Enemy had nearly all filed off from the Puerto de
> Echelar – ...

*

Meanwhile, an assault on San Sebastian had failed bloodily on 25 July.
The town lay on the northern coast of Spain, across the neck of an
isthmus that jutted out from the mainland. To the north, at the head of
the isthmus, stood the Monte Urgull, a rocky outcrop 120 metres high
and crowned with a castle. The town had a population of less than
10,000 and was built in the shape of a square, with each face 350 metres

long and with its walls adjoining a bay to the west and the estuary of the River Urumea to the east. It had a large hornwork outside the southern face to strengthen it against the most obvious line of attack, directly along the isthmus. Another outwork, the fortified Convent of San Bartolomé, stood on a hill 550 metres further south.

San Sebastian had been blockaded by land since 28 June and by sea since 3 July. But the Royal Navy was overstretched by the war that had broken out between Britain and the United States of America in 1812 and was unable to seal San Sebastian off from supplies and reinforcements brought at night by coasting vessels from France, just 25 km along the coast. The town's Governor, General Louis Rey, was a capable and determined commander and enjoyed considerable support from the inhabitants, who had been under French occupation for five years and had close trade links with France.

Wellington entrusted the operations against San Sebastian to Sir Thomas Graham, with the 5th Division and a Portuguese brigade, and visited him on 12 July. He agreed that the town should be assaulted in the east, its most vulnerable side. The walls here could be breached by artillery firing from the hills on the opposite side of the River Urumea and troops could reach the breaches by advancing along a stretch of the river bed, left exposed beneath the walls at low tide for four hours. Unfortunately, their route would lie directly under the eastern face of the hornwork.

The preliminary approaches were made from the south, along the isthmus, to clear the French from their most outlying works, including the Convent of San Bartolomé, which was stormed on 17 July. Batteries opened fire on the town itself on the 20th and breached the walls three days later. Graham did not make an immediate assault, partly as the parallel from which the storming troops would emerge had yet to be completed and partly as he wanted to add a second breach, which was done later that day. The assault was scheduled for the morning of the 24th, but had to be postponed another day, as the siege batteries had set fire to the houses immediately behind the breaches, making it doubtful whether the troops would be able to enter the town. The delay gave the French time to prepare additional defences. At both breaches, the front of the walls had collapsed outwards leaving the back of them intact, with a drop of up to six metres into the street. General Rey destroyed all the steps leading up to the ramparts, prepared the nearby houses for defence

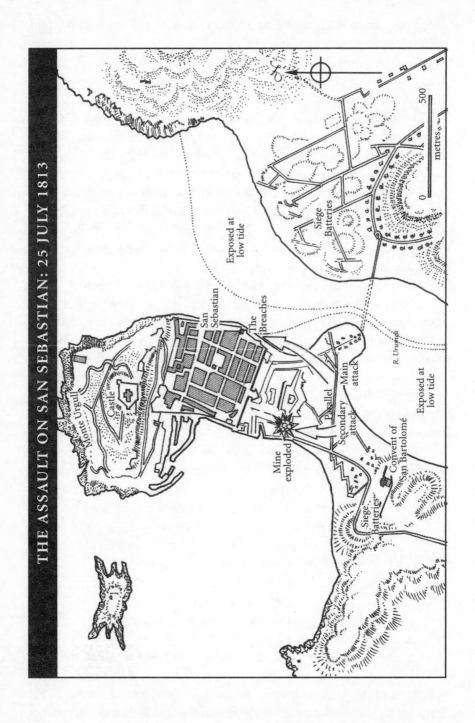

THE ASSAULT ON SAN SEBASTIAN: 25 JULY 1813

Monte Urgull

Castle

San Sebastian

The Breaches

Mine exploded

Parallel

Secondary attack

Main attack

Convent of San Bartolomé

Siege Batteries

Siege Batteries

R. Urumea

Exposed at low tide

Exposed at low tide

0   500

metres

and sealed off the breached walls on either side to prevent the stormers from working their way along them. Marksmen and shells were placed on the eastern side of the hornwork ready to assail the attackers as they passed below on their way to the breaches.

Graham for his part planned to explode a mine in an empty aqueduct under the western corner of the hornwork to divert attention. The assault was made early in the morning of 25 July and failed dismally. The mine proved surprisingly effective, bringing down the counterscarp on the western side of the hornwork. But the besiegers were unprepared to take advantage of this unexpected success, while the assault on the breaches was mismanaged and became disjointed in the pre-dawn darkness. It was made by Major-General Andrew Hay's brigade of the 5th Division. In a letter written the next day, Hay shed light on the attitudes of the senior officers responsible for ordering the attack:

... the greatest misfortune is that the attack did not succeed, indeed it was *impossible* if the garrison did their duty tolerably well. however fortunately for me *I* was only the acting person as General Oswald [the divisional commander] was looking on & Sir Thomas [Graham] & soon after the thing was over the chief [Wellington] arrived [from his headquarters at Lesaca] & was perfectly satisfied that what *men* could do had been done & they showed that as no man flinched but went on till they were either knocked down by a tremendous fire of musqutry, grape shells & hand grenades & large stones from behind walls & breast works or till we received orders to retire which they did in the best possible order & the officers & men obeyed implicitly every order I gave them & which I was at great pains to explain to them all before we began, Col [illegible] & [Brevet Lieutenant-Colonel Edward] Miles of the 38[th Regiment] all safe & behaved in the most gallant stile advancing to support the Royal [Scots] by a nearer cut till they were nearly drowned in the sea they are safe and thank God We are not to make any more such [illegible], at the same time I do not think any blame can attach to the planners of the attack as till you *try* you never can *know* the physical difficulties. To give Oswald Credit he always had an extreme bad opinion of the busyness I certainly considered it extremely hazardous but I had no right to give an opinion as I was only to carry it into execution & I have seen things that appeared impossible carried out by the sheer bravery of british troops but that is *only* when you can *touch* the enemy, but when they are behind walls & loop holes they demolish [you] without your having any opportunity of annoying them . . .

Hay's comments are put into perspective by Wellington's complaint to Lord Bathurst that he understood 'that the General and superior officers were so indiscreet as to talk before their men of the impossibility of success, and that they still continue the conversation.'*

The repulse cost 571 casualties. The siege was then suspended, leaving a blockade in place, but was resumed on 24 August. San Sebastian was successfully stormed a week later, with heavy losses. After the failure of the assault by Hay's brigade in July Wellington had called for volunteers from the other divisions to show the 5th how to storm a breach. The response had been overwhelming, but Lieutenant-General Leith, the 5th Division's new commander, had insisted that the assault should be led by one of his own units, Major-General Frederick Robinson's brigade. After the storming, Robinson was infuriated by the low profile of his brigade in Graham's report to Wellington and claimed that Hay had been principally responsible for the slight. He furiously claimed that Hay was 'a fool and I verily believe, with many others on my side, an arrant Coward – That he is a paltry, plundering old wretch is established beyond doubt – That he is no Officer is as clear, and that he wants spirit is firmly believed, ergo, he ought not to be a General'.†

Hay was neither the most dynamic of generals nor the most hospitable of hosts, but did not in fact deserve so damning an indictment. Lieutenant-Colonel William Gomm of the Quartermaster-General's Department, a future field marshal, wrote that he had a high respect and regard for him.‡

After its capture, San Sebastian was gutted by fires started by the bombardment and fanned by the strong wind. General Rey retired to the Castle on Monte Urgull, but capitulated on 8 September.

---

* J. Fortescue, *A History of the British Army* (London, 1899–1930), v. 9, p. 353.

† C. Atkinson, 'A Peninsular Brigadier: Letters of Major-General Sir F. P. Robinson, K.C.B., dealing with the Campaign of 1813', in *Journal of the Society for Army Historical Research (JSAHR)* 1956, v. 34, p. 168.

‡ F. C. Carr-Gomm, ed., *Letters and Journals of Field-Marshal Sir William Maynard Gomm, G.C.B.* (London, 1881), p. 336. See also S. Monick, ed., *Douglas's Tale of the Peninsula and Waterloo by John Douglas (former Sergeant, 1st Royal Scots)* (Barnsley, 1997), p. 28.

The fortress of Pamplona, 62 km inland, had simply been blockaded and was starved into surrender on 31 October.

*

Wellington resumed the offensive on 7 October when he crossed the River Bidasoa into France. He surprised Soult by attacking near the coast. The Light Division spearheaded an assault at Vera, 12 km inland, while the 1st and 5th Divisions led attacks near the mouth of the river. The 5th Division forded the Bidasoa nearest the sea, at Fuenterrabía, where local shrimpers had informed Wellington that it could be crossed at low tide. This outflanking attack eased the advance of the 1st Division, which crossed near Irun, 2.5 km upriver.

Ensign John Blackman of the Coldstream Guards described the 1st Division's assault in a letter to his parents dated 9 October:

You will no doubt look more than twice at the date of this letter [dated from France], but it is [a] real fact that we are actually in France, and as well as I am able to describe how this glorious movement was made, you shall have it – I will in the first place assure you of my perfect safety, that you may read with more composure the joyful news: – [Lieutenant-General] Sir John Hope joined us about a week ago: – on Wednesday last (Octr 6th) we heard such a move was in contemplation, and that it was to take place either on that night or very early on Thursday morn^g – I observed several Orderly's going in different directions which of course confirmed it in my mind – The pontoons were moving up all night, and on the morn^g of the 7th about 2 O'clock the order came for us to move at ½ past 3 and assemble on the road near Irun and wait there till day-light. We then took a circuitous march round Irun, and came into the road near the broken or I should say burnt bridge [at Béhobie] of the Bidassoa, which divides France from Spain, in the meantime we observed the 5th division fording that river (Bidassoa) near Fontarabia without any or at least very feeble resistance, and we (the 1st division) forded near the bridge through nearly 3 feet [of] mud under a very slack fire – We soon obtained firm footing in France, and we drove the enemy entirely from *all the high* ground about here, the 5th division preceding us – during this our pontoons were established, and our cavalry and heavy guns passed over – about 11 O'clock we had quiet possession of the heights, and the Noble

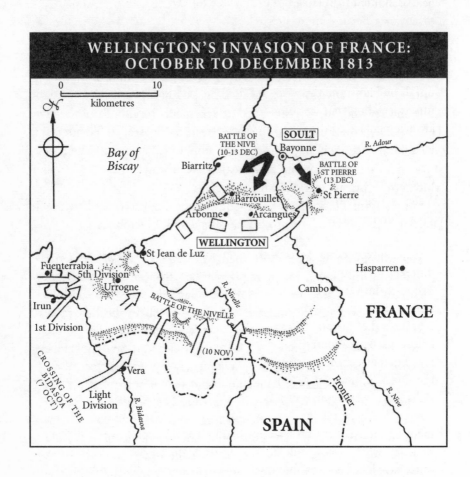

WELLINGTON'S INVASION OF FRANCE: OCTOBER TO DECEMBER 1813

0   10
kilometres

N

Bay of Biscay

BATTLE OF THE NIVE (10-13 DEC)

SOULT

Bayonne

R. Adour

Biarritz

BATTLE OF ST PIERRE (13 DEC)

St Pierre

Barrouillet

Arbonne   Arcangues

WELLINGTON

St Jean de Luz

Hasparren

Fuenterrabia

5th Division

Urrogne

R. Nivelle

Cambo

Irun

1st Division

BATTLE OF THE NIVELLE

FRANCE

(10 NOV)

CROSSING OF THE BIDASOA (7 OCT)

Vera

Light Division

R. Bidasoa

Frontier

R. Nive

SPAIN

Marquis [Wellington] came riding by who was greeted with very hearty shouts of applause[.] Lord Wellington thought it not prudent to advance beyond these heights, but took his position so that the enemy might not see us the next morn^g ([illegible] ½ expecting (to use his expression) that the enemy would come capering along, to try and drive us back, not thinking that our guns & cavalry were well up[)], but however this did not happen, au contraire, they were in full expectation that *we* should make another attack, and made their arrangements accordingly – to day we are all quiet remaining in our position on the heights, with the enemy in the valley – . . .

Captain William Coles belonged to a squadron of the 12th (or Prince of Wales's) Regiment of (Light) Dragoons supporting the 5th Division's attack at Fuenterrabía:

. . . the advance was extremely well arranged, the Heads of the different Columns moving in a paralel line, preceded by the light Troops, who very soon gaind possession of the opposite bank of the river & facilitated the movements of the Army, it is strange to say that instead of the opposition we expected, the Enemy retird regularly before us & abandon'd the strong positions they occupy'd on the Heights that command the River, if such was their intention before the attack I think if the left Columns had mov'd quicker to their right flank we might certainly have brought them to action if not intercepted their retreat, tho so much difficulty attended the movement of the Artillery on account of the extreme narrowness of the Road by which we advanc'd, that in attempting a rapid march we must have left it & consequently have fought to great disadvantage . . .

Soult fortified a new position 10 km to the east on the hills above the River Nivelle. He expected that he would again be attacked near the sea and concentrated a disproportionate amount of his strength in the west. But Wellington on 10 November attacked his central and eastern sectors and merely demonstrated in the west, as Assistant-Surgeon Thomas Maynard of the Coldstream Guards described in a letter written the next day to the father of his friend Ensign Blackman. The Guards, along with five King's German Legion battalions, constituted the 1st Division, which was placed in the western sector between the 5th Division on the left and, on the right, a Portuguese brigade and an independent brigade of

British infantry under Major-General Lord Aylmer. Maynard begins by describing the lead-up to the battle in early November:

... The Surrender of Pamplona on the 1st set us at liberty to advance, but the heavy rains which fell on the 30 31 & 1st so deluged the country and destroyed the roads over the mountains to the right that our movements were deferred until the waters had time to run off & dry. A succession of fine weather from the 2nd to 7th did the needful and on the 8th we went to bed under the idea of attacking on the following morning; a sudden counter order during the night however awakened us to disappointment, and we had to endure two more days of anxious impatience. The 8th & 9th were bright sunny days with brisk winds and the order for attack was resumed on the 10th. We moved under cover of the dark as near as possible to our allotted point of attack to support the Light brigade of German Legion, day dawned and the Horse artillery flying in every direction [&] the beautiful burst of fire that opened at one moment [a]long the lines was the most beautiful thing I ever saw[.] In a little time our advancing fire proclaimed them flying, we drove them thro' Urogne [Urrugne] & to their strongest works. We moved forward now & occupied some heights to the left of Orogne [Urrugne] while the fields & hedges below were filled with our skirmishers, theirs lining the high road[.] Here we remained – A brigade under Lord Aylmer of the Coldstream were employed against a hill, on the right of [Ur]rogne, crowned with a tremendous strong battery and covered with columns. In vain they assailed it and were ordered to retire – The vagabonds followed them with repeated cheers and thinking they had now done it, advanced in great strength and theatened the Village. The left wing of the Coldstream was moved down & they soon retired. After this nothing but skirmishing among the hedges followed, and all on the left ceased. we never once got fairly into fire and I need not say John [Blackman] is quite well[.] Ensn [Windham] Anstruther of the Coldstream attached to the Lt Infantry is the only officer wounded, he not badly, in the calf and is under my care at present. We lost one man & 8 wounded – While these diminutive operations were going on on our flank, the right were more nobly engaged, Hills next to inaccessable, batteries impregnable, columns innumerable, were carried, stormed & turned one after another, and night put an end to a contest which was terrible and bloody ...

As a result of the battle Wellington broke out of the Pyrenees and arrived south of the city of Bayonne, where he would be able to spend the winter on lower ground. There was no more serious fighting for a month, but Major John Duffy of the 43rd revealed how his regiment lost heavily in a minor action on 23 November:

This morning at daylight heard that we were to be employed in driving in the Enemys line of Piquets – & to be supported by the [Light] Division – about 8 O Clock the 5 Companies on Piquet advanced and drove the Enemy before them – Our left was to rest about the Centre of a sloping hill about half a mile in front – The right only to advance about 300 yards to a Green Hill – These points were gained with only the loss of 3 or 4 men wounded on our part – The Enemy however collected a large Force on a Hill in front where they appear'd to have a strong work – It was some hours before the precise line we intended to occupy was agreed upon and during this delay the Enemy kept up a pestering fire, but as our men were directed to cover themselves in the Ditches &c we did not suffer much – particularly on the right – but by some mistake the two Companies stationed for the purpose of keeping up the communication in the Centre enter'd a wood in front and afterwards proceeded to the further extremity of it when they suddenly found themselves close under the Enemy's works – here they remained shelterd for some time – but as the whole were orderd back it was found nearly impossible to extricate them without loss – The signal by Bugle was at last given to retreat – the Enemy knowing the sound immediately rushed forward – flanked the wood and kept up a destructive fire – The result was L^t [Mackay] Bailie killed – Capt [Samuel] Hobkirk and about 15 men taken Prisoner, & L^t [Alexander] Steele wounded & about 60 non com off^{rs} & Privates killed & wounded –

The firing continued till about 3 O Clock in the afternoon – We returned to our Cantonments in the Evening –

Wellington was hemmed in between Bayonne to the north, the Atlantic to the west and the River Nive to the east. He therefore pushed part of his army over to the east bank of the Nive on 9 December. Colonel John Elley, the Assistant Adjutant-General of the British Cavalry, explained the objective in a letter of the 14th:

... On the Evening of the 8th an arrangement was made known to the Generals of Division, detailing the operations for the following day, with a view to occupy the right Bank of the Nive, to circumscribe the Enemy, prevent him detaching to the Interior, and to gain on our part a considerable accession of territory, thereby enabling Lord W to operate with the Enemys Communication, and oblige him to retire and uncover Bayonne ...

Knowledge of the impending operation seems to have leaked out surprisingly early, for Major Duffy recorded on 27 November that he had heard of an intended move across the Nive. Captain Richard Brunton of the 6th Caçadores was unlucky enough to be involved in bitter fighting on the far bank. His experiences were unusual in that Wellington lost fewer than 300 men in establishing himself across the river:

... On the 9th of December it was determined to ford the River, altho' the water was still very deep, and accordingly we formed with the utmost silence before day break, and on the signal (a distant Gun on our left) we dashed into it; the French Picquet and their Sentries which were within a few yards fired on us and retired. – The River was deeper than was expected, and part of the first two or three Sections were washed off their legs and carried down the stream; the remainder by locking each others arms got safe over, and their ammunition being carried on their heads was kept dry – the Enemy opposed us but feebly and in our advance during the day we had only some partial skirmishing; but in the evening we came upon them in position, altho' they had evidently tried to conceal their Force, – and it was determined to make them shew it, – accordingly two Companies of my Battalion of which mine was one, were ordered to dislodge them from some Houses, which they occupied on the main road near Villafranca. We effected it, but the Enemy pouring down reinforcements, the struggle became a very severe one, and the other captain was immediately wounded and taken to the rear – I maintained my ground, until the object in view had been attained; but it was the sharpest work for a few minutes that I ever was engaged in, – the 2 Companies had 12 men killed, and 26 wounded, an unusually large proportion of the former, – but it is accounted for by the fact, that our men and the French at one time, were actually firing at each other through the same hedge. – ...

Soult launched a counter-offensive on the west bank of the Nive on the morning of the 10th. One of his thrusts was eventually checked by the Light Division at the village of Arcangues. A famous incident occurred when the 43rd Regiment, posted inside the church, drove off French artillery with musketry at an extreme range of 350 metres. The men were able to create a devastating hail of shots by firing from three levels: from behind the wall of the churchyard, from the ground-floor windows and from the upper-storey windows of the women's galleries. Major John Duffy described how:

> Before day light this morning the Sentries on Piquet reported that they heard the moving of Guns on the roads in front – At day light we observed Troops passing a part of the road in front – but generally supposed they were filing off to reoccupy their former line of Piquets to the left [having been driven in the day before by a strong reconnaissance]. – however about 9 O Clock they burst upon our left Piquets from behind a Hill where they had formed strong Columns and we were obliged to fall back as quick as possible – The right 5 Compys under my own Command were not pressed – The Division assembled on a Position about half a mile to the rear occupying the Chateau & Church of Arcangoes [sic] in force – the Enemy followed but were kept in check by a heavy musquetry fire from the Church[.] He afterwards brought some Guns to bear upon the Church but was obliged at last to desist from the heavy fire of musquetry poured upon him – . . .

Lieutenant James Gairdner of the 1st Battalion, 95th Rifles revealed the serious errors made by his commanding officer during this fighting. His account adds new details to the previously published accounts from the 95th:

> Ab^t two hours after day break the enemy in great force attacked and drove in our Piquets & those of Genl Hopes Corps on whom they made a desperate attack, with us there was a terrible confusion, and tho the Piquets had observed the enemys force collecting in their front for some time yet when the [French] did attack, they took some of them Compleatly by surprise when our compy arrived at the Chateau d'Arcangues we were ordered to halt there for that the division was to maintain that position – the rest of the batt^n came in by companies as the[y] could but our Compy was sent out from the

Chateau to occupy the ridge in front of it in order to support the
3^d batt^n who were actually *retiring from the ridge when we recieved
the order to occupy it to support them*, this was mentioned to the
commandant who however had not sense to comprehend that it was,
not only useless but dangerous to send one company up to occupy a
ridge on which we were not able to communicate right & left however
were were [sic] ordered to go leaving a subdivision at the house
below the chateau; [Lieutenant John] Hopwood and myself went up
with the advanced subdivision and felt our way to the top of the
ridge with a few men, the enemy had not yet occupied it but were
close to it and immediately after we arrived there one ball went
through the heads of both Hopwood & Serjt [William] Brotherwood
(Thus died uselessly two as brave soldiers as ever stepped I have since
heard our commandant attempt to maintain that it was not his
intention we should occupy this place That however I will always
assert whenever I hear the subject mentioned to be false both
Hopwood & myself were too well aware of the useless danger we
were going to meet, to have run into it without an order, I said and
always shall say it that Hopwood lost his life through the ignorance
of the commanding officer and if Colonel Barnard had commanded
the Regiment this day poor Hopwood Brotherwood and the other
sufferers of the company this day would have been spared.)

I went up to Hopwood as soon as I saw him fall took him by the
hand and called him by his name, he half opened his eyes which
were closed but never spoke, his brains were knocked out of the
wound. – This melancholy event left me in command of the company, as I was under the eyes of the commanding officer and so
situated that it was in his power by sound of bugle to order me to
retire when he thought proper (though I knew that every moment
I remained there hazarded the loss of the whole subdivision which I
had there for we could not see ten yards before us, and as we were
advanced considerably out of the line of skirmishers the enemy were
on our right & left in our rear I confess I never expected to return
with a sound skin.) [I was] determined not to quit this place untill I
was either driven from it or ordered from it – the former of which
happened very soon for the enemy seeing we were unsupported and
out of our place sent some men who came through the hedge on our
left & fired into us we ran into the road & retired to the house the
other subdivision was at and I certainly never run quicker in my life,

a help of that kind gives a man a wonderful agility. – we kept the house beyond which we ought never to have advanced & were relieved at dusk by another compy this house is established as a Piquet house & the line drawn from it right & left a very good one when relieved we returned to the Chateau – . . .

While the main French thrust was checked at Arcangues, a secondary attack made unexpected progress further west near Barrouillet. The sector commander, Lieutenant-General Sir John Hope, had left a chain of outposts supported by only two Portuguese infantry brigades and had withdrawn his other units between 5 and 16 km to the rear. Yet Colonel Elley's testimony indicates that the possibility of an attack ought to have been suggested by Soult's moves on the evening of the 9th:

> . . . The Position occupied by Sir R Hills Corps [on the east bank of the Nive] is very commanding, looks into Bayonne and affords a View of every movement, into, or out of that Town –
>
> On the Evening of the 9th from this Point the Enemy was seen filing through Bayonne, which continued on the morning of the 10th in the direction of Anglet – This menace on our Left, brought our Troops out of Cantonments into Position, but not before our advanced Picquets were hastily driven in, by immense Clouds of the Enemys Tirailleurs [skirmishers], and some impression on our proper Ground was made – which however was soon recovered but not without a loss too heavy for such an Affair . . .

In fact, the fighting lasted some hours and might have ended disastrously had it not been for the arrival of units from the rear.

The morning of 11 December found Barrouillet shrouded in fog. Wellington before leaving this area ordered Hope to drive back the French outposts. Colonel Elley in describing the fighting that occurred later that day highlighted the controversy that again surrounded Hope's dispositions:

> . . . On the 11th about Noon, the Enemy reinforced his right, and shewed some Appearance, by forming heavy columns of an intended attack on Sir J. Hope, who had in the Early part of the Day, driven the Enemys Post's off their Grounds, and on which instead of occupying it *light* – he had placed too many Troops, being Ground difficult to defend and more difficult to retire from – Thus was our

Left situated at 3. *P.M.* – Lord W came to the Ground[.] I was looking out, and on reporting what I had observed – His Lordship observed 'Depend on it – if they are forming Columns, it is for an Attack had the Formation been in Line, it would have been for defence – we must therefore get off this bad Ground as well as we can' – I took the liberty to observe that to all Appearances the Enemy would not Attack, should we *continue our Ground* – Lord W very prudently did not wish to risk the requirement of holding such bad Ground till dusk, and gave orders for the advanced Division to retire on the Position – Immediately the Enemy perceived our reserve in retreat – He opened a heavy fire of Cannon, and musquetry, advancing with rapidity – Some Portuguese on the Left went back rather quick, but the 9th Regiment, shewing a steady countenance, impeded the Enemy, and prevented much mischief – This movement was not however, by any means well executed – Skirmishing continued till dark which terminated the affairs of the 11th . . .

The fighting on the following day was less serious but, as Elley described, costly mistakes were still being made:

. . . On the morning of the 12th the 1st Division composed of the Guards &c. took the Picquets relieving the 5th the latter having sustained heavy losses – The Enemy the same as the preceeding Evening a Brigade of Nine pounders had been brought into Position the officer commanding had orders not to fire unless any movement of the Enemys evinced an attack, unluckily an officer on duty with two Guns, saw a Battalion in motion to relieve Picquets, which he mistook for an attack, and opened – This induced the Enemy to conclude the attack was on our Part which brought on an Affair of Posts – Two Battalions of the 1st and 3rd Guards on Picquet *not well posted* suffered rather severely having Lt Col [Samuel Coote] Martin and Capt [Charles William] Thom[p]son of the 1st and Capt [Henry Robert] Watson (adjt) of the 3d killed several officers wounded and from 3 to 400 men k and w.

About noon Lord W. ordered our Picquets to cease firing the Enemy took the Example and did the same, and nothing more occurred during the 12th – . . .

Soult, having failed to make any significant impact on the west bank of the Nive, switched his attention to the opposite side, where Hill was posted with 14,000 men. He passed troops over the bridges at Bayonne ready for an offensive on the morning of the 13th. Wellington had warned Hill on the 10th that he was very likely to be attacked in force on any of the subsequent nights. Indications of an impending attack were also picked up by the outposts. Major Duffy recorded on 12 December:

> ... I observed from the top of the Chateau [of Arcangues] this Evening just before dark part of a Column near Bayonne in reserve moving through the Entrenched Camp [the French fortifications outside that city] towards our right[.]
>
> 13th At two O Clock AM. the Enemy found to have retired from our front – and just after day break a Cannonade heard across the Nive in front of General Hill's Corps – ...

Similar indications were detected by Captain Richard Brunton of the 6th Caçadores. He explains in his narrative that after the crossing of the Nive on 9 December, the French had withdrawn in the night, allowing the 2nd Division to occupy the village of St Pierre. The 6th Caçadores formed part of Brigadier-General Charles Ashworth's Portuguese infantry brigade:

> ... Our Caçadores being scattered, as outposts in the Farm Houses in front, both on the 11th and 12th, we were obliged to turn out as the Enemy reconnoitred us and shewed a disposition to attack, but they did not advance far enough to come in contact with us, altho' our artillery made some good practice among them. – On the night of the 12th I was on the outlying Picquet, and having in the Evening observed some movement, I remained nearly the whole night with my advanced sentry, and altho' it was very dark, could perceive in the Enemy's Bivouac, large Bodies of Troops continually in movement, which I was enabled to do, by observing them pass their numerous watch fires; and [seeing] those constantly to increase, I reported that circumstance, several times during the night to General Ashworth, and I hope with some utility, as it afterwards appeared that nearly the whole of the French army had been withdrawn on that night, from before Lord Wellington who was a considerable distance on our left, and on the opposite side of the river, and had been concentrated in our front, with the intention of overwhelming Lord Hill; they found him however prepared as the result of that

glorious day proved. – Just as day was beginning to break on the morning of the 13th a numerous Staff galloped up to a small knoll close to where I was with the Sentry, on which I ordered him to fire, and not many minutes elapsed before we were envelopp'd in a mass of Sharpshooters and hotly engaged, very shortly after, whilst retiring disputing every inch of ground with my Picquet, I received a severe wound in the leg, which closed my career in the Peninsula. – I was taken back to Cambo [a general hospital 12 km to the south-east], and no hopes being entertained of my recovering the use of my leg, I embarked at Passages [Pasajes, near San Sebastian], and landed in England on the 6th of January 1814, having been absent from it since May 1809, nearly 5 years, an uninterrupted period of Service in the Peninsula, of which I believe very few can boast. . . .

Ashworth's own account records that the French made a strong reconnaissance on the 11th. He added on the 12th that many French generals, including Marshal Soult, were reconnoitring all day. Unfortunately, he does not state if any action was taken that night following Brunton's warnings.

Thick fog initially screened the French on the morning of the 13th. Hill was dangerously outnumbered and could not immediately be reinforced from the west bank of the Nive for the nearby pontoon bridge had been swept away by the swollen river the previous evening. Wellington instead had to direct reinforcements to another bridge 4 km upstream. Luckily, Soult failed to use all his available troops and both his outer prongs were checked. In the centre, he attacked Ashworth's brigade, which was progressively reinforced by units of Major-General Edward Barnes's British brigade. Despite stubborn resistance, the French made headway, particularly when the cowardly commander of the 71st Regiment, Lieutenant-Colonel Sir Nathaniel Peacocke, ordered it to withdraw. Ashworth during these critical moments took local command after Barnes was wounded. Hill then counter-attacked with his last reserves and rolled the exhausted French troops back down the slopes. Ashworth was wounded at this time, by one of the shots fired by the retreating French, and like Brunton was taken to the hospital at Cambo. Wellington at the end of the fighting arrived with reinforcements, but declined to take over command from Hill, who in fact had managed to defeat the French with just the troops he had in hand. Six days later, the commander of the 2nd Division, Lieutenant-General Sir William Stewart, wrote to Ashworth:

Nothing less than the incessant occupation wh^h the consequence of the late action has given me, could plead my apology for Having been so tardy in expressing to you the warm sentiments of admiration which I have felt for the gallant conduct of yourself & of the brave Brigade under your Command on that occasion.

The obligation which I individually was under for your valuable support on the 13th Ins^t – was trifling in comparison of that which I conceive our Cause, & the Portugueze army in particular to have been placed under by your exertions & excellent arrangements previous to & during the action –

– To the very judicious manner in which you had posted your Picquets & supported them by your Battalions, & to the just *rèconnaissance* which you had made of your position the 12th Ins^t I attribute very much of the Success of our proceedings on the succeeding day –: the alertness of your corps at it's several alarm Posts, & finally the distinguished gallantry of your officers & men crowned with success one of the most hard contested affairs in which the allied forces have been engaged –

I have felt it to be my duty to express my Sense of your merit & of the Portugueze troops both to Sir Rowland Hill & to Marshal Sir Wm Beresford, & have perhaps only failed inadequately expressing all that is due & half that I have felt upon the occasion – I have called the attention of these my superior officers to the admirable conduct of your three Commanding officers, Lieut. Colonel [Maxwell] Grant & [Peter] Fearon, & the late Major Joze [?] – I have likewise recommended very warmly Captains Borges [?] & [Hugh] Lumley of the 18th Reg^t – & shall be gratified if you give me an opportunity of being acquainted with any other officers' names who may claim your approbation for their good conduct on the 13th Ins^t – If it be your wish I shall be happy to be the conveyor of your Sentiments in their favor either to Sir Rowland Hill or to Marshal Beresford –

I infinitely regret the deprivation of your services & trust that your wound is doing well: if I can further your wish on any subject connected with the Brigade under your Command I need scarcely assure you that it will be a source of gratification to be so called upon by you.

Ashworth's brigade had suffered 471 casualties, about 17 per cent of its strength. But after four days of fighting, Soult's offensive on the Nive had been soundly repulsed. A lull now ensued. Wellington awaited the spring before he renewed his offensive, partly for logistical reasons and partly because of the poor condition of the roads. He was also wary of over-extending himself in case Napoleon managed to secure an armistice with the Continental Allies, led by Russia, Prussia and Austria, in northern Europe, thus releasing reinforcements for Soult.

*

Limited clashes occurred on the outposts in the New Year as the two sides gathered forage. Lieutenant Standish O'Grady of the 7th Hussars wrote on 17 January 1814 to his father from Hasparren, 18 km south-east of Bayonne:

Here we are about three miles from the French army and on the Right of the English we have had some work and I am sorry to say have lost some very good officers. You have heard I suppose of poor [Captain Robert] Boltons death he was wounded severely & taken Prisoner the French officer sent in to say that every care should be taken of him & to request that a Surgeon from the 18th [Hussars] should be sent to see him[.] But the poor fellow was dead [on 19 December] before he arrived – He was followed to his Grave by sixteen French officers and buried with all possible military honors a debt which they said they owed a Brave man altho' an enemy – we are obliged to send half the Reg^t to forage and have very severe work to get any – these rascals carry on a hedge & ditch warfare – on our part we can get little honor & run a good chance of some hard blows – a ball struck [Colonel Edward] Kerrisons stirrup iron and did him no harm – Yesterday morning Poor [Captain Peter] Heyleger as fine a fellow as ever lived was shot thro' the arm and the ball lodged in his side close to his back bone it was extracted immediatly and he is doing as well as possible[.] I hope he'l do well we cannot afford to lose him as he is one of the best officers in the Reg^t & *of course* in the army. This outpost duty is more harrasing than dangerous for the ground we occupy we are ordered not to defend and the French could be in our bed rooms in two hours – the fighting ground lies about a mile behind us – As I am now in a situation where they do not scruple to shoot a Gentlemans son I shall write to you constantly and should any thing occur to hinder my doing so you may be certain I am well, and *well employed*, which will be the only excuse I shall ever make for not writing – . . .

Wellington knew by 10 January that the Russian, Prussian and Austrian armies had crossed the River Rhine. To help cover Paris Napoleon withdrew 14,000 troops from Soult, leaving him with just 62,500. In contrast, Wellington now had 82,000. He planned to thrust eastwards and force Soult to withdraw inland by relentlessly outflanking him to the south. Once Soult had fallen back, part of Wellington's army under Lieutenant-General Sir John Hope would isolate the garrison of Bayonne.

Wellington launched his offensive on 14 February. In a letter written the day before, Captain William Coles of the 12th Light Dragoons highlighted some of the reasons why Wellington did not move earlier:

> . . . in consequence of the advance of the Allies & Bonaparte having been oblig'd to detach a part of the Army of Soult in order to strengthen the Grand Army, I think it probable we shall soon attempt the passage of the Adour, Lord Wellington is making great preparations for the Event the Pontoons &c have for some time past been moving to the Front & Magazines are forming on the Nive to render supplys when the Weather is sufficiently dry to admit of the advance of the Army
>
> . . .
>
> as it [the Adour] is a considerable river & consequently presents a great Barrier much difficulty must attend our crossing it; however his Lordship will manage for the best. The troops are in high condition & health & are anxious to bring affairs at this important crisis to a consummation which I trust may be done before the expiration of Four Months –
>
> . . .
>
> We have been very badly off for Forage for the Cavalry of late, on the right of the Army I hear that even the supply of corn without any Hay or straw has been very short in consequence of the extreme bad state of the Roads, however the weather is now improving & will facilitate the transport of all supplys which must have failed had it continued bad much longer . . .

Soult fell back 40 km and concentrated his army in a strong position near the town of Orthez on the north bank of the Gave de Pau. On 25 February Wellington arrived south of Orthez with the right wing of his army under Hill, as an unidentified correspondent described in a letter of 5 March:

> ... about mid day the Light division made its appearance upon the heights above Orthes, Lt Col Ross's troop, (R^l H.A.) [Royal Horse Artillery] which accompanied it, was ordered up by his Lordship to open upon the Enemy; the moment the advanced guard of this Column (the light division) was seen by the Enemy, a mine was exploded to destroy the Bridge. (this attempt we soon learned proved ineffectual)[.] The Enemy at the commencement of our Cannonade appeared to be in the greatest confusion, Columns of Infantry & Cavalry, Carriages of all descriptions, baggage &c, &c, were blocking up the roads, & pressing into the Town from the direction of Pau & Dax, Peyrehorade, &c, the roads were equally crowded beyond the Town, as the troops retired through it, our fire considerably increased the confusion, but it was not judged prudent to push them by, endeavouring to possess ourselves of the Town, as the Enemy's Force was very considerable in, & near it, a party of Light troops was sent to possess themselves of the Houses upon this side [of] the Bridge, to try & prevent the Enemy from effectually destroying it. ...

The French on the morning of the 26th made another ineffectual attempt to destroy the fortified medieval bridge that guarded the access into Orthez. But Wellington did not try to force his way over it; instead his left wing under Beresford crossed the Gave de Pau 24 km to the west of Soult's position and advanced eastwards along the north bank.

Wellington hence outflanked Soult and was able to attack him on the north bank on the 27th. During the battle, Picton's 3rd Division attacked Soult's position frontally up two spurs and gained the crest after bitter fighting. Captain James Oates of the 88th Regiment was with Major-General Thomas Brisbane's brigade on the eastern spur:

> ... as to the cause of my promotion to the rank of Major at Orthes, the 88th which was then commanded by Col, now Majr Genl [John] Taylor, with the two Majors present, McPherson & [James] McGrigor, we were ordered with the rest of Sir Thos Brisbanes brigade to attack upon the centre of Soults position

– The 88[th] were marched up a narrow road in sections of threes right in front, my compy (Gr[enadier]s) of course were the first formed after leaving the road and had to sustain a heavy fire while the remainder of the regt were forming on my left – I perceived a dense column of the enemy returning in disorder in a hollow close on my right and wishing to bring the whole fire of my company upon this column where every shot could tell, but from the rapid firing of musketry and artilery I could not stop them, upon which I went in front of my com[pany] as the only effectual way of closing it and was directing there fire in the way I wished when I received a severe wound through my right thigh, however I had the satisfaction of seeing before I was carried to the rear that the fire of my company was taking full effect as I wished – I threw my sword as far as I was able in front as the enemy was at this time very close to us and desired the men never to see my face again without they brot me back my sword – it is unnessary to say that I received it, it was delivered to me the same day by Serjt Brazil who was severely wounded himself about two minutes after me – . . .

The Battle of Orthez did not go entirely as Wellington had planned, but ended with the French retreating in disorder. The pursuit was handicapped by the enclosed nature of the countryside and by a French musketball that temporarily incapacitated Wellington by striking his sword hilt violently against his thigh. Only the 7th Hussars had any significant success during the pursuit, as Lieutenant Standish O'Grady described to his father on 11 March:

As it was not possible for me to write so as to send my letter with the Dispatches I did not hurry myself and waited untill I could get halted for a day or two[.] by the Dispatches you saw I was safe and for the four or five days after an action the Cavalry are so well employed that they never get into quarters until 9 or 10 at night and we have had more than once to Bivouacke – on the 27th the 7th were the only Cavalry Reg[t] engaged and we did our business in the most Fox hunting style crossed the country after them and cut off seven hundred and eighty[.] the infantry cheered us as we returned Sir S Cotton Returned thanks to Colonel Kerrison and the Officers of the Reg[t] in General Orders in the most handsome manner – the ground on which the Battle was fought is most beautifull and every man could see the whole of the action . . .

Soult withdrew towards the city of Toulouse, 175 km to the east. Captain Edward Keane was serving as ADC to Colonel Hussey Vivian, the commander of a brigade of hussars. He made clear in his diary entry for 2 March the strain that the marching was putting on Wellington's troops: 'A Halt this day, much wanted to our wearied Limbs. Wrote to my father for the first time since the Army moved it being the first opportunity – dined at home – '

Lieutenant Gairdner recorded in his diary on 18 March that Wellington no longer had to rely on transported supplies and that the army was fed entirely on what the country furnished, which was paid for by sending money by the commissaries. In contrast, the French troops antagonized their own countrymen with their unbridled looting, as an unidentified correspondent explained in a letter dated 5 March:

> ... I must not omit to acquaint you with the pleasing sensation that has been excited amongst the people upon our appearance, in every Village & town we have passed through, we have been hailed as the deliverers of an oppressed people, the marks of gratitude & kindness are numerous that we have experienced[;] upon the other hand, the retreat of the French Army has been marked by atrocities disgraceful to human nature, the system of rapine & plunder that has been pursued in their own Country has never been surpassed, & has justly brought upon their heads the imprecations of their Countrymen. . . .

On 7 March Wellington detached Beresford with two divisions to occupy Bordeaux, 120 km to the north. The response of the city's inhabitants testified to growing local support for a restoration of the Bourbon monarchy. Captain Keane recorded on the 12th:

> Entered Bordeaux at half past 10. o.c. to the great joy of the people (to all appearance) they hoisted the white Flag & white [Bourbon] Cockades & made the Air resound again with Vive le Roi Vive les Anglais – dined with the Marshall [Beresford] went to the Theater – & there received with the greatest Acclamations of joy –

Beresford rejoined the main army on 18 March, leaving a division at Bordeaux.

On the 26th Wellington arrived west of Toulouse, but could only attack Soult, who was established in the city, by crossing the River

Garonne to the east bank. Initial attempts to cross south of Toulouse failed dismally. Wellington then established a bridge 18 km north of the city. It was broken by the swollen Garonne, but repaired on 8 April, enabling Wellington to push southwards on Toulouse. Colonel Hussey Vivian's brigade of hussars led the advance. The 18th Hussars made a brilliant charge to capture a bridge over the River Ers north-east of Toulouse. Vivian was wounded at the start of the attack, but Wellington was so delighted at its success that he exclaimed, 'Well done, the Eighteenth. By God, well done.'* The regiment thus restored its reputation following its disgrace at Vitoria.

Captain Keane recorded in his diary on the 9th:

> All tolerably quiet to day, the Enemy appear to be working as hard as they can on the heights [of Calvinet] on this [eastern] side of Toulouse – Ld Wellington reconnoitered both Positions for a long time this day, a little skirmishing on the River [Ers] to our left in consequence of our sending some Light Troops to take possession of a Bridge which the Enemy reoccupied in the afternoon & blew it up at ½ past 5°C – Col V. as well as can be expected after so severe a wound, & every hopes are entertained by all the Medical men that his Arm will be saved, Numerous Visitors to day of all Ranks, from a Marshal [Beresford] downwards – in rather a bad house, obliged to dine in the Kitchen –

Next day was Easter Sunday. Wellington now had his army west and north of Toulouse and demonstrated on both these fronts. He delivered his real attacks against the fortified Calvinet Heights east of Toulouse, as they commanded the city. Two Spanish divisions were bloodily repulsed, but Beresford with the 4th and 6th Divisions advanced and gained the southern end of the heights and then, after a lull, pushed along them. During this contest, Major-General Denis Pack's brigade of the 6th Division was heavily engaged at the Colombette and Tour des Augustins redoubts. The 42nd (or the Royal Highland) and 79th Regiments of Foot took them both, but were driven out by a French counter-attack, obliging Pack to bring up his reserve, the 91st Regiment of Foot. The French were expelled, again recaptured the redoubts and were finally driven out when the last brigade of the 6th Division joined the fight. The 42nd and

---

* Fortescue, *History of the British Army*, v. 10, p. 76.

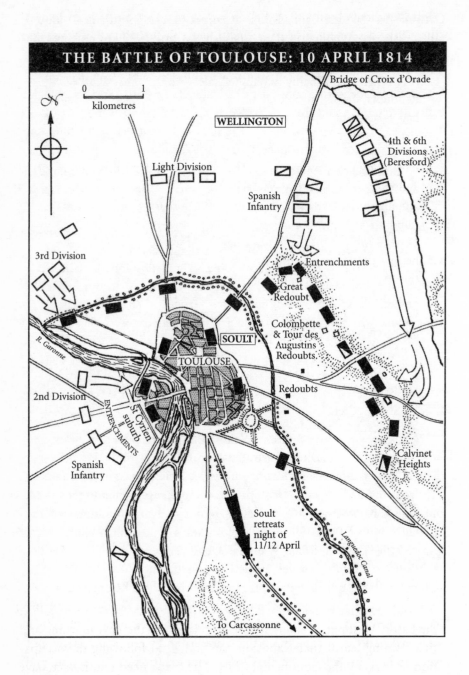

THE BATTLE OF TOULOUSE: 10 APRIL 1814

Bridge of Croix d'Orade

0   1
kilometres

N

WELLINGTON

Light Division

4th & 6th
Divisions
(Beresford)

Spanish
Infantry

3rd Division

Entrenchments

Great
Redoubt

R. Garonne

SOULT

Colombette
& Tour des
Augustins
Redoubts.

TOULOUSE

Redoubts

2nd Division

St Cyrien
suburb

ENTRENCHMENTS

Calvinet
Heights

Spanish
Infantry

Soult
retreats
night of
11/12 April

Languedoc Canal

To Carcassonne

79th Regiments both suffered appalling losses. Lieutenant John Ford of the 79th described his experiences after the Highlanders took the redoubts for the first time:

> ... When the Enemy attempted to recover possession of the Redoubts, I was in a kind of Fleche or outwork of the one we had taken, but separated from the main part of it by a deep farm road
>
> ...
>
> one French Regiment marching up that road cut off my retreat and that of Seven men who were with me. – one of the number attempted, and possibly did escape? – another had the presence of mind to cry out 'Sit down', and if the words had come from a General Officer they could not have been more promptly obeyed – he saw the Enemy before we did, (They came up on our left,) and the cry of 'the French Sit down.' did not require to be often repeated. – we immediately sat down close to the Parapet. – at this moment we heard a cheering and that portion of the Enemy, then close to us, appeared panic struck, went to the right about & immediately retreated. –
>
> One French Officer looked at us and shrugged up his Shoulders (supposing we were wounded and thereby intimating that he could not afford us any assistance) and a French Soldier attempted, while retreating, to pull off the Epaulettes from Capt John Camerons Coat as he lay dead a few yards from us, but did not succeed. – (Cap^n J. Cameron commanded the Company I belonged to.) –
>
> It was altogether but a momentary business, the cheering came from the 91st then advancing to meet the Enemy, for Lieut [Alexander] Roberton at the head of a party of his Regiment immediately entered the work, and surprised at seeing us there, said, Ford are you wounded? – Having been thus released we joined our Regiment where it had reformed, having had a narrow escape of being bayonetted or dragged along as Prisoners with the retiring French army. – ...

Soult evacuated Toulouse on the night of 11/12 April as a result of the battle. Wellington entered the city in triumph the next morning and that evening learnt that Napoleon had abdicated following the occupation of Paris by the Continental Allies. The battle need not, in fact, have been fought.

On 17 April, Soult agreed to an armistice which formally ended hostilities, but not before an unnecessary sortie on the 14th by the French garrison of Bayonne had inflicted another 1,500 casualties. The city was held by 12,000 men, but had been blockaded by Lieutenant-General Sir John Hope's detachment since the end of February. Reports of an impending sortie had been largely disregarded. Captain John Blackman of the Coldstream Guards had written to his parents on 26 March:

> ... It is daily expected that the Garrison will attempt a sortie from the Citadel to try & retake the Church of St Etienne, or some other object they may have in view; this comes from reports of deserters &c – I do not much expect it myself, but of course it keeps us all on the alert. – ...

Hope was surprised by the French attack in the early hours of 14 April. Wellington was not personally present and Major-General Andrew Hay, who was on duty that night as commander of the outpost line, was shot dead at the start of the action. His death adds poignancy to a letter that he had written a day earlier to his wife, who had brought their three daughters from England and had arrived three days before at the nearby village of Biarritz:

> I really at last think you have brought *peace* with you as since my people went on duty last night they have not fired a shot at us.
>
>   ...
>
>   in a couple of days this tour of duty ends[.] when I have We shall be able to make your stay in france more comfortable & then we shall *all* be able to return soon to England ...

Hope himself was wounded and captured after riding as usual into the thick of the fight. The French were eventually repelled and capitulated on 26 April.

*

After several years of war, it took time to adjust to peace. Assistant-Surgeon Thomas Maynard of the Coldstream Guards wrote to Captain Blackman's father from Boucau near Bayonne on 20 May:

> ... The change in the face of things is wonderful and when you meet French Soldiers walking about arm in arm with our men and mixing with us you can scarcely fancy it reality. Instead of looking well into

what direction you are travelling and keeping well out of sight of this
& that point you now ride about fearless and unconcerned what lane
your Horse turns into. . . .

But how important a contribution had the Peninsular War made in
toppling Napoleon? Most obviously, it had helped drain his resources of
money and manpower and had also undermined his reputation. The
initial French defeats in the Peninsula, including Wellington's victories
at Roliça and Vimeiro, were the first major, clear-cut reverses suffered
by Napoleon's Empire. These and subsequent French setbacks encouraged the Continental Allies to challenge Napoleon and were particularly
instrumental in Austria's decisions to go to war in 1809 and to join
Russia and Prussia in the field in August 1813. The Peninsula between
1812 and 1814 was a secondary theatre, for Napoleon's fate was decided
mainly in central and eastern Europe, but it was crucial in tying down
as many as a quarter of a million troops who would at the very least
have prolonged the war elsewhere. Napoleon's key mistake was to invade
Russia in 1812 without having first subdued the Peninsula, which he
could eventually have done by committing sufficient reinforcements.
Instead, he saddled himself with a two-front war at opposite ends of
Europe and his subsequent refusal to seek a negotiated peace on either
front made his downfall inevitable.

Wellington's Peninsular victories were essential in boosting morale in
Britain and in bolstering the Tory Government, which was committed
to a resolute prosecution of the war. They also strengthened Britain's
position as part of the Allied Coalition against Napoleon. It was not
enough for Britain to pay financial subsidies to the Continental Allies
to enable them to maintain their armies in the field: many of her allies
suspected that she was more concerned with her global maritime and
commercial interests than with sharing the burden of the military
struggle against Napoleon in Europe. Wellington's campaigns helped
allay these suspicions and Britain enjoyed a high standing within Europe
by the end of the Peninsular War. This gave her statesmen, including
Wellington himself, a strong hand in negotiating the successful post-war
settlement at the Congress of Vienna.

Wellington through his campaigns also gave the British army a solid
bedrock of experience and an unshakeable self-confidence. He was
gazetted Duke on 3 May, but the honour had been long expected, for

Lieutenant-Colonel Murray of the 18th Hussars had written to his wife as early as 9 August 1813:

> ... They say here that Ld. Wellingt^n is made a Duke, what will they do as he has beat the French twice since that. The soldiers on parade the other day were talking to what new honor Ld W. was to be advanced. A Serjeant said that he thought that he ought to be made a Prince of the blood for he was sure he had shed enough of it. . . .

Wellington visited Paris for a week at the beginning of May to confer with the victorious Allied powers. He was then sent by them to Madrid in an unsuccessful attempt to moderate the reactionary outlook of the newly restored Spanish King Ferdinand VII. (Napoleon had detained Ferdinand in France during the war and had only released him on 24 March 1814.) Ferdinand had soon repudiated the Constitution that the Spanish Parliament, or Cortes, had passed in Cadiz in 1812 and had made clear his determination to rule as an absolute monarch. This aggravated Spain's instability, which had already been worsened by the catastrophic economic, social and political impact of the Peninsular War. Portugal likewise suffered from decades of political upheaval.

Wellington was justifiably proud of his achievement in bringing his Peninsular army by 1814 to a peak of efficiency. He felt that in the end he could have done anything and gone anywhere with that army and that it was the most complete machine for its numbers in Europe. But it was swiftly broken up, with the Portuguese and Spanish troops returning home and some British units being sent across the Atlantic to fight the United States, with whom war had broken out in June 1812.

Gunner Andrew Phillips of the Royal Artillery wrote from Portsmouth on 16 October 1814 to inform his parents that he expected to be discharged within three or four weeks. He had no regrets:

> ... we ar[e] all Discharged at this place, then We have eighty two mils to march to London then I may be a Day or two thear befor a packt Sail for with – But as sun as I git my Discharge I will writ you the Day I march from portsmouth then I will think I am free for once[.] I have served my king and Cuntrey long anuff for nothing[.] Now I am gitting into years and I hop I will spend the remander of them in a mor beneficel mennar for my Self and every other One that belongs me . . .

He added a note on the same letter on 23 October, in which he revealed one of the hazards awaiting discharged soldiers, namely press gangs that forcibly impressed men for service in the Royal Navy:

> Dear father[,] I am taking Short in my opinion since I wrot this letter[.] My Discharge is Com and I am to recive it on monday the 24th of the month[.] I will march on teusday the 25th for london I expect to be in your hous befor a fortnight if I am not taken with the Press Gange[.] the[y] have taken a great number of our men that was Discharged befor but I hope I will have the luk to pass . . .

Wellington himself had a hero's welcome when he returned to England in June 1814. He was appointed Ambassador to the French Court the following month and took up his post in August, but found that it was not the most tactful of appointments, as assassination plots made clear. He was transferred in January 1815 to take Lord Castlereagh's place as Britain's representative at the Congress of Vienna, which was negotiating a settlement for post-war Europe.

9

The Waterloo Campaign

1815

During the final months of the Peninsular War, British troops had also been in action in Holland. Insurrection had broken out following Napoleon's catastrophic defeat at Leipzig in October 1813 and the British saw an opportunity to seize the great naval base of Antwerp. But they had difficulty finding the necessary numbers of soldiers and Lieutenant-General Sir Thomas Graham sailed with an expedition composed largely of poorly equipped and inexperienced second battalions. He was also delayed by adverse winds, and by mid-December, the French had reinforced the garrisons of both Antwerp and Bergen-op-Zoom, the two main fortresses.

Graham hoped to operate against Antwerp in conjunction with a Prussian corps under General Friedrich von Bülow, but found him a difficult and unpredictable ally. After two abortive advances, Bülow marched off into northern France. Graham then attempted a surprise attack on Bergen-op-Zoom on 8 March 1814, but narrowly failed, partly because of the blunders of his subordinates.

Captain William Walton of the Coldstream Guards wrote to his mother on the 9th:

A most unfortunate attack has been made upon Bergen op Zoom, with attempt to Storm the place. it was at first attended with success, but owing to our Troops not being sufficiently supported, we were forced to give up what part of the Town we had got possession of & return – our loss has been dreadful, as you will see by the Gazette – but I must just hint to you that most of *those* who are returned as *missing*, are either *killed* or *wounded* – only the Light Infantry of the *Colds*ᵐ were engaged, and Captⁿ [Charles] Shawe is among the sufferers, but his wound I am happy to say is slight – thro' the thigh, and the bone not injured – I understand there is to be an exchange of Prisoners immediately. it is certainly a most unfortunate Affair –

Graham lost four Colours and 2,550 men, over half of whom were unwounded prisoners. But his defeat did not affect the outcome of the war, for the main Allied armies entered Paris at the end of the month. Napoleon abdicated and was exiled to the Mediterranean island of Elba.

A British force remained in Belgium and Holland, which became the United Netherlands under Dutch rule. Sergeant John Gray of the 33rd (or the 1st Yorkshire West Riding) Regiment of Foot wrote to his brother from Antwerp in May 1814:

... I supose you have heard before now of the Entrance of the Brittish Army into Antwerp on the 5 Ins^t the Brigade our Regiment is attached to was the First brigade that entered the City and the 33^d & 54th Regiment took the Garrison Duty for the Day[.] I Releived a Guard of one Sergant and 12 Privates of the French at one of the Outer Gates the[re] were a great many of the French in the Town when we entered but most of them Marched out in a few Days after[;] there are several French ships of war and a great many on the stocks building –

I hope the Great Change of affairs in Europe will make an alteration for the better in regard to your Trade and the Price of P[r]ovisions as it is what has been very much wanted in England a long Time –

We have been under Orders for Ireland we suppose for America but that Order has been Counter manded and we received another order to march to Ostend to embark for England before we came to this Place but I suppose that is likewise Counter manded but I think if affairs is not soon settled with America that we shall most likely go there a great many of the men are in high spirits expecting their Discharges but I shall not apply for mine if we Go to England as I'am very well off w[h]ere I am my Captain [h]as given me the Payment and Charge of the Company since the 24th January for which I have nearly 6^d p^r Day extra to the other sergants and he has promised me a Coulour the First vancancy which will be 6^d more besides Perqusites which will be nearly 1-£ p^r Week equal to half as much more with you who have every thing to pay for at the full value. – ...

The rank of colour sergeant had been introduced in July 1813 to reward distinguished service and was given to one sergeant in each company.

The war with the United States officially ended with the signing of the Peace of Ghent on 24 December 1814. The willingness of the American delegates to negotiate had been increased by the end of the Peninsular War, which enabled the British units already in North America to be reinforced by some of Wellington's veterans and by powerful elements of the Royal Navy. Unfortunately, the news of the peace took one and a half months to cross the Atlantic and in the meantime the British suffered a costly repulse at New Orleans on 8 January 1815 when they made a direct attack on strongly entrenched American positions.

Following the end of hostilities in North America, a new crisis almost immediately broke out in Europe. Napoleon escaped from exile in February and within a month had regained power in France. The European powers remobilized against him. Wellington left Vienna and arrived at Brussels on the night of 4/5 April to assume command of an army that was assembling there.

Lieutenant Standish O'Grady of the 7th Hussars was delighted at the prospect of renewed fighting and on 16 March wrote to his father from London:

> ... now for another of my follies which is my anxiety for a new war, what a stylish fellow Boney has shewn himself at last, the accounts yesterday were particularly good for *us*. I should not be at all surprised to find him in Paris and that too very shortly, Sir H Vivian [the brigade commander] told me yesterday that our next order in all probability would be one to hold ourselves in readiness for foreign Service[.] Lord Wellington is certainly ordered to take the command of our army on the Continent and it must be made as respectable as possible or it is worse than nothing at all –
>
> ...
>
> all here are betting on Bonaparte and thousands have Given 20 Gui[nea]s to receive a hundred if he was on the throne befor the end of this year – all this Town is in astonishment and every military man is in expectation of being ordered for Brussels to form our army there, I think it not unlikely but we may get the rout[e] also and every thing considered It would make me the happiest man in the

world – Boney deserves the thanks as well as applause of all the British army, and I give him mine with the greatest cheerfullness, He has regained his character & [proved] himself a real game fellow at last – If he is to die I hope he'll have a run for his life, it would be a thousand pities to have him chopped in cover and If he does give a run it will be one of the most *varmint* that has been heard of for the season –

In contrast, Lieutenant Gairdner of the 95th Rifles was annoyed, even if confident of the outcome. He wrote to his father on 23 April:

This cursed war has knocked all my plans in the head; I thought a month ago that by this time I should have been on my way to see you, but this scoundrel Bonaparte to the astonishment of the world has as it were by magic reseated himself without spilling a drop of blood on that throne which it cost Europe just twelve months ago so much blood and treasure to pull him down from. Our Regiment has recieved orders to embark for Flanders and we sail from this place [Dover] the day after tomorrow – The Campaign will doubtless be an active one but it ought not to be a long one; It is very fortunate that peace is made with America – . . .

But the Allies were not ready to launch an immediate invasion of France and feared that Napoleon might make a pre-emptive strike against the United Netherlands. For Britain, this was a key region in both protecting Antwerp and maintaining the European balance of power.

The British soldiers found the Belgians hospitable, but were unsure of their loyalties. Belgium had been under French occupation from 1794 to 1814 and many Belgians had served in Napoleon's armies. Lieutenant-Colonel Murray of the 18th Hussars later wrote:

. . . The inhabitants were very simple & friendly: many used to caution us not to rely upon the Netherland Troops, who (they said) in adverse circumstances would certainly forsake us from their attachment to the French.

The prevailing extent of Farm Buildings & the ample resources they possess, are peculiarly calculated for the easy cantonment of Cavalry: Besides the Flemish Peasant is naturally equestrian, one's horse therefore as one'self has every where a hospitable welcome in the Netherlands.

Lieutenant Gairdner wrote from Ghent on 29 April:

... The people of this country *say* that they wish well to the cause
but of their sincerity I am not yet able to judge, they are generally
accused of preferring the French to the Dutch[.] They are of Course
sorry for the war and annoyed at the Prospect of having their country
made a thorough-fare for troops – They hate both the Russians and
Prussians and seem only to like the English so far as that they
consider them somewhat better than the others – When you say that
England is at a great expense, they say that at present she must lay
out a great deal of money but that she will end by being the gainer,
in fact they seem to dislike their own situation and to distrust every
nation – ...

Much of the expense sprang from having to repair the frontier
fortresses, which had mostly been destroyed during the Wars of the
French Revolution (1793–1802). Wellington himself had inspected the
defences of Belgium in August 1814; officers of the Royal Engineers had
also been active in reconnoitring and ascertaining what needed to be
done to place the frontier in a permanent state of defence. Acting on
their recommendations, the defences of Ypres, Menin, Tournai, Courtrai,
Ath and Mons were now hurriedly repaired. Captain John Oldfield was
one of the handful of Royal Engineer officers in the country:

... With this limited [Royal Engineer] establishment before Bonaparte reached Paris on the 20th. of March nearly ten thousand men
[mostly local peasants] were put to work upon the fortifications in
the Netherlands. At Ypres from the supposed impossibility of Napoleon reaching Paris the excitement had rather subsided and with the
exception of a strong working party repairing some breaches in the
escarp and draining out the ditches, matters were going on in their
usual course ...

While the fortifications were being repaired with renewed effort, the
country around Tournai was inundated to prevent the French just across
the border from seizing it from the weak garrison by a sudden attack.
The intact fortresses of Antwerp, Ostend and Nieuport were strengthened
and Ghent was also prepared for defence. Temporary bridges were
established at strategic points. The pontoons used at Avelghem to span

41. Napoleon in 1815.

42. The crossroads at Quatre Bras, looking north along the paved highroad to Brussels. Note the graves on the right.

43. The Château of Hougoumont, drawn a month after the Battle of Waterloo. This was Wellington's main strongpoint and it was defended throughout the battle by the British Foot Guards and detachments of German infantry.

44. Charge of the Scots Greys at Waterloo, amid the guns of Napoleon's great battery.

45. Captain Edward Kelly of the 1st Life Guards despatching a French cuirassier at the Battle of Waterloo by running him through the neck with his sword. Kelly famously killed a cuirassier colonel and took his epaulettes as trophies.

46. Wellington orders the general advance of his army at the end of the Battle of Waterloo.

47. Wellington (right) and the Prussian commander, Field Marshal Gebhard Leberecht von
Blücher, greet each other as victors at the end of the Battle of Waterloo.

48. Wellington riding through the lines at Waterloo.

49. Lieutenant-General Henry William Paget, second Earl of Uxbridge and Marquess of Anglesey. He commanded Wellington's cavalry at Waterloo.

50. Captain William Tyrwhitt-Drake, Royal Regiment of Horse Guards, c. 1815. He joined the regiment in September 1805 and served with it in the Waterloo Campaign. He retired from the army in May 1826 and died in 1848.

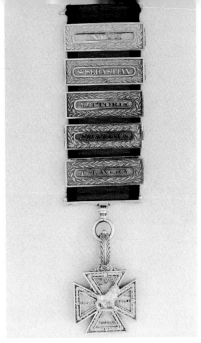

51. Colonel Sir William Howe De Lancey. He served with the Quartermaster-General's Department during the Peninsular War and was mortally wounded at Waterloo. He is wearing his Army Gold Cross.

52. Colonel De Lancey's Army Gold Cross, awarded to senior officers who had distinguished themselves in the Wars against France.

53. An officer of the 52nd (or the Oxfordshire) Regiment of Foot (Light Infantry) in Paris immediately after Waterloo.

54. Colonel Sir John Colborne, c. 1819. He served in the Peninsula and, as the commander of the 52nd Regiment, helped defeat Napoleon's Imperial Guard at Waterloo.

55. Life in the Army of Occupation in northern France after Waterloo. Caricature of two hussar officers thrown from their carriage near Étaples, while charging to a ball at Boulogne, c. 1818.

56. Wellington, c. 1820, in the cloak that he wore at Waterloo.

57. Napoleon's tomb on the island of St Helena, 1821.

58. A soldier relating his exploits in a tavern, 1821. The soldier wears the Waterloo Medal and is pointing to a picture of the battle.

the River Scheldt were found in store and had apparently been left behind by the Duke of York's army in 1794.

Captain Oldfield shed light on Wellington's relations with his engineers in a letter dated 30 April:

... The Duke lost no time after assuming the command of the army in visiting the frontier fortress[es], & I was not a little gratified to find that he was well satisfied with Ypres, and with the selection I had made of the detached works to be retained or levelled[.] His Grace approved generally of the exertions of our department; having made a tour of inspection in the last summer and decided upon the points to be occupied no time was lost in deliberation, but the works immediately commenced. The Com[mandin]ᵍ Engineer [Lieutenant-Colonel Sir James Carmichael-Smyth] also had employed his officers in reconnoitring all the principal positions in the country, and in obtaining a map of local information which now came into use – he had also studied the campaigns of former years, & from his knowledge of the Low Countries gained the good opinion & confidence of the Duke, a confidence rarely, if ever, ill-bestowed – That His Grace sometimes takes prejudices, and has an unfortunate memory of an unlucky occurence the following anecdote will prove – in going round the works at Ypres, The C.R.E. [Commanding Royal Engineer] and an officer were immediately before the Duke, the officer with great want of tact was enquiring of the Colonel the news of the day, and was with difficulty silenced; on leaving the works & getting into the carriage, the Duke turned to the C.R.E. and said 'If you had not silenced the gentleman who was enquiring for news, I was about to tell him, he was not in a coffee room. I remember him well in the Peninsula instead of looking after his positions, he was amusing himself riding over the Country'[.] His Grace proceeded to relate an anecdote of another officer in the Corps, who being asked among [various] questions, which he was not prepared to answer, if an inundation was fordable, and upon his answering in the affirmative the Duke ordered him to pass it, upon which the unlucky officer got in, horse & all and escaped with a good ducking: Colonel Smyth expressing his regret that the Duke should have had so much occasion to express dissatisfaction with the officers of the Corps, His Grace replied, that with our Corps such instances were solitary instances; whereas in the service generally they were very frequent proceeding to pass enconiums on us that coming from another, than the Duke of Wellington we might have considered as undeserved. . . .

The Royal Engineer officers in the United Netherlands numbered no more than 61 even after being reinforced following Napoleon's return from exile. Ten companies of the Royal Sappers and Miners were also present to carry out the work supervised by the Royal Engineers and formed a total of 10 officers and 772 other ranks. Two of these companies constituted part of the army's pontoon train. Once the frontier defences were restored and as the army prepared to invade France, arrangements were made to ensure that each Anglo-Hanoverian infantry division had proper engineer support to avoid a repetition of the difficulties experienced in the Peninsula. Oldfield explained on 1 June:

> During the month of May I was constantly on the move, inspecting the progress of the works on the Frontier: every effort was made to organize an efficient Engineer establishment to move with the Army[.] The exertions of the commanding Engineer and of the Department generally were appreciated by the Duke, and the supply of the wants of the Department thoroughly urged upon the ministers & upon the Master General [of the Ordnance] by His Grace. Engineer Brigades were organized for each division of the Army: consisting of six waggons carrying entrenching tools for 500 men, with 4000 sand bags and a proportion of Engineer stores, to each Brigade was attached a company of Sappers with its Officers. . . .

Two bridges, each of twenty pontoons, were horsed and horses were demanded for two further bridges:

> . . . The British never before had so complete an Engineer Establishment. We had twenty thousand peasants besides strong military working parties employed on the frontier – . . .

Captain Oldfield concluded in a letter written in May:

> . . . From Namur to Nieuport the distance was 120 miles, and although it could not be expected what we had done could prevent an enemy from penetrating a frontier of such extent, that was done which would give the army time to assemble.

Wellington's army was inferior to the one that had been broken up and dispersed at the end of the Peninsular War. Only 40 per cent of his troops were British or from the King's German Legion. The remainder had been contributed by the United Netherlands and the German states of Hanover, Brunswick and Nassau. It was a composite force of mixed quality and experience, but Wellington exaggerated when he protested on 8 May that he had 'an infamous army'. Of the thirty-three British battalions he had under his command by the start of hostilities, as many as eighteen had served in the Peninsula. He also managed to combine his British, King's German Legion and Hanoverian brigades to form divisions which each had a backbone of reliable units to bolster less experienced ones.

A Prussian army under Field Marshal Prince Gebhard Leberecht von Blücher had deployed to the east of Wellington to help cover Brussels. Wellington and Blücher could field a combined strength of 210,000 men, but had to guard 160 km of frontier in order to cover all the potential invasion routes. Thus Napoleon, who could assemble a strike force of 124,000 troops, had a window of opportunity in which to maul the Allies piecemeal before they could concentrate all their units.

Wellington had a powerful cavalry force, which by June numbered over 14,000, nearly 60 per cent of whom were British or from the King's German Legion. Lieutenant O'Grady of the 7th Hussars wrote on 27 March to his father from London:

> ... there is some satisfaction in knowing that we are destined to act in a Capital cavalry Country and much a better one for campaigning than the one we last had the happiness of operating in & as the Country is thickly inhabited we shall not have to carry much canteens or other baggage[.] Ld Uxbridge they say is to have the Command & Vivian will most likely have one brigade[;] so far we are uncommonly lucky I think our Campaign will be very short but we shall not be idle – How like a play it looks to see such extraordinary changes – just as we thought our task at an end we find it is only just beginning but there is nothing so delightfull as uncertainty and I think half the pleasures of the army consist in it – ...

Wellington wrote to Lieutenant-General Sir Stapleton Cotton, now Lord Combermere, from Brussels on 7 April, indicating whom he wanted to command his cavalry:

I received both your letters when [Major-General Sir Henry] Torrens
[the Military Secretary to the Duke of York] was here, and I
immediately spoke to him about you; as I assure you that I am most
anxious to have the assistance of all those to whom upon former
occasions I have been so much indebted. We shall have I hope an
enormous body of Cavalry of different Nations; and I trust that
Torrens will be able to make an arrangement which will be satisfactory to you.

But the Prince Regent pressed for the appointment of one of his
favourites, Lieutenant-General Henry Paget, the Earl of Uxbridge (later
the Marquess of Anglesey). Uxbridge was duly appointed on 15 April. In
fact he worked smoothly with Wellington, as they were both pragmatic
men. But Wellington made his feelings clear in a letter to Combermere
on 3 December 1817:

... You are as well aware as I can make you of the nature & cause of
the arrangements for the Command of the Cavalry last war. The
Prince Regent entertains a high opinion of Lord Anglesey's Interests;
and Lord Anglesey more than once told me at the time that he had
not wished to come out. I certainly should have been satisfied to say
the least with my old friends & Assistants; but I could not object to
another arrangement proposed by such authority. . . .

The British cavalry were quartered in the villages of the fertile valley
of the River Dender, with Uxbridge's headquarters at the town of
Ninove, 22 km west of Brussels. On 29 May, they were reviewed in the
fields opposite the village of Schendelbeke, 10 km south-west of Ninove.
Lieutenant O'Grady wrote:

... all the British Cavalry and the horse artillery were inspected by
the Duke of Wellington the day before yesterday there never was so
fine a sight – we all assembled in a plain in three lines each near a
mile long[.] Ld Wellington *Blucher* the Prince of Orange the Duke de
Berri [nephew of the French King, Louis XVIII] & Ld Uxbridge were
the remaining officers[.] old Blucher said he never saw such a sight
in his life & valued the horses at 3 million of money he said he
should shut himself up when he went back to the Prussians for three
days to endeavour to forget how inferior they were to us – Lord
Wellington said the 10th [Hussars] were the most beautiful horses he

ever saw but that he could account for that & then turning to Ld Uxbridge said the 7th [Hussars] were out & out the most soldierly and best turned-out Reg^t in the field to which Lord Uxbridge added in his short way 'Damn it the 7th cant be improved they are perfect' – It was really beautiful to see Ld Uxbridge manuvering 46 Squadrons on ground that could but just hold them but he can do it in capital Style – I have dined with him sometimes and like him much he is quite as familiar as one of ourselves – . . .

The fact that Uxbridge was the Colonel of the 7th puts Wellington's remarks in perspective.

Captain Henry Grove of the 23rd Regiment of (Light) Dragoons added more details of the review:

. . . The weather was perfect, and the field was high grass, saving us from dust – it was a brilliant sight – Lord Uxbridge paid £200 for the use of the ground, saying that many old women laid out as much for a Soirée – at one oclock the Duke with Marshal Blucher, and a host of distinguished characters, arrived; and were received with a Salute of 21 guns, and having gone down each line, we broke into columns of Half Squadrons, and marched past – We had 46 Squadrons, besides the six Troops of Horse Artillery, and no Troops ever appeared in better order – We left the Field at 4. °Clock and got back to St Quintin at ½ past 7, having been on our Horses 14½ hours.

Lieutenant-Colonel Murray, the commander of the 18th Hussars, wrote to his wife on 7 June:

. . . We had the other day a Review of the Cavalry, about 7 thousand including Horse Artillery. They were in three lines, & nothing could be more brilliant. Blucher said that he should not be able to look at his own people for a fortnight afterwards. The Duke of Wellington, the Prince of the Netherlands, Marshal Blucher, &c. dined afterwards with Lord Uxbridge. Blucher was in a green Uniform & rode a fine dappled Grey Horse at the Review. I sat within one of him, General Dornberg an Officer of Hussars only being between, at the Dinner, but as he spoke in German I could not profit by it. The Dinner was sumptuous without ostentation, not even servants in Livery, but everything as good as it could be, which I think in better taste for at dinner I prefer good living [?] even to finery (it being however well understood I like the latter to be on myself)

. . .

We have races once a week, Brigade Field days three times a week, & race dinners where people get very drunk, & ride home across the country, killing their Horses, & getting half drowned themselves. I dont partake of the later festivities of the day & retire early after a few *Tumblers* of Champaigne. . . .

At the same time, Wellington's army prepared for hostilities. Ensign Edward Macready of the 30th Regiment claimed that he was drilled out of all patience and that he longed for war as a respite from fatigue:

> . . . the Prince of Orange [commander of Wellington's I Corps] kept us hard at work – he prepared for a campaign by filling the Hospitals – twice a week we marched two miles to the heath of Casteau near Mons and were drilled in Corps or division. These parades with our return to quarters often lasted from three in the morning till six in the afternoon. Our men sometimes fainted and more frequently pretended to faint from heat and fatigue so much so that it became a standing trick if I may be allowed the expression for some old hand to drop as the Prince past the line. This had always a good effect & we soon marched home . . .

British heavy cavalrymen sharpened their swords to a spear point to make them more effective in thrusting, for they knew that many French cavalrymen would be protected from slashing strokes by armour. A General Cavalry Order issued at Ninove on 12 June read:

> 1 The swords of every Regiment of Cavalry are to be ground & pointed according to the Pattern recieved by the Troop Serg^t Majors and Men assembled this Day at Cavalry Head Quarters: –
> 2 This Order must be carried into execution without Loss of Time

Another concern was the time it would take the army to concentrate from its widespread cantonments should Napoleon invade. Murray issued an order to the 18th Hussars on 11 May:

> The Officers must take every means to make their Troops acquainted with the name of the Village where they are stationed, & of the Head Quarters of the Regiment.
> Not a private to day could tell the Lieut. Colonel the name of the place where he was quartered, & as the soldiers in general seemed

equally unacquainted with the direction of the roads going out of their own quarters it is evident what difficulties would arise to the assembling [of] the Regiment on any immediate urgency.

Captain Grove took similar precautions the day after joining the 23rd Light Dragoons from England on 21 May:

> ... The day after I joined, when my Tent had been pitched, and all put in good order, I wanted to try my baggage saddle, and see how my horses would work when loaded; and also to see how my servants could manage the matter – I suddenly ordered every thing to be got ready for a march – we were soon off, and when they had got three miles we returned, and all things again put in order. . . .

Officers of the Royal Staff Corps reconnoitred the main routes in the country. Their reports contained detailed notes on the state of the roads and the adjacent ground, of the width and depth of the rivers and the means of crossing them. In addition, they noted the numbers of men and horses that could be quartered in towns and villages. Besides mapping the routes that they reconnoitred, they sketched the view of the horizon from at least one side of the road. They also reported on the defences of towns such as Oudenaarde and Courtrai.*

Lieutenant-Colonel William Nicolay, the Commanding Officer of the Royal Staff Corps, wrote on 17 May to Major-General John Brown, the unit's Colonel, to inform him of developments, particularly those concerning the Corps:

> ... Sir H. Lowe, who has shewn every disposition I could wish towards the Corps, is about to quit us in a day or two, on a particular Service – this seems to be arranged chiefly from an idea that Sir G. Murray may probably come out here, tho' by no means certain[.] In the mean time Sir Wᵐ Delancey will carry on the Duties of the [Quartermaster-General's] Department – & from the little I have seen of him, I make no doubt but we shall proceed with a perfect good understanding –
>
> . . .
>
> The cross roads, are bad, being quite a sandy soil, & a little of our Hythe Shingle would be very desirable – On this account all the

---

* NAM. 1968–07–137.

principal Roads are paved in the middle for use in bad weather –
with another road at each side, for dry weather, which answers
therefore very well – and almost universally there are rows of trees
on both sides of the roads – . . .

Major-General Sir Hudson Lowe, Wellington's original Quartermaster-
General, did not have his confidence and left on 2 June. Unfortunately,
Major-General Sir George Murray, Wellington's trusted Quartermaster-
General from the Peninsula, was now in North America. Until he could
return, the Department was entrusted to Colonel Sir William De Lancey,
who returned to his old Peninsular post of Deputy Quartermaster-
General.

On 15 June Napoleon suddenly struck at the junction of Wellington
and Blücher's armies. Wellington, in Brussels 48 km to the north, was
slow to react, for he thought that it might be a feint and feared that the
real attack would come against his western flank. That evening, he calmly
went to a ball given by the Duchess of Richmond, who had invited many
of his officers, along with prominent local citizens and several of the
British residents of the city. Many British civilians had moved to Brussels
after Napoleon's fall in 1814 to take advantage of the lower cost of living
or simply to visit the Continent, from which they had been excluded
since the short-lived Peace of Amiens of 1802–03. The ball was cut short
by news that the French had attacked one of Wellington's brigades at the
crossroads of Quatre Bras, just 32 km south of Brussels.

Magdalene, Lady De Lancey vividly captured the atmosphere of those
tumultuous moments in a precis of her famous narrative. She had been
married to Sir William De Lancey for just over two months and had
come to join him in Brussels:

I arrived at Brussels on Thursday the 8th June – & was surprised at
the peaceful appearance of that town & the whole country fr[om]
ostende – we were billeted in the House of Count de Lannoy in the
Park – I saw very little of the town & still less of the inhabitants for
nothwithstanding Sir W's belief that we should remain quietly there
for a month at least – I have the comfort of remembering that as
there was a chance of our seperating in a few Days I wasted no time
in visiting or going to Balls – which I did not care for –
    fortunately my husband had scarcely any business to do & he
only went to the office for about an hour every Day, I then used to

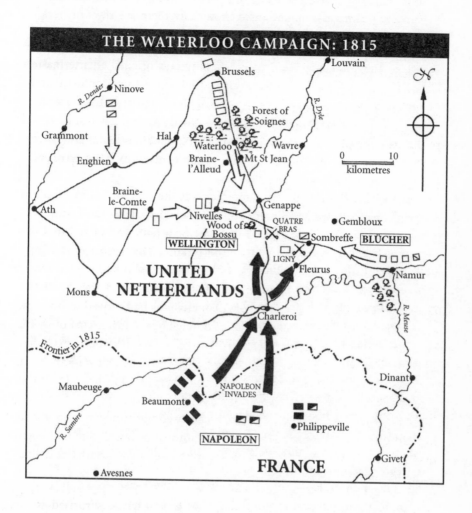

THE WATERLOO CAMPAIGN: 1815

Louvain

Brussels

R. Dender Ninove

Grammont

Hal

Forest of
Soignes

R. Dyle

Enghien

Waterloo
Braine-
l'Alleud

Wavre

Mt St Jean

0   10
kilometres

Braine-
le-Comte

Ath

Nivelles
Wood of
Bossu

Genappe

QUATRE
BRAS

Gembloux

Sombreffe

BLÜCHER

WELLINGTON

LIGNY

Fleurus

UNITED
NETHERLANDS

Mons

Namur

Charleroi

R. Meuse

Frontier in 1815

Dinant

Maubeuge

Beaumont

NAPOLEON
INVADES

R. Sambre

Philippeville

NAPOLEON

Givet

FRANCE

Avesnes

sit & think with astonishment of my being transported into such a scene of happiness so perfect so unalloyed, feeling that I was entirely enjoying life, not a moment wasted how active & how well I was! –

I scarcely knew what to do with all my health & spirits, now & then a pang would cross my mind at the approaching campaign, but I chased away the thought resolved not to lose the present bliss by dwelling on the chance of future pain –

on Wednesday 14th I had a little alarm in the Evng with some public papers & Sir William went out with them, but returned in a short time and it passed by so completely that Thursday afternoon was the happiest day of my life but I cannot recollect a Day of my short married Life that was not perfect – I shall never get on if I begin to talk about what my happiness was but I dread to enter on the gloomy past, which I shudder to look back upon – I often wonder I survived it – We little dreamt that Thursday was the last we were to pass together & that the Storm would burst so soon – Sir Wm had to dine at the Spanish Embassadors, the first invitation he had accepted from the time I went – he was unwilling to go & delayed & still delayed till at last when near 6 I fastened all his medals and Crosses on his Coat, helped him to put it on & he went – I watched at the Window till he was out of sight & then I continued musing on my happy fate – I thought over all that had passed & how grateful I felt[.] I had no wish but that this might continue – I saw my husband loved & respected by every one, my life gliding on like a gay dream in his care – when I had remained at the window nearly an hour I saw an A.D.C. ride under the Gateway of our House – he sent to inquire where Sir W. was dining – I wrote down the name & soon after I saw him gallop off in that direction – I did not like this appearance but I tried not to be afraid – a few minutes after I saw Sir W. on the same Horse gallop past to the Dukes which was a few Doors beyond ours – he dismounted & ran into the House & left the Horse in the middle of the Street – I must confess my courage failed now & the succeeding two hours formed a contrast to the happy forenoon –

about 2 [a.m. on the 16th] Sir Wm went again to the Dukes & he was sleeping sound – at 3 the troops were all assembled in the Park & Sir Wm & I leant over the Window seeing them march off so few to return – it was a clear refreshing morng & the scene was very solemn & melancholy[.] The Fifes played alone & the Regiments one after the other marched past & I saw them melt away, through the great Gate at the end of the Square [the Place Royale] – shall I ever forget the tunes played by the shrill Fifes & the Bugle horns which disturbed that night – at six in the mor^n I went to Antwerp – . . .

Wellington left Brussels for Quatre Bras on the morning of the 16th, which was now held by the 2nd Dutch–Belgian Division. In the afternoon, Napoleon attacked the Prussians with the bulk of his army at Ligny, 10 km south-east of Quatre Bras. He instructed his detached left wing under Marshal Ney to drive back Wellington and send forces south-eastwards to help encircle the Prussians. But Wellington in the battle that ensued at Quatre Bras managed to keep control of the strategic crossroads. He was initially outnumbered, but was reinforced from Brussels to the north and from his other cantonments in the west. By the end of the battle, he had 37,000 troops on the field and switched to the offensive, driving back Ney's now outnumbered forces.

Lieutenant George Simmons of the 1st Battalion, 95th Rifles arrived from Brussels at about 3.00 p.m. As the riflemen passed through fields of corn taller than themselves, they were greeted by a few roundshot and were suddenly checked by a thick, thorny hedge. Simmons peered through and saw grassland intersected with ditches and also some French infantry who opened fire. Simmons saw a rifleman wounded nearby and knew the battalion had to press on before it took more casualties. He took a few steps to the rear, ran at Sergeant Underwood and butted him through:

> . . . Underwood gathering himself up, who the hell sent me through this hedge in that manner? – I did Sir! We must have no fine Ladies here, look at these rascals, the field is too small to hold us. Underwood deliberately fired at one of them. The company rushed through the gap like a flock of sheep following its leader, the French were now handed along very unceremoniously through several fields intersected with Ditches & low embankments, affording us good ground for Rifle practice. The Enemy were now in force behind some straggling houses, so we called a halt in a good position, behind an embankment with a ditch in front. Lieut [Jonathan] Layton who was close to me received a hit in the wrist, & side by musket balls the wounds were not severe, but they bled freely. I tore off part of the sleeve of his shirt & wound it round his wrist, telling him to go to the Doctor. George Simmons you must hit the

fellow first. I see him now pointing with his finger[.] I took a rifle,
laid down & fired over the stump of a tree, several men were doing
the same from the embankment. I knew some of them were punished because they began to hide themselves. After firing in this way
3 or 4 shots, a serjeant said fire my Rifle Sir. I sprang up & said fire
it yourself. Layton intreated me to do so, [but I said] not this time.
The serjeant then placed his Rifle over the stump, I pointing at
(almost bent over him) a man at the corner of a wall. At this
moment a round-shot struck him in the face, dashing his head into
long shreds or ribbons & throwing him backwards a distance of
10 yards. It was quite marvellous his smashed head did not touch
me, only a little sprinkling of blood. Layton & [Lieutenant Orlando]
Felix were close by observed George Simmons you really have a
charmed life. In my excitement, I said Men look at that glorious
fellow, our comrade & brother soldier, he now knows the grand
secret, he has died nobly for his Country & without a pang of
suffering. My boys I trust he is on the high road to heaven. May
God in his mercy bless *him*. . . .

The 95th were posted on Wellington's far eastern flank to keep open
his communications with the Prussians along the high road to Ligny.
The riflemen had a Brunswick battalion in support and were reinforced
towards 5.00 p.m. by a Hanoverian brigade under Major-General Kiel-
mansegge, part of the 3rd Division. Lieutenant Simmons continued his
account:

> . . . A column of Germans now came near & halted. [Lieutenant-]
> General Sir Charles Alten com^g the 3rd Division was on horseback in
> front with his staff. This great & kind man [had been] comdg the
> Light Division in Spain. I no sooner espied him, than I ran & seized
> his hand, saying God bless you my General. Ah! my Light Division
> officer. I wish I had my old Division here now[.] Gentlemen, this is
> one of my dear old friends. Simmons where is [Lieutenant-Colonel
> Sir Andrew] Barnard [the commanding officer of the 1st Battalion,
> 95th Rifles]. I want him to cover my advance, look Sir, there he is &
> you know he will be pleased to do so. I hope we shall soon receive
> the order to clear your front, soon after we jumped the Ditch &
> drove the Enemy from the houses as Rifle men are wont to do,
> reader this was not done without having some [illegible] on the
> green, a necessary evil connected with glorious War. – Several

Columns advanced covered by Riflemen & Light Infantry. The columns were now & then compelled to form square to resist the French Cavalry. . . .

Lieutenant Gairdner, who was also in the 95th, described subsequent events in more detail than Simmons. He had arrived at Quatre Bras after the rest of the Battalion, having been left at Brussels to bring up its stragglers:

... We took a wood from the enemy [the Bois de la Hutte, along the south-eastern edge of the battlefield] which they might have defended better, when we arrived at the extremity of which we saw them in [illegible] Columns and as we were without support we of course lay down to watch them, indeed I wonder much at their giving up the wood so easily and as we were only ab^t 400 Skirmishers without support I felt very uneasy, while thus situated the Adjutant [Lieutenant John Kincaid] came with an order for us to retire and occupy some houses on a ridge in our rear there was no order for the Brunswickers to retire. however they came away with us the consequence was that the French Crowded into the wood when they saw us leave it and followed up, we were obliged to halt on a bare ridge above it and there make a stand. I there recieved a wound in the foot and went to the rear, I afterwards heard that three attempts were made to Retake the wood that night but the French kept it after all. Our Reg^t suffered much this day as did the whole [of Picton's 5th] Division particularly the Highland Reg^{ts} which were several times charged by French Cavalry . . .

Private Edward Costello was in the same company as Gairdner, whom he called 'a worthy little officer'. His account, published in 1852,* suggested that he and Gairdner were wounded at the same time, when they unexpectedly received a volley as they were advancing after driving the French from the wood. But Gairdner clarifies that he himself was wounded slightly later, after the company had fallen back. That night, he remained with the other wounded in houses just behind the position and the following morning returned to Brussels in a hired cart as he was unable to walk.

Ensign Macready of the 30th Regiment reached Quatre Bras in the

---

* E. Costello, *Adventures of a Soldier* (London, 1852).

late afternoon. He and a small party had been left behind by mistake in
the village of Naast 26 km west of the battlefield when the 3rd Division
moved off. But they marched on their own initiative to rejoin the rest of
Major-General Sir Colin Halkett's brigade and quickened their pace on
hearing the distant gunfire. By the time they neared the battlefield of
Quatre Bras, the men had begun to faint very fast. They were told by a
staff officer that the rest of the 30th had arrived about a quarter of an
hour before and were on the other side of the wood of Bossu. Macready's
detachment marched for the crossroads:

... We soon reached Quatre bras where the Brunswickers and some
of Picton's people were in square and on turning the end of the
wood found ourselves in the hurly burly of the battle. The roaring
of great guns and musquetry – the bursting of shells and shouts of
the combattants raised an infernal and indescribeable din while the
galloping of horses – the mingled crowds of wounded and fugitives
(Belgians) – the volumes of smoke and flashing of fire struck out a
scene which accorded admirably with the music. As we passed a spot
where the 44th our old chums had suffered considerably the poor
wounded fellows raised themselves up and welcomed us with faint
shouts 'push on old Thirtieth – pay em off for the poor 44th you're
much wanted my boys – success to ye my darlings'[.] Here we met
our old Colonel [Lieutenant-Colonel Alexander Hamilton] riding out
of the field shot through the leg[.] the Highlanders were crossed like
the marks of their plaid on some spots – Hamilton shewed us our
Regiment and we reached it just as a body of Lancers and Cuirassiers
had enveloped two faces of its square. We formed up to the left and
fired away. The tremendous volley our square which in the hurry of
formation was six deep on the two sides attacked, gave them, sent
off these fellows with the loss of a number of men and their commanding officer. He was a gallant soul – he fell while crying to his men
'avencez [sic] mes enfan[t]s – courage – encore une fois Français'[.]
I dont know what might have been my sensations on entering this
field coolly, but as it was I was so fagged and choked with running &
was pass'd so suddenly into the very thick of the business that I can't
recollect thinking at all except that the Highlanders (over whom I
stumbled almost every step) were most provokingly distributed. On
our repulse of the Cavalry Sir Thomas Picton rode up and thanked
us warmly as this body had cut up two or three regiments – I think

the men I saw had belonged chiefly to the 11th Cuirassiers – they
were savage looking fellows – . . .

Of Wellington's cavalry, only the Brunswickers and a Dutch–Belgian
brigade actually fought at Quatre Bras, for the British horsemen did not
begin to arrive until the closing stages. They had a long and arduous
march from their quarters in the Dender valley. The 15th (or The King's)
Regiment of (Light) Dragoons (Hussars), for example, covered over
72 km in 16½ hours.* Captain William Tyrwhitt-Drake of the Royal
Regiment of Horse Guards recorded the weight carried by a trooper's
horse of his regiment on 10 June when in complete marching order.
He calculated the average weight of a trooper at eleven stone and
added all equipment and horse appointments, including helmet, boots,
saddle, weapons, cloak and blanket. The total came to 19 stone 10 lb.
In addition, the horse would have to carry two days' forage (48 lb)
and the trooper's rations (5 lb), which increased the overall weight to
23 stone 7 lb.

While on the march, several cavalry regiments discarded their forage
to lighten the weight, as Captain Grove of the 23rd Light Dragoons
described in his journal for 16 June:

> After being very merry last night with my friends Jeremey [? James]
> Hay of the 16th [Light Dragoons] Simpson, and Entwis[t]le, I was not
> inclined to be called at 4 oclock to meet the Enemy – We were
> ordered to turn out and march immediately, as the French were on
> the move – Simpson went back to his wife at Brussels, but Entwisle
> had an inclination to see the armies meet, from which we called him
> the amateur. We began our march at 7 °Clock and at Enguhein
> [Enghien] found the Cavalry assembled – We went on to Sart de
> Marelines [Sart Dames-Avelines, a village immediately north of the
> battlefield of Quatre Bras], and 8 miles from which, we were ordered
> to trot, as our services were required – We threw away our forage,
> and after great exertion, and a march of 30 miles, we did not arrive
> in time to be of any use – I thought myself fortunate in seeing even
> the close of the action which had been very severe
>
> . . .

* H. Wylly, *XVth (The King's) Hussars 1759 to 1913* (London, 1914), pp. 240–1.

At 10 P.M. we returned to within a mile of Nivelles, and remained
in a clover field with a heavy dew on it for the night.

The 23rd's return to near Nivelles was apparently to guard Wellington's
western flank against French patrols or a potential outflanking move.

The Prussians had meanwhile suffered a heavy but indecisive defeat
at Ligny and pulled back during the night towards the town of
Wavre, 22 km to the north, to regroup. Captain William Cameron, a
deputy-assistant quartermaster-general who had previously served with
the 1st Foot Guards in the Peninsula, sheds light on these events. He
left Brussels, apparently on 15 June, for the city of Namur, 56 km to
the south-east, where Blücher's headquarters were located. He arrived
on the 16th and:

... I learnt that the french had crossed our lines but only as a
Reconnaissance that the garrson [sic] had left Namur in consequence
but that nothing serious was apprehended. not relying on this I
pushed on and came up to the Prussians in action at Fleurus engaged
in the battle of Ligny as the french call it, there being mistaken for a
frenchman I was taken to the general of division Thielman [com-
mander of the Prussian III Corps] I enquired of him where the
English troops were and learnt that the shortest way to join them
was by the high Road but that the road was patroled and I might be
taken prisoner they were then at Quatre bras but if I went to the
Rear I might join them by some cross roads. This I objected to,
wishing rather to remain with the general, till the High Road was
cleared passibly by the advance of the Prussian troops instead of
which the Prussians were obliged to retreat to Gembloux before
which Lord then [Lieutenant-]Col [Sir Henry] Harding[e, the British
liaison officer with the Prussian army] lost his hand and wrist by a
cannon shot at the close of the action. I fell back with the Prussian
troops to the village of Gembloux and at day break endeavoured to
join the E_[English] army by the cross roads but the map mislead
me and I returned again to Gembloux w[h]ere I learnt that it was
fortunate I had not been taken prisoner as the french were patroling
through the villages by which I had endeavoured to pass. At Gembloux I procured a guide and then went on to Wavre occupied by
another portion of the Prussian army, I then pushed on to Waterloo
which I reach[ed] about 5 Evening 17th and reported myself to the
Quarter Quarters [Master] General Col de Lancey. I took up my

quarters the same night in the stable with my horse in the village of Waterloo at day light in the morning I mounted but found my horse quite exhausted from his work 2 days before. Then in the imergancy secured a horse of a Belgian commisariate officer laying my own in exchange – This horse was killed *early* in the action [of Waterloo] (was twice wounded)

But the outcome of the Battle of Ligny was not immediately known at Quatre Bras. On the evening of the 16th, Lieutenant-Colonel Murray accompanied a picket that his brigade commander, Major-General Sir Hussey Vivian, sent out to the east of the battlefield:

> ... Slight rain came on during the night, & word was brought to me that there was a Prussian Officer in a house just by, & who was on his way to Head Quarters.
>
> I went from the open ground where I was with the Picket to the house where I found the Prussian Officer.
>
> He told me that a very severe action had been fought by the Prussians (Battle of Ligny) he spoke despondingly – He said that he had been in all the former campaigns against the French, but had never before seen them fight with anything like the same determination – & that their force of Artillery was quite overwhelming.
>
> The Prussian Officer then went on to the Duke of Wellington.
>
> & I returned to my Picket – which the French did not attack until next day. . . .

Despite the disheartening tone of his message, this Prussian officer does not seem to have left Ligny before Blücher had actually been defeated. On the morning of 17 June Wellington expected to be able to take the offensive in conjunction with Blücher, now that they had managed to concentrate powerful numbers of troops. He first heard of the Prussian retreat after sending an ADC, Lieutenant-Colonel the Hon. Sir Alexander Gordon, to reconnoitre. He then realized the exposure of his position and resolved to make a corresponding withdrawal, nearly 13 km northwards to a shallow ridge south of the village of Waterloo.

Captain John Oldfield, the Brigade-Major and second-in-command of the Royal Engineers, provides crucial evidence in his account about the selection of the Waterloo position. He described how on the morning of 16 June at Brussels:

... Between seven & eight o'clock, Sir George Wood [the commander of the Royal Artillery] & Lieut. Colonel Smyth [the commanding Royal Engineer] drove out in [the] calêche [light carriage] of the latter, saying to their Brigade Majors, they would drive out & see what was going forward, that they did not anticipate anything that day, that if any thing did occur they would send in for us, they took lead [led] horses with them, but expected to be back in two hours. Colonel Smyth did not even take his sword. He left orders for me to execute in case he did not return by noon, at which hour he had made an appointment with Major Tyleden [Tylden, commanding the pontoon train] & others[.] As soon as Colonel Smyth had departed I ordered my horse to be saddled & with my orderly & a led horse to be ready at a moments warning – the Adjutant [Lieutenant John Sperling] gave the same direction to his servant – When the firing commenced in the afternoon [Captain H.] Baynes the Brigade Major of Artillery & I were most anxious for tidings from our chiefs, as without orders we could not move, the firing appeared much more than it really was the reports were various, towards evening many wounded came in: Bruxelles was in a state of great excitement. Shortly after my Chief had joined Head quarters he sent into me for the plan of the position of Waterloo, which had been previously reconnoitered, the several sketches of the officers had been put together & one fair copy made for the Prince of Orange – a second had been commenced in the Drawing room for the Duke, but was not in a state to send. I therefore forwarded the original sketches of the Officers – No further tidings arriving from our chiefs we separated for the night, ordering our horses to be ready at a moments warning[.] We had in the course of the afternoon sent off our Artillery Mounted Orderly with a note stating our anxiety to join our chiefs. About midnight my orderly who passed the night in my anteroom, awoke me to give me a dispatch which had arrived from Sir Geo. Wood & Colonel Smyth for Baynes & myself[.] My note from the Col: said that the affair of the day (16th) had been a sharp one, that the enemy were repelled on all sides, that a forward movement was anticipated the following morning, & that Sperling & myself might join him, he begged me to communicate the contents of his note to his Friend General Francis Dundas who would probably ride out with me. In less than a quarter of an hour we were in our saddles, the old general with us & on our way to the Front. My English groom I left at Bruxelles with my baggage & two of my horses My Sapper orderly accompanied me, mounted on one of my horses & leading another, I gave him also Col. Smyth's sword to carry to the field, as the Col: had left it at Bruxelles[.] We breakfasted & feed our horses at a small inn, in the Village of Waterloo about daybreak on the morning of the 17th & then proceeded to the front through the village of Genappe. In the three miles between Genappe & Quatre Bras we passed several corps of cavalry & field batteries halted on the ground. The Duke & his [illegible] Major were immediately in rear of the Village of Quatre Bras – the French army immediately in our front. A wounded horse of Col: Freemantle's was limping about on three legs between the two armies – The farm yard of Quatre Bras was full of wounded the 92nd were bivouacking under the wall of the enclosure. The [Brussels] road between the farm house & the public house opposite was covered with dead. . . .

Lieutenant-Colonel John Fremantle was one of Wellington's ADCs. Oldfield in a subsequent letter explained that on the morning of the 17th:

. . . Upon my joining Col. Smyth he desired me to receive from Lieut. [Marcus] Waters the plan of the [Waterloo] position, which according to his desire, I had sent to him from Bruxelles, the preceeding day and of which I was told to take the greatest care, it had been lost in one of the charges of the French Cavalry and recovered – Lieutenant Waters who had put it in his cloak before his saddle, was unhorsed in the melée & ridden over, upon recovering himself he found the Cavalry had passed him, and his horse was no where to be seen, he felt alarmed for the loss of his plan. to look for his horse he imagined was in vain, and his only care was to avoid being taken prisoner which he hoped to do, by keeping well towards our right, the enemy being repulsed in his charge was returning by the left to the ground from which he had advanced. After proceeding about fifty yards, he was delighted to find his horse quietly grazing on the vegetables in a garden near the farm house at Quatre Bras; he thus fortunately recovered his plan and with it rejoined the Colonel[.] The retreat of the Prussians upon Wavre rendered it necessary for the Duke to make a corresponding movement, and upon the receipt of a communication from Blucher he called Col: Smyth and asked him

for his plan of the position of Waterloo, which I immediately handed
to him

. . .

The Duke then gave directions to Sir William De Lanc[e]y to put
the army in position at Waterloo, forming them across the Nivelles
and Charleroi chaussées which coming from Bruxelles divided at
this point[.] We were consequently in a line with the Prussians at
a distance of about eight miles and eight miles in rear of Quatre
Bras. . . .

Other evidence suggests that the position that De Lancey was directed
to take up was in fact a more southerly ridge either side of the inn of
La Belle Alliance. De Lancey found that this was too extensive for the
numbers of troops available and therefore selected the now famous ridge
of Mont St Jean 1.5 km further north.

*

Wellington was not immediately attacked on 17 June and was able to
begin his retreat at 10.00 a.m. Napoleon detached 32,000 men under
Marshal Emmanuel de Grouchy to follow the Prussians and then
belatedly linked up with Ney at Quatre Bras early in the afternoon.
Wellington's rearguard was entrusted to his cavalry under Lord
Uxbridge, which withdrew in three columns on, and either side of, the
Brussels high road. Lieutenant-Colonel Murray and the 18th Hussars
were with the light cavalry brigades of Major-Generals Sir Hussey Vivian
and Sir John Vandeleur, which formed the eastern column about 1.5 km
from the high road. Murray recorded:

. . . The Brigade [of Vivian], however, had not commenced its march
when the Enemy bore on the wood where the Picket was posted.
An officer of the 18th sent to report that the Enemy were moving in
force on this point, found the Duke of Wellington – who said 'he
did not expect them there so soon' – The Duke then asked 'for
the last English Newspapers' which he began reading with perfect
leisure.

After skirmishing a while the Picket was withdrawn – receding
under Capt. [Richard] Croker's command, – very gradually the
Enemy thus became in full possession of the wood.

The Brigade leaving its ground the 18th were the Rear Regiment.

It was then that issuing from the neighbourhood of the wood the Enemy's cavalry advanced with acclamation of 'Vive l'Empereur.' & it is a curious circumstance that the sound of it resembled the Allah! Allah! with which the Turks animate their courage. . . .

Murray had fought the Turks in Egypt as part of a British expedition there in 1807. His column successfully retired across the River Dyle to the east of the village of Genappe and its pursuers then switched their attention to the Brussels high road. Here, Uxbridge's central column consisted of the Household and Union Brigades, the 23rd Light Dragoons and the 7th Hussars. A fierce clash occurred at Genappe, 4 km north of Quatre Bras. Captain Thomas Wildman of the 7th Hussars was serving as ADC to Lord Uxbridge. He described the action in a letter of 19 June:

. . . All our cav^{ly} had arrived during the night & when the arrangement was made to retire the Cav^{ly} were ordered to cover our retreat. this move commenced about 1 PM with the Inf^y & ar^y & lastly the cava^{ly} moving off from the left so that the 7th being the right reg^t covered the whole[.] when the Inf^y were all gone the French began to move & soon after advanced with an immense column of cav^{ly} the lancers & cuirassiers in front 3 reg^{ts} of each we skirmished with them till we had passed the Village of Ge*n*appe . . . when they advanced so strong that it was thought necessary to charge them[.] this fell to the 7th & Major [Edward] Hodge moved down with his Sq^{dn} & the 2 others. the lancers were however so wedged in the Street of Genappe & with so large a column in their rear that they were obliged to stand at all events & our sq^d not making any impression was repulsed[.] when we retired they pursued some men were killed & wounded. Major Hodge [Captain James] Elphinstone & [Lieutenant Arthur] Myers were prisoners[.] [Lieutenant] John Wildman [his brother] & [Lieutenant Edward] Peters were also taken & stripped of their pelisses belts & money but just at that moment the 1st Life G^{ds} made a most gallant charge & drove the Lancers in confusion in which the two young gents made their escape Elphinstone got away last night & arrived here & Lord U. sent to the Enemys advance posts to enquire about the Major & Myers whom report had good naturedly killed & was informed they were both prisoners the Major slightly & Myers severely wounded – they are doing well. . . .

Wildman added on 10 July that nothing had been heard of Hodge or Myers since and that they were supposed dead. Captain Grove commented on the sometimes wild rumours about how Hodge met his end:

> ... Some years after, I was talking to an old man named Williams, (whose son was in the 7th) when he remarked that Hodge had been killed by a cannon shot while sitting on a Truss of Hay eating bread & cheese! I asked him where the Truss of Hay & Bread & cheese came from! ...

Private Samuel Boulter of the 2nd (or Royal North British) Regiment of Dragoons, the famous Scots Greys, was with Uxbridge's central column as part of the Union Brigade. He was not engaged during the retreat, but vividly described his experiences in a letter to his brother from Rouen on 23 September. This extract begins with the action at Genappe, after which the French pursuit slackened:

> ... the 7th Hussars attacked them but the French out numbering them so very much they lost a good number and was obliged to retreat but the life Guards made some very pretty charges on them but the road being so very muddy the men was almost smuthered with Dirt and as the 7th Hussars was chiefly attacked in a small village near Gennappe that the [cobble] ston[e]s was so very slippery that I really believe they lost more men with the horses falling and being rode over and at the same time a most Dreadfull Thunder Shower came on with such rapidity that we was completely wet through in the course of a few minutes and it continued to rain the whole of the Night that I can assure you we was in a most Deplorable state by the morning we had not a Dry thread upon us and the Horses was in the same situation for they could not lie Down and had not been Down then from the 16th night. We could get plenty of Green Forage for them but as for ourselves we had not got any thing for about 48 hours and could not get any provisions up We was then on our position of Waterloo and can assure you it was a position we Did not intend to move from untill we had been beat but thank God that Day has not arrived yet, however we begun to put ourselves in readiness about 5 o'Clock in the morning the 18th ...

One of the few men to keep dry that night was Lieutenant Simmons of the 95th. He was summoned on the evening of the 17th by his battalion commander, Sir Andrew Barnard. He found Barnard established in a weaver's shop, with plenty of food that had just arrived from Brussels. Barnard told him to feed away and then to take up a position near the fire for the night. But Simmons protested: 'Why Sir, if I were to stay here the Company would have a contempt for me, I must go & rough it with them.' Barnard was an excellent officer, but was taken aback by Simmons' reply and told him he was a strange fellow. Simmons returned to the bivouac and plastered a muddy blanket with thick clay. He and Volunteer Charles Smith each wrapped themselves in a blanket and then had the clay-plastered one laid over them both. Simmons awoke next morning quite dry after a good night's sleep. In contrast, Captain Grove wrote:

> ... The rain continued incessantly all night, and our Bivouac [was] any thing but agreeable; lying down ancle deep in water in our wet cloaths, without baggage or provisions – I believe no Soldier ever passed a night of greater hardship and fatigue – A party of 13 were standing round a fire, contrived to get a bottle of French wine among them, and [Captain James] Maxwell Wallace gave me a Pipe of tobacco. The retreat and false reports of the French marching to Brussels, caused considerable confusion on the road; great part of the baggage was plundered and destroyed, and the road near Brussels was blocked up.

As a result of sleeping on the wet ground Captain Grove was suddenly attacked by rheumatism three months later after arriving at Amiens in France and was not relieved of it for eight years despite trying various remedies. Similarly, Private Richard Armstrong of the 51st (or the 2nd Yorkshire West Riding) Regiment of Foot (Light Infantry) wrote to his mother and sister from the Bois de Boulogne outside Paris on 1 September 1815 with the sad news of a friend's death following a cold caught at the time of Waterloo:

> ... I am sorry to relate to you the following sad account – my Poor but dearest Freeind Serjeant Edward Serjeant after a severe Cold wich he got in and previous to the Battle of Waterloo wich turned to a fever terminated his period of life – this morning he departed leaving behind Him a poor [illegible] and faithful widow and a Charming Fatherless Boy whome we consider as the very model of the Father and also amongst His Friends is adored as such – I have wrote this

to you previous to Her writing as she is in such a state at present grieving after her lost partner that she cannot be spoke to in any reason – but as soon as she is a little composed we intend writing for Her to His Parents and we sincerely hope they will not forget it their duty to look upon Her and the poor orphan as sufferers of Water-loo[.] She has a deal of His accounts to setle in the Regiment wich will detain Her some time hear after wich we would prevail upon her to visit her deseased Husbands Friends – Know [Now] I hope you will not neglect a moment to acquent his sister Nancy of his death and beg of her to forward the account to Poor Neds Mother and be asured He was not so destitute of Friends but he will be Honorably intered although in a Foreign Country where in General Soldiers are Buried in the Earth without Coffin but we will see him intered desantly because he is worthy of it and much regreted – . . .

10

The Battle of Waterloo

18 June 1815

Assured of Prussian support, Wellington resolved to give battle at Waterloo on Sunday, 18 June. Lieutenant-Colonel Murray noted how rumours and nervous tension pervaded the army that morning:

> ... There was a rumour of an intended general action – rumours also that the French were about to attack & that the Duke of Wellington was absent having gone to the Prussian army.
>
> The same ignorance which had disfigured the movement of the previous evening – was abroad with idle fears its offspring. ...

Napoleon's army began to deploy at 10.00 a.m. on the opposite side of the valley. Ensign Macready was stationed in the centre of Wellington's front line. His journal reveals that he and his comrades at regimental level were unaware at the start of the battle that Prussian support would be forthcoming:

> ... We (I mean the multitude) were not aware that Blucher could afford us any assistance as we heard that he was completely beaten and hotly pursued – but no British soldier could dread the result when Wellington commanded – our poor fellows looked wretchedly but the joke and laugh were bandied between them – heartily & thoughtlessly as in their happiest hours. About eleven o'clock some rations and spirits came up – the latter was immediately served out to the men but I dared not drink on my empty stomach – I had just stuck a ramrod thro' a noble slice of bull beef & was fixing it on the fire when an Aid de Camp galloped up and roared out 'Stand to your arms'. We were in line in an instant; Considerable movements were perceptible among the enemy's columns and from the number of mounted officers riding to and from one group of Horsemen I should think Napoleon was there issuing his decrees. Our artillery

arrived full galop and the guns were disposed on the most favorable ground in front of their respective Divisions. The Regiments formed column and marched a little to the rear under cover of the brow of the hill. Our company and [the] 73rd['s company of] Grenadiers were ordered as coverers to Cleves and Lloyds brigade[s] of guns. Our men were in a great measure protected by the crest of the hill but the whole French army with the exception of its reserve was exposed to our Artillery. . . .

Wellington's primary fear was for his western flank. He had detached 17,000 men under Prince Frederick, a son of the Dutch King, at Hal and Tubize 13 km west of Waterloo. He had also placed the 3rd Dutch–Belgian Division in reserve at Braine-l'Alleud, 1.5 km west of the battlefield. Captain Oldfield of the Royal Engineers reveals that on the morning of the 17th:

> . . . The Duke at the same time [as ordering De Lancey to put the army in position at Waterloo] ordered Col: Smyth to give directions for Braine Le Leud [Braine-l'Alleud] to be entrenched & made defensible. Lieut. [John] Sperling was forthwith despatched to Halle to Captain __ [actually Lieutenant Faris] to move immediately with his Company of Sappers & Brigade of entrenching tools from the Engineer Park [depot] at Halle for Braine le leud which place, he was to put in the best possible state of defence, the time would permit, by throwing up flêches to cover the entrance to the town; or taking such steps as he might consider advisable to make the place tenable[.] This order was clearly delivered to Lieut. Sperling in my presence, and clearly understood by both of us; the order he stated was delivered by him to Captain __ who to extenuate his non-compliance with the order, stated that he did not understood it[.] By Capitaine's Carte de la Belgique it appears there is a good road from Braine le Leud directly upon Bruxelles, with several others diverging from it into the Bois de Loignee [Soignes]; had our position at Waterloo been forced by the enemy, the occupation of Braine le Leud would have been of the greatest importance to us, and secured a safe retreat for at least one of our columns –
>
> . . .
>
> The Captain stated that he understood from Lieut. Sperling that he was to fortify the position of Braine le leud; that he had proceeded there & hearing from the Mayor that the British Troops had left it

the preceeding day, he moved his people forward to Waterloo, which he considered as part of the position & was looking about him when Col. Smyth came up – The Col. when riding with the Duke had previously seen some sappers straggling about the village, he pulled up & ascertained to whom they belonged. They had fortunately not been observed by the Duke[.] The Captain was not with them, but was seen afterwards by the Colonel & placed immediately in arrest. The Sappers were ordered to collect & move into the village halting near the church, at the extremity of the place on the Bruxelles side to be in readiness when called upon – as their services would probably be required.

. . .

The Company remained only a short time near the church, but without orders proceeded on their way to Bruxelles losing most of their entrenching tools. Col. Smyth very properly refused to include the officers & men attached to this Company as entitled to the Waterloo Medal[.] The error of the Captain whose dislike to being in the rear and anxiety to see what was doing in the front, might have led to the most unfortunate results had we experienced any reverse. As it was the Sappers would have been in action had they remained in the Village, as I had subsequently orders to send them to the front. . . .

Before the opening of the campaign Wellington had rejected the idea of entrenching his position on the grounds that this would reveal where he intended to fight. He rarely used field fortifications as they tended to immobilize troops in fixed positions and he preferred to use more flexible and aggressive defensive tactics. Yet on the morning of Waterloo he partly relented. He apparently decided that it was now too late for Napoleon to carry out any large-scale manoeuvres and that some field fortifications were therefore warranted to strengthen his position against frontal attack. Lieutenant-General Sir Henry Clinton, the commander of the 2nd Division, claimed that at about 11.00 a.m. two of his brigades were ordered to supply working parties to throw up breastworks to cover the guns: 'but when they arrived the officer with the intrenching tools was not present, and before these works were begun the enemy had commenced his attack. So the guns had no cover.'*

* C. Chesney, *Waterloo Lectures* (reissued London, 1997), p. 207.

Oldfield's account both confirms and clarifies Clinton's claim. He explained how he had been left at the village of Waterloo and how not long afterwards:

> ... a Staff officer brought me a message to say the Duke was desirous some cover should be thrown up for our troops on the Plateau to the right of our centre, opposite the farm of La Haye Sainte & that I was to forward to that spot Captain __ [Lieutenant Faris'] Sappers and whatever officers I could collect. I immediately dispatched [Captain] Sir George Hoste [who had just arrived from Antwerp] & Lieut: Sperling and going to give orders to the Sappers, found they had moved from the church, & upon enquiry heard they had been seen at some distance from Waterloo on their road to Bruxelles. Finding there was no chance of falling in with them without going myself considerably to the rear I rode up to the field to make my report to Col. Smyth from whom I learnt the Duke had relinquished the idea of an entrenchment & from the circumstance and my having been several times during the day on the plateau, I can confidentially [sic] state that not a shovel full of earth was stirred & deny the assertion of having fought the battle of Waterloo, in an entrenched position or of a redoubt being constructed on the plateau ...

On the morning of the battle Napoleon sent General François Haxo, the commander of his Imperial Guard engineers, to reconnoitre and see if Wellington had erected any earthworks. Haxo reported in the negative and this probably encouraged Napoleon in attacking only frontally, although his opportunities for an outflanking move at this late stage were limited, particularly given the waterlogged nature of the terrain.

Napoleon's attacks started at about 11.30 a.m. with a preliminary assault on the farm of Hougoumont, Wellington's strongpoint in the western sector of the battlefield. The garrison of British guardsmen and German infantry successfully held out all day, despite desperate fighting around both the building block and the adjacent wood, garden and orchard. Among those killed in the defence was Captain John Blackman of the Coldstream Guards. He was twenty-one. Another of the defenders, Private William Pritchard of the 3rd Foot Guards, wrote to his wife Mary on 12 July:

> I take this oportunity of addressing you with a few lines which I hope will find you in Good Health as this leaves me at this Period. I

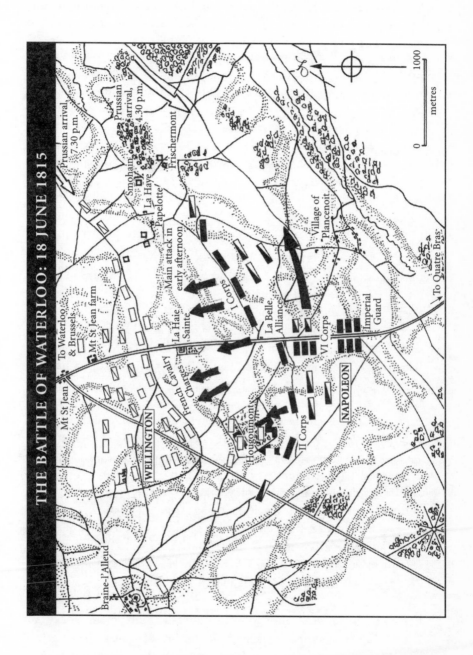

THE BATTLE OF WATERLOO: 18 JUNE 1815

Braine-l'Alleud

Mt St Jean

To Waterloo & Brussels

Mt St Jean farm

WELLINGTON

French Cavalry Charges

La Haie Sainte

I Corps

Main attack in early afternoon

La Haye

Papelotte

Smohain

Prussian arrival, 4.30 p.m.

Prussian arrival, 7.30 p.m.

Frischermont

Hougoumont

II Corps

La Belle Alliance

Village of Plancenoit

NAPOLEON

VI Corps

Imperial Guard

To Quatre Bras

N

0   1000

metres

suppose you must have heard of A Battle that has Been Fought by this. I asure you it was A Bloody one and any Person that were in it neaver could expect to come out of it Alive seeing there Comarades fall on each side of them at such A Tremendous Rate I for my own Part thought of nothing But Fighting and Gaining the victory and it Pleas'd the all mighty to grant my Request and keep me from being Injured thanks be to him for his Preservation[.] on Saturday the 17th of June we marched A very heavy Day s march after Fighting nearly all the Day before[.] we lay in A Been Field that night and it Rained in Torrents we all being so Fatieug'd we were forc'd to lay Down and in less than an Hour we were allmost Drown'd in water and in that condition lay'd all night[.] in the Morning about 8 oClock we saw the French on A Hill in Front we were on one hill and they on another they advanc'd our Cannon Play'd on them they [advanced] toowards A wood by A Farm house [Hougoumont] as soon as the General saw there intentions the Brigade of Guards were sent there imediately we came into the wood when it began very sharp in less than 3 Hours we could hardly go along for Dead Bodies we Charg'd them and Drove them But in less than an ½ Hour we were forced to retreat into an apple orchard where [we] remained in Breast works some small time being reinforc'd by A small Party of German Legions [elements of Colonel Charles du Plat's King's German Legion brigade] we again Charg'd them and drove them and afterwards kep our Position untill about 7 oClock in the Evening when Wellington perceived there Right Gave way we again Charg'd them and they Ran in all Directions we follow'd them as long as we Could see and after we halted the Prussians had Came up they Follow'd Killed and took Prisoners A Great amount we hear there were taken 30000 Prisoners and upwards of 200 Peices of Cannon I cannot say any thing Perticular more Concerning it so I hope and trust you will make yourself Happy on my account as I am in hopes all things are nearly setled and I have not the least Dowt But Peace will once more be restord to our native Isle and I may say to all [E]urope. I hope my little Daughter is in Good Health and all the Family

Early in the afternoon Napoleon unleashed his main attack on Wellington's eastern wing, preceded by the fire of a massed battery of guns. This was smashed by a decisive charge of the Union and Household Brigades of British heavy cavalry.

Captain William Elton commanded a squadron of the 1st (or The King's) Regiment of Dragoon Guards, in Major-General Lord Edward Somerset's Household Brigade. In a letter of 15 July, he described how he charged the cuirassiers who had been covering the western flank of the French attack:

> ... The Enemy stood very well till we came within 20 yards: They had every appearance of being picked men, extremely large & well mounted, which I believe was the case as they were Cuirassiers of the Imperial Guard. Our men setting up a general shout, many of them went about immediately. Those who could escape lost no time, the others were blocked up in a corner, a large fence on one side & a broad ravine on the other: These were all killed by our people, but their cuirass secured them to such a degree that not one blow told out of five. Here Lord Uxbridge had a turn with one of their Officers & tho' two of our men charged him & gave him plenty of cuts & thrusts on both sides, the man escaped into the Lane where he was killed by the others. Lord E. Somerset who charged with us crossed the ravine & was followed by all of us whose horses could leap in such slippery ground[.] Many Dragoons lost their lives in falling in, others went round[.] The Lane leading from the Duke of Wellingtons position into the plain was quite choked up with Cuirassiers & our men mixed & engaged with each other[.] at length it was tolerably well cleared and Lord Edward having heard that the quarter part of the K.D.G[uards] were broke & gone away without order into the Enemys lines ordered me to rally & halt as many as possible, which was done but too late, as no one seemed to know what was become of the right Squadrons & other broken troops & the ground in the plain where they had so far advanced was covered with immense columns of the enemy ...

The British heavy cavalry had charged too far and, having exhausted their horses, were counter-attacked and lost heavily.

Napoleon had now discovered that the Prussians were descending on his eastern flank from Wavre and he was forced to detach some of his reserves to counter this threat. The leading Prussian units emerged on to the battlefield at 4.30 p.m., but encountered stiff resistance. Nonetheless, they were continually reinforced throughout the rest of the battle and tied down as many as 13,000 of Napoleon's troops.

Wellington badly needed this diversion, as waves of French cavalry led by Marshal Ney had begun to assail his centre at 4.00 p.m. Ensign Macready provides some fascinating details of this phase of the battle. He had been deployed in the valley with his company and some other light infantry to skirmish, but withdrew at the start of the French charges to a hollow square formed by the 30th and 73rd Regiments. This was the standard formation for infantry against horsemen and was usually impregnable when assailed by cavalry alone:

> ... Their first charge was magnificent. As soon as they quickened their trot into a galop the Cuirassiers bent their heads so that the peak of their helmets looked like visors and they seemed cased in armour from the plume to the saddle – not a shot was fired till they were within thirty yards when the word was given – and our men fired away at them. The effect was magical – thro' the smoke we could see helmets falling – cavaliers starting from their seats with convulsive springs as they received our balls horses plunging & rearing in the agonies of fright and pain and crowds of the soldiery dismounted – part of the squadrons in retreat but the more daring remainder backing their horses to force them on our bayonets. Our fire soon disposed of these gentlemen. The main body reformed in our front were reinforced and rapidly and gallantly repeated their attacks. In fact from this time (about four o'clock) till near six we had a constant repetition of these brave but unavailing charges. There was no difficulty in repulsing them but our ammunition decreased alarmingly – at length our artillery waggon galloped up emptied two or three casks of cartridges into the square & we were all comfortable. The best cavalry is contemptible to a steady and well supplied Infantry regiment – even our men saw this and began to pity the useless perseverance of their assailants and as they advanced would growl out 'here come these damned fools again'. . . .

Lieutenant James Hamilton of the 2nd Line Battalion of the King's German Legion vividly described his experiences in a letter of 20 July. As part of Colonel du Plat's brigade of the 2nd Division, he initially stood in reserve:

> ... at 10 Oclock the Artillery moved to the Heights, we fell in and in five minutes [there] commenced a most terrible Cannonade from 500 pieces of Artillery, which never ceased or diminished until nine

at night, Our Brigade was formed in open Column of Companies on the right and a little in rear of the first Division – we continued in this Position suffering much from the Cannonade until two, when we observed the Regiments of the first Line form Squares to repel Cavalry – this movement was scarcely executed when the French Cavalry made a dashing charge. They were received with a severe and galling Fire, that did much execution. They did not however retire immediately, but finding they could make no impression on the 52ⁿᵈ [Regiment] which received their charge They galloped down the Line of Squares, perhaps in the Idea of finding some Corps in Confusion but they were at every point repulsed with the greatest Steadiness.

. . .

our Cavalry observing the opportunity cut in amongst them and completed the Havock previously made by the Infantry. those that escaped were immediately supported by numerous Forces, and our Cavalry were obliged to retire in their turn. At this charge the French had passed within our Artillery, and many of the men were cut down at the Guns, others escaped by creeping under and the moment the French had repassed jumped up and fired with the greatest coolness and gallantry. It was also at this charge the Duke of Wellington and his Staff were exposed to considerable hazard of being taken Prisoners. He had been riding on the Summit of the Hill (where some Batteries of Artillery were placed) the whole morning. the best spot, where a general View could be had of the Battle – but certainly by far the most dangerous Post in the Field – The French Cavalry came on so rapid that the Duke had scarcely time to get within the protection of the Squares[.] His personal danger, great exertions, and Gallantry were conspicuous to the whole Army throughout the Day. . . .

At the height of the French charges Du Plat's brigade was called forward with the rest of the 2nd Division to strengthen Wellington's front line. The brigade moved over the ridge crest to occupy an advanced position immediately north of the farm of Hougoumont:

. . . the right was now closely engaged against superior numbers. Our Brigade, two English Brigades were ordered up to support – the numerous charges of French Cavalry, in every direction, made it necessary we should advance in Squares, this was done in admirable order and the whole Line now advanced with Cheers two hundred

Yards beyond their Original Position. I believe at this moment was displayed the grandest Sight and most heroick Courage and firmness ever witnessed, on *both sides* – in my View there was at least 20,000 Infantry Occupying a Space of half an English mile each Regiment formed into Squares four deep, the two Front Ranks kneeling. between the Intervals of Squares were placed a few Regiments of Cavalry. we were advanced a little below the Summit of the Hill toward the Enemy, who were formed on an ascent 200 Yards in our Front with their Skirmishers advanced close upon our Squares – our Artillery about 20 yards behind and above us the Shot from which just cleared above our Heads. The French Skirmishers were *immediately* dispersed, they then advanced heavy Columns of Infantry, who came on with much shouting and in good order to within a few yards, when a severe firing took place and we advance[d] to the charge with the Bayonet which the French did not await but retired in the greatest confusion, losing more than half their numbers. they now charged with two Regiments of Lancers. these we received with loud cheers, and a murderous Fire when within 20 Yards and as the Smoke cleared, we saw them routed and galloping away in all directions. This charge however was directly followed, by a Body of Cuirassiers and five or six Regiments of them charged us successively, *in good order* and with determined firmness and Courage. they could not however break any Regiment – and they galloped twice down the Line (within ten paces distance) and under a most murderous Fire of musketry until they were *Completely destroyed* – and Horses and men were laying in heaps throughout the whole Line. . . .

Lieutenant Hamilton added about his battalion:

> . . . This Regiment in the mor^g of the 18 mustered 300 Bayonets – in the Evening after the Battle when we formed – we had six officers and Thirty four Private Soldiers left with the Colors – Many joined us the next day who had assisted to convey away the severely wounded – . . .

Wellington's cavalry repeatedly counter-attacked to give the infantry squares some respite. Lieutenant William Turner of the 13th Light Dragoons described the battle in a letter on 3 July. In it, he mentioned the famous 'G' Troop Royal Horse Artillery, which was ordered into the front line from reserve towards 5.00 p.m. The troop's acting commander, Lieutenant-Colonel Alexander Macdonald, was in charge of the six troops that were attached to the British cavalry. The actual command of 'G' Troop therefore rested with Second Captain Cavalié Mercer:

> ... about 10 AM the French began to move large Columns of troops in our front and about ½ past 11 the battle began, we were put with the 15th Hussars and commanded by [Major-]Genl [Sir Colquhoun] Grant, we were on the right of the great road and nearly the right of our line, we covered the artillery of Capt Macdonald's troop who behaved well, before 2 we had 3 officers and several men killed by Cannon Balls and Shells, we were then put close to some Belgian artillery to keep them to their guns and there we suffered from musketry and round shot, then moved to the right of the line to charge the French lancers [General Marie-Guillaume Piré's light cavalry division, demonstrating west of Hougoumont] but they retired. We then came back to our place close to the artillery which the French Imperial Guard à Cheval [cavalry] & Cuirassiers had taken[.] we immediately with the 15th formed up in line (gave three cheers) and went at them full speed; they – [sic] immediately and we charged after them all down their position up to their infantry when we were ordered to retire which we did but in confusion; we formed and told off again having lost a good many men; I shot one [of the enemy] with my pistol but did not use my sword (I had the misfortune to break the double barreled one in marching up the country or else I should have shot two)[.] at 4 PM the French Cavalry came up again but on our trotting to meet them they immediately retired, we then came back on our side [of] the Hill beyond our Guns; the battle was now most dreadful and the field covered with dead and dying in all directions. Lord Wellington repeatedly passed us when we huzzared him; the French Cavalry advanced again to the muzzle of our Guns, the Gunners were ordered to retire and we charged them again in the grandest style between our masses of Infantry, they retreated and we charged them close to their Infantry who were formed in squares the same as ours ...

Lieutenant Turner lost his mare wounded in this charge, but managed to return to the rear of the artillery and mounted a dragoon's horse. The havoc was dreadful:

... one Cannon Ball killed Gen¹ Grant's horse, [Lt-]Col [Leighton Cathcart] Dalrymples [of the 15th Hussars] horse and took off his [Dalrymple's] leg it then passed close between [Lieutenant John] Wallace and me; we remained here still exposed every minute some man or horse falling my Capt [Frederick] Goulburn at whose side I in general was had just mounted a trooper after having had his horse badly wounded when he was knocked off by a spent ball but fortunately without injury, about ½ past 6 PM we charged again down the Hill and then retreated to our guns again; about 8 PM the great attack was again made when they were repulsed and we were immediately ordered to charge again as our Infantry were retiring. Gen¹ Hill came in our front and called out now 13ᵗʰ come on, he took off his hat with several other Generals, we immediately huzzared with the whole of the Infantry and charged them, they retired in the greatest confusion, our Infantry kept us at [the] trot for three miles when when [sic] (the whole of the Cavalry) pursued them about three miles further when darkness at 9 PM put an end to the slaughter, the last charge was literally riding over men and horses who lay in heaps ...

Captain Grove reveals what happened to the 23rd Light Dragoons. The regiment, part of Major-General Wilhelm von Dörnberg's brigade, was engaged in the centre of the battlefield:

After the desperate weather during the night, neither men nor Horses looked worth a shilling a peice – the horse I rode was knocked up, and I sent him to Brussels; and not being able to find either of my others, I was obliged to ride a Trooper, and of course I did not pick out the worst. At 12 o'clock (some say Eleven) this memorable battle began – our Brigade, and probably others, remained under cover of the hill in close Column dismounted, for four hours, exactly within range of the French Guns, and suffered severe loss – At 4 we advanced into the Plain, where our Infantry were formed in Squares, with the Cavalry and Artillery in the Intervals, making the most beautiful Feild day which can be fancied. Tho our Cavalry dealt destruction among the Curassiers, our loss was great. One Battalion of German Rifles was annihilated, with the exception of the commanding officer, who came up to me saying he had brought his Regᵗ complete into action, but that he was the solitary remains,! and asked my advice, which was that he should go to the 'Horse Guards' [the headquarters of the British army, in London] and asked [sic] for another....

Fortunately for Wellington, Ney failed to move up infantry and guns to support his cavalry until too late. He did so only in the evening, after capturing the farm of La Haie Sainte, and by then his cavalry were too exhausted to take advantage of this destructive close-range fire.

Captain Oldfield reveals an example of the consequences of the wide range of uniforms worn by the various contingents of Wellington's army and the similarity of some of them to those of the French:

> ... During a charge of Cavalry the enemy had penetrated to our second line, and in the melée I had the good fortune to save a Dutch Hussar from being cut down by one of our own, I believe of the 10th, the uniform was very similar to that of a French Corps with which we were engaged, but being perfectly acquainted with the Dutch uniform, I rode up in time to prevent mischief in this instance; our Hussar however telling me he had sabred two or three in that uniform – ...

At the end of the day, Napoleon tried a final attack using his crack Imperial Guard. But Wellington defeated this assault and then ordered a triumphant general advance into the valley, routing Napoleon's exhausted army.

The decisive nature of the victory was immediately obvious. Captain Thomas Wildman of the 7th Hussars wrote from Brussels on 19 June:

> ... I will now send you an account of a victory so splendid & important that you may search the annals of history in vain for its paralel nor is it only extraordinary in the effect it must produce upon the present state of Europe & the blow it has given to all Napoleon's expectations but as a grand military affair it will probably for ever stand unrivalled and alone....

Similarly, Lieutenant-Colonel Sir William Gomm, an assistant quartermaster-general attached to the 5th Division, wrote triumphantly to his sister Sophia on 19 June:

> I know what satisfaction it will give you all to learn that I have been with the 5th Division, and therefore in the hottest of all this 'Glorious

Business' and have escaped with two Blows which are of no Consequence, and two Horses wounded which is of *great consequence* –

The Prussians are marching upon Charleroy, and we move upon
Nivelles immediately –

I consider the French army as utterly destroyed, and we shall be
in Paris as fast as our legs can carry us – tell aunt so, and recommend
her to leave off croaking –

I am writing this unintelligibly enough, but it would be still worse
by *word* of mouth, at this moment, for I am so hoarse with *hurraaing*
all yesterday, that I can scarcely articulate –

I have been four days without washing *face* or *hands*, but am in
hourly expectation of my lavendar water &c &c &c

I am very tired – adieu dear Sophia, I hope this will reach you
early, for I will know how anxious you will all be about me –

. . .

We have done nothing like it since Blenheim and the Consequences are likely to be far more important . . .

Captain William Staveley of the Royal Staff Corps wrote to his
mother the day after the battle:

After the most Tremendous Contest ever known we have completely
beaten Buonaparte at the Head of his army 120,000 men – We have
taken the whole of their Guns 160 & their Baggage – the loss on both
sides is dreadful, it is impossible to conceive the obstinacy with which
the Battle was fought. Blucher formed [?] with his army at the close
of the day & is now pursuing them.

I escaped having only a spent shot in the guts which did not
penetrate.

Lieutenant-Colonel Sir John Colborne, the commander of the 52nd
(or the Oxfordshire) Regiment of Foot (Light Infantry), wrote on the
19th to his stepsister, Miss Fanny Bargus:

You will be anxious to hear of us after the most severe conflict I have
ever witnessed, and I think it will be the most important in its result
– [Ensign] William Leeke is very well. The Infantry behaved nobly,
and the 52^d as usual.

I have only time to write you these few lines – You will be
surprized at the Gazette we have lost some of our most valuable
Officers.

Captain Philip Wodehouse of the 15th Hussars wrote to Miss Parry on 19 June, resting the piece of paper on the top of a drum:

> Though I cannot persuade myself that the wish that you once so kindly expressed is still as lively as then, yet not to use you as you appear to use me, I write to say that I suffered no harm from the affair of yesterday *even although the charm* has *not* arrived. How brilliant & decisive it was, the Gazette will inform you; I only send you these few lines written according to your desire in hurry & confusion to assure you that in spite of your forgetfullness, my affection for you is as strong as ever, & that if a cannon ball hits me tomorrow I believe I shall die thinking of you.

He instead married Lydia Lea in 1832.

The soldiers in their letters were also preoccupied by the scale of the slaughter. Private John Abbott of the 51st Regiment wrote on 12 November to Miss Anne Bank:

> I Take this most Pleasing opportunity of Sending these few Lines to you Still hoping to find you and All Friends well as this Leaves us Both very well In health and Spirits at present thank God for all his Mercies[.] My Dr Friend we may properlly think of his Great Mercies after Escaping such a Tremendous Battle which Partly I will relate To You. But theres one Thing to remark you don't properlly understand the miserable Nature of a Battle when I First Left home I had verry Little Idea of Seeing So many of my fellow Creatures Destroy^d By the Dreadful Sword . . .

Private Samuel Boulter of the Scots Greys was likewise horrified by the carnage:

> . . . [Those of the French] that Did get away run as if the Devil had been hard after them, threw off their Nabsacks and left every thing they was possessed off and can assure you no small number was lying on the Ground the next Day[.] But it was a very affecting scene to see so many men lying Dead in the such a short time for my part I cannot ascribe it to any thing else than a Judgement of God and indeed a great many lay Wounded which called for Water but we could not supply them all some were lying with legs off some Wounded all over the Body in such a manner that they was not able to move a yard[.] We buried all of ours that was Dead that we could

find and the Wounded was taken off and Medical assistance was rendered them immediately[.] I can assure you some of the poor fellows was most terribly cut up several has Died since of their Wounds and almost every one that had a limb amputated has Died. However I have reason to thank that Superintending providence that [h]as hitherto guarded me from all Dangers and hope that matters will take such a turn as will soon restore all people to their homes . . .

In fact, the statistics for a British surgeon, Charles Bell, show that only 27 per cent of his patients died after undergoing primary amputations and 47 per cent after secondary, or delayed, ones. Among those who survived an amputation was Lord Uxbridge, who was wounded by one of the last shots of the battle. Captain Wildman, who was one of his ADCs, wrote:

. . . But one only serious misfortune prevents me from saying that it was the proudest, happiest day I ever knew. But the loss the British army has sustained in the services of Lord Uxbridge must be felt by all & you may conceive how much more strongly so by me who always admired & looked up to him as an officer & have lately learned to respect esteem & love him as a Man His conduct the whole day beggars all description. His arrangement firmness & intrepidity surpassed what had been expected of him & not in cavalry movements & attacks alone but he frequently rendered the most judicious & timely assistance in affairs of Infantry where any sudden danger was to be apprehended.

. . .

I must now again revert to that w^h throws a damp upon what would otherwise have been the most glorious most satisfactory moment of our lives. Just as Sir Hussey Vivians brigade was going down to the charge Lord Uxbridge was struck by a grape shot from the Enemys guns on the right knee which shattered the joint all to pieces. I did not see him fall & went on the charge but soon missed him[.] I found [Captain Horace] Seymour [another of Uxbridge's ADCs] taking him to the rear[.] he told me immediately that he must lose his leg & then began conversing about the action & seemed to forget his wound in the exultation for the Victory[.] when the surgeons examined it they all agreed it would be at the imminent danger of his life to attempt to save the limb he only said 'well gentlemen I thought so myself[.] I have put myself into your

hands & if it is to be taken off the sooner it is done the better.' He
wrote a short note to Lady U. saying that if he had been a young &
a single man he would probably have run the risk but that he would
preserve his life for hers & his children sake if possible. During the
operation he never moved or complained no one ever held his hand,
he said once perfectly calmly that he did not think the instrument a
very sharp one. When it was over his nerves did not seem the least
shaken & the Surgeons said his pulse even was not altered. He said
smiling 'I have had a pretty long run I have been a beau these 47
years & it would not be fair to cut the young men out any longer'
& then asked if we did not admire his vanity. I have seen many
operations but neither [Lieutenant-Colonel] Lord Grenock [Assist-
ant Quartermaster-General to the cavalry] nor myself could bear
this we were obliged to go to the other end of the room. Thank
God he is doing as well as possible he has had no fever & the
surgeons say nothing can be more favorable. I began this [letter] on
the 19 the Even^g we brought Lord U here [Brussels] in a litter, this
is the morn^g of the 21st. He has had it dressed for the first time &
the surgeons report is as favorable as ever the steady firmness &
calm courage of his disposition will assist his recovery more than
any thing. The regret of the army is beyond bounds, Inf^y & cava^{ly}
all saw him & all admired him[.] How he escaped with life I can
hardly imagine. He was every where in the hottest fire when the day
was doubtful he cheered & assisted the Inf^y & I saw him & was by
him when he put himself at the head of a squadron of cavalry &
charged a solid mass of their Inf^y The fire was terrific & destroyed
many The rest would not go on & he rode on & struck their
bayonets before he turned & yet escaped. It was hard to have him
wounded at last after so many escapes. [Colonel] Sir John Elley [the
Deputy Adjutant-General] one of the bravest soldiers & as grand an
officer as ever lived is here with 3 stabs & a sabre cut when I went
to see him he cried like a child in speaking of Lord U. & said that
he rejoiced his valuable life had been preserved yet the loss to the
British army was irreparable. His emotion was so great that I was
obliged to leave him for his own sake after trying in vain to change
the subject The loss on our side has been immense but the Enemys
army has been annihilated. There never yet was known such a battle
& probably never will again at least much as I rejoice at having
shared in this I hope I never may see such another – . . .

Wildman's claim that Uxbridge's fall was widely regretted is confirmed by other accounts. After Uxbridge was created Marquess of Anglesey, Lieutenant-Colonel Murray wrote that he was delighted at this well-deserved honour, as Uxbridge's energy and example on the 18th had been almost above human exertion.

The army had considerably less admiration for Wellington's despatch announcing the victory to Earl Bathurst, the Secretary of State for War and the Colonies. Among those antagonized by its terseness was Lieutenant-Colonel Murray, who complained on 4 July:

> ... But I cannot say much for the warmth of the praise the Duke bestowes [on] him [Uxbridge], it is as cold as ice & as heartless.
>
> Though Ld. Wellington does not very much for us, read Bonaparte's despatch, he does us justice, & remark the cavalry charge at ½ past 8 or at the end of the day it was our Brigades. 10th & 18th [Hussars.]

Murray was referring to the French Official Account, issued from Paris on 21 June.* Wellington's despatch simply stated that 'The Earl of Uxbridge, after having successfully got through this arduous day, received a wound by almost the last shot fired, which will, I am afraid, deprive His Majesty for some time of his services.'†

Equally bitter controversies arose from allegations of cowardice. Captain William Clayton of the Royal Horse Guards felt obliged to justify himself in a letter to his commanding officer:

> Reports detrimental to my Character having gone forth, It thus becomes necessary for me to request you will take the *earliest* opportunity of communicating the contents of this letter to the Officers of the Regiment, whose prejudice against me, is carried to some extent, in consequence of the various reports, daily engendering & circulating respecting my conduct, & which have been received with much avidity, & I must add, illiberality, & dispersed with the greatest industry – Two causes appear to have operated, in favor of the general credence given to these statements; The 1st is, in consequence of the mistake which has arisen in my not being gazetted as

* C. Kelly, *A Full and Circumstantial Account of the Memorable Battle of Waterloo* (London, 1831), p. 70.
† W. Siborne, *History of the Waterloo Campaign* (reissued London, 1990), p. 582.

wounded; & 2[ndly] the nature of the injury I received, by a slight concussion of the brain, not producing visible marks of a wound – Immediately therefore after M[r] [David] Slow's [the Surgeon's] arrival with the Reg[t] I addressed the following letter to him, which I have enclosed, also his answer – . . .

This reply was dated 21 July and was signed by both Mr Slow and William Maurice, Hospital Assistant of the Royal Horse Guards:

In reply to your letter of this day, I hasten to inform you, that when M[r] Maurice & myself saw you, & heard your description of the indisposition caused by a blow received on the back of the neck, in the field on the 18th Ult. we were of opinion, though there were no exterior marks of injury, that the contusion was to such a degree, as to require medical treatment, which induced me to report you slightly wounded –

Clayton resumed his letter:

. . . and here indeed, I should close my letter, conceiving the statement of the Surgeons, as amply sufficient to remove all doubt, as to the propriety of my Conduct – But, as I know, how apt we all are to prejudge, & that the force & effect of prejudice, when the mind of man is warped, naturally leads him to listen to every idle calumny in circulation – Those unknown 'friends,' anxious I conclude to traduce my character, who have kindly stated that I ought not to have left the field, can surely be little aware, of the extent, & nature of the injury I received, or of the violent & acute pains produced by even the slightest concussion or oppression on the brain; during three days I kept my bed, & my sufferings were great, & to this day, Sir, I feel severely at times the effects of the Injury – No human being can sympathize in the sufferings of his neighbour, & therefore how can any man venture to assert, that I had not sufficient cause for quitting the field – Had I merely sought for an excuse to go to the rear, I should have done so on receiving the blow, & not have continued with the Reg[t] during 3½ hours afterwards, the greatest part of the time, under as heavy a fire, as it was possible for the enemy to direct against us, during which time, I was suffering much, & at last became so faint, & weak, that I was in expectation of falling from my horse – I quitted the field, Sir, I should think near 7 °Clock in the Evening, from total inability any longer to perform my Duty there – It was my misfortune for in consequence, & according I am fully aware, to the rules of the Service, I have lost that promotion which could I have continued in the Field, I should have received – Sir, I lost not a moment in joining my Reg^t & left Bruxelles, even before I had permission from the Surgeon to go – Sir, I was during two days an efficient member of an Army, which has accomplished an Event, so glorious to Britains [sic], so important to the whole world, & I feel (as every one must do) a laudable pride in the honourable performance of the sacred duty which I owed to my country, my friends, & myself, & that person who would intentionally endeavour to wring from me my portion of the hard earned laurels acquired on the 17th & 18th does me an irreparable injury which 'enricheth not him & makes one poor indeed' – When Sir I made an application for the majority of the Reg^t vacant by the death of our ever to be lamented brother Officer [Major Robert Packe], there was a probability of a continuance of the War, & Captn [John] Thoyts being a prisoner on parole [having been captured by the French at Waterloo], would have been, according to the rules of the Service, incapacitated, I therefore applied in order to prevent the introduction of an Officer from another Reg^t & not I assure you from the most distant wish or inclination to supersede Captn Thoyts, whose seniority & greater length of service would have given him of course a prior claim, if exchanged in time – no application therefore of mine could possibly have affected Captn Thoyts – This, Sir, is another report, I understand, circulated against me, & perverted & misconstrued in the most unhandsome manner – In short, Sir, if after the documents I have herewith produced, & the statements I have made, any man means to arraign my conduct let him do so – But if henceforth any man traduces, stigmatizes, or calumniates my character either directly or indirectly, (I will not state to you as my Commanding Officer) the measures I shall adopt, to call him personally to account for his conduct – Sir, if I had a thousand lives, I would sacrifice them all, rather than permit such *unmerited* reproach & censure any longer to exist; & I shall feel obliged to those of my friends in the Reg^t to *do their* endeavours, from time to time to *correct the errors* which have gone abroad

A similar allegation can be found in a letter from Captain Edward Kelly of the 1st Life Guards. Kelly distinguished himself at Waterloo by killing a French cuirassier colonel and taking his epaulettes as trophies. He was later wounded and wrote to his wife from Brussels on 6 July:

I have at length had the pleasure of receiving two letters from you after having almost given up the idea of hearing from you at all – and if I had not something to remind me that I am not immortal your praise and the manner in which you are pleased to over rate my little Services [at Waterloo] would almost turn my Brain – My wound though not at all dangerous is I am sorry to say likely to prove tedious and painful and the Chief medical officer here has been to inspect the wounded officers to have those sent to England whose Cure is likely to be protracted and I am sorry to say my name is among the number. The small bone of my leg is fractured and before the wound which is very large can heal Exfoliations of the bone must take place –

However I bear my sufferings better than my confinement and now that I am out of bed that also becomes less irksome –

The wounded officers are almost all doing well and nothing can equal the kindness of the inhabitants of this Town to us all – The best families in the Town have all been employed in making bandages and lint &c – and the people at whose house I was quarter'd at Ninove [before the start of hostilities] have come over here to see me.

The Gallant Marquis of Anglesea is gone to England with his Lady who came here to Him and He sent me word by His aide de camp the day He went away that He had already mentioned my name to the Duke of Wellington and that on his arrival in London He would also mention me to The Prince [Regent] and to The Duke of York – so that I think there will be a race between me and [Captain John] Whale for the Lᵗ Colonelcy [vacant following the death at Waterloo of Lieutenant-Colonel Samuel Ferrior] and God knows I won it fairly in the Field but I think there is no chance of my getting it –

The men and those officers who fought with me in the Field are enthusiastic in my favor but there are some officers who were absent from some idle excuse or other who are envious of my praises, one you mentioned in your last letter [apparently Captain Whale], might have been in the Field on Sunday [18 June] but He reported himself wounded from a scratch and when he found Ferrior was killed, He posted off to take the command of the Reg^t immediately. *This [to be kept] to yourself* – I offered the French Colonels Epaulettes to Lord Uxbridge but He said he could not think of depriving my family of them –

I got his horse also, a most noble one but being attacked by a number of French at the same time I was obliged to let him go and should have been killed but for our Corp^l Major who fought bravely by my side till we laid them down never to rise again.

I have recommended him to Lord Ha[r]rington [the Colonel of the 1st Life Guards.]

In about another week I shall [be] able to give you a more exact account of myself – I shall avoid going home if I can but if I am to be six weeks or two months laid up I had better be in England than here as all the wounded are going who have not a prospect of joining the army soon –

Lord Combermere will put me on the Staff here when I am able to do duty at least He promised He would before I came out – How lucky I was not on the Staff before or I should have lost this glorious opportunity which I sought to distinguish myself – The weather here is most delightful and I pine like a child to be out – When I go to England, I shall write for you to meet me on the other side of the Water – and do not forget to let me know about the Bills, whether you received them or not[.] The years pay will set up my affairs again and as Jem says I *got it with my Blood*. . . .

Kelly then mentioned various family matters and assured his wife that:

. . . the greatest pleasure I desire from my conduct is that I hope it will make me worthy of such a wife as you are and before I went into action, I took a farewell of you and my children in my warmest imagination . . .

He added that many officers had lost all their baggage and horses in the confusion, but that he himself had lost only his bed and tent and that he was very lucky since the tent was public property. He wrote that the great discharge from his wound kept him very low, so that he was allowed three glasses of wine each day. But he hoped in a day or two to hop out a little on a pair of crutches.

*

The situation in the rear of the army during the battle had been excruciatingly tense. Lieutenant Gairdner had spent the day at Brussels after being wounded at Quatre Bras and revealed in his diary how defeatist the mood had been in the capital:

> The bloodiest, hardest contested and most decisive victory was gained this day on the position of Waterloo. I was at Brussells all day in which there were many reports and alarms spread[.] I felt uneasy as I was unable to walk well & had no horse to ride[.] it was universally believed at one time that the French would be in Brussells in the evening, and I believe that the people generally speaking were glad of it, however tho' they looked on the British army as conquered (and certainly the disorder and confusion with which the baggage and stragglers retired thro' the place warranted such conclusions) yet I saw no disposition to insult. –

Also in Brussels was Edward Heeley, the fourteen-year-old servant to Lieutenant-Colonel Sir George Scovell of the Quartermaster-General's Department. He recorded in his journal for the 18th:

> During the morning I went several times towards the park to see all I could, as this was the most public part of the town. It was in a great bustle, but people seemed astonished at not hearing any cannonading, but between 10 and 11 o'clock the thundering commenced, but not very loud at first, yet it did not require to go on the ramparts to hear it for it could be heard any where quite plain. What seemed to astonish people very much was the almost unbroken procession of every description of vehicle loaded with ammunition. These were artillery carts and waggons, the waggon train waggons and the country people's carts of every description, and everyone was chalked upon to tell what they contained. . . .

By 1.00 p.m., the cannonade was tremendous and in the evening about 5,000 to 6,000 French prisoners arrived escorted by British dragoons:

> . . . The poor fellows cut a sorry figure, they must have fought gallantly for scarcely one of them had a hat or cap on, and nearly all of them were more or less wounded, principally sabre wounds. They were all drenched to the skin with rain and covered with mud. A few thoughtless people insulted them, with 'Where's Boney now' and such like, but speaking generally they were more pitied than anything

else. They marched straight through the town to Antwerp, and were there put on board our ships. It is almost incredible to anyone when told the condition the men were in. Our cavalry, though mounted on such high horses, were so completely plastered with mud that the red of their coats could only be seen in patches.

. . .

We'll call it now 9 o'clock, and the roar of the cannon had gradually died away. People were crying 'Is it over? Who's won, Are they only stopped on account of darkness etc.', when all at once the welcome news arrived, that Wellington had gained the day, and the French were flying in all directions. This news dispelled all the gloom, every one was smiling, the wounded were being caressed and the poor women comforted as much as possible. All the past calamities of the day were being made quite light of, and no one looked so proud as the British soldier. . . .

Lady De Lancey had gone for safety to Antwerp, where she received a succession of conflicting reports on the fate of her husband, William, who had in fact been grievously wounded. She travelled to Brussels on 20 June and learnt that William had been struck on the back by a cannon shot and had been taken to a cottage in the village of Mont St Jean. The roads were congested with a mass of vehicles, horses, wounded and runaways:

. . . We were soon out of Brussels again & on the road to Waterloo – it is 9 miles & we took 3 hours & a half – Mr H. [William Hay, a former captain in the 16th Light Dragoons] rode before with his sword drawn & obliged them to let us pass – We often stood still for 10 minutes[.] The Horses screamed at the smell of corruption, which in many places was offensive at last when near the village Mr H. said he would ride forward & find the House & learn whether I should still proceed or not – I hope no one will ever be able to say they understand what my feelings must have been during the half hour that passed till he returned – how fervently & sincerely I resolved that if I saw him alive for one hour I never would repine – I had almost lost my recollection with the excess of anxiety & suspense, when Mr H. called out 'alls well I have seen him he expects you' – when we got to the Village Sir G. Scovell met the Carriage & opening the Door, said stop one moment – I said, 'is he alive?' – 'alive yes & the surgeons are of opinion that he may recover but I wish to warn you of one thing – you must be aware that his life hangs on a very slender hold & therefore an agitation would be injudicious, now we have not told him you had heard of his death we thought it would afflict him therefore do not pretend to have heard of his death['] – I promised & he said, – now come along – I sat down an instant in the outer room & he went in, when I heard my husband say – 'let her come in['] – then I was overpaid for all the misery – I was surprised at the strength of his voice for I had expected to find him weak & dying – when I went into the room where he lay he held out his Hand & said 'Come Magdalen[e] this is a sad busyness, is it not?['] – I could not speak but sat down by him & took his Hand this was my occupation for six Days. – . . .

On 26 June William gave a little gulp and died. Magdalene returned to Brussels that same day. William was buried two days later at the cemetery of St Josse Ten Noode near the city. Magdalene visited the grave on 4 July and departed for Ostend to return to England, three months to the day after her wedding. She remarried in 1819, but died three years later, aged twenty-eight.

11

Aftermath

1815–52

Wellington and Blücher exploited their victory at Waterloo with an immediate advance on Paris. Captain Grove of the 23rd Light Dragoons wrote that on the day after the battle:

> At an early hour we advanced a short distance, & halted for some time; during which large columns of Prussians passed us; and here my never failing friends of the 7th Hussars, sent to me to say that 'Breakfast was ready'[.] I soon obeyed the summons, tho' I feared it was a Hoax – I had scarcely touched a thing to eat or drink since 4 o'clock in the morning of the 16th (72 hours at least) I found these jolly fellows sitting in a circle on the ground, with plenty of Pigeon Pie and Brandy, having by chance got hold of Tom Wildmans baggage horse, with these good things; and knowing that he was well off, not much ceremony was used in securing the Prize – this made a new man of me, and it was very kind of these men to think of me at such a time – Although we had nothing to eat the previous night, the weather was so perfect, and our cloaks had in some degree recovered [from] the drenching of the 17th, we made ourselves comfortable by forming a tent with some of them, and the time passed in high spirits – . . .

Captain Wildman had been wounded while serving as an ADC to Lord Uxbridge.

Wellington crossed into France on 21 June and subsequently breached the three lines of fortresses guarding the north-eastern frontier. Cambrai was swiftly taken on the 24th and Péronne two days later. Wellington was determined to preserve order and discipline and so advanced more slowly than his Prussian allies, who left behind a trail of devastation.

Captain William Walton of the Coldstream Guards wrote to his mother from before Paris on 2 July:

We arrived before the good City of Paris yesterday afternoon – the French seem inclined to defend it. If they persist the City I make no doubt will be reduced to ashes – This the Prussian army has sworn to do if the[y] meet with any opposition[.] At all event[s] not a Shot has been fired against the English since the Battle of Waterloo [a slight exaggeration] and a most tremendous Battle it was – never did I see such Slaughter, the heaps of dead were quite dreadful to behold. The French fought with the most obstinate Courage – but all would not do – Buonaparte charged himself at the head of his Imperial Guards he has nearly twenty six thousand of them when they came on the field, and very few were left to tell the tale of their defeat – I was particularly lucky to escape, as I was riding about the field all the day – as soon after the action began I was appointed Brigade Major [to the 2nd Brigade of Guards], in Consequence of the Officer who held that situation having his arm taken off by a Cannon shot and is since dead – so I conclude the Duke of York will approve of my continuing to fill that situation when I arrive in England – It has been a most glorious business for the Prussians and English, they have done it quite by themselves. The Russians, & Austrians not having yet come up, negotiations of some description are going on. The French have a large force yet in Paris and on the Heights of Montmartre but I do not see what they can do but capitulate. We have now with us nearly two hundred thousand men, and in less than a week shall double that number. Something more will be known tomorrow but as Letters go to night I must conclude – I do not think another Shot will be fired – If it is Paris is lost twice over –

In the wake of his crushing defeat Napoleon had abdicated and left Paris. The Provisional Government signed a Convention on 3 July under which the French army would evacuate the capital and retire south of the River Loire. Lieutenant-Colonel Murray of the 18th Hussars wrote to his wife on 4 July from before Montmartre:

... The business is at an end I fancy, an armistice has taken place. I saw Paris today from the Out Posts.

We rather expected to have entered it yesterday but now I hear no Troops are to go in. However the Officers will be able to go in.

Nothing can exceed the pitiless devastation of property which marks
the Prussian advance, by this we ourselves suffer, for nothing is to be
had, the Prussians I dare say have played the very devil in the China
manufactory at Sere, & in the village adjoining our encampment not
a soul remains to tell us the name of the Place.

I am told all this is very just & quite as it ought to be, but I think
it is a very inconvenient way of carrying on the War to say no worse.

We however commit no excesses, & the name of British humanity
remains as unsullied as their valour. . . .

Wellington's and Blücher's armies occupied Paris on 7 July and King
Louis XVIII was restored to his throne the next day. The Treaty of
Paris formally brought peace on 20 November 1815. One of its terms
was that a multinational Army of Occupation of 150,000 men should be
stationed at French expense in north-eastern France between Calais
and the Swiss border. Its presence would ensure European security and
foster the stability of the restored Bourbon regime. This army would
remain for five years, but the need for its continued presence would be
reviewed after three. The command was entrusted to Wellington, who
established his headquarters at Cambrai.

By the end of January 1816, all the Allied troops had left Paris and
moved to their sectors in the occupation zone. The British contingent
contained 30,000 men, the infantry being commanded by Hill and the
cavalry by Combermere, who had arrived in July 1815 to replace the
wounded Uxbridge.

British officers particularly enjoyed hunting and racing, but it was,
ultimately, an Army of Occupation and the potential for unrest was
taken seriously. A General Cavalry Order, issued on 20 December 1815,
stressed the desirability of cultivating the best understanding with the
inhabitants. Complaints should be immediately attended to, but calmly
and dispassionately and using a French-speaking officer. The order also
observed that the cessation of war was not an excuse for indolence.
The field movements and exercise of the troops should be in strict confor-
mity with the regulations and brigade commanders were immediately
to adopt measures to put their regiments into the most effective state
of equipment. The order stressed that the troop officers had to pay
attention to the health of the men; vegetables would in future form part
of the daily rations. In order to counter drunkenness, addicted men were

to be separated from the others and employed incessantly during the day in all the drudgery to the relief of those with good conduct.

Major-General Sir Hussey Vivian served in the Army of Occupation as the commander of the 2nd Cavalry Brigade. His papers provide a good case study of how relations were managed between British units and the French inhabitants. The brigade contained the 7th and 18th Hussars and the 12th Light Dragoons, which became the 12th (or Prince of Wales's) Royal Regiment of (Light) Dragoons (Lancers) in March 1817. The 18th returned to England in November 1816, but the 7th and 12th remained until the end of the occupation in November 1818. The brigade's area of occupation was near Boulogne and Montreuil in the Pas de Calais and the 12th received their Waterloo Medals in 1816 on the nearby battlefield of Agincourt. According to Wellington, a Grenadier Guards officer bought the right to dig on the battlefield and found items such as spurs and stirrup-irons at the place where the French knights were said to have been buried. But after two or three weeks, Wellington learnt that these activities were upsetting the French and had to hint to the officer that he should stop digging.*

Discipline was strict, for Wellington wanted to set an example within the British contingent for other elements of the Army of Occupation. On 11 August 1815, Colonel George Quentin in the temporary absence of Vivian had issued a Brigade Order at Beauvais, 61 km north of Paris:

> It having been reported to the officer commanding the Brigade that many of the men have been constantly offending the Inhabitants by repeated cries of Vive l'Empereur [Long live the Emperor] & other Expressions of the same kind – he calls upon the officers & non Commissioned officers of the Brigade, immediately to put a stop to so improper a custom – He is aware that nothing is meant by them but a foolish joke – But it is nevertheless a circumstance that may have the most injurious effects by involving the men in Quarrells with the Inhabitants & by giving His Grace the Commander of the Forces (to whom it has been reported) an opportunity to find fault with them. He feels confident that after this caution he shall hear of no farther complaints of the sort. This order to be read to the men by Commanding officers of Troops.

* Earl Stanhope, *Notes of Conversations with the Duke of Wellington 1831–1851* (London, 1938), pp. 83–4.

Vivian was careful to prevent trouble wherever possible. For example, his Brigade-Major, Lieutenant-Colonel Michael Childers, wrote to the Sub-Prefect of Montreuil and Boulogne on 9 April 1817, asking that the owners of village cabarets should not allow soldiers to remain in them after 9.00 p.m.

In July 1816 Vivian took a dim view of Lieutenant Thomas Prior of the 18th Hussars, who caused an affray in a theatre at Boulogne by insulting a performer. Vivian explained in a letter to Combermere on the 30th that after Prior was knocked down, two other officers of the 18th intervened. But the National Guard arrived, along with the Commandant and, apparently, some gendarmes. This prompted several Englishmen, not belonging to the Army of Occupation, to rush onto the stage. Vivian acknowledged that the initial fault was Lieutenant Prior's, but also criticized the violent conduct of the National Guard in attacking unarmed men with drawn swords and fixed bayonets. The affray ended only after one of the Englishmen had been severely wounded.

An even more serious incident occurred on 11 May 1818 at Long-villers, 9 km north of Montreuil, in which eight soldiers were badly hurt. Investigations found that the troops were not to blame and that they had shown forbearance in not using their weapons against the numerous body of inhabitants who had attacked them with stones.

Vivian took a firm line with the French to maintain respect for the British army. He set out his firm and even-handed approach in a letter to the Sub-Prefect of Montreuil on 20 February 1816:

> Herewith I have the honor to forward to you a letter from Lt Col [James] Bridger the officer who commands the 12th Lt Drags, at Fruges, together with a complaint of Lieut Leech of that Regt against a French gentleman on whose house that officer was quarterd,
>
> Insolence such as is therein described must not and cannot be submitted to, Lieut Leech conducted himself prudently and in conformity to orders in not attempting personally to resent such conduct, but in order to prevent a recurrence of a circumstance of this sort I trust you Sir will immediately take such measures as will protect British officers from the insults of the disaffected and ill disposed, whilst on the one hand, it will be my endeavour to prevent by the strictest discipline, any misconduct on the part of the Troops under my command, and to redress any complaint that may be made against them, on the other I look with confidence to the

civil authorities of the Country, to punish those who in defiance of those authorities, and in transgression of the Laws of civility and hospitality so demean themselves as to endanger the harmony, which it must be desirable to all parties should subsist. . . .

Vivian had already protested to the Sub-Prefect a week before about the poor quality provisions supplied by French contractors:

> . . . I beg in the strongest manner possible, to call your attention, to the circumstance of, most of the Troops of the 7th Reg^t of Hussars, quarterd at Etaples, and adjacent villages, having now, actually been two days without meat, some even so much as five, the meat which was provided, being perfectly unfit for use.
>
> The Troops are ordered to preserve the strictest discipline, but circumstances of this sort, naturally compel the soldier to ask for provisions in the House where he is quarter'd to prevent his starving[.] I could wish therefore, that in the event of a recurrence of such a circumstance, directions may be given to the mayor of each village, to furnish meat, on the requisition of the Officer Commanding.
>
> The Bread of which you sent me a sample by Lieut Col Childers is sour, and very full of sand, and I do not consider it sufficiently good for the soldiers, nor shall I allow it to be received

Vivian was keen to maintain standards of drill, smartness and discipline. In a Brigade Order of 8 May 1816, he noted that as a result of the dispersed nature of the brigade's regiments, only the utmost exertion of every officer could ensure that they were kept in a creditable state. Every fit man and horse should assemble for exercise twice a week. In addition, each troop had to have one, or if possible two, riding drills near their quarters. Officers were on no account to absent themselves from these duties without the utmost necessity. Vivian warned that when he made his half-yearly inspection, he would be ready to make allowances for the inconveniences under which his regiments were placed, but not for any neglect of those means which were still within the power of the officers.

The training undertaken by each unit was supplemented by the annual reviews that Wellington held in the autumn to give his men experience in large-scale manoeuvres.

Wellington decided that it was both possible and desirable to reduce the strength of the Army of Occupation in 1817. Each Allied contingent was reduced by one-fifth. This was followed by the end of the occupation altogether by 30 November 1818. It had fulfilled its objectives and was no longer necessary, particularly as the frontier fortresses to protect the United Netherlands were nearly complete.

*

Waterloo was the greatest day in the history of the British army. Captain Grove reveals the gusto with which the 23rd Light Dragoons marked the anniversary in 1816:

> ... The first anniversary of the Battle of Waterloo was not forgotten – Clocks differ, but 12 o'clock on the night of the 17th of June 1816, was earlier than usual – the men were eager to commence the Cannonade, imitated with wonderful success, by standing at each bedstead, which they raised, and banged to the floor with all their strength – fancy the noise through a large Barrack. – The Band went down to the town, and played under the windows of the commanding Officer ([Lieutenant-Colonel John] Cutcliffe) and his wife – Four large Barrels of the strongest beer, brewed for the occasion were served out to the men in the Riding house; from whence a deputation came to the Mess soon after dinner, to request [name missing] would go down and drink with them; but without waiting for his answer, he was hoisted upon their shoulders, and carried off – they wanted to take us all in turn, but we begged to decline the honor and they left us. –
>
> Every Officer was carried by the men to the Messroom. – When they came to me, I apologized for not being ready, and advised them to take [the] Veterinary Surgeon first, but on no account to put him into a wheel barrow; this tickled their fancy, and away they went for Dr [John] Ship, and brought him in triumph, with all the implements of his craft in front. –
>
> In the Evening there was a Ball, and the Band were bound in honor not to get drunk that day; but the following day they had a special good dinner, and liquor enough to swim in –
>
> Some of us came home at 7 in the morning in a carriage; galloping round the Barrack yard; none of us of course being perfectly sober. – Some of the men were round a fire in the middle of the Barrack yard, where they had bivouac'd during the night, and had finished their beer – they held up a can upside down in token of wanting a fresh supply – they went to the messman and told him

they had my orders to get more, and he was donkey enough to give it, but I did not pay for it. –

For three days all duties were suspended from necessity, as hardly a man could be found; they were lying about in the fields in a state of intoxication – all that could be done was, for the Serjeant Major to collect a few of the best men, to assist in feeding the horses; as for cleaning or giving them exercise, that was out of the question. –

At last all shook right, and every thing went on as well as usual. – . . .

The British army was drastically reduced in strength following Napoleon's final defeat. The 23rd Light Dragoons, for example, was one of the eight cavalry regiments that had been disbanded by 1822.

Captain Standish O'Grady of the 7th Hussars wrote on 23 January 1816 to inform his father that one troop in each of the cavalry regiments stationed in France was to be reduced:

> . . . this order makes me almost a private gentleman, and I fear I have little chance of being able to prevail on any of our Captains to exchange with me
>
>   . . .
>
> I should be most unfortunate to be put on the H.P. [half pay] list now as I only want about a year & a half of having served my time for a Majority, and no one is ever promoted from Half pay. I hardly thought so shabby a piece of economy would have been resorted to, as the reduction of one Troop, & that too in Reg^{ts} now serving abroad[.] My profession was my own choice and I have never repented having made it, since I have Entered the Army I have made a great many acquaintances, & amongst them some friends, I have also been fortunate enough to insure the good opinion of all my Commanding Officers, it is not therefore to be wondered at, that I should feel allied to a profession in which I have never met any thing but success. I should certainly rather remain with the 7th untill I left them for promotion, & even then I shall quit them with regret – . . .

Captain O'Grady went on temporary half-pay that May. He subsequently served in the 18th Hussars, but was again put on half-pay when the 18th was disbanded in 1821.

*

Napoleon had meanwhile arrived in October 1815 on the island of St Helena in the South Atlantic, where he spent the remaining five and a half years of his life as a prisoner of the British. Catherine, the wife of Captain Robert Younghusband of the 53rd Regiment, was living on the island and on 4 January 1816 wrote a letter to her aunt in which she described a fascinating dinner with Napoleon at his house, Longwood:

Altho' I wrote to you a very long letter only three weeks ago I am certain you will be glad to hear from me an account of my having dined by invitation with the great Bonaparte. – The invitation came to me alone for Napoleon makes it a rule never to invite husbands & wives the same day. Sir George Bingham [the commander of the troops on the island] & myself were the only two invited. I went accompanied by Marshal & the Countess Bertrand – She professes the greatest love for me & acknowledgements for the attentions I have been able to pay her.

We arrived at Longwood at 7 – The Emperor was walking but he came in & seemed very cheerful. 'you are come to live in Camp Madame – ah c'est tres bien.' He then asked me to try a grand Piano Forte of Stodards arrived from England the day before. 'I want your opinion, tell me if it is as good as the Piano at Plantation House [the residence of the Governor, Lieutenant-General Sir Hudson Lowe].' I told him it was better – He was pleased – 'come try it – ' ['] I will teach you to pronounce Italian.['] He then read the words of a Song I was about to sing. After I had sung two songs he asked me to play at Tric Trac with him, being told this was Backgammon I sat down, but I found it was different & said I could not play. 'Ah c'est domage! will you teach me English Backgammon[.]' The idea of my instructing the great Napoleon threw me into a flutter, but he found placing the men so difficult that he gave it up. [Di]nner was announced. I was placed to Bonapartes right hand. The party consisted of Marshall & Countess Bertrand, General & Countess Monthulon [Montholon], Baron Gourgaud, Count Las Cases, and his Son, and Sir G^e Bingham. During the whole dinner no one uttered a syllable but the Emperor & myself. A dead silence prevailed. The Emperor asked me a number of questions about India, & several about camp. The first course was off Silver. The dinner excellent. The servants magnificently dressed. Nothing was out at Table. Every thing carved by the Servants & brought round. Bonaparte eat of about ten different dishes and drank very little. He took a glass of wine before his Soup. The Vegetables were eaten seperate, & after the meat. The desert or second course was off the most superb Seve [Sèvres] china. The plates all solid Gold. The sweetmeats were exquisite. The Emperor filled a Plate with his own hand & sent them to Camp. 'Carry these to the little girl who sings so well, from *Me*' said he to the servant. I own I felt highly pleased at this kindness & rememberance of Emily. He offered me several things with his own hand, which did not strike me at the time, but Count Las Cases told me yesterday [that] it was the highest mark of his favor. A thing said he the Emperor would not have done to a Queen in Paris – [']& I assure you he paid you more attention than he has done to many Queens – & as for Princes, I have seen seven Princes waiting in the anti:room & not able to gain admittance.' –

But to return – dinner was no sooner over, & we all got up, when the Emperor rose & returned to the drawing room. A Table was laid out with a coffee set – the most beautiful & superb I imagine in the world! The Cups & saucers were 25 guineas *each*. Every cup had a beautiful view of different parts of Egypt – & saucers a highly finished miniature of the different Bays [Beys] of Egypt. They were made at Seve, & presented to the Emperor by the City of Paris. He took great pleasure in shewing & describing them. He then asked me if I could play at Renversé (a game like whist) I said I could not. He then made his party, & General Monthulon, Countess Bertrand, Sir G^e Bingham & myself made a whist table. The Emperor was in high glee. he sung all the the [sic] time he was playing. He won a great deal & seemed to pay the greatest attention to the Game & to be entirely interested in it. It was near Eleven when the party broke up. Bonaparte observes the same etiquette & state with his Court here as at Paris, none of them sit down or speak in his Presence. He makes a sign when he chooses they should sit. They dress every day as if at Court. He took notice of my dress which was a silver muslin of a peculiar pattern. 'I know said he, that is Indian.'

. . .

Bonaparte said Cap^tn Younghusband was one of the handsomest men he ever saw – 'Ah! c'est un homme superb'! He marked him out from all the officers of the 53^d who were introduced to him in a body last week. He rides out every day but has particular limits when unattended by one of our officers. He rides up & down precipices where no mortal but himself would choose to venture. He looks best on Horseback. His smile is particularly agreeable but the usual turn of his countenance is heavy & grave. He hates Longwood & fancies the Water there disagrees with him. . . .

Captain Basil Hall of the Royal Navy visited St Helena in August 1817 while returning from a voyage of discovery in the Far East. He was the brother of Magdalene, Lady De Lancey and the son of Sir James Hall, who had received lessons at the Brienne Military Academy in France at the time that Napoleon had been there. He was granted an interview with Napoleon at Longwood on the 13th:

> . . . On being ushered into the Room, I observed Bonaparte standing before the fire. He was leaning his head on his hand, with his elbow resting on the mantle piece. He looked up, and immediately advanced a pace towards me, returning my bow in a quick, careless manner.
>
> . . .
>
> Bonaparte has been always supposed to have had a strong taste for every thing Oriental, – and for whatever related to Voyages of Discovery in particular. I can fully believe that this is correct, for he appeared deeply interested by the account which I gave him of what we had seen: and he carried on his enquiries with a fervor and an anxiety to be informed which I have never met with in any other person.
>
> It would be in the highest degree satisfactory to be able to give his questions in the order and in the very words they were put, but this is unfortunately not in my power. They were very numerous and sagacious, – not thrown out at random, but ingeniously connected with one another, so as to make every thing assist in forming a clear comprehension of the subject. – I felt that there was no escaping his scrutiny, – and such was the rapidity and precision with which he apprehended the subject, that I felt at times as if he were as well or better informed upon it than I was myself, – and that he was interrogating me with a view to discover my veracity and powers of description. –
>
> . . .
>
> He was in high spirits while putting these questions and carried on his enquiry with so much cheerfulness, not to say familiarity, that I was more than once thrown completely off my guard, and caught myself unconsciously addressing him with the freedom and confi-

dence of an equal. When I checked myself upon these occasions and became more formal and respectful, he encouraged me to go on with so much real cheerfulness, that I soon felt myself quite at ease in his presence.

On his desiring me to tell him what these Loo choo People knew of other Countries, I said they knew a little of China, and a little of Japan – 'But of Europe?' said Bonaparte; – I told him that they had never heard of France, nor of England – [']nor' continued I emboldened by his extraordinary familiarity and good humour, [']have they even heard of you!' – Bonaparte appeared highly amused by this piece of impudence; The implied compliment seemed to flatter his vanity more than the impertinence of the remark hurt his dignity, for he laughed heartily for a minute or two at what I had said.

. . .

There was not the least appearance of a wrinkle either on his brow or at the corners of his eye. Were it not for an occasional lighting up of the eyes, and a sort of determined commanding glance, which pierced as it were into ones most hidden thoughts, I should have been disposed to describe his look as being placid or gentle, and at all times lively, but never stern.

Nor was there the slightest trace of care visible in his face or in his manner, – on the contrary his whole deportment, conversation and expression of countenance indicated a mind perfectly at ease.

. . .

His air was that of a character quite unsubdued – and far above being affected by the ordinary accidents of life. – This tranquillity was probably assumed, – but if so he certainly played his part most skilfully, – for I could discover nothing during the Interview which betrayed the least ill humour, or impatience at his situation. Indeed he made no allusion to it whatever, – directly or indirectly. . . .

Napoleon died at St Helena on 5 May 1821 and was buried at the centre of the island next to a spring shaded by willows. The signature book for visitors to his tomb in 1836–7 is filled with entries, mostly by British and French passengers on passing ships. They included Captain Holt of the 75th Regiment of Foot, who recorded that he had fought against the hero whose tomb he visited on 29 September 1836. A fortnight earlier, two British visitors wrote: 'Washington was a great man[,] Napoleon a greater but *Wellington* the greatest.'

Someone with less admiration for Napoleon crossed out 'greater' and added 'not so great'. Others dwelled on what little now remained except the memory of his past grandeur.

In contrast, Wellington had another thirty years of life ahead of him and he lived them to the full. He never fought another battle, but joined the Earl of Liverpool's Cabinet as Master-General of the Ordnance in December 1818 and served his country with varying fortunes as a diplomat and statesman. He saw himself as a public servant rather than a party politician, but grew more reactionary in outlook as a result of the disorder that accompanied Britain's post-war economic distress. In international affairs, Wellington believed firmly in the Concert of Europe, by which the great powers acted together to preserve peace, and in the principle of non-interference in another country's internal affairs. But he was increasingly dismayed as George Canning, the Foreign Secretary from 1822, pursued a more detached policy. Wellington failed at the Congress of Verona in 1822 to avert French intervention in Spain to restore the authority of King Ferdinand VII. Similarly, during his mission to Tsar Nicholas I at St Petersburg in 1826 he had only limited success in securing a Russian undertaking not to intervene in the Greek War of Independence against Turkey.

Wellington resigned from the Cabinet in April 1827 when Canning became Prime Minister, but was himself appointed to the premiership in January 1828 following Canning's death in August and the resignation of his successor, Viscount Goderich. During his two-year ministry, Wellington resolved one of the great issues of the day by forcing through Catholic Emancipation to allow Catholics to sit in Parliament. This probably averted a civil war in Ireland, even if it increased the divisions in the Tory Party and obliged Wellington to fight a duel with one of his most vocal critics, Lord Winchilsea, to quash accusations that he had acted dishonourably. He was less successful in handling demands for Parliamentary reform and resigned in November 1830.

Wellington subsequently led the opposition to Whig attempts to pass a reform bill through the House of Lords as he feared that reform would lead to revolution and then to a dictatorship. His position made him so unpopular that he had to have shutters fitted to protect the windows of his London home, Apsley House, from stone-throwing mobs. Political stalemate threatened to provoke an uprising in May 1832 until Wellington pragmatically persuaded his supporters to allow the passage of the Reform Bill to avert the danger and preserve the existence of the Lords.

After the dismissal of the Whigs in 1834, Wellington served as Foreign Secretary during Sir Robert Peel's first, four-month, premiership. From 1841 to 1846, he had a Cabinet seat without office in Peel's second ministry, but then retired from active political life. He received a shower of other honours and appointments, including those of Colonel-in-Chief of the Rifle Brigade and Lord Lieutenant of Hampshire (1820), Constable of the Tower of London (1826), Colonel of the Grenadier Guards (1827), Lord Warden of the Cinque Ports (1829), Chancellor of Oxford University (1834), and Ranger of Hyde Park and St James's Park (1850). He held the post of Commander-in-Chief of the British army for two brief periods in 1827–8 and again for the remainder of his life from August 1842, but as a result of financial constraints and his own conservatism and failing health he failed to carry out the sweeping reforms that were necessary. The army's deficiencies became clear during the Crimean War (1854–6) two years after his death. Yet he skilfully organized the defence of London during the Chartist unrest of April 1848 and helped avert the threat of riots. He became known as 'The Duke', a national institution in his own right, and his dedication to the service of crown and country enabled him to be increasingly aloof from party politics. He twice refused the premiership, in 1834 and 1839, and became a trusted adviser to Queen Victoria. His restored popularity was confirmed when he was mobbed by enthusiastic crowds at the Great Exhibition of 1851 and he died aged eighty-three at Walmer Castle in Kent on 14 September 1852.

Wellington was buried in St Paul's Cathedral on 18 November after a magnificent state funeral with one and a half million people lining the route from the Horse Guards. The massive bronze funeral car bore the names of twenty-five of his victories, while the procession included eighty-three Chelsea Pensioners and a detachment from every regiment in the British army.

As the body was lowered through the Cathedral floor into the vault, the eighty-four-year-old Field Marshal the Marquess of Anglesey, formerly the Earl of Uxbridge, was openly in tears. He suddenly stepped forward and impulsively laid his hand on the coffin in a final farewell to an unforgettable commander.

Select Bibliography

Seventh Marquess of Anglesey, *One-Leg: the Life and Letters of Henry William Paget* (London, 1961)

Anon, *List of Officers of the Royal Regiment of Artillery from the year 1716 to the present date* (Woolwich, 1869), revised edition

Anon, *The Waterloo Medal Roll: Compiled from the Muster Rolls* (Dallington, 1992)

C. Atkinson, 'A Peninsular Brigadier: Letters of Major-General Sir F.P. Robinson, K.C.B., dealing with the Campaign of 1813', in *Journal of the Society for Army Historical Research* (*JSAHR*) 1956, vol. 34, pp. 153–70

M. Ball, 'An Artist's Road to Waterloo: The Sketch-Book of Ensign Robert Batty, 1813–14', in A. Guy, ed., *The Road to Waterloo: the British Army and the Struggle against Revolutionary and Napoleonic France, 1793–1815* (London, 1990)

P. Boyden, 'The Postal Service of Wellington's Army in the Peninsula and France, 1809–1818', in A. Guy, ed., *The Road to Waterloo: the British Army and the Struggle against Revolutionary and Napoleonic France, 1793–1815* (London, 1990)

A. Brett-James, *General Graham, Lord Lynedoch* (London, 1959); *Wellington at War, 1794–1815* (London, 1961)

N. Cantlie, *A History of the Army Medical Department* (London, 1974), vol. 1

F. C. Carr-Gomm, ed., *Letters and Journals of Field-Marshal Sir William Maynard Gomm, G.C.B.* (London, 1881)

D. Chandler, *The Campaigns of Napoleon* (London, 1966)

A. Chaplin, *A St. Helena's Who's Who: or a Directory of the Island during the Captivity of Napoleon* (London, 1919), 2nd ed.

M. Combermere and W. Knollys, *Memoirs and Correspondence of Field-Marshal Viscount Combermere* (London, 1866), 2 vols

C. Dalton, *The Waterloo Roll Call* (London, 1904; reissued 1978)

D. Davies, *Sir John Moore's Peninsular Campaign, 1808–1809* (The Hague, 1974)

R. Edwards, ed., *Roll of Officers of the Corps of Royal Engineers. From 1660 to 1898* (Chatham, 1898)

C. Esdaile, 'The British Army and the Guerrilla War in Spain', in A. Guy, ed., *The Road to Waterloo: the British Army and the Struggle against Revolutionary and Napoleonic France, 1793–1815* (London, 1990); *The Duke of Wellington and the Command of the Spanish Army, 1812–14* (London, 1990); *The Wars of Napoleon* (London, 1995); *The Peninsular War: A New History* (London, 2002)

V. Esposito and J. Elting, *A Military History and Atlas of the Napoleonic Wars* (New York, 1964; reissued 1999)

I. Fletcher, *Galloping at Everything: the British Cavalry in the Peninsular War and at Waterloo 1808–15 a Reappraisal* (Staplehurst, 1999)

J. Fortescue, *A History of the British Army* (London, 1899–1930), 13 vols

N. Gash, ed., *Wellington: Studies in the Military and Political Career of the First Duke of Wellington* (Manchester, 1990)

D. Gates, *The British Light Infantry Arm c.1790–1815* (London, 1987)

M. Glover, *Wellington as Military Commander* (London, 1968); *Britannia Sickens: Sir Arthur Wellesley and the Convention of Cintra* (London, 1970); 'Purchase, Patronage and Promotion in the British Army at the time of the Peninsular War', in *Army Quarterly* 1972–3, vol. 103, pp. 211–15, 355–62; 'The Purchase of Commissions: a Reappraisal', in *JSAHR* 1980, vol. 58, pp. 223–35

W. Grattan, *Adventures with the Connaught Rangers 1809–1814* (London, 1902)

J. Gurwood, ed., *The General Orders of Field Marshal the Duke of Wellington, K.G.* (London, 1832); *The Dispatches of Field Marshal the Duke of Wellington during his Various Campaigns in India, Denmark, Portugal, Spain, the Low Countries, and France, from 1799 to 1818* (London, 1834–8), 13 vols.

C. Hall, *British Strategy in the Napoleonic War, 1803–15* (Manchester, 1992)

P. Haythornthwaite, *The Armies of Wellington* (London, 1994)

M. Howard, *Wellington's Doctors: The British Army Medical Services in the Napoleonic Wars* (Staplehurst, 2002)

J. Hyden, 'The Sources, Organisation and Uses of Intelligence in the Anglo–Portuguese Army, 1808–14', in *JSAHR* 1984, vol. 62, pp. 92–104, 169–75

M. Lewin, *Napoleon and his British Captives* (London, 1962)

E. Longford, *Wellington: the Years of the Sword* (London, 1969)

J. McGrigor, *Autobiography and Services of Sir James McGrigor* (London, 1861)

T. McGuffie, ed., *Peninsular Cavalry General: the Correspondence of Lieutenant-General Robert Ballard Long* (London, 1951)

J. Maurice, ed., *The Diary of Sir John Moore* (London, 1904), 2 vols

C. Mercer, *Journal of the Waterloo campaign* (London, 1870; reissued 1985)

D. Miller, *Lady De Lancey at Waterloo: a Story of Duty and Devotion* (Staplehurst, 2000)

J. Mollo, *The Prince's Dolls: Scandals, Skirmishes and Splendours of the first British Hussars, 1793–1815* (Barnsley, 1997)

R. Muir, *Britain and the Defeat of Napoleon 1807–1815* (London, 1996); 'From Soldier to Statesman: Wellington in Paris and Vienna, 1814–15', in A. Guy, ed., *The Road to Waterloo: the British Army and the Struggle against Revolutionary and Napoleonic France, 1793–1815* (London, 1990)

A. Mullen, ed., *The Military General Service Roll 1793–1814* (London, 1990)

F. Myatt, *British Sieges of the Peninsular War* (Tunbridge Wells, 1987)

W. Napier, *History of the War in the Peninsula and the South of France* (1828–40), 6 vols

C. Oman, *A History of the Peninsular War* (Oxford, 1902–30), 7 vols; reissued in 1995–97 with two new complementary vols; *Wellington's Army 1809–14* (London, 1912; reissued 1993)

F. Page, *Following the Drum: Women in Wellington's Wars* (London, 1986)

R. Parkinson, *Moore of Corunna* (Abingdon, 1976)

B. Perrett, *A Hawk at War: the Peninsular War Reminiscences of General Sir Thomas Brotherton, CB* (Chippenham, 1986)

A. Roberts, *Napoleon and Wellington* (London, 2001)

I. Robertson, *Wellington at War in the Peninsula 1808–1814: an Overview and Guide* (Barnsley, 2000)

H. Robinson, *Memoirs of Lieutenant-General Sir Thomas Picton* (London, 1836)

B. Robson, ' "Warranted Never to Fail": The Cavalry Sword Patterns of 1796', in A. Guy, ed., *The Road to Waterloo: the British Army and the Struggle against Revolutionary and Napoleonic France, 1793–1815* (London, 1990)

R. Routh, *Observations on Commissariat Field Service and Home Defences* (London, 1852) 2nd ed.

H. Siborne, *The Waterloo Letters* (London, 1891; reissued 1983)

W. Siborne, *History of the Waterloo Campaign* (London, 1848; reissued 1990)

D. Smith, *The Greenhill Napoleonic Wars Data Book* (London, 1998)

L. Smurthwaite, 'Glory is Priceless!: Awards to the British Army during the French Revolutionary and Napoleonic Wars', in A. Guy, ed., *The Road to Waterloo: the British Army and the Struggle against Revolutionary and Napoleonic France, 1793–1815* (London, 1990)

Earl Stanhope, *Notes of Conversations with the Duke of Wellington 1831–1851* (London, 1938)

H. Strachan, 'The British Army's Legacy from the Revolutionary and Napoleonic Wars', in A. Guy, ed., *The Road to Waterloo: the British Army and the Struggle against Revolutionary and Napoleonic France, 1793–1815* (London, 1990)

G. Teffeteller, *The Surpriser: the Life of Rowland, Lord Hill* (Newark, 1983)

R. Thoumine, *Scientific Soldier: a Life of General Le Marchant, 1766–1812* (London, 1968)

A. Uffindell, *Great Generals of the Napoleonic Wars and their Battles, 1805–1815* (Staplehurst, 2003)

A. Uffindell and M. Corum, *On the Fields of Glory: the Battlefields of the 1815 Campaign* (London, 1996; reissued 2002)

S. G. P. Ward, *Wellington's Headquarters: a Study of the Administrative Problems in the Peninsula, 1809–14* (London, 1957)

E. Warre, ed., *Letters from the Peninsula, 1808–1812* (London, 1909; reissued 1999)

J. Weller, *Wellington in the Peninsula* (London, 1962; reissued 1992); *Wellington at Waterloo* (London, 1967; reissued 1991); *On Wellington* (London, 1998)

Second Duke of Wellington, ed., *Supplementary Dispatches, Correspondence, and Memoranda of Field Marshal Arthur Duke of Wellington, K.G.* (London, 1858–72), 15 vols

Note:

Relevant regimental histories can be identified in A. S. White, *A Bibliography of Regimental Histories of the British Army* (London, 1965; reissued 1994)

Index of Contributors

Ranks and units are those which, as far as can be ascertained, were applicable when the contributors are first mentioned. The figures in round brackets are the National Army Museum Accession numbers of the papers from which extracts have been taken.

General Index

Entries are filed word-by-word.
Bold locators refer to illustration
caption numbers, as listed on pages
xiii–xix. Battles, peaces and treaties are
listed under their individual names.
Modern placenames are given in
brackets after the name in use at the
time.

Abbreviated ranks

The ranks given are those the individuals
held when first mentioned in the book.

Pte – Private
Cpl – Corporal

Sgt – Sergeant
Ens – Ensign
2/Lt – Second Lieutenant
1/Lt – First Lieutenant
Lt – Lieutenant
2/Capt – Second Captain
Capt – Captain
Maj – Major
Lt-Col – Lieutenant-Colonel
Col – Colonel
Brig-Gen – Brigadier-General
Maj-Gen – Major-General
Lt-Gen – Lieutenant-General
Gen – General
FM – Field Marshal